Colonial Catoctin

Colonial Developmental Dynamics on or about the
Potomac River at Catoctin Creek up to Waterford

Loudoun County, Virginia

1728-1829

Volume
2

Roberto Costantino

WILLOW BEND BOOKS
2006

WILLOW BEND BOOKS
AN IMPRINT OF HERITAGE BOOKS, INC.

Books, CDs, and more—Worldwide

For our listing of thousands of titles see our website
at
www.HeritageBooks.com

Published 2006 by
HERITAGE BOOKS, INC.
Publishing Division
65 East Main Street
Westminster, Maryland 21157-5026

Copyright © 2006 Roberto Costantino

Other books by the author:

Colonial Catoctin: The Fairfax Family and Freeholders of Piedmont Manor and Shannondale Manor, Loudoun County, Virginia Land Book, 1743-1820, Volume 1

Miscellaneous Road Cases, Loudoun County, Virginia, 1758-1782, Loudoun County Circuit Court, Clerk of Circuit Court, Archives, Miscellaneous Road Cases, Files No. 38 to 48, Leesburg, Virginia

The Quaker of Olden Time: The Life and Times of Israel Thompson (d. 1795). His Land, Plantation, Mills, Tanyard and Mansion House, and the Rise of Wheatland, Loudoun County, Virginia

All rights reserved. No part of this book may be reproduced or transmitted in any form or by any means, electronic or mechanical, including photocopying, recording or by any information storage and retrieval system without written permission from the author, except for the inclusion of brief quotations in a review.

International Standard Book Number: 978-0-7884-4317-8

Table of Contents

Introduction, p. 3

Chapter One- Richard Wood's Tract (circa 1728-1729), p. 5

Chapter Two- Francis Awbrey on the Potomac River at Catoctin Creek (circa 1731), p. 9

Chapter Three- John Colvill's Catoctin Tract (circa 1731), p. 25

Chapter Four- John Mead's Tract from Catesby Cocke (circa 1731), p. 45

Chapter Five- Richard Brown & Co. on Catoctin Creek (circa 1741), p. 60

Chapter Six- John Hough's Catoctin Lands (circa 1747), p. 90

Chapter Seven- The Earl of Tankerville's Catoctin Manor (circa 1759), p. 122

Chapter Eight- Catesby Cocke's 591-Acre Tract (circa 1745), p. 143

Chapter Nine- Catesby Cocke's 2,672-Acre Tract (circa 1741), p. 149

Chapter Ten- Catesby Cocke's Partition from Cocke & Mercer Tract (circa 1742), p. 161

Chapter Eleven- John Mercer's Partition from Cocke & Mercer Tract (circa 1742), p. 187

Chapter Twelve- Waterford (circa 1781), p. 218

Index, p. 241

Introduction

The confluence of the Potomac River at Catoctin Creek is situated about thirty four miles upriver in a northwesterly course along the shore from Great Falls, which itself is about sixteen miles above the port of Alexandria. It's about twelve and a half miles downriver from Harpers Ferry, West Virginia. The Catoctin Creek is a tributary of the Potomac River located in northwestern Loudoun County, Virginia. Its watershed occupies about 59,000 acres of land under the Blue Ridge. Generally, the ground here is fertile, well watered, and suitable for agriculture, animal husbandry, and woodland industries.

Close by the convergence of these bodies of water lies a large island in the Potomac River opposite Point of Rocks called Heaters Island or Conoy Island. One of the Conoy tribes, the Piscataway, had settled here by the early eighteenth century. As early as circa 1712, the Baron Christoph von Graffenried (d.1743) led an expedition of colonials through here. This would result in the publication of maps and descriptions of the upper reaches of the Potomac River. The record from the American Indians' point of view is missing.

There were crossing places near here for travelers and transportation over the swift river. On both shores of the river were essential paths and roads. On the Maryland side of the river there was an important route down the Monocacy River from the Susquehanna Valley whereas on the Virginia side there was a main way from points south to and from the Potomac River. These routes would offer access as well to nearby towns or villages such as Frederick Town in Maryland or Leesburg in Virginia. It would seem that this site was ripe for building and development.

Nevertheless, during the colonial period up to the end of the French and Indian War this locality was heavily forested, sparsely populated, and largely uncultivated. Development here had lagged as it was a backcountry remote from navigable waters. Besides, growth had been sluggish as a consequence of the presence of large tracts of land, which in many cases were controlled by absentees. Subsequently, as the yeomanry would come to be pushed into the Piedmont region by the local economies of the Tidewater region, this country would come to be suitably populated for a surplus producing agrarian economy by about 1790. The population then remained more or less stable over the next one hundred and thirty years.

The people in this locale made clearings in the forest and cultivated patches of land. Crops of cereals, grasses, and to a lesser extent tobacco were the principal agricultural products. Fruits were raised in abundance. Animal husbandry resulted in an increased number of cattle, hogs, sheep, and horses. Travel and transportation on land was done on foot or by horse, while canoes and scows or flats were used in water. Villages and stores developed around millseats and crossroads.

The references to gentry here are for absentees. Among the relatively small number of upper middle class working people here were freeholder planters, merchants, professionals, and high artisans. Among the relatively large number of middle class working people here were freeholder planters, husbandmen, and common artisans. Among the relatively large number of lower middle class working people here were free husbandmen, common artisans, servants, and laborers. Among the relatively large number of lower class working people here were hunters and trappers, fishermen, peddlers, laborers, and bound servants. Slavery was introduced, which further marginalized servants.

The Negro inhabitants were by statute in a grouping of their own. In turn, they were further divided by their legal status into free Negroes, enslaved Negroes, and fugitive Negroes slaves. The free Negroes possessed a piece of paper on which it was officially stated that they were free; some possessed land and a dwelling house whereas others were landless. The enslaved Negroes were separated in a descending social order into people of mixed European and Negro ancestry; people of Negro descent born in the Western Hemisphere; and Negro people brought from Africa. Likewise, the Negro people brought from Africa were categorized in a pecking order by experience and their particular ethnicity. The record from the slaves' point of view is missing.

Colonial development happened here. This book comprises a history of such dynamics on or about the Potomac River at Catoctin Creek or the Lower Catoctin Creek from circa 1728 to 1829. The varied dates were those actually published in the records of the respective courts of law in many cases without adjustments for the Gregorian calendar. Moreover, the given dates make no estimates for delays in applying for grants to their own lands by stubborn pioneers as the same typically occasioned making improvements and paying taxes.

Colonial Catoctin, *Volume* 2, is a comprehensive study of a land area stretching from the Potomac River at Catoctin Creek up to the South Fork of Catoctin Creek including Waterford (established 1781). It traces more than 190 legal instruments that broke up tracts of land, which had been patented to grantees and subsequently were separated into parcels or lots of land as well as the following further divisions of such lands into pieces of land. Included are transcriptions of legal instruments with complete boundary descriptions and consideration monies, ninety-four measured drawing illustrations of the same, roads and paths, footnotes, and an index to names, places and subjects.

Richard Wood's Tract (circa 1728-9)

The parceling of land on and about a certain tract or parcel of land containing at least 260 acres of land, which was surveyed for and granted to Richard Wood by a patent out of the Proprietor's Office of the Northern Neck of Virginia dated 3/13/1728/9. More than a decade afterwards the said Richard Wood would transfer 260 acres to a certain Thomas John as was recorded in Prince William County by deeds bearing date 5/8/1739. Later, it came into the legal possession of Thomas John & Samuel and Mary Harris.

This was an inland property situated on and about Catoctin Mountain and a drain of Limestone Run. During the Colonial Period it was marked at times with various boundary symbols such as RW for Richard Wood, CM for Cocke & Mercer, and JA for another. By 1760 this piece of land was identified as adjoining to Joseph McGeach's 600-acre tract of land lately from Catesby Cocke by Aneas Campbell, which was previously part of a larger tract surveyed for Coke & Mercer (see Deed Book A, pp. 496-501).

1. 3/13/1728-1729, The Proprietor of the Northern Neck of Virginia of the one part to **Richard Wood** of the other part, Patent for a certain tract of land.

2. 1/1 and 1/2/1768, **Thomas John** and **Samuel Harris** of the County of Loudoun Colony and Dominion of Virginia and **Mary** wife of the said **Samuel Harris** of the one part to **Joseph Janney** of the said County and Colony of the other part. Witnesseth that for and in consideration of the sum of 41 pounds and 8 shillings current money of Virginia to the said **Thomas John, Samuel Harris** and **Mary** his wife in hand paid by the said **Joseph Janney** at or before the sealing and delivery of these presents the receipt whereof they doth hereby acknowledge, hath granted bargained sold aliened and confirmed and by these presents doth grant bargain sell alien and confirm unto the said **Joseph Janney** his heirs and assigns all that tract or parcel of land situate in the County of Loudoun and bounded as followeth viz. Beginning (blank space) red oaks on a knoll marked **JA** a corner to the original survey or (blank space) corner to land **George Gregg** purchased of **Catesby Cocke** extending thence with one of the original marked lines S 43° E 71 poles to (blank space), then through an old field of the said **Harris** S 31° W 130 poles to a line near a corner of **George Gregg's** on a hill, then with the line of marked trees N 27° W 44 poles to a spanish oak corner to **John Hanby's** late purchase of the said **Thos. John,** then with the said **Hanby's** line N 50° E 40 poles to three small gums by a swamp, then with another of his lines N 33° W 75 poles to two red oak saplings by the **mountain road** corner to said **Hanby,** (then) N 55° E 62 poles to the beginning containing 46 acres of land, being part of a larger tract granted to **Richard Wood** by a patent from the Proprietor's Office for the Northern Neck dated the 13th day of March, 1728/9 and by the said **Richard Wood** transferred to the said **Thomas John** by good and sufficient deeds bearing date the 8th day of May, 1739, and the said **Thomas John** having in part conveyed the said land unto the said **Samuel Harris** but not so fully as to complete a sure title in fee simple, therefore the said **Thomas John** is

joint in the conveyance, and all houses buildings orchards ways waters watercourses profits commodities hereditaments appurtenances whatsoever to the said premises hereby granted or any part thereof, and also all the estate right title interest use trust property claim and demand whatsoever of them the said **Thomas John**, **Samuel Harris** and **Mary** his wife of in and to the said premises and all deeds evidences and writings touching or in any wise concerning the same. To have and to hold the lands hereby conveyed and all and singular other the premises hereby bargained and sold and every part and parcel thereof with their and every of their appurtenances unto the said **Joseph** (blank space) his heirs and assigns forever, **Thos.** his T mark **John, Samuel Harris**, and **Mary** her X mark **Harris**. Sealed and delivered in the presence of **John Hough, Alex. McIntyre, Adam Carnahan**, and **John Hanby**. Proven on 6/13/1768. Lease and Release, Loudoun County Deed Book F, pp. 337-342

3.   3/4 and 3/5/1773, **Samuel Harris** of the County of Loudoun and **Mary** his wife of the one part to **Joseph Janney** of the County aforesaid of the other part. Witnesseth that for and in consideration of the sum of 467 pounds current money of Virginia to the said **Samuel Harris** and **Mary** his wife in hand paid by the said **Joseph Janney** at or before the sealing and delivery of these presents the receipt whereof he doth hereby acknowledge, have granted bargained sold aliened released and confirmed and by these presents doth grant bargain sell alien release and confirm unto the said **Joseph Janney** and to his heirs all that tract or parcel of land situate in the County of bounded as followeth viz. Beginning at a large leaning white oak at the head of a valley or drain of **Limestone Run** on the **Kittocton Mountain** extending thence S 24° W 245 poles to a hickory in a gully corner to **George Gregg**, then with his line N 46° W 180 poles to a heap of stones by a fence corner to said **George Gregg**, then N 30° E 50 poles to a locust stake corner to said **Gregg**, thence N 22° E 131 poles to a sassafras sapling corner to said **Joseph Janney's** other land and in a line of other land of **Gregg's**, then with the said line S 42° E 24 poles to a hickory stump **Gregg's** corner, then S 72° E 139 poles to the first station containing 214 acres of land being part of a tract formerly granted to **Richard Wood** and lately the property of **Thomas John** deceased, who in his lifetime conveyed the fee thereof to the said **Samuel Harris** as will more fully appear among the records of Loudoun County Court, the said **Thomas John** hath also by his last will and testament divided the same to the said **Samuel Harris** his heirs and assigns forever reference thereto being had will more fully and at large appear, and all houses buildings orchards ways waters watercourses profits commodities hereditaments and appurtenances whatsoever to the said premises hereby granted or any part thereof belonging or in any wise appertaining. To have and to hold the land hereby conveyed and all and singular other the premises hereby granted and released and every part and parcel thereof with their and every of their appurtenances unto the said **Joseph Janney** his heirs and assigns forever, **Samuel Harris** and **Mary** her M mark **Harris**. Sealed and delivered in the presence of **Thomas Mathews, Abel Janney**, and **John Kavanaugh**. Proven on 3/15/1774. Lease and Release, Loudoun County Deed Book K, pp. 96-101

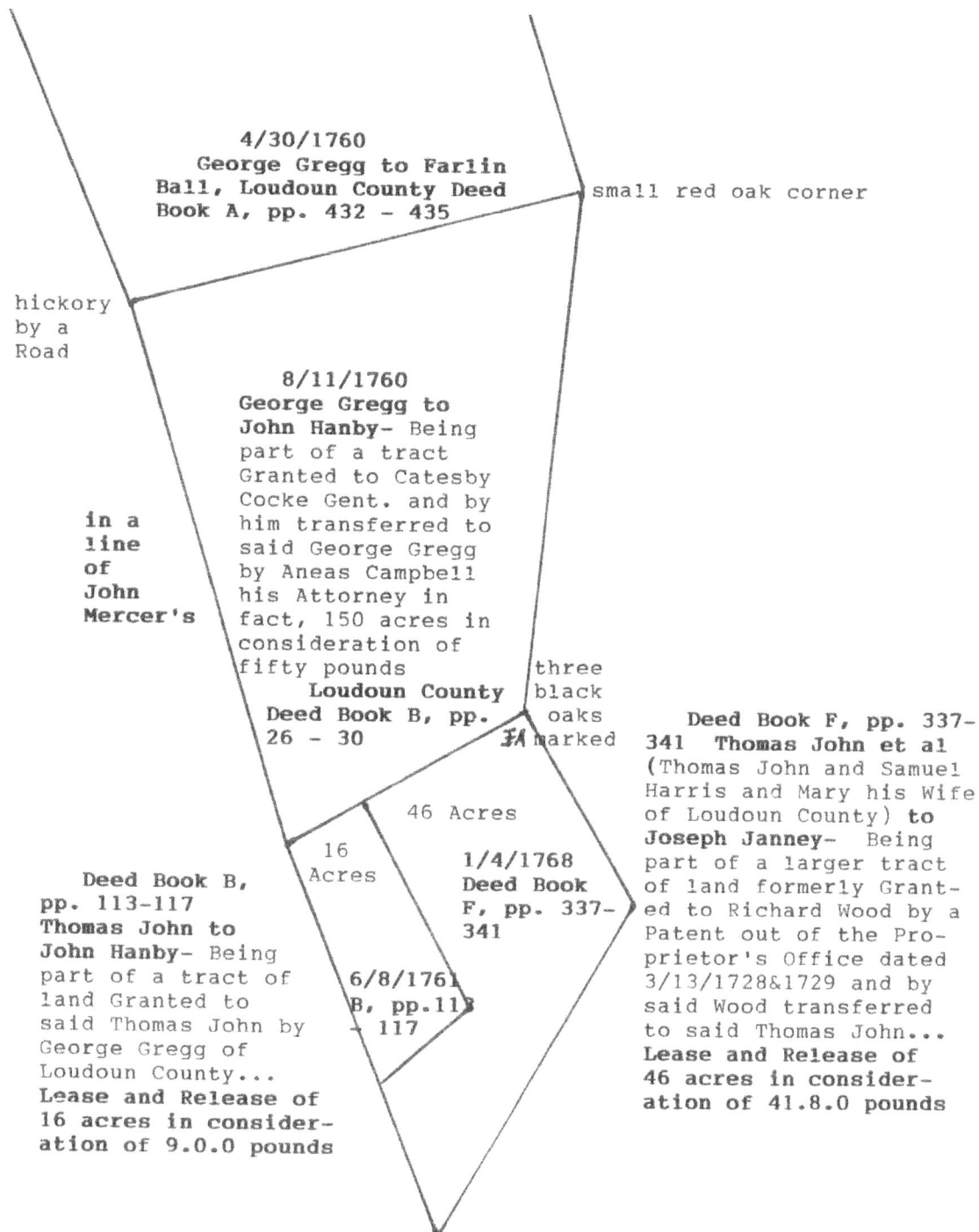

Loudoun County, Virginia   1 in. = 50 poles

Being part of a tract formerly granted to Richard Wood and lately the property of Thomas John deceased, who in his lifetime conveyed the fee thereof to the said Samuel Harris

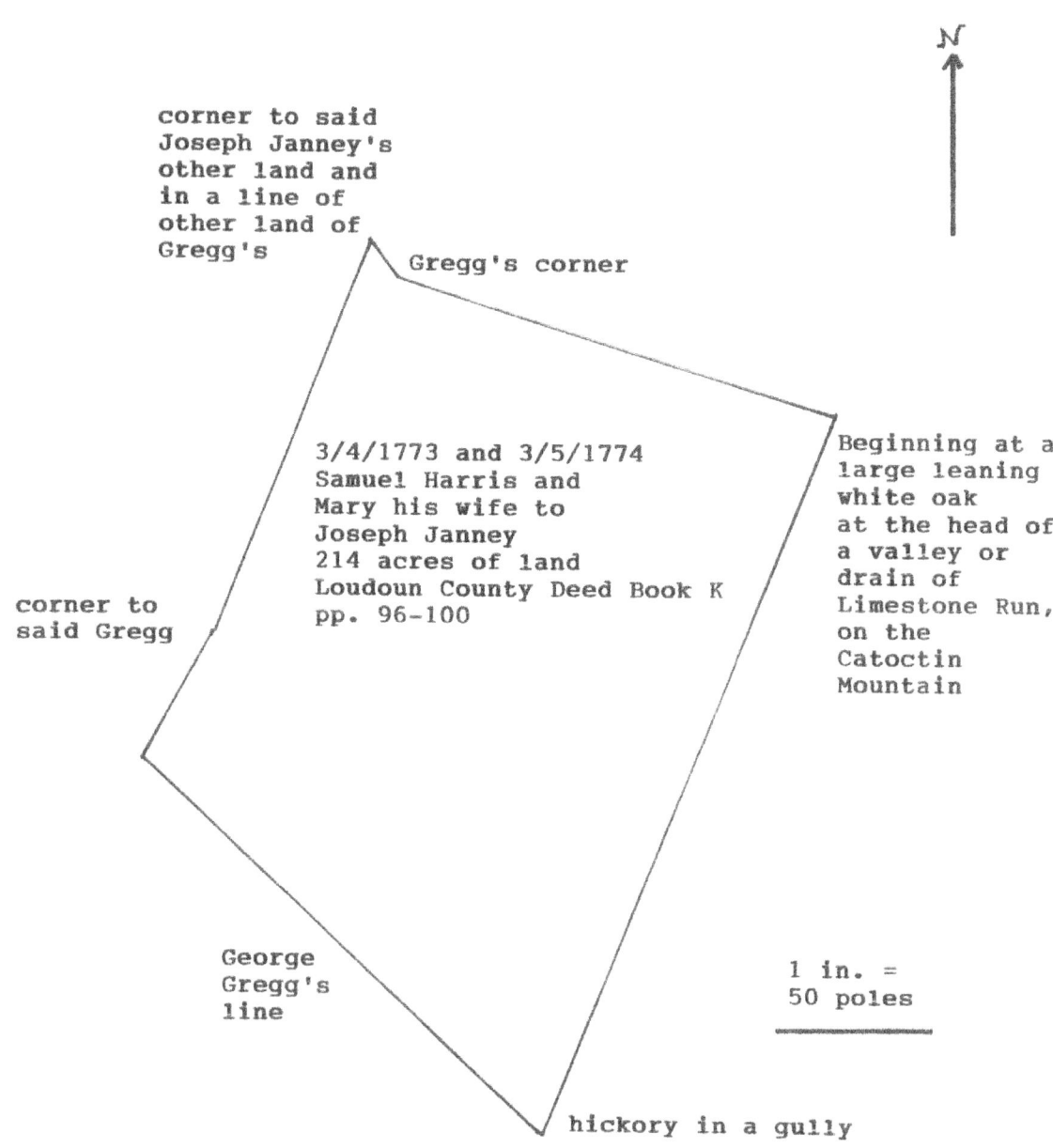

Francis Awbrey on the Potomac River at Catoctin Creek (circa 1731)

The earliest colonials on or about the Potomac River at Catoctin Creek undoubtedly remain unidentified. Generally, it was only the well-to-do who left a paper trail of their private property who've received such recognition. They were usually at the head of a company of people including family and peers, substitutes and replacements, servants and slaves. Francis Awbrey was recognized contemporary to the Colonial Period as an early settler on or about the Potomac River at Catoctin Creek. As a measure of the same, William Mayo's map of the Northern Neck of Virginia dated in 1736 includes the names "Awbrey" and "Sinclaire" on the Virginia shore of the Potomac River in the vicinity of "Canoy Island".

Francis Awbrey was a native of the Potomac River Valley. He was originally from the Lower River in Westmorland County, Colony of Virginia (b. 1690). In circa 1710 he was married to Frances Tanner of the aforesaid county. During his lifetime he became a ferry master and a real estate speculator primarily on the Upper River. It appears as if his family or people were invested with a know-how regarding the operation of ferry services, boats and scows.

Francis Awbrey and company were particularly active in contemporary land speculation on the Upper Potomac River from Four Mile Run in present-day Arlington County up to Catoctin Creek in contemporary Loudoun County. Beth Mitchell wrote that Francis Awbrey obtained landholdings from the Proprietor's Office in Fairfax County on the waters of Horsepen Run of Broad Run; Cubb Run and Rocky Cedar Run; and on the forks of Pohick Creek.[1] Otherwise, Francis Awbrey also possessed a grant for a vast tract of land under Short Hill. During his lifetime he conveyed the same to John Tayloe of Richmond County.[2]

Francis Awbrey invested in Maryland lands to a lesser degree. He mentioned in his last will and testament of his real property lying in Maryland, "over the bay". At the time of his decease according to his last will and testament he was in anticipation of possibly receiving deeds or grants for land from the land office in Maryland, for any quantity or quantities of land, "on the mail or islands".[3]

Circulation with Maryland at that time was of enough importance that Francis Awbrey was above all acquiring strategically located landholdings in such places where the crossing of the river was facilitated such as on the Potomac River at Catoctin Creek. The mouth of Catoctin Creek is about six miles west of the mouth of the Monocacy River and across the Potomac River from Point of Rocks, Maryland. At the turn of the third decade of the 18th Century the Catoctin Creek was largely uncharted ground. Awbrey's several properties in this locale fell above Goose Creek and depending on the particular tract or parcel of land they were on the waters of Big Spring Branch or Awbrey's Spring

---

[2] Bertrand Ewell, A Plat of Colo. John Tayloe's Kittockton Land, Loudoun County Deed Book A, p. 232: James McIlhaney to Andrew Reed, Bargain and Sale, Loudoun County Deed Book X, pp. 62-64
[3] Janet Green Ariciu, Transcription of Francis Awbrey's Last Will and Testament from the Virginia State Library, Richmond, Va., Janet's Genealogy, www.geocities,com/janet-ariciu/Awbrey.html?20057

Branch, Limestone Run, Clark's Run, Indian Cabin Branch of Catoctin Creek, and Catoctin Creek itself.[1]

According to case at law of John Colvil v. Thomas Aubrey heard by the Fairfax County Court dated in 1750, the late Francis Awbrey had held an interest in various lands on the Greater Catoctin Creek. The plaintiff, John Colvill, produced a deed of release from Francis Awbrey to him dated 3/18/1734, for 745 acres of land on the Potomac River with an exception for the defendant, Thomas Awbrey. The accompanying survey and description of the same reveals that this land under Catoctin Mountain joined the defendant's fence and was bounded by Indian grave sites as well as a dwelling house of Moberly's, later the Widow Pyburn's, at the mouth of Catoctin Creek. Across the mouth of Catoctin Creek was a path by a fence. This tract joined John Colvill's land from the Proprietor's Office bearing date 5/18/1731, for 4,063 acres on the Catoctin Creek. Meanwhile, the defendant Francis Awbrey produced a Proprietary deed to him in the name of Tutons dated 9/10/1731, by which he claimed 224 acres of land under Catoctin Creek.[2]

Besides, John Colvill possessed a further grant bearing date 5/13/1739, by virtue of a warrant and survey and promise of a deed to Francis Awbrey containing 4,403 acres of lands on Catoctin Creek, which was registered in the Proprietor's Office Book E, Folio 49 and 53. It is not clear how this land came into the possession of John Colvill. Nevertheless, it would come to be parceled and traded in the name of John Colvill or his estate.[3]

Additionally, Francis Awbrey owned a parcel of 100 acres of land through a William Piercy from Richard Wood, originally. It was specifically referred to in his last will as lying above Goose Creek. His heir, John Awbrey, would give his wife Mary the power to convey the same to another, which she accomplished as a widow to George Gregg dated in 1745.[4] What is more, it seems Francis Awbrey acquired a grant from the Proprietor's Office for 330 acres of land above Goose Creek, which joined the lands of Richard Averill, and Amos Sinclair and company.[5] It is noted that dated in 1745 the late Francis Awbrey's son, Thomas Awbrey, was grantee of some 207 acres above Goose Creek, which land joined the land of John Tuton, and Margaret Hawling and company.[6]

Francis Awbrey died in 1740-1741. The subject properties were at that time under the jurisdiction of Prince William County. Within a couple of years the County of Fairfax was formed along the Potomac River up to Difficult Run (1798 Line). Based on the somewhat puzzling text of his last will and testament probated on March 24, 1740/1741, he had resided at that time it seems on his plantation under the mouth of Catoctin Creek. He left his wife a combination of income, personal property including slaves and a servant, as well as a life estate in their dwelling plantation as she had three minor children to care for including Sarah, George, and Samuel. But, the deceased actually left his dwelling plantation to his son Thomas. Also, the deceased had reserved

---

[1] Loudoun County, Commonwealth of Virginia, Surveyed and Drawn by Eugene M. Scheel for the Loudoun Association of Realtors, Inc., Multiple Listing Service Committee, 1990
[2] Fairfax County Circuit Court, Archives, Record of Surveys 1742-1856, John Colvil v. Thomas Awbrey 5/14/1750, pp. 58-61
[3] John Colvill to John Hough, Lease and Release, Fairfax County Deed Book B, pp. 280-282
[4] Mary Awbrey to George Gregg, Lease and Release, Fairfax County Deed Book A, Part 1, pp. 366-369
[5] Ariciu, p. 64
[6] Ariciu, p. 65

for Thomas the contingent sum of fifty pounds from land sales so as for him to purchase "tow Negros". One of his daughter's called Elizabeth at that time was married to Philip Noland. Otherwise, the deceased would separately leave slaves and or servants to his children Thomas, Richard, Samuel, and Sarah.

The late Francis Awbrey left his other lands above Goose Creek as follows.
At the time of his decease Francis Awbrey was expecting to receive a deed for land upon the Potomac River at Clark's Run joining to Richard Roberts place, from which land he gave to his son Richard Awbrey the lower half-part above Clark's Run where one Samuel Hull lived, which joined Sinclair's land. Richard Awbrey's share of the land was distinguished by the presence thereon of a ferry road to a ferry landing place. Whereas the deceased gave to his sons Thomas and Samuel Awbrey, to be divided between them, the other half-part of the land, which stretched from Richard Awbrey's given inheritance up to the mouth of Catoctin Creek.

It is noted that the Potomac River and islands therein fall entirely in the jurisdiction of Maryland; for this reason the given ferry landing should be distinguished from a ferry service. In his last will and testament Francis Awbrey had specifically mentioned his ferry and ordinary at the falls whereas he had referred to his ferry road and ferry landing on his land above Clark's Run. The author surmises that this was a ferry landing for a ferry service that was licensed in Frederick County, Maryland, which belonged to another, possibly, John Nelson.

There was a public ferry from near Point of Rocks, which was recognized as Nelson's Ferry during a session of the Court of Frederick County, Maryland, in June of 1749.[1] Such a ferry service would have utilized Conoy Island (Heaters Island) to cross the Potomac River. In fact, a tract on Conoy Island had been surveyed as early as 1724 for Arthur Nelson of the same Nelson families.[2] By the November Court of 1755 this site was identified as that place where John Nelson formerly kept a ferry.[3] Also, there was a road nearby. In 1733 the antecedent authority of the Prince George's County Court had appointed John Nelson as overseer of the road from the mouth of Monocacy to the first mountain.[4]

Later, in 1755 the given records of Frederick County Court acknowledged the site as the nearest and best way for travelers from Fredrick Town to cross the River. Likewise, it was known for being of convenience to people traveling in and out of Virginia. But, the then ferry master, Phillip Noland, had lately removed his ferry lower down the River as there was no fitting wagon road to access the site.[5] As a consequence of which John Trammell Jr., had petitioned the Court the year before for authority to keep a ferry as a replacement for Noland's as his land was conveniently situated at or near Conoy Island.[6]

Additionally, Francis Awbrey by his last will and testament left to his son Henry a one-half part of that tract on the Potomac River containing 762 acres of land by virtue of

---

[1] Rice, Millard Milburn, This Was The Life, Monocacy Book Company, Redwood City, CA, 1979, p. 11
[2] C.E. Schildknecht, Monocacy and Catoctin, Vol. III, Family Line Publications, Westminster, MD, 1994, p. 164
[3] Rice, p. 170
[4] Schildknecht, C.E., Monocacy and Catoctin, Vol. II, Family Line Publications, Westminster, MD, 1998, p. 198
[5] Rice, p. 171
[6] Rice, p. 147

a deed dated 2/12/1739, which joined the land of Clapham and the plantation where George Williams had formerly lived. He gave the other half-part to their son George, whose share included the plantation and improvements including houses and outhouses where Andrew Greenhorn lived. Lastly, he left their daughter Sarah all that tract of land to three white oaks being Sinclair's corner, where Jonathan Richardson lived.[1] By about 1750 some such land had been conveyed to Mrs. Mason.[2]

The deceased left some other lands down the Potomac River as follows. The late Francis Awbrey bequeathed a tract of land imprecisely referred to as "at the falls", in separate shares to his sons John and Richard. Was this Great Falls or was it Little Falls or something else? John's share was where one Poultney lived. Richard's 50-acre share was one containing the aforesaid ferry and ordinary. Francis Awbrey maintained a licensed public ferry and an ordinary at a site on the mouth of Pimmit Run by 1738.[3] The author supposes that pertaining to meaning; especially Awbrey's meaning in the given writing they were one and the same.

Plus, the deceased left land on the Potomac River at Four Mile Run, which was bequeathed in half parts each to his sons Richard and Henry.[4] This site would become a landing place for a ferry service over the Potomac River via Analostan Island to and from the vicinity of Georgetown in modern day Washington, D.C., which is memorialized with a historical marker in modern Arlington County for Awbrey's Ferry. Another son, Francis Awbrey, was bequeathed all that tract of land he then lived upon at Pohick Creek together with personal stock and household goods.[5]

The subject Francis Awbrey was the father-in-law of Phillip Noland (b. circa 1718 – 1794) who became the master of a popular ferry over the Potomac River during the 18th Century, which was commonly known as Noland's Ferry. Phillip Noland had married the former Elizabeth Awbrey around 1740. The ferry service under Phillip Noland had commenced operations upriver by 1750. His ferry service at that time was described as being situated by "Noland's Island".[6] As was noted above, he moved his ferry further down the river by 1755. His ferry service landing place would then be on the Virginia shore near present day Noland's Ferry Road (Rout 660).

It is further noted that Thomas Awbrey aspired to develop a ferry service. By 1770 there was an order of court for a public road from William Kirk's Mill to the mouth of Catoctin Creek for the benefit of Awbrey's proposed ferry. But, as the road was generally not considered beneficial by the inhabitants of those parts, it was objected to by at least 38 such freeholders who signed a petitioned in rejection of the notion. The Court of Loudoun County heard the case and made an order bearing date September 11, 1770, in which the designated overseer of the road was commanded to let the road lie not cleared until said Awbrey had a proper boat and a suitable road in Maryland for such access.[7]

Lastly, on March 2, 1785 an advertisement in The Virginia Journal and Alexandria Advertiser indicated an upcoming public sale agreeable to the last will and

---

[1] Ariciu, p. 32
[2] Catesby Cocke to John Mercer, Deed of Partition, Fairfax County Deed Book C, pp. 99-106
[3] Ariciu, p. 35
[4] Ariciu, p.32
[5] Ariciu, p. 33
[6] Rice, p. 62
[7] Loudoun County Circuit Court, Archives, Miscellaneous Road Cases 1758-1782, File No. 42

testament of William Douglass Esq., at his late dwelling house, partially to the effect of the sale of 30 acres of land called the Smith's Shop Field contiguous to said dwelling house, which was purchased of Thomas Awbrey. And, 70 acres of land adjoining the Smith's Shop Field purchased of Thomas Awbrey. And, all the estate right and title of 535 acres of land on the Potomac River purchased of John Sinclair and known by the name of Hawling's Bottom, in which the said William Douglass died in possession of a 365-acre share. Also, a vacancy in 8 acres of land with a deed, which adjoined said Hawling's land. Also, 12 acres of land lying on the Potomac River adjoining the said 8 acres of land, which was purchased of Thomas Awbrey.[1]

---

[1] Wesley E. Pippenger and James D. Munson, The Virginia Journal and Alexandria Advertiser, Volume I, Willow Bend Books and Family Line Publications, Westminster, MD 1998

1. 3/12/1728, The Office of the Proprietor of the Northern Neck of Virginia of the one part to **Margaret Hawling** of the other part. Patent for land registered in the Proprietor's Office in Book B, Folio 215
2. Date unknown, The Office of the Proprietor of the Northern Neck of Virginia to **Francis Awbrey**, grantee. Patent for a tract containing 330 acres above **Goose Creek** adjoining **Richard Averill** and **Amos Sinclair.** Library of Virginia, Archives, Northern Neck Grants E, p. 136 (Reel 291), p. 138 (Reel 291).
3. 9/10/1731, The Office of the Proprietor of the Northern Neck of Virginia to **Francis Awbrey.** Patent for a tract containing 224 acres of land. Fairfax County Circuit Court, Archives, Record of Surveys 1742-1856, pp. 58-61
4. 3/18/1734, **Francis Awbrey** to **John Colvill.** The conveyance of a certain tract containing 745 acres of land with an exception. Deed of Release, Fairfax County Circuit Court, Archives, Record of Surveys 1742-1856, pp. 58-61
5. 5/18/1739, The Office of the Proprietor of the Northern Neck of Virginia to **John Colvill.** A grant by virtue of a warrant and survey and promise of a deed to **Francis Awbrey** containing 4,403 acres of land registered in the Proprietor's Office in Book E, Folio 49 and 53. See **John Colvill Gent.** to **John Hough**, blacksmith, bearing date 10/7/1747, Fairfax County Deed Book B, pp. 280-282
6. 3/24/1741 (probate date), **Francis Awbrey**, Last Will and Testament, Virginia State Library, Richmond, Virginia, as transcribed by Janet Green Ariciu for Janet's Genealogy.
7. 6/22/1744, The Office of the Proprietor of the Northern Neck of Virginia of the one part to **Margaret Sinkler (Sinclair)**, of the other part. Proprietor's deed registered in the Proprietor's Office in Libra F, Folio 82
8. 7/18/1744, **Margaret Sinkler** of Fairfax County, widow, of the one part to **Mary Richardson**, the wife of **David Richardson**, of the same County of the other part. All that tract or parcel of land containing 150 acres. It being a part of a larger tract of land surveyed for **Margaret Halling** now **Sinkler (Sinclair)** containing 586 acres of land. Lease and Release for and in consideration of the sum of 5 pounds sterling. Fairfax County Deed Book A, Part 1, pp. 223-227
9. 7/18/1744, **Margaret Sinkler**, widow, of Fairfax County of the one part to **Elizabeth Morris**, the wife of **Samuel Morris** of Prince Frederick County in

the Colony of Virginia of the other part. All that tract or parcel of land being a part of a larger tract surveyed for **Margaret Halling (Hawling)** now **Sinkler (Sinclair)**. Lease and Release, Fairfax County Deed Book A, Part 1, pp. 227-231

10. 5/13/1745, **Mary Awbrey**, widow, of Fairfax County and executrix of the late **John Awbrey** of the County of Fairfax of the one part to **George Gregg** of Fairfax County of the other part. All that tract or parcel of land containing 100 acres of land. Lease and Release for and in consideration of the sum of 10 pounds sterling. Fairfax County Deed Book A, Part 1, pp. 366-369

11. 6/17/1745, The Office of the Proprietor of the Northern Neck of Virginia to **Thomas Awbrey**, grantee. All that tract or parcel of land containing 207 acres above **Goose Creek** bordering **John Tuton**, and **Margaret Hawling**. Library of Virginia, Archives, Northern Neck Grants F, pp. 224-225 (Reel 292).

12. To all Christina people unto whom this present writing shall come, I **Francis Awbrey** of the Government of Georgia sendeth greeting. Know ye that I the said **Francis Awbrey** for and in consideration of the love and affection which I have and bear towards my loving brother **Samuel Awbrey** of the Parish of Cameron and the County of Fairfax and Colony of Virginia and for diverse other good causes and valuable considerations me hereunto moving, have given and granted and by these presents do fully freely clearly and absolutely give grant alien make over and confirm unto the said **Samuel Awbrey** his heirs executors administrators and assigns all and singular my right title interest trust property claim and demand whatsoever to me belonging or in any wise appertaining or which either me or my heirs executors administrators or assigns may can might would could should have either in law or equity in and to a certain parcel of land bequeathed and demised unto him the said **Samuel Awbrey** being the half part of the land joining to **Potomack River** above the land given to my brother **Richard Awbrey**, which land was left to my brothers **Thomas Awbrey** and **Samuel Awbrey** to be equally divided between them as will appear by my father **Francis Awbrey's** last will and testament bearing date 12/14/1741. To have and to hold all and singular the aforesaid parcel of land hereditaments and appurtenances and every part and parcel thereof unto him the said **Samuel Awbrey** his heirs and assigns as aforesaid from henceforth to his and their own proper use and uses forever. In witness whereof I the said **Francis Awbrey** have hereunto put my hand and seal this 3/8/1749-1750, **Francis Awbrey**. Signed sealed and delivered in presence of us, **Thos. Awbrey**, **William** his W mark **Hall**, and **Sarah** her X mark **Hall**. Proven on 3/27/1750. Fairfax County Deed Book C, Part 1, pp. 28-29.

13. To all Christina people unto whom this present writing shall come, I **Francis Awbrey** of the Government of Georgia sendeth greeting. Know ye that I the said **Francis Awbrey** for and in consideration of the love and affection which I have and bear toward my loving brother **George Awbrey** of the Parish of Cameron and the County of Fairfax and Colony of Virginia and for diverse other good causes and valuable considerations me hereunto moving, have given and granted and by these presents do fully freely clearly and

absolutely give grant alien make over and confirm unto the said **George Awbrey** his heirs executors administrators and assigns all and singular my right title interest trust property claim and demand whatsoever to me belonging or in any wise appertaining or which either me or my heirs executors administrators or assigns may can might would could should have either in law or equity in and to a certain parcel of land bequeathed and demised unto him the said **George Awbrey** by his father **Francis Awbrey deceased** in his last will and testament bearing date 12/14/1741, reference being had thereunto full and more at large appear, and now in possession of him the said **George Awbrey** situate in the Parish and County aforesaid joining to the **River of Potomack** and thence running along the **Widow Sinclair's** line containing 386 acres be the same more or less. To have and to hold all and singular the aforesaid parcel of land hereditaments and appurtenances and every part and parcel thereof unto him the said **George Awbrey** his heirs and assigns as aforesaid from henceforth to his and their own proper use and uses forever. In witness whereof I the said **Francis Awbrey** have hereunto put my hand and seal this 2/24/1749-1750, **Francis Awbrey**. Signed sealed and delivered in presence of us, **Thos. Awbrey**, **Paul Noland**, **William** his W mark **Hall**, and **Sarah** her X mark **Hall**. Proven on 3/27/1750. Fairfax County Deed Book C, Part 1, pp. 28-29.

14. May 14, 1750, Fairfax County. In Ejection Tierra, **John Colvil v. Thomas Awbrey**. The Plaintiff and Defendant both agreed to survey the lands in dispute though the day in the order is past and the jury is not present. The Plaintiff produced a deed of release from one **Francis Awbrey** to him dated the 18th of March, 1734, for 745 acres of land with an exception (see the deed) then proceeded to survey the above 745 acres viz. Beginning at a hickory on **Potomack River** at A, thence S 3° – 30 minutes E 82 poles when corrected to B, a large corner white oak, thence N 55° W 123 poles to C, four small corner hickories, thence N 10° W 60 poles and 12 links to D, a corner red oak on a point, thence N 59° W 170 poles no corner found at E, thence SW 50 poles no corner found at F, thence S 78° W 17 poles when corrected to G, a corner white oak by the Defendant's fence, thence South 70 poles to H. Then the Plaintiff desired me to survey from here according to the courses in **John Warner's** plat to find the corner at the **Indian grave** viz. West 82 poles to J, thence North 79 poles to No. 9, thence N 16° E 76 poles to No. 10, a white oak and chestnut at the **Indian grave**, thence N 41° W 31 poles to a white oak and a gum stump when corrected at No. 11, thence N 80° W 77 poles to a corner chestnut tree at No. 12, thence N 40° W 98 poles at the foot of the Mountain at No. 13. And, then the Plaintiff desired me to go no further in this line but measure down to **Potomack River** at right angle that is N 50° E 32 poles to No. 61, and so to lay down the meanders to the beginning hickory, which the Plaintiff says includes all the land the Defendant should have in the said 745 acres deeds as per the exception. Thence up the River the meanders thereof N 43-½° W 27 poles and 11 links, N 22° – 30 minutes W 18 poles, N 42-½° W 40 poles and 22 links, N 14-½° W 27 poles and 3 links, N 25° W 78 poles and 20 links, N 46° – 15 minutes W 69 poles and 15 links to **Moberly's** now **Widow Pyburn's** at the

mouth of **Kitocton Creek**, thence N 63-½° W 63 poles, N 20° - 30 minutes W crossing the said Creek 9 poles to a corner poplar and white oak at No. 14, thence N 50° E 26 poles to a path by a fence at No. 62, thence N 70° W 80 poles no corner but continued the course 32 poles further to a corner red oak, white oak, and beech trees showed by the Defendant at No. 59, thence N 60° E 96 poles to **Potomack River** at No. 60, and then down the meanders of the River to the first station at A. The Plaintiff produced a deed from the Proprietor's granted him bearing date the 18th of May, 1731 for 4,063 acres, and (illegible) for the second corner thereof, a poplar by **Kitocton Creek** side by a large cliff of rocks at No. 2, thence S 22-½° E 15 poles to a white hickory corner when corrected at No. 3, thence S 48° E 67 poles to a red oak at No. 4, thence S 19° E 61 poles when corrected to a red oak and hickory at No. 5, thence S 59° E 256 poles when corrected crossing the Mountain to three red oaks and a hickory at No. 6, thence N 32° E 164 poles when corrected to a white oak on the north side of the **Indian Cabin Branch** to No. 7, thence N 20° E 118 poles when corrected to a white oak to No. 8, thence S 72° - 30 minutes E 144 poles when corrected to a red oak at the Defendants fence at No. 9, thence the other courses laid down by the lines per the 745 acres at No. 10, No. 11, No. 12, No. 13, and No. 61, and so up the meanders of the River and Creek to the poplar and white oak as aforesaid at No. 14, thence from the aforesaid poplar and white oak S 60° W (at 74 poles crossed the Creek) 90 poles no corner to No. 16, thence S 65° W 122 poles no corner at No.17. And, then the Plaintiff desired me to survey no further as this part of the land is out of dispute and to plat of the remaining courses as per this plat from (illegible) at No. 17, No. 18, No. 19 and so on to No. 58 and from thence to (illegible), and from No. 1 to No. 2 where we began at for this deed and the courses distances & c. may be seen in the said 4,063 acres deed. Then the Defendant required me to lay down a line from the chestnut tree at No. 12 to the poplar and white oak at No. 14 represented in this plat by a red line bears N 36° - 30 minutes W 419 poles which he says ought to be extended. And, claims all the land in the 745 acres deed below **Kitocton Creek** as from the beginning hickory at A the several courses to the said chestnut tree at No. 12 and so to No. 14 and down the meanders of the said Creek and River to the said hickory at A. And, then the Defendant desired me desired me to reverse a line from the **Indian grave** at No. 10 to the red oak at No. 9 and found some marked trees not far out of line which he did not desire to be laid down in this plat. The Defendant produced a Proprietor's deed dated the 10th of September, 1731 for 224 acres granted to **Francis Awbrey** called **Tutons** under which he claims and desired me to plat the same as described in this plat by the following red letters and black figures viz. A, B, C, D, E, No. 9, No. 8, No. 7, and F. The Defendant claims also all the land which the Plaintiff holds below **Kitocton Creek** in the 4,063 acre-deed and also in the 745-acre deed as mentioned before. The place showed for the trespass is at the letter T where **John Watts** lately lived, **John West**, The Surveyor of Fairfax County. Sworn Chain Carriers for the Plaintiff, **David Richardson**, and **Saml. Moberly** and **David Smith**. Sworn Chain Carriers for the Defendant, **Saml. Moberly** and

Joseph Kelly. Fairfax County Circuit Court, Archives, Record of Surveys 1742-1856, pp. 58-61.

15. 8/13/1759, **John Hough, Isaac Hollingsworth, and Elenor Poultney** of Loudoun County, executors of the last will and testament of **John Poultney deceased** late of the said County of the one part to **Lee Massey** of Fairfax County of the other part. All that tract or parcel of land containing 305 acres situated formerly in Truro Parish in the County of Fairfax but lately in Cameron Parish in the County of Loudoun, which was sold and conveyed to the said **John Poultney** by a certain **Richard Abril (Richard Averill)** by indentures of lease and release bearing date 11/17/1747. Beginning at a white oak corner tree of **Francis Awbrey** standing at the head of a drain near the **Great Road** also the beginning tree of the said **Richard Abril's** tract and further bounded as in and by said recited indentures. Lease and Release for and in consideration of the sum of 320 pounds current money of Virginia. Loudoun County Deed Book A, pp. 320-327

16. 9/29/1759, **Ann Mason** of the Parish of Overwharton in the Count of Stafford, widow, and **Thomson Mason** of the same Parish and County of the one part to **David Smith** of the County of Loudoun of the other part. Witnesseth that the said **Ann Mason** and **Thomson Mason** hath demised granted and to farm let into the said **David Smith** his heirs and assigns one certain messuage tenement or parcel of land in the tenure and occupation of the said **David Smith** containing 100 acres be the same more or less. It being part of a larger tract now in the possession of the said **Ann Mason** and **Thomson Mason** lying and being in the Parish of Cameron and County of Loudoun, originally taken up and patented by **Francis Awbrey deceased**. The same to be laid off and bounded by the said **Thomson Mason** as he shall think fit including the dwelling plantation wherein the said 100 acres is to be laid off as not to hinder the settlement of any other plantation messuage or tenement now settled on the aforesaid tract. Lease for Lives, Loudoun County Deed Book B, pp. 39-44.

17. 7/13/1761, **Margaret Sinclear (Sinclair)** of Loudoun County, widow, of the one part to **John Tramel** of the same County, planter, of the other part. All that tract or parcel of land containing 178 acres more or less. The same being the residue and remainder of a larger tract of land said to contain 586 acres granted to the said **Margaret Sinclear** by Proprietor's Deed dated the 22nd day of June, 1744, which said last mentioned land hath been sold and the greatest part thereof conveyed by the said **Margaret Sinclear** in the following manner viz. 150 acres part thereof to **Mary Richardson** now the property of **William Jones**, 150 acres other part thereof to **Elizabeth Morris** and is now the property of **William Tramel**, and 108 acres another part thereof to **John Hanby** to whom it still belongs, and all the rest residue and remainder of the said tract is sold by the said **Margaret Sinclear** to **John Tramel** party to these presents and is the land intended to be hereby granted released and conveyed. Lease and Release in consideration of the sum of 71 pounds current money of Virginia. Loudoun County Deed Book B, pp. 221-225

18. 8/10/1761, **John Hanby** of Loudoun County, farmer, of the one part to **John Trammell** of the same County, planter, of the other part. All that tract or parcel of land lying and being in Loudoun County formerly Fairfax County. It being a parcel of a larger tract granted by the Proprietor of the Northern Neck to **Margaret Halling** (afterwards **Sinclair**), the same being sold and conveyed by the said **Margaret Sinclair** unto the said **John Hanby** by deeds of lease and release bearing date the 24th and 25th days of October, 1751. Lease and Release in consideration of the sum 100 pounds Pennsylvania currency, Loudoun County Deed Book B, pp. 212-216

19. 8/10/1761, **John Trammell** of Loudoun County, planter, of the one part to **William Jones** of Loudoun County, farmer, of the other part. Three tracts or parcels of land in the said County of Loudoun viz. The first tract containing 425 acres. It being the same formerly granted to **David Richardson** by Proprietor's Deed dated 12/8/1742, and by the said **David Richardson** and **Mary** his wife sold and conveyed unto the said **John Trammell** by deeds of lease and release bearing date the 11th and 12th of September, 1758. The second tract being a parcel of a tract surveyed for **Margaret Halling** now **Sinclair** containing 150 acres. It being the same formerly sold and conveyed by the said **Margaret Sinclair** to the said **Mary Richardson** wife of the said **David Richardson** by deeds of lease and release dated the 18th and 19th of July 1744, and by the said **David Richardson** and **Mary** his wife sold and conveyed unto the said **John Trammell** by deeds of lease and release bearing date the 13th and 14th of September 1758. The third tract containing 190 acres. It being the parcel of a greater tract granted by the Proprietor's deed to **Catesby Cocke** and by the said **Catesby Cocke by Aneas Campbell** his attorney in fact sold and conveyed unto the said **John Trammell** by deeds of lease and release bearing date the 11th and 12th of August 1760. Lease and Release in consideration of the sum of 675 pounds current money of Pennsylvania, Loudoun County Deed Book B, pp. 206-212

20. 8/10/1761, **John Hanby** of Loudoun County, farmer, of the one part to **John Trammell** of the same County, planter, of the other part. All that tract or parcel of land lying and being in Loudoun County formerly Fairfax County. It being a parcel of a larger tract granted by the Proprietor of the Northern Neck to **Margaret Halling** (afterwards **Sinclair**). The same was sold and conveyed by the said **Margaret Sinclair** unto the said **John Hanby** by deeds of lease and release bearing date the 24th and 25th days of October, 1751. Lease and Release in consideration of the sum 100 pounds Pennsylvania currency, Loudoun County Deed Book B, pp. 212-216

21. 6/12/1769, **Samuel Mobley** of the one part to **William Griffith** of the other part. I hereby assign convey and make over to **William Griffith** a lease I had of **Samuel Awbrey** for 150 acres of land on **Potomack River** dated 7/20/1758, for and in consideration of the sum of 27 pounds Pennsylvania currency to me in hand paid the receipt whereof I do hereby acknowledge and in witness thereto affix my hand and seal the day above. **Samuel** his X mark

Mobley. Present, **Josias Clapham**, **Richard Roach**, and **Henry Brown**. Proven on 6/13/1769. Assignment, Loudoun County Deed Book G, p. 142

22. 9/11/1770, Loudoun County Circuit Court, Archives, Miscellaneous Road Cases 1758-1782, File No. 42, Leesburg, Virginia

23. 8/6/1771, **William Griffin** of Loudoun County of the one part to **James Paxton** of the said County of the other part. All that lease hold tenement or tract of land lying on **Potomac River**. It being a tract of land formerly leased by **Samuel Awbrey** to **Samuel Mobley** and conveyed by the said **Mobley** by deed of assignment to the aforesaid **William Griffin.** Assignment, Loudoun County Deed Book H, p. 209

24. 6/3/1785, **John Compton** of Frederick County and State of Maryland of the one part to **John Cummings** of Virginia of the other part. Whereas **Samuel Awbrey** of Loudoun County in an indenture bearing date 9/12/1758 did devise grant lease and let to **Mathias Gossett** a certain messuage tenement or parcel of land containing 150 acres of land laid off as follows. Running down **Potowmack River** from the mouth of **Kittockton Creek** till it comes to the mouth of a spring that is the dividing line between the said premises and **Samuel Mobley**, then such a course as said **Mobley's** line run up the mountain so far as running to **Russell's** line, and with the said line to the Creek so as to contain 150 acres of land. Lease for Lives for and during the natural life of the said **John Compton** and his wife **Mary** and their son **John Gossett**, which lease was sold by said **Gossett** to **John Trammell** as appears by deed bearing date 9/14/1762. Now, this indenture witnesseth that the said **John Compton** for and in consideration of the sum of 5 shillings hath granted bargained sold assign and set over by these presents unto the said **John Cummings** all and singular the said messuage or tenement and premises above mentioned and every part and parcel thereof with the appurtenances. Assignment, Loudoun County Deed Book P, Part 1, pp. 292-294

25. 6/23/1810, **Isaac Steere Jr.** and **Rebekah** his wife and **Thos. Steere** of the County of Loudoun of the one part to **William Brown** of the County aforesaid of the other part. All that tract or parcel of land containing 295 acres of land. It being the tract of land formerly the property of **John Steere deceased** and directed by the last will and testament of the said **John Steere** to be sold by the executor therein mentioned, in pursuance of which the present sale was made. Beginning at a maple, oak, and gum, in **Steere's** line formerly **Sinkler** and further bounded as in and by said recited lease it doth more full and at large appear. Bargain and Sale for and in consideration of the sum of $ 5,763.34 lawful money of the Commonwealth of Virginia. Loudoun County Deed Book 2M, pp. 82-85

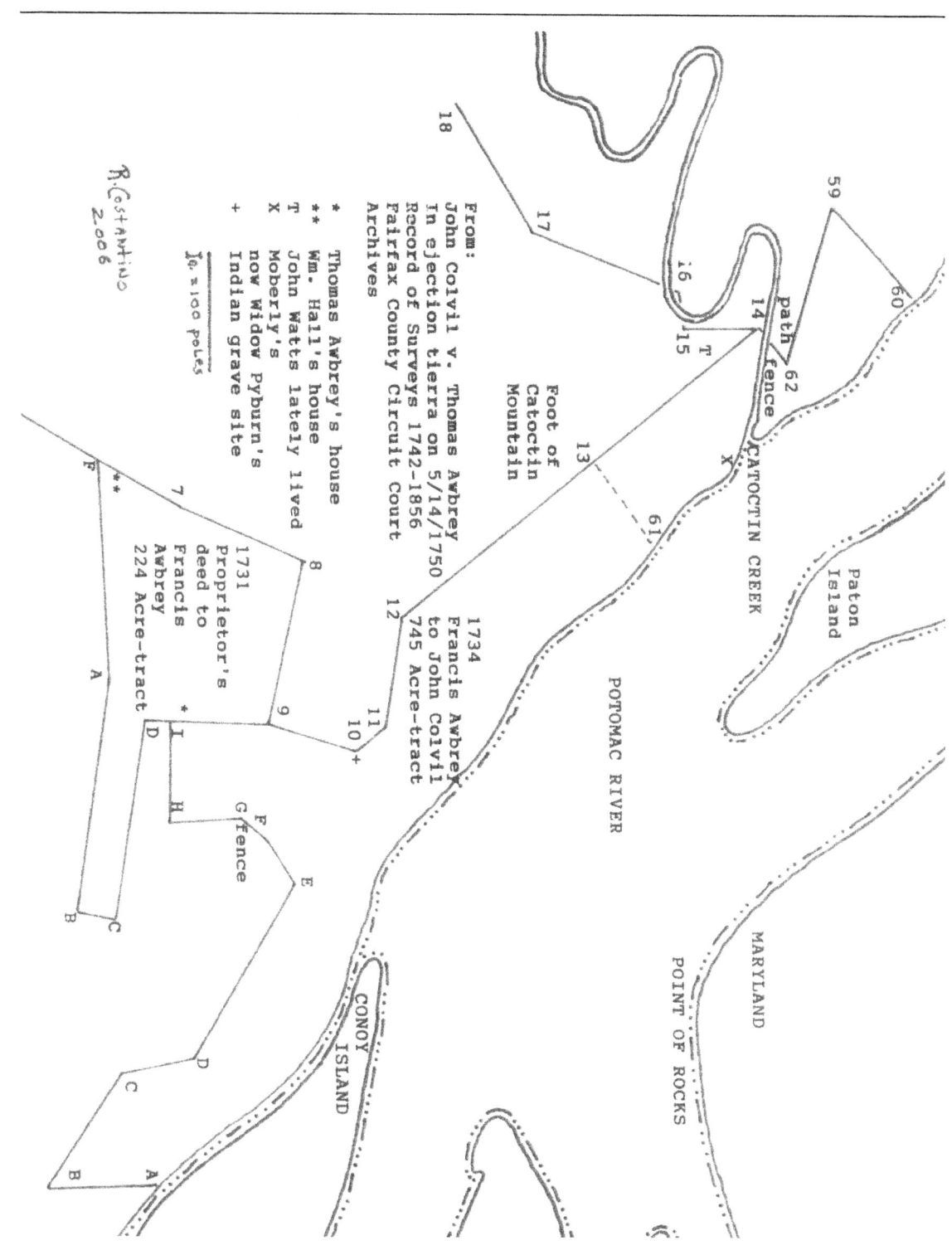

(being part of the aforesaid Margaret Sinkler's Tract) which was confirmed to her by a Patent out of the Proprietor's Office duly recorded bearing date 3/12/1728 and Registered in the Proprietor's Office in N°. B, Folio 215 and also confirmed to her by another Patent out of the Proprietor's Office bearing date 6/22/1744 in Lib. F, Folio 82

Beginning at a black oak standing in the second line of the entire tract about about fifty two poles from the second corner of the entire tract and marked for a dividing line between Eliz. Morris and the said Mary Richardson and extending thence...

...to a stake and heap of stones corner to said Morris thence...

7/11/1744
Margaret Sinkler of Fairfax County to Mary Richardson the Wife of David Richardson of the same County, Lease and Release of 151 Acres of land, Fairfax County Deed Book A, Part 1, pp. 223-227

Note: Margaret Sinkler on tract surveyed for Margaret Halling, lately, Sinkler ("Widow Halling")

...to a red oak by a Great Rock in the side of the entire tract thence...

...to a white oak near a drain of Clark's Run thence...

...about 15 or 16 miles above Goos(e) Creek and about 2 miles below Kitocton Mountain and being part of a tract of land Surveyed for Margaret Halling(now Sinkler) containing five hundred and eighty six acres...

Future: 6/23/1810, Isaac Steere Junior and Rebekah his wife & Thomas Steere to William Brown, 295 acres land, Loudoun County Deed Book 2M, pp. 82-85

This Indenture made 5/13/1745, Mary Awbrey widow & executrix of John Awbrey late of the County of Fairfax in the Colony of Virginia to George Gregg of the County & Colony aforesaid, yeoman, Lease and Release, all and singular that Tract or parcel of land and bounded as followeth for and in consideration of the sum of ten pounds sterling, Fairfax County Deed Book A, Part 1, pp. 366-369

Witnessed by R. Boggess
　　　　　　Jos Mageath
　　　　　　John Gregg

...the which tract or parcel of land was conveyed to William Peircy by Richard Wood it being a part of his Tract & by the said Peircy sold to Capt Francis Awbrey in his lifetime & by him left in his Last Will & Testament to the above said John Awbrey who by his Last Will and Testament awarded her the said Mary Awbrey with full power to convey the same to the above said George Gregg

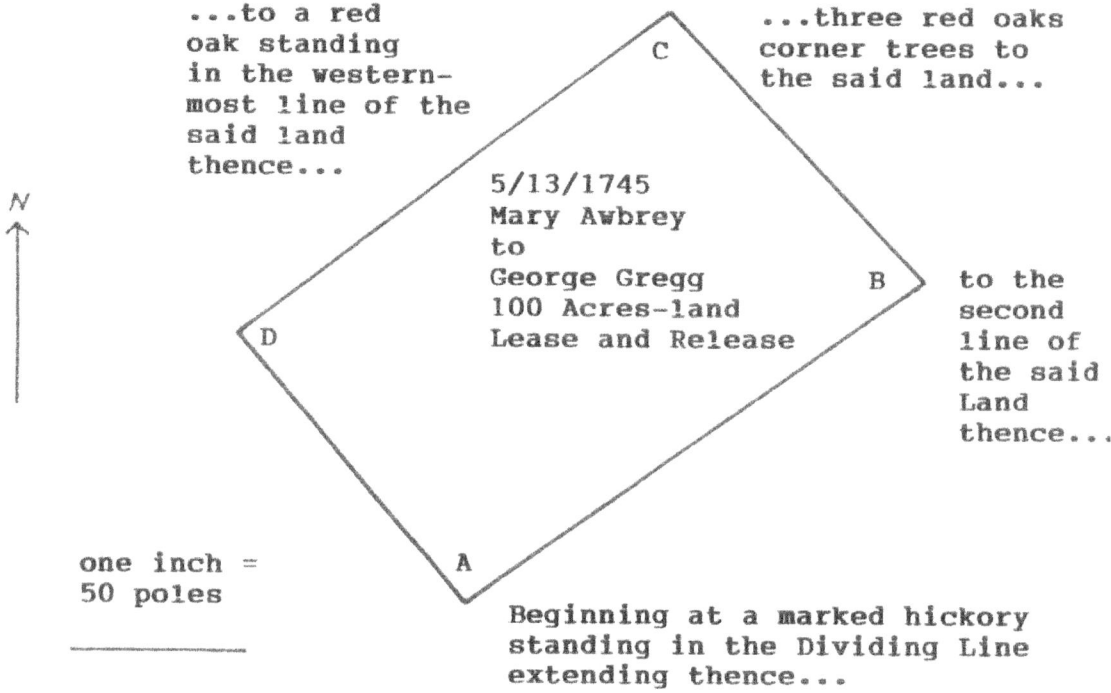

Fairfax County, Colony of Virginia
(Loudoun County)

This Indenture made 8/13 & 14/ 1759, Do Grant bargain and sell unto Lee Massey all that Tract or parcel of land with appurtenances formerly sold and conveyed to said John Poultney by a certain *Richard Abril by Indentures of Lease and Release dated 11/16 & 17/1747 and bounded as follows

...to a double bodied red oak in the line of the Widow Halling thence...

Beginning at A a white oak Corner Tree of Francis Awbrey standing at the head of a Drain near the Great Road also the Beginning tree of the said *Richard Abril's Tract of land extending thence...

a dead white oak between two live oaks thence...

B) ...a white oak and spanish oak in or near a Drain of Limestone Run near a Corner of Mr John Mercer also a corner of the said Abril's Tract thence...

8/14/1759
John Hough
Isaac Hollingsworth
and Elenor Poultney
Executors of
John Poultney dec.
to Lee Massey
305-Acre Tract for and in consideration of 320 pounds, Lease and Release, Loudoun County Deed Book A, pp. 320-326

red oak

1 in. = 50 poles

* Apparently, Richard Averill (Richard Averill and John Mead)

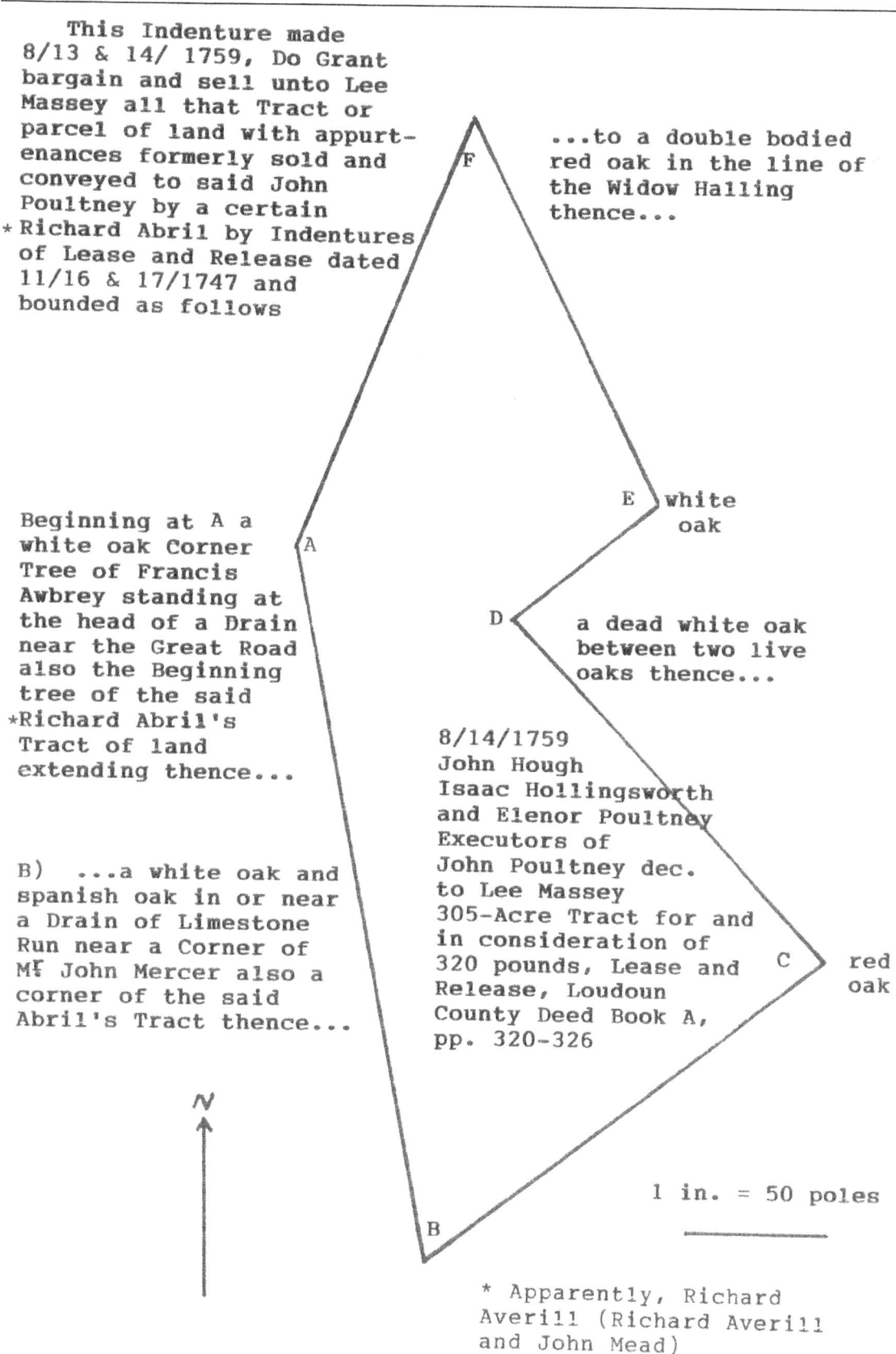

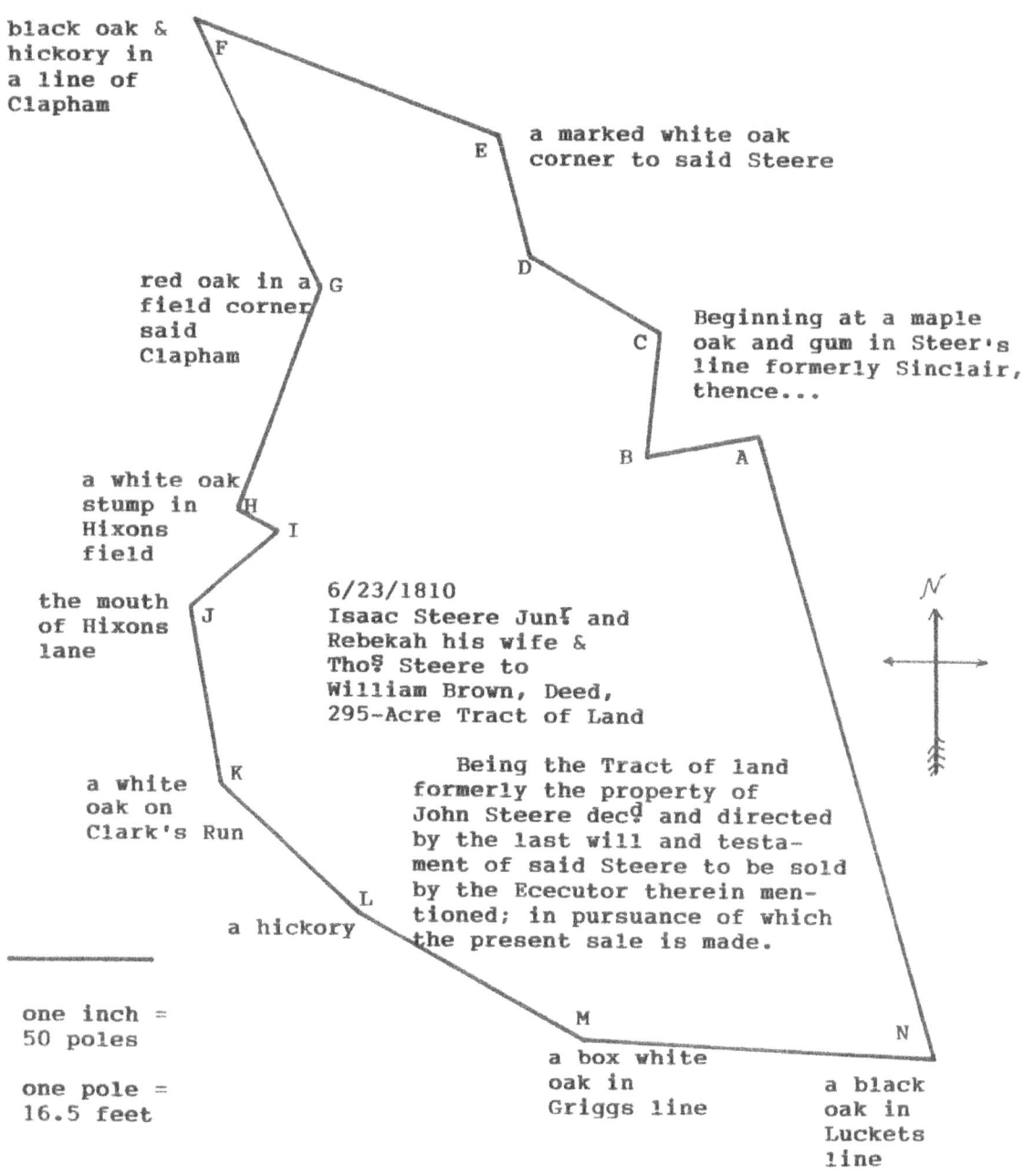

This Indenture made 6/23/1810, Isaac Steere Jr. and Rebekah his wife & Thos. Steere in consideration of $ 5,763.34 from William Brown, Deed, 295-acre Tract, Loudoun County Deed Book 2M, pp. 82-85

John Colvill's Catoctin Tract (circa 1731)

John Colvill (b. circa 1690) has been described as a mariner by some and a merchant by others. More precisely, he was the captain of a ship and a transatlantic merchant from an old home place in Newcastle upon the River Tyne, England, G.B. On another level, John Colvill was an adventurer who sought wealth and social position by unscrupulous means.

It's clear that John Colvill once earned a lucrative income of distributions in kind and dividends of ready money and sterling for commanding a marine vessel and trading in combinations of raw goods, finished goods, slaves, servants, and passage. Such merchant ships were primarily business organizations. Stockholders invested large sums of capital in consideration of future returns. He would have regularly been in charge of the organization of a somewhat large number of hands compelled to cooperate on complex synchronized tasks under a hierarchical order.

The said John Colvill was probably the same such person who was written about in the April 8, 1746 issue of the Maryland Gazette, a sea captain. It was reported that a Richard Piercy in St. Mary's County, Maryland, had said that one Henry Walley had come from London about 14-15 years before as a passenger on board a ship commanded by Capt. John Colvill, and that Piercy had an important message for Walley.[1] In another instance, Captain John Colvill ("Colvil") was reported to have been trading on the Potomac River aboard the ship Tankerville ("Tankervil").[2] He was likely the Capt. John Colvin who was reported about 1734 to have delivered personal goods directly to the Collector of Customs for the South Potomac on behalf of Thomas, Lord Fairfax.[3]

John Colvill's arrival in Northern Virginia coincided more or less with the 1724 sanctioning of an official tobacco warehouse at a Potomac River landing at Great Hunting Creek. The shallow bay fronting the site was a relatively important upriver anchorage location. It was suited for scows, droughers, and flats, while but a short distance farther out the depth of the river allowed for seagoing ships to anchor.[4] According to Beth Mitchell, John Colvill acquired real estate holdings on the waters of Great Hunting Creek from the Proprietor's Office bearing date in 1731.[5] Donald A. Wise indicates he had previously lived by 1729, in Charles County, Maryland.[6]

During the second quarter of the 18th Century, John Colvill acquired assorted landholdings from the Northern Neck Proprietary from the Potomac River at Great Hunting Creek up to the Shenandoah River. Mitchell has written about some such grants and patents including those of Colvill's up to Difficult Run. Besides, he possessed such

---

[1] Karen Mauer Green, The Maryland Gazette 1727-1761: Genealogical and Historical Abstracts. The Frontier Press, Galveston, Texas, 1989, p. 22

[2] Donald A. Wise, "Colonel John Colville (ca 1690-1755)", Don Wise- An Online Compilation of Historical Documents: This Article abstracted from the Yearbook of the Historical Society of Fairfax County, Virginia, vol. 16, 1980, pp. 94-103

[3] Stuart E. Brown, Jr., Virginia Barron: The Story of Thomas, 6th Lord Fairfax, Chesapeake Book Co., Berryville, Va., 1965, p. 48

[4] Donald G. Shomette, Maritime Alexandria: The Rise and Fall of an American Entrepot, Heritage Books, Inc., Bowie, Maryland 2003, , pp. 12-14

[5] Beth Mitchell, Beginning at a White Oak...: Patents and Northern Neck Grant of Fairfax County, Virginia, Third Edition. April 1988, Fairfax, Virginia, p. 68

[6] Donald A. Wise

landholdings and others from speculators, which rambled on from Catoctin Creek up to the Shenandoah River, the residual of which would become the deceased's Catoctin Tract ("Catacton Tract") as it was referred to in his final papers. He had other lands from speculators on Accotink Creek and on Tuscarora Run. Moreover, he acquired about 6,300 acres of land on the Maryland shore of the Potomac River. John Colvill took advantage of his circumstances to explore, locate, and identify potentially valuable real estate and to heavily speculate in such landholdings with the liquidity afforded him by his high station in life.

John Colvill was considered a gentleman, which is how he was commonly styled in legal documents. John Colvill served in the House of Burgesses for Prince William County from 1744-1747.[1] According to extracts from the Truro Parish Vestry Book, a John Colvill or Colo. John Colvill served on the vestry in 1737 and from 1739 to1741, 1743, and from 1745 to1748. On September 23, 1734, it was noted that John Colvill Gent., vestryman, was bound for England as he had promised to use his interest to procure a "discreet and godly" minister of the Anglican Church to come over to Virginia and settle in the said parish.[2]

Naturally, given his high status he had important friends and acquaintances; notably, the Proprietor's cousin and agent, Colonel William Fairfax of Belvoir. Author and historian Stuart E. Brown indicates they were partners in the land business.[3] John Colvill and John Minor promoted a scheme in 1745 to lay out a settlement at the navigable head of Great Hunting Creek called "Cameron", which plan was not approved.[4]

The evidence suggests that John Colvill lived comfortably in the Colony of Virginia. He mostly resided at his dwelling plantation called Cleesh on a branch of Great Hunting Creek. John Colvill recorded its name as "Cleesh" whereas his brother and heir, Thomas Colvill, referred to it as "Clish". It was an improved landscape site with a frame and brick house.[5] Some of the other buildings upon his plantation were a mill and a brewery distillery.[6] Its fields were cultivated with grain and tobacco.[7] The List of Tithing for 1749 indicates that John Colvill was classified a Presbyterian and was charged 5 tithes for some combination of free or indentured people and 29 tithes more for enslaved people. It was further noted he was a Colonel in the militia, a justice of the peace, and formerly was a vestryman.[8]

The names John Colvill and Thomas Colvill used for their main dwelling plantation of "Cleesh" or "Clish" may provide some further insight into their background.

---

[1] Donald A. Wise

[2] F. Edward Wright and Wesley E. Pippenger, Early Church Records of Alexandria City and Fairfax County, Virginia, Family Line Publications, Westminster, Maryland 1996, pp. pp. 98-99

[3] Stuart E. Brown, Jr., p. 102

[4] Donald A. Wise

[5] John Colvill, Inventory, Fairfax County Will Book B, Part 1, pp. 135-141: see "11 Brick moulds- 6 Iron'd" , p. 136

[6] The Right Honorable Charles Astley Bennett the Earl of Tankerville of the Kingdom of Great Britain to John Patterson, Letter of Attorney, Loudoun County Deed Book C, p. 98: Beth Mitchell, Beginning at a White Oak…: Patents and Northern neck Grants of Fairfax County, Virginia, Third Printing, April 1988, Fairfax, Virginia, p. 126 ("the remains of old brewhouse" 1/15/1790)

[7] Charles, Earl of Tankerville to John Patterson, Letter of Attorney, Loudoun County Deed Book C, Part 1, pp. 98-109

[8] Donald A. Wise

There has been in Great Britain a familial line of Colville of Cleish recorded as early as the 16th Century. Some of them would have been of comparatively high birth and the head of the clan would have resided in Cleish Castle, Kinross, Scotland. The now restored castle has been described as a five story tower standing on the northern slopes of the Cleish Hills.[1] Kinross, the town and the only small burgh in the county is of considerable antiquity. Kinross-Shire is bounded on the north and west by Perthshire, on the southwest by Clackmannanshire, and on the south and east by Fife. In modern time it has been the least populated county in Scotland and the second to the smallest.[2]

On John Colvill's paternal side his line came from Norman ancestors. It seems that some such as Colvill had come to permanently settle in Great Britain as early as the 12th Century, especially in Scotland and Ireland. His last name which he spelled Colvill was and is commonly spelled Colville. Some other variations in the colonial records of his family name are Colvil, Colvell, Colwell, and even Colvin. Genealogical research indicates that the clans Colville have a connection with the clans Colvin. John Colvill would have come from a class of lesser gentry, merchants and nascent manufacturers, who tended to be Whigs.

John Colvill had some contemporary near relatives in his orbit. He had a brother in the aforesaid Thomas, who it appears was a merchant. They had a sister named Esther who had married Captain Mathias Giles. Their mother Catharine Colvill had died in Newcastle around 1719. Thomas Colvill's brother in law was George Colvill from Newcastle. They were allied through marriage in someway with Charles Bennett, Earl of Tankerville of the Kingdom of Great Britain.

As events would turn out, Thomas Colvill would live out his final years in Fairfax County. Thomas Colvill described aspects of his background in his final papers published in Fairfax County bearing date 10/8/1766. He was originally from Newcastle on the Tyne, England, lately from Cecil County, Maryland, but at that time from Fairfax County, Virginia. He indicated in his final papers he had maternal relations in Durham, England, named Stott, Wills, Richardson, and a woman named Catherine Smith.

Thomas Colvill of Fairfax County was in his own right an accomplished man. It appears he was lately Thomas Colvill with the tracts of Horn Point and Knowlwood in Cecil County as was listed in Debt Books. In 1752 Thomas Colvill was a taxable person in Cecil County while in possession of three slaves. There was a Thomas Colvill listed as a commissioner in Cecil County who was empowered on August 6, 1730, to lay out a town on Broxen's Point called Ceciltown, which was on the Bohemia River. In 1742 he was a commissioner appointed to carry out the incorporation of Charlestown, which was to be laid out at Long Point on the North East River.[3] There was a Thomas Colvill of Cecil County who was recorded in the deed records of Baltimore County between 1743 and 1748.[4] It was reported in the Maryland Gazette in 1745 that Colo. Thomas Colvill was elected to serve in the General Assembly of Maryland.[5] In another issue dated in 1749 it was reported in the Maryland Gazette that Colo. Thomas Colvill and others were

---

[1] Clan Colville Society Homepage, www.geocities.com/clancolville/
[2] Encyclopedia Britannica, Volume 13, William Benton, Publisher, Chicago, 1959
[3] Henry C. Peden, Inhabitants of Cecil County, Maryland 1649-1774, Family Line Publications, Westminster, Maryland 1993
[4] John Davis, Baltimore County, Maryland, Deed Records Volume Two: 1727-1757, Heritage Books, Westminster, Maryland 1996
[5] Karen Mauer Green, p. 13

then representatives for Cecil County in place of others.[1] Additionally, Colo. Thomas Colvill or Thomas Colvill was recorded in the Proceedings and Acts of the General Assembly for Cecil County, Maryland.[2]

At the time of his death, John Colvill was seemingly unmarried. In his final papers was mentioned his brother in law, George Colvill, which suggests he had intermarried a family member. He recited in his last will and testament about having resided for a time with a certain freed servant woman named Mary Foster, by whom they had at least one surviving illegitimate daughter called Catharine. Mary Foster had come into the country on the testator's ship and when freed from her indenture, she continued to live with him for several years.[3]

John Colvill may have become the target of scandal for his apparent indiscretions. In 1752 the grand jury of Fairfax County reported its findings as to whether or not a certain John Colvill had lived in fornication with Mary Carney.[4] What is more, John Colvill became cash poor with outstanding liabilities, which he could not afford to settle. It's obvious from his final papers that he died heavily in debt, first and foremost to the Earl of Tankerville, and, secondly, to his brother Thomas Colvill. John Colvill left a paper trail of personal faults and financial shortcomings.

Thomas Colvill in his final papers published charges against John Colvill along with their sister Esther of having concealed from him through neglect or carelessness a legacy of one hundred pounds sterling left to him by their mother in Newcastle around 1719. He wrote it was kept entirely from his knowledge until he accidentally examined a box of old papers left in his possession many years before by John Colvill, wherein he found correspondence between his brother in London and his sister in Newcastle dated in 1719, and a copy of their mother's will and papers, and thereby uncovered proof of his evident deficiency. At the time of this apparent malfeasance, John Colvill had been staying in London acting in the capacity of the executor for their late mother's estate in Newcastle, England, while Thomas Colvill was away in Virginia.[5]

It seems likely that John Colvill had probably anticipated his own imminent death when he made his last will and testament bearing date of 5/6/1755. He died in early 1756. John Colvill deceased selected both the Earl of Tankerville and Thomas Colvill as executors of his last will and testament while concurrently appointing his brother as his acting executor. In an action towards settling with the deceased's principal creditor he being the Earl of Tankerville, the deceased conveyed unto him a rich and valuable estate in lands and slaves in Virginia, but withal subjecting the lands and slaves (his dwelling plantation slaves excepted) towards the payment of all his just debts.[6]

The first piece of real estate referenced in John Colvill's will implying a primacy of some sort was the residue of the deceased's tract of land upon the branches of Accotink Creek in Fairfax County called the Hither Quarter. It contained at that time

---

[1] Karen Mauer Green, p. 61 (see p. 67)
[2] Archives of Maryland Online, Proceedings and Acts of the General Assembly, Volume 40, p. 169, p. 429, p. 518; Vol. 42, p. 238; Vol. 46, p. 52; Vol. 63, p. 12
[3] Charles, Earl of Tankerville to John Patterson, Letter of Attorney, Loudoun County Deed Book C, Part 1, pp. 98-109
[4] Donald A. Wise
[5] Thomas Colvill, Last Will and Testament, Fairfax County Will Book B, pp. 424-432
[6] Charles, Earl of Tankerville to John Patterson, Letter of Attorney, Loudoun County Deed Book C, Part 1, pp. 98-109

about 650 acres of land, which during his lifetime John Colvill had bought from Edward Emms and otherwise taken up from the Proprietary. The deceased's Hither Quarter had neighbored William Fairfax's 1,400-acre tract of land called Springfield or Springfield Manor, which was on and about the site of the first actual courthouse building in Fairfax County as well as an ordinary and other houses. It appears that much of John Colvill's once Hither Quarter is overlaid in modern times by Merrifield.[1]

The deceased did give and bequeath the Hither Quarter to Thomas Colvill together with the appurtenances and slaves and stock of all kinds. This land was devoted to agricultural production by slaves, which were supervised by overseers or a foreman. A quarter in this context was a farm worked by some combination of free, indentured and enslaved people. The Hither Quarter would have included from one to a few simple domestic buildings and structures devoted to the accommodation of people that provided both functional and social separation between slaves, servants, and those they served.[2]

The second piece of real estate referenced in John Colvill's will was the deceased's dwelling plantation called Cleesh on Great Hunting Creek in Fairfax County, which at that time contained about 1,000 acres together with neighboring waste land taken up from the Proprietary and the mill with appurtenances thereto belonging, and all houses, utensils, slaves and stock. It was John Colvill's will it be conveyed to his brother Thomas Colvill during his lifetime before descending to the Earl of Tankerville. John Colvill added the proviso to the bequest that the remaining slaves inhabiting the plantation would remain attached to the subject land.

The third piece of real estate referenced in John Colvill's will was the deceased's Catoctin Tract ("Catactin Tract") in Fairfax County (Loudoun County est. 1757), which he left in entirety save a 1,000 acres reserve near John Hough to the Lord of Tankerville. It was transcribed for his will that it contained 16,000 acres of land whereas his surviving brother, Thomas Colvill, would later estimate it to include 16,290 acres. It was at that time inhabited by slaves and was stocked with horses, cattle and hogs. The Catoctin Tract had been joined together by John Colvill during his lifetime beginning around 1731, from different tracts of land he had acquired in real estate transactions from probably at least four sources including Francis Awbrey, Amos Janney, Proprietor's Office of the Northern Neck of Virginia, and, most likely, John Gregory.[3]

In fact, John Colvill had resold more land on the Greater Catoctin Creek than he retained. Bearing date 5/17/1739 John Colvill had acquired a landholding of 17,296 acres on the waters of Catoctin Creek from the Proprietor's Office, which he afterwards sold to William Fairfax bearing dates 5/17 and 5/22/1740. Similarly, John Colvill had acquired about 29,120 acres of land, which rambled from the North Fork of Catoctin

---

[1] Kenton Kilmer and Donald Sweig, The Fairfax Family in Fairfax County: A Brief History, Fairfax County Office of Comprehensive Planning, Third Printing, January, 1992, pp. 75-77

[2] Carl R. Lounsbury, An Illustrated Glossary of Early Southern Architecture & Landscape, Oxford University Press, New York 1994

[3] John Colvill to John Hough, blacksmith, Lease and Release, Fairfax County Deed Book B, Part 1, pp. 280-282: John Hough, blacksmith, to George Gregg, yeoman, Lease and Release, Fairfax County Deed Book B, Part 1, pp. 413-416: Fairfax County Circuit Court, Archives, Record of Surveys 1742-1856, John Colvil v. Thomas Awbrey, In Ejection Tierra, pp. 58-59: Charles, Earl of Tankerville to John Patterson, Letter of Attorney, Loudoun County Deed Book C, Part 1, pp. 98-109: Joseph Cadwallader by Septimus Cadwallader to Obed Pierpoint, Bargain and Sale ("survey made for John Gregory now Tankerville"), Loudoun County Deed Book W, pp. 200-202

Creek at Short Hill to the Shenandoah River. Likewise, he sold it to William Fairfax. One generation later they would be called and known as George William Fairfax's Piedmont Tract or Piedmont Manor and Shannondale Tract or Shannondale Manor.[1]

The fourth piece of real estate referenced in John Colvill's will was the deceased's tract or parcel of land lying on the branches of Difficult Run in the County of Fairfax containing about 1,500 acres of land as also his 2/9ths share of the copper mine, and 200 contiguous acres of land he held in the company of others. One of the said branches would appear to have been Colvin Run. Mitchell wrote that sometimes Colvin is written instead as Colvill, which the author hereby confirms.[2] It was John Colvill's will that such lands be handed down to the said Charles, Earl of Tankerville. These lands are overlaid in modern times by the authority of the Great Falls post office.[3]

The fifth piece of real estate referenced in John Colvill's will was a patent for a tract called Merryland on the shore of the Potomac River, Maryland. Originally, it was surveyed for Benjamin Tasker and contained 5,000 acres of land. Shortly afterwards, John Colvill ("John Colville") of Newcastle on the Tyne bought it and had it resurveyed in 1732 to include 6,300 acres of land.[4] It was John Colvill's will that it be sold by his executor or executors to be applied towards paying his debts and legacies.

The sixth piece of real estate referenced in John Colvill's will was the deceased's tracts or parcels of land lying on or about Four Mile Run in Fairfax County containing about 1,400 acres. It was John Colvill's will that it be disposed of by his executors in such manner as most might tend to be advantageous to his estate on behalf of the Earl of Tankerville and his heirs.

The seventh piece of real estate referenced in John Colvill's will was his tract of land and plantation lying on the branches of Tuscarora in Fairfax County (Loudoun County est. 1757), which the deceased had bought from Middleton Shaw containing 178 acres together with one-half the horses, cattle and hogs. It was John Colvill's will that it be handed down to the aforesaid Mary Foster, "in full consideration of her services and demands".[5]

The eighth piece of real estate referenced in John Colvill's will was the aforesaid reserve of 1,000 acres of land near John Hough. The deceased bequeathed the same to his daughter Catharine by Mary Foster, who was at that time married to John West Jr., together with 15 slaves, "old and young". This property was from such a tract or parcel of land, which the deceased had bought from Amos Janney.

Dated in 1747, John Colvill had sold a piece of his Catoctin Tract containing 500 acres of land to John Hough, blacksmith. The subject deed indicates that Colvill had assigned the land to Hough for and in consideration of a reserve of the late Francis

---

[1] Costantino, Roberto, Catoctin: The Fairfax Family and the Freeholders of Piedmont Manor and Shannondale Manor, Willow Bend Books, Westminster, MD, 2006 (publication is scheduled for September, 2006)
[2] Mitchell, p. 68
[3] Kenton Kilmer and Donald Sweig, pp. 62-65
[4] Grace L. Tracey and John P. Dern, Pioneers of Old Monocacy: The Early Settlement of Frederick County, Maryland 1721-1743, Genealogical Publishing Company, Inc., Baltimore, Maryland, 1989, pp. 37-39. C.E. Schildknecht, Editor, Monocacy and Catoctin, Volume II, Family Line Publications, Westminster, MD, 1998, p. 45
[5] Charles, Earl of Tankerville to John Patterson, Letter of Attorney, Loudoun County Deed Book C, Part 1, pp. 98-109

Awbrey's.¹ In turn, John Hough, blacksmith, conveyed one-half part of the given tract of land on the same day to George Gregg, yeoman, for and in consideration of a settlement made to the satisfaction of the administrators of Amos Janney.²

Dated in 1760, the House of Hough in the name of John Hough (surveyor) reacquired by deed of release those 250 acres from the House of Gregg in the names of John Gregg and Elizabeth his wife for monetary consideration.³ There can be but little doubt that the given transaction was made in anticipation of John Hough's further acquisition of the given 1,000 acres from Catharine and John West Jr., which conveyance was actually consummated dated July 20, 1761, by deed of release from John West Jr. and Catharine his wife to John Hough (surveyor) for monetary consideration.⁴ These several transactions resulted in John Hough's (surveyor) control of about 1,500 contiguous acres on the waters of Catoctin Creek.

A survey and plat of those 1,000 acres of land was made by George West, which was published in Loudoun County bearing date June 8, 1762. The sworn chain carriers had been Thos. Dodd and Levi Wells. It shows within the nucleus of the boundaries of the outer 1,000 acre tract of land the given 500 acres tract of land marked, "Hough's 500 Acres". The boundary description indicates that the lines were marked with at least one marker seemingly for Francis Awbrey and John Colvill as in FA-JC, and another apparently for John Mead and John Hough as in JM-JH.⁵

Otherwise, John Colvill left a conditional bequest of 40 pounds sterling to the heir or heirs of his brother in law, the late George Colvill of New Castle on the Tyne, England. It was his stated intention to thereby provide for the descendants of George Colvill with cash in lieu of all or any of them inheriting or enjoying any other part of his estate. And, the deceased handed down to the trustees or managers of the Charity School of All Saints Parish in New Castle the sum of 40 pounds sterling to be used and disposed of for the benefit of the school.

On January 20, 1756, the Earl of Tankerville made an agreement with John Patterson Gent. of the Parish of Saint James, Westminster, County of Middlesex, to depart from England for Virginia, and there take possession and management of the said several estates and affairs for and in behalf of and as steward, agent or manager for the Earl of Tankerville. John Patterson was thereby authorized to be the Earl of Tankerville's lawful attorney and in his name to enter into and upon and take possession of all and singular the estates, plantations, mills, works, tracts of land, tenements, shares of mines, slaves, hereditaments, stock of all kinds, and all matters and things belonging to the Earl in Virginia and Maryland.⁶

Among his varied responsibilities John Patterson was charged with receiving from the acting executor, Thomas Colvill, an exact account of all his receipts relating to the

---

¹ John Colvill to John Hough, blacksmith, Lease and Release, Fairfax County Deed Book B, Part 1, pp. 280-282
² John Hough, blacksmith, to George Gregg, yeoman, Lease and Release, Fairfax County Deed Book B, Part 1, pp. 413-416
³ George Gregg to John Hough, Lease and Release, Loudoun County Deed Book A, pp. 406-410
⁴ John West and Catharine his wife to John Hough, Lease and Release, Loudoun County Deed Book B, pp. 242-247
⁵ Survey and Plat by George West, Loudoun County Deed Book C, pp. 270-272
⁶ Charles, Earl of Tankerville to John Patterson, Letter of Attorney, Loudoun County Deed Book C, Part 1, pp. 98-109

estate of John Colvill. Moreover, he was certified to jointly collect or cause to be collected all and every part of the personal estate and debts that were due to the deceased John Colvill, and to pay and satisfy in due course all the debts and legacies due and owing from the said John Colvill to the Earl of Tankerville. John Patterson was obliged to make a remittance of the produce every six months.

An inventory of the personal estate of Colo. John Colvill deceased was made dated February 6, 1756 and recorded in Fairfax County dated March 17 and April 10, 1756.[1] It was prepared and arranged by location, building by building and room by room. The specified locations covered in the account included his dwelling plantation or Cleesh, Tom's Quarter, and Joe's at the New Quarter. His estate possessed seemingly a surplus of slaves, finished goods and raw goods as he had been a merchant. It appears there were 20 slaves residing on his dwelling plantation. Otherwise, there were 10 slaves who belonged to the deceased at what was called Joe's on the New Quarter, and 11 more slaves belonging to him at Tom's Quarter for a total of 41 slaves. The subscribers to the record were Nick Minor, John Moss and Phil Noland.

The estate of John Colvill possessed many merchantable hardware goods, especially heavy metals. There were among other goods, 61 small narrow axes, 68 unsorted cart boxes, 67 large grubbing hoes, 17 large narrow hoes, 94 pair-cross hinges, 53 pair-locks & hinges, 28 pair-hinges without hooks, 436 lbs. of new iron, 509 lbs. of old iron, 50 lbs. of new iron hoops, 186 lbs. of sheet & pipe lead, 17 lbs. of steel, 206 lbs. of cart tiers and hoops, 92 lbs. of ox chains, 36 lbs. of pipe lead, 11 dozen glass-gallon bottles, 6 dozen pewter buttons, nails and brads and so on. There were hardware goods too with nautical applications such as 5 ship carpenter axes, 26 ships scarper and one large and valuable chain.

Cleesh was a dwelling plantation or compound. It appears the late John Colvill's dwelling house contained four rooms with a loft above the stairs. There was also an overseer's house with a chimney-fireplace at Cleesh, which was equipped with among other things a bed and rug, 3 chairs and an old chest, cooking goods and tongs, two guns and 1 whip saw. There was a shed with a room used for storage. Cleesh was equipped with tools for making fires, cooking, cleaning, dairying, spinning, clearing, farming, shearing, carpentry, cooperage, masonry and blacksmithing. The estate had on hand 80 bushels of salt and 16 bushels of corn beans. The deceased owned a valuable wagon and harness for four horses with a riding chair. It was previously noted there was a mill and a brew house on his dwelling plantation.

The late John Colvill's dwelling house was composed of a hall or room, a stove room, little room, deceased's room, and a loft above the stairs. The stove room was fitted with a bed and contained a pantry, two tables, and house-ware goods. The little room was fitted with a bed and contained a trunk, chest, table, looking glass, chair, sugar-box with lock, flatware, spy glass, and various fabric goods. The deceased's bedroom was fitted with a bed and contained a desk, case-of-drawers, 2 tables, chair, large balance scale, small balance scale, chest and lock, hair trunk, flatware, silver hilted sword, iron hilted sword, pair of pocket pistols, and a parcel of doctor's means (instruments). The hall was fitted with a bed and contained a desk, looking glass, 2 tables, 6 chairs and 1 armchair, glassware, china and dinnerware including 7 delft plates and 2 japanned

---

[1] Colvill, Colo. John, Gent., Fairfax County Will Book B, Part 1, pp. 135-141 as transcribed for http://GunstonHall.org

serving boards, and a collection of 20 painted flowers and 38 unpainted canvasses it seems, and 6 large prints and 7 small prints of different sorts. The loft above the stairs was fitted with a bed and contained an armchair, trunk, blunderbuss, troopers' saddle pistols with holsters and holster caps and bridle, 8 small hunting saddles, 8 horse collars, 20 basket hilted cutlasses, fabrics, and miscellaneous goods.

At a place called Joe's on the New Quarter there was personal property belonging to John Colvill's estate. Aside from the aforesaid slaves there was livestock on the site, which quarter was equipped with 2 felling axes and an old axe, 50 lbs. of old iron and pots and hooks. At a place called Tom's Quarter there was personal property belonging to the deceased. Aside from the aforesaid slaves there was livestock on the site, which quarter was equipped with a table, fabrics, azimuth compass, book case with sundry books, silver watch, glass gallon bottles and quart bottles, farming tools, felling tools, 20 yards sail cloth, one box 40 lbs. red lead, 20 lbs. window lead, 300 lbs. drop shot.

Finally, the personal estate of the deceased included much livestock. There were upon his dwelling plantation on Great Hunting Creek 27 of several types of bovine, 7 of several types of equine, 16 of several types of swine, and 34 sheep. There were upon Tom's Quarter; 15 of several types of bovine, 4 equine, and 55 of several types of swine. Finally, there were at Joe's on the New Quarter; 3 equine and 8 of several kinds of bovine.

About nine years later, Thomas Colvill made a reference in his final papers to the plantation whereon he had lately lived or Cleesh and another plantation near it called Tom's Quarter, which indicates that Tom's Quarter as well was to be found on and about Great Hunting Creek.[1] For this reason, one may deduce that Joe's at the New Quarter was elsewhere, possibly, on the Catoctin Tract as the deceased's accounts included charges against his estate for appraisers at "Catacton".[2]

As was stated the Lord of Tankerville and Thomas Colvill were constituted and appointed the executors of John Colvill's last will and testament. But, as the bulk of the debts were owed and due to persons in England and to Thomas Colvill in sterling money, power was therefore given Thomas Colvill for his security as acting executor to sell the tract called Merryland and to raise any deficiency from the sale of any Virginia lands or slaves he should think fit in full satisfaction of all the deceased's just debts; except, his Lordship would take upon himself the payments thereof, which his Lordship refused to do.[3]

Under the authority of the Earl of Tankerville, there appeared an advertisement in the June 12, 1760 issue of the Maryland Gazette more or less as follows: John Patterson, agent, at Fairfax County, Virginia, has land for rent, property of Charles the Earl of Tankerville, lying on Potomack River and Kittockton Creek in Loudoun County, Virginia. Apply to Patterson at William Kirk's on Kittockton Creek or Andrew Adams, merchant, in Leesburg.[4]

By the summer of 1760, John Patterson began to raise monies from new revenues sources by indentures of lease for lives for land to farm on and about the Catoctin Creek. The Earl of Tankerville as represented by John Patterson had styled the former Catoctin

---
[1] Thomas Colvill, Fairfax County Will Book B, pp. 424-432
[2] John Colvill, Fairfax County Will Book B, pp. 442-445
[3] Thomas Colvill, Fairfax County Will Book B, pp. 424-432
[4] Karen Mauer Green, p.255, p. 276

Tract as Catoctin Manor ("Catoctian Manor"). Typically such indentures of lease for lives were made for the term of three lives. They included in the terms and conditions of the respective lease a clause, which required the lessee to only use a water suit mill built by or for the Earl of Tankerville on Catoctin Manor provided it be and within five miles of the lessee's place under penalty of forfeiture of lease.

In his authority as the agent for the Earl of Tankerville, John Patterson traded indentures of lease for lives for land to farm in the names of men named Samuel Coombs for 150 acres,[1] William Braddock for 100 acres,[2] James Ferguson for 100 acres,[3] Samuel Schooley for 100 acres,[4] another to Samuel Schooley for 100 acres,[5] William Grant for 113-1/2 acres,[6] James Hamilton for 109 acres and 13 perches,[7] Adam Count for 100 acres,[8] Henry Count for 100 acres,[9] Henry O'Daniel for 100 acres,[10] David Foxal for 100 acres,[11] Joseph Teel for 100 acres,[12] Joseph Teel Junior for 100 acres,[13] William Henderson for 100 acres.[14]

The boundary description of the given lease to Samuel Coombs dated June 14, 1760, made a reference in the boundary description to an adjacent spread of land called John Patterson's Reserve. There were a total of 14 lots leased from the Earl of Tankerville by John Patterson on and about Catoctin Creek amounting to about 1,472 acres of land, which were entered into the records of Loudoun County. Moreover, Patterson leased at least one other lot to William Trammell, which was on Difficult Run (presently in Fairfax County).[15]

---

[1] Charles, Earl of Tankerville by John Patterson to Samuel Coombs, Lease for Lives, Loudoun County Deed Book B, pp. 346-350

[2] Charles, Earl of Tankerville by John Patterson to William Braddock, Lease for Lives, Loudoun County Deed Book B, pp. 350-354

[3] Charles, Earl of Tankerville by John Patterson to James Ferguson, Lease for Lives, Loudoun County Deed Book B, pp. 355-359

[4] Charles, Earl of Tankerville by John Patterson to Samuel Schooley, Lease for Lives, Loudoun County Deed Book C, pp. 5-10

[5] Charles, Earl of Tankerville by John Patterson to Samuel Schooley, Lease for Lives, Loudoun County Deed Book C, pp. 10-14

[6] Charles, Earl of Tankerville by John Patterson to William Grant, Lease for Lives, Loudoun County Deed Book B, pp. 342-346

[7] Charles, Earl of Tankerville by John Patterson to James Hamilton, Lease for Lives, Loudoun County Deed Book C, Part 1, pp. 277-282

[8] Charles, Earl of Tankerville by John Patterson to Adam Count, Lease for Lives, Loudoun County Deed Book C, Part 1, pp. 272-276

[9] Charles, Earl of Tankerville by John Patterson to Henry Count, Lease for Lives, Loudoun County Deed Book C, Part 1, pp. 282-287

[10] Charles, Earl of Tankerville by John Patterson to Henry O'Daniel, Lease for Lives, Loudoun County Deed Book C, Part 1, pp. 287-292

[11] Charles, Earl of Tankerville by John Patterson to David Foxal, Lease for Lives, Loudoun County Deed Book C, Part 1, pp. 297-302

[12] Charles, Earl of Tankerville by John Patterson to Joseph Teel, Lease for Lives, Loudoun County Deed Book C, Part 1, pp. 302-307

[13] Charles, Earl of Tankerville by John Patterson to Joseph Teel Junior, Lease for Lives, Loudoun County Deed Book C, Part 1, pp. 307-312

[14] Charles, Earl of Tankerville by John Patterson to William Henderson, Lease for Lives, Loudoun County Deed Book C, Part 1, pp. 292-297

[15] Charles, Earl of Tankerville by John Patterson to William Trammell, Lease for Lives, Loudoun County Deed Book C, Part 2, pp. 660-664

An examination of the contemporary record of tithing in Cameron and Shelburne Parish under a name such as the Earl of Tankerville reveals that his Lordship was regularly liable for tithing charges for slaves residing on his Catoctin Manor. Possibly, the slaves were remains from the days of John Colvill's Catoctin Tract. On a list of tithes taken bearing date in 1761, there were 6 charges for slaves to the Earl of Tankerville. On a list of tithes taken bearing date in 1765, there were 8 charges for slaves to the Earl of Tankerville ("The Honorable Charles Earl Tankerville's Quarter"). Also, there was a coded notation for 12,369 acres of land, which was assigned to hm. On a list of tithes taken bearing date in 1767, there were 8 charges for slaves to the Earl of Tankerville. Also, there was a coded notation for 13,369 acres of land, which was assigned to him. On a list of tithes taken bearing date in 1768, there were 8 charges for slaves to the Earl of Tankerville. On a list of tithes taken bearing date in 1771, there were 3 charges for slaves to The Earl of Tankerville.[1]

It is noteworthy that the given 1765 tithing record had in fact referred to the Earl of Tankerville's quarter. A quarter as such would have been an improved landscape site, which could have been enclosed. It would have included a few simple buildings or structures and objects of low quality committed to the storage of stock of all kinds and the accommodation of people.[2] Eugene M. Scheel wrote about a landscape site in Loudoun County between Lovettsville and Taylorstown (Taylor Town) on Route 667 or Tankerville Road known as Tankerville, which by about 1830 was the site of a post office.[3]

The Earl of Tankerville's agent had a rival in Thomas Colvill as he objected to having been being excluded from participating in the given solicitations of tenants. So in response to John Patterson, Thomas Colvill ran an advertisement in the October 15, 1761 issue of the Maryland Gazette, wherein he maintained that Patterson as agent for the Earl of Tankerville had advertised land for rent in Virginia without permission, which was devised to his Lordship by the will of the late John Colvill but was subject to payment of the deceased's debts.[4] In a later issue of the same publication dated November 5, 1761, John Patterson, at that time in Leesburg, responded to the same.[5] Around the same time, Charles, Earl of Tankerville, died. By his last will and testament bearing date 8/13/1762, he devised unto his two sons, Charles, Earl of Tankerville and Henry Astley Bennett, both of the Kingdom of Great Britain, the authority to sell the aforementioned lands if they should agree to sell the same, as by the said will of record in the Dumfries District Court did more filly appear.

As for the aforesaid Merryland Tract, at one time Thomas Colvill seemingly intended to divide the tract into lots of land for men named Lee, West, Magruder, and Philpot. Accordingly, Charles Beatty made a plat of it in 1762, which subdivided it into

---

[1] Marty Hiatt and Craig Roberts Scott, Loudoun County Virginia Tithables 1758-1786, Volume 1-3, Iberian Publishing Company, Athens, Georgia 1995
[2] Carl R. Lounsbury, An Illustrated Glossary of Early Southern Architecture & Landscape, Oxford University Press, New York, 1994
[3] Eugene M. Scheel, Loudoun Discovered: Communities, Corners & Crossroads, Volume 5, Presented by The Friends of Thomas Balch Library, 2002, pp. 87-91
[4] Karen Mauer Green, p. 276
[5] Karen Mauer Green, p. 277

22 lots averaging about 286 acres of land.[1] Apparently, such transactions were not entered into the records of the Court of Frederick County, Maryland.

Subsequently, Thomas Colvill by October 28, 1764 learned that John Hough's son had come to a piece of land and marsh adjacent to Cleesh ("Clish") to survey it pursuant to a warrant directed to him from John Patterson, which land John Colvill during his lifetime had taken up from the Proprietor. Thomas Colvill would formally complain to Thomas Bryan Martin, Agent for the Proprietor of the Northern Neck of Virginia, of the same as the warrant had not made the least mention either to his Lordship or Colville. Thomas Colvill charged John Paterson with having obtained the given warrant for a survey of the land under false pretenses.[2]

According to Thomas Colvill's account of it, his Lordship's agent had for a long time been fermenting disputes and differences between his Lordship and himself by false reports. Thomas Colvill accused John Patterson with villainy. But, he openly declared his Lordship's (Earl of Tankerville) innocence from all causes of his complaints. It was Thomas Colvill's opinion that Patterson had imposed himself upon his Lordship at a time when he was sick and abroad.

Thomas Colvill was tenacious. The estate of his brother John Colvill had been indebted to him for many years and he had wanted satisfaction from the Earl of Tankerville by John Patterson. Thomas Colvill went to the September Court for 1761 in Fairfax County in a legal action against the Earl of Tankerville's side, before whose justices he produced accounts of his administration of the said estate and inserted his account of the subject debts he was due in the amount of 829 pounds and seventeen shillings sterling, which case was decided in his favor. His Lordship's agent then appealed from the judgment to the General Court at Williamsburg, where it got hung up for several years. During April, 1765, upon a hearing before the General Court, the judgment of the Fairfax County Court was confirmed.

Apparently, information and data about the same got back to the Earl of Tankerville. John Patterson's potentially lucrative business venture as agent for the Lord of Tankerville came to a screeching halt; the Catoctin Manor was no more. Consequently, after an exchange of correspondence between Thomas Colvill and representatives for the Lord of Tankerville, including his Ladyship, Thomas Colvill would come to offer reconciliation to Charles, Earl of Tankerville. They reached a settlement whereby the Earl of Tankerville obliged himself to Thomas Colvill in the net amount of 687 pounds and 16 shillings and 11 pence sterling. What's more, Thomas Colville remained the acting executor for the estate of the deceased John Colvill while simultaneously becoming the agent for the Earl of Tankerville.[3] Shortly afterwards Thomas Colvill assigned such authority over to George West.[4] Nevertheless, it seems that formal transactional activity on Catoctin Manor had come to a halt.

Thomas Colvill died in late 1766 and his will was probated on January 19, 1767. The executors for the deceased's last will and testament were his widow Frances Colvill, George Washington Esquire, and John West Jr. It was Thomas Colvill's will that what

---

[1] Grace L. Tracey and John P. Dern, p. 38
[2] Mitchell, pp. 125-126
[3] Charles, Earl of Tankerville to Thomas Colvill, Power of Attorney, Loudoun County Deed Book E, pp. 31-48
[4] Thomas Colvill to George West, Power of Attorney, Loudoun County Deed Book E, pp. 115-116

was left of his lands at Accotink be sold together with some slaves. It appears that the deceased's estate included 22 slaves and their infant children. It was Thomas Colvill's will that such monies as above when recovered from the Earl of Tankerville be applied towards the payment of all his just debs and legacies. It was Thomas Colvill's will that his executors sell so much of the remaining landed estate of his deceased brother John Colvill, as would satisfy all his just debts. Thomas Colvill left the sum of 100 pounds to executor John West Jr. for his trouble and 100 pounds to George Washington.

Thomas Colvill would have been around sixty-five years of age at the time of his decease. He was lately of Cleesh Plantation on Great Hunting Creek in Fairfax County.[1] He left his widow Francina, alias Frances Colvill, the plantation whereon the deceased had lately lived and the plantation near it called Tom's Quarter including 450 acres of land. And, from his personal estate the deceased left her his household furniture including a clock, either three or four horses and a chair and harness, and varied interests in 15 slaves and their young children. He left a half interest in one such slave named Ben who was to be trained as a blacksmith to John West Jr. But, at the decease of his wife or her widowhood the said 450 acres with slaves and stock would descend to her niece, Sarah Savin. Additionally, he left his wife's niece Sarah Savin, the sum of 250 pounds current money and a slave girl called Teeny.

Otherwise, Thomas Colvill left other bequests to among others Benjamin Moody who was to receive two hundred acres out of his Accotink Tract and a young slave woman called Daphne. He left a slave girl named Sarah to Ann, the daughter of Capt. William Ramsay, who was already in her possession. He left a slave girl named Monica to Sarah Johnston, the daughter of Capt. Geo. Johnston. He left a slave girl named Nan to Catharine, the daughter of John West Jr. He left a slave boy named Spencer to Thomas, son of John West Jr. He left Isabella Hollingsbury the sum of 20 pounds current money and the use of the deceased's tract of land containing 150 acres near Pimmit Run. He left the sum of 80 pounds sterling to the youngest daughter of William Anderson, merchant in London. Lastly, in the event there be any surplus in the deceased's estate it was Thomas Colvill that it be divided into four equal parts among his late mother's given relations in Durham and Catharine Smith or their descendants.

In 1765 Thomas Colvill had attempted to sell the tract called Merryland intact to John Semple for and in consideration of 2,500 pounds sterling. But, whereas Thomas Colvill died before receiving the consideration monies and prior to having executed any actual formal conveyance of the same to John Semple, the sale went into an indeterminate state. Being that Thomas Colvill's estate was indebted for varied sums of money and legacies, which could not be paid until the executors actually received the liabilities from John Colvill's estate, his executors published prayers the General Assembly of Maryland would pass such a law as would allow them to make a sufficient deed to Semple or his assigns so the respective wills of John and Thomas Colvill could be complied with. Merryland was ultimately conveyed intact dated in 1772 to Adam Stewart, Thomas Montgomery, and Cumberland Wilson.[2]

---

[1] Charles, Earl of Tankerville to Thomas Colvill, Power of Attorney, Loudoun County Deed Book E, pp. 31-48

[2] Archives of Maryland Online, Proceedings of the Acts of the General Assembly, Volume 63, page 110, Volume 63, page 293

Although in the short run the lands in John Colvill's estate had not produced sufficient income to anyone's satisfaction, nevertheless, there is no doubt that over time there was a substantial capital appreciation in the value in the assortment of land. And, whereas the said Charles, Earl of Tankerville and Henry Astley Bennett mutually agreed to sell the aforesaid lands, they by their letter of attorney dated December 22, 1789, did constitute and appoint Robert Townsend Hooe and Charles Little, their attorneys for them and each of them to dispose of and convey the lands and estate to which John Colvill deceased had or might have had any right, title or claim. As a result, the properties were systematically liquidated piece by piece to diverse freeholders.

1. 5/18/1731, The Office of the Proprietor of the Northern neck of Virginia to **John Colvill**, a tract containing 4,063 acres of land, Fairfax County Circuit Court Archives, Record of Surveys 1742-1856, pp. 58-61

2. 9/10/1731, The Office of the Proprietor of the Northern neck of Virginia to **Francis Awbrey**, a tract containing 224 acres of land, Fairfax County Circuit Court Archives, Record of Surveys 1742-1856, pp. 58-61

3. 3/18/1734, **Francis Awbrey** to **John Colvill**, a tract containing 745 acres of land with an exception, Deed of Release, Fairfax County Circuit Court Archives, Record of Surveys 1742-1856, pp. 58-61

4. Date unknown, The Office of the Proprietor of the Northern neck of Virginia to **John Colvill**, a tract containing 2,250 acres of land, Fairfax County Circuit Court Archives, Records of Surveys 1742-1856, pp. 58-61

5. 5/18/1739, The Office of the Proprietor of the Northern Neck of Virginia to **John Colvill**, a grant by virtue of a warrant and survey and promise of a deed to **Francis Awbrey** containing 4,403 acres of land and registered in Book E, Folio 49 and 53. See indenture **John Colvill Gent.** to **John Hough**, blacksmith, bearing date 10/7/1747, Fairfax County Deed Book B, pp. 280-282

6. 10/7/1747, **John Colvill, Gent.** of Fairfax County and Colony of Virginia of the one part to **John Hough** of Fairfax County, blacksmith, of the County and Colony aforesaid of the other part. Whereas there is a certain tract or parcel of land situate lying and being in the County of Fairfax aforesaid on the **North and South Forks of Kittocton** viz. Beginning at a white hickory corner to **John Mead** extending thence N 27° E 300 poles to a stake, thence N 68° W 225 poles to a hickory or stake, thence S 19° W 403 poles to a stake on a hill, thence S 70° E 196 poles to a stake in a bog, thence N 14° E 100 poles to the first station containing 500 acres of land, and whereas the same is part of a tract that was granted to the said **John Colvill** his heirs and assigns forever by a good sufficient deed from the Proprietor of the Northern Neck of Virginia by virtue of a warrant and survey and promise of a deed to **Francis Awbrey** containing 4,403 acres the said patent bearing date the 18th day of May, 1739 and registered in the said Proprietor's Office in Book E, Folio 49 and 53, under certain rents reservations and exceptions in the said grant expressed as by the said patent more fully and at large appears. Now this indenture witnesseth that the said **John Colvill** for and in consideration of a **Reserve** of the late **Francis Awbrey** made with the said **John Colvill** agreed to by the said **Colvill**, whereof the said **John Colvill** doth hereby acknowledge full satisfaction thereof and for every

part thereof, doth acquit and discharge the said **John Hough** his heirs and assigns by these presents hath granted bargained sold alienated released and confirmed and by these presents doth bargain sell alien release and confirm unto the said **John Hough** and his heirs and assigns all and singular the 500 acres of land situate bounded and being as is above set forth and described, together with all the houses barns buildings orchards gardens ways waters watercourses woods meadows swamps fishings fowlings hawkings huntings rights liberties privileges improvements advantages hereditaments and appurtenances with the rents issues profits of the same. To have and to hold the said 500 acres of land hereditaments and premises hereby granted alienated released or confirmed or mentioned or intended to be granted and release with the appurtenances unto the said **John Hough** his heirs and assigns forever, **John Colvill**. Sealed and delivered in the presence of us, **Hugh West Jr.**, **Francis Hague**, and **Saml. Mead**. Proven on 11/17/1747. Lease and Release, Fairfax County Deed Book B, Part 1, pp. 280-282

7. 10/17 and 18/1748, **John Hough** of Fairfax County in the Colony of Virginia, blacksmith, and **Sarah** his wife of the one part to **George Gregg** of the same place, yeoman, of the other part. Whereas there is a certain tract or parcel of land situate lying and being in the County of Fairfax aforesaid on and near **Kittockton Creek** viz. Beginning at a white oak and stake near the **Lower Beaver Dam Branch of Kittockton** extending thence S 19° W 187 poles to a stake and black oak, thence S 68° E 202 poles to a stake and white oak, thence N 27° E 186 poles to a stake, thence N 68° W 225 poles to the first station containing by estimation 250 acres being the half part of a tract said to contain 500 acres of land conveyed to the above said **John Hough** by **John Colvill Gent.** by lease and release bearing date the 7th day of October, 1747 recorded in Libra B, Folio 281. And, whereas the said 500 acres is part of a tract that was granted to the said **John Colvill** his heirs and assigns forever by good sufficient deed from the Proprietor of the Northern Neck in Virginia by virtue of a warrant of a survey and promise of a deed to **Francis Awbrey** containing 4,403 acres the said patent bearing date the 18th of May, 1739, and registered in the said Proprietor's Office in Book E, Folio 49 and 53, under certain rents reservations and exceptions in the said grant expressed as by the said patent more fully and at large appears, now this indenture witnesseth that the said **John Hough** and **Sarah** his wife for and in consideration of a settlement and satisfaction made to the administrators of **Amos Janney** late of the County of aforesaid deceased by the said **George Gregg** whereof the said **John Hough** doth hereby acknowledge as full satisfaction and therewith fully satisfied contented and paid, hath granted bargained and sold alienated released and confirmed and by the presents doth bargain sell alien release and confirm unto the said **George Gregg** and his heirs and assigns all and singular the said 250 acres of land more or less situate lying and being as is above set forth and described, together with all and singular the barns buildings orchards gardens ways waters watercourses woods meadows swamps fishings fowlings hawkings huntings rights liberties privileges improvements advantages hereditaments and appurtenances with the rents issues and profits of the same. To have and to hold the said 250 acres of land

hereditaments and premises hereby granted alienated released or confirmed or mentioned or intended to be granted and released with the appurtenances unto the said **George Gregg** his heirs and assign forever, **John Hough** and **Sarah Hough**. Sealed and delivered in the presence of **Francis Hague, John Hanbey**, and **Martha Harris**. Proven on 11/15/1748. Lease and Release, Fairfax County Deed Book B, Part 1, pp. 413-416.

8. May 14, 1750, Fairfax County. In Ejection Tierra, **John Colvil v. Thomas Awbrey**. The Plaintiff and Defendant both agreed to survey the lands in dispute though the day in the order is past and the jury is not present. The Plaintiff produced a deed of release from one **Francis Awbrey** to him dated the 18th of March, 1734, for 745 acres of land with an exception (see the deed) then proceeded to survey the above 745 acres viz. Beginning at a hickory on **Potomack River** at A, thence S 3° – 30 minutes E 82 poles when corrected to B, a large corner white oak, thence N 55° W 123 poles to C, four small corner hickories, thence N 10° W 60 poles and 12 links to D, a corner red oak on a point, thence N 59° W 170 poles no corner found at E, thence SW 50 poles no corner found at F, thence S 78° W 17 poles when corrected to G, a corner white oak by the Defendant's fence, thence South 70 poles to H. Then the Plaintiff desired me to survey from here according to the courses in **John Warner's** plat to find the corner at the **Indian grave** viz. West 82 poles to J, thence North 79 poles to No. 9, thence N 16° E 76 poles to No. 10, a white oak and chestnut at the **Indian grave**, thence N 41° W 31 poles to a white oak and a gum stump when corrected at No. 11, thence N 80° W 77 poles to a corner chestnut tree at No. 12, thence N 40° W 98 poles at the foot of the Mountain at No. 13. And, then the Plaintiff desired me to go no further in this line but measure down to **Potomack River** at right angle that is N 50° E 32 poles to No. 61, and so to lay down the meanders to the beginning hickory, which the Plaintiff says includes all the land the Defendant should have in the said 745 acres deeds as per the exception. Thence up the River the meanders thereof N 43-½° W 27 poles and 11 links, N 22° – 30 minutes W 18 poles, N 42-½° W 40 poles and 22 links, N 14-½° W 27 poles and 3 links, N 25° W 78 poles and 20 links, N 46° – 15 minutes W 69 poles and 15 links to **Moberly's** now **Widow Pyburn's** at the mouth of **Kitocton Creek**, thence N 63-½° W 63 poles, N 20° - 30 minutes W crossing the said Creek 9 poles to a corner poplar and white oak at No. 14, thence N 50° E 26 poles to a path by a fence at No. 62, thence N 70° W 80 poles no corner but continued the course 32 poles further to a corner red oak, white oak, and beech trees showed by the Defendant at No. 59, thence N 60° E 96 poles to **Potomack River** at No. 60, and then down the meanders of the River to the first station at A. The Plaintiff produced a deed from the Proprietor's granted him bearing date the 18th of May, 1731 for 4,063 acres, and (illegible) for the second corner thereof, a poplar by **Kitocton Creek** side by a large cliff of rocks at No. 2, thence S 22-½° E 15 poles to a white hickory corner when corrected at No. 3, thence S 48° E 67 poles to a red oak at No. 4, thence S 19° E 61 poles when corrected to a red oak and hickory at No. 5, thence S 59° E 256 poles when corrected crossing the Mountain to three red oaks and a hickory at No. 6, thence N 32° E 164 poles when corrected to a white oak on the north side

of the **Indian Cabin Branch** to No. 7, thence N 20° E 118 poles when corrected to a white oak to No. 8, thence S 72° - 30 minutes E 144 poles when corrected to a red oak at the Defendants fence at No. 9, thence the other courses laid down by the lines per the 745 acres at No. 10, No. 11, No. 12, No. 13, and No. 61, and so up the meanders of the River and Creek to the poplar and white oak as aforesaid at No. 14, thence from the aforesaid poplar and white oak S 60° W (at 74 poles crossed the Creek) 90 poles no corner to No. 16, thence S 65° W 122 poles no corner at No.17. And, then the Plaintiff desired me to survey no further as this part of the land is out of dispute and to plat of the remaining courses as per this plat from (illegible) at No. 17, No. 18, No. 19 and so on to No. 58 and from thence to (illegible), and from No. 1 to No. 2 where we began at for this deed and the courses distances & c. may be seen in the said 4,063 acres deed. Then the Defendant required me to lay down a line from the chestnut tree at No. 12 to the poplar and white oak at No. 14 represented in this plat by a red line bears N 36° - 30 minutes W 419 poles which he says ought to be extended. And, claims all the land in the 745 acres deed below **Kitocton Creek** as from the beginning hickory at A the several courses to the said chestnut tree at No. 12 and so to No. 14 and down the meanders of the said Creek and River to the said hickory at A. And, then the Defendant desired me desired me to reverse a line from the **Indian grave** at No. 10 to the red oak at No. 9 and found some marked trees not far out of line which he did not desire to be laid down in this plat. The Defendant produced a Proprietor's deed dated the 10th of September, 1731 for 224 acres granted to **Francis Awbrey** called **Tutons** under which he claims and desired me to plat the same as described in this plat by the following red letters and black figures viz. A, B, C, D, E, No. 9, No. 8, No. 7, and F. The Defendant claims also all the land which the Plaintiff holds below **Kitocton Creek** in the 4,063 acre-deed and also in the 745-acre deed as mentioned before. The place showed for the trespass is at the letter T where **John Watts** lately lived, **John West**, The Surveyor of Fairfax County. Sworn Chain Carriers for the Plaintiff, **David Richardson**, and **Saml. Moberly** and **David Smith**. Sworn Chain Carriers for the Defendant, **Saml. Moberly** and **Joseph Kelly**. Fairfax County Circuit Court Archives, Record of Surveys 1742-1856, pp. 58-61.

9. 5/6/1755, **John Colvill deceased** of Fairfax County was seized in fee of several tracts of land in **Fairfax County**, **Virginia**, and **Frederick County**, **Maryland**. By his last will and testament among other things the deceased did bequeath unto his daughter and son in law, **Catharine** the wife of **John West Jr.** and their heirs forever, a certain tract or parcel of land containing 1,000 acres being part of his **Catoctin Tract** ("**Catactin Tract**"), which would be laid off adjoining to **John Hough's** land, which he had bought from **Amos Janney**. Moreover, the deceased would devise the residue of his Virginia lands including the bulk of his **Catoctin Tract** unto his creditor, **Charles Bennett**, **Earl of Tankerville** of Great Britain his heirs and assigns forever. Last Will and Testament, **John Colvill** (John Colville), Fairfax County Will Book B, p. 97: Inventory, Fairfax County Will Book B, p. 135, p. 141: Estate Account, Fairfax

County Will Book B, p. 395, p. 442, Fairfax County Will Book E, p. 334, p. 280, p. 282

10. 3/5/1759 The Right Honorable **Charles, Earl of Tankerville** of the one part to **John Patterson** of the other part. Power of Attorney, Loudoun County Deed Book C, Part 1, pp. 98-109

11. 3/10 and 3/11/1760, **George Gregg** of the County of Loudoun and Colony of Virginia and **Elizabeth** his wife of the one part to **John Hough** of the said County of the other part. Witnesseth that the said **George Gregg** and **Elizabeth** his wife for and in consideration of the sum of 66 pounds and three shillings current money of Virginia the receipt whereof the said **George Gregg** and **Elizabeth** his wife doth hereby acknowledge, hath granted bargained sold aliened released and confirmed and by these presents doth fully freely and absolutely grant bargain sell alien release and confirm unto the said **John Hough** and to his heirs and assigns forever, all that tract or parcel of land containing 250 acres of land situate lying and being in the County of Loudoun aforesaid on the **Kittocton Creek** including the main fork thereof and bounded as followeth viz. Beginning at a stake near a marked hickory sapling and a spanish oak on hill corner to the said **John Hough's** land above his lane and extending thence N 19° E 190 poles to a hickory and red oak, thence S 68° E 225 poles to a stake in a line of **John Mercer** crossing the said Creek, thence with said **Mercer's** line S 27° W 188 poles to a white oak and red oak on hillside corner to said **Hough,** thence with his line N 68° W 200 poles to the first station crossing the said Creek below the said **Hough's** meadow, together with all members and appurtenances thereunto belonging and the reversion and reversions, remainder and remainders, rents issues and profits thereof and all the estate right title interest claim and demand whatsoever both in law and equity to him the said **George Gregg** and **Elizabeth** of in and to the said premises above mentioned with the appurtenances. To have and to hold the said 250 acres of land with the appurtenances unto the said **John Hough** his heirs and assigns forever, **George Gregg** and **Elizabeth Gregg**. Proven on 5/13/1760. Lease and Release, Loudoun County Deed Book A, pp. 406-410

12. These indenture made these 20th and 21st days of July, in the year of our Lord Christ 1761, and first year of the reign of our **Sovereign Lord, George the Third,** by the grace of God of Great Britain, France and Ireland, King, Defender of the Faith and so forth, between, **John West, Gent**. of the County of Fairfax in the Colony and Dominion of Virginia and **Catharine** his wife of the one part to **John Hough, Gent**. of the County of Loudoun in the Colony and Dominion of Virginia aforesaid of the other part. Whereas **John Colvill Gent**. late of the County of Fairfax aforesaid, deceased, by his last will and testament bearing date the 6th day of May, 1755 amongst other things therein contained did give and bequeath unto his daughter the wife of the said **John West** and their heirs forever, 1,000 acres of land part of his **Catactan Tract** to be laid off adjoining to **John Hough's** land which he bought of **Amos Janney,** in such manner as his executors in the said will mentioned should appear as by the said last will and testament duly proven recorded and enrolled in the Court of the County of Fairfax by inspection may at large appear. And, whereas the said

executors nominated and appointed in and by the said will hath not laid off unto the said **John West** and **Catharine** his wife the said 1,000 acres of land nor marked the same with particular metes and bounds, but it still remains to be done according to the above bequest. Now this indenture witnesseth that they the said **John West** and **Catharine** his wife for and in consideration of the sum of 327 pounds and 10 shillings current money of Virginia to them in hand paid by the said **John Hough** the receipt whereof they the said **John West** and **Catharine** his wife do hereby confess and acknowledge and for diverse other good causes and consideration them thereunto moving, they the said **John West** and **Catharine** his wife have granted bargained and sold aliened released and confirmed and by these presents do grant bargain and sell alien release and confirm unto the said **John Hough** and to his heirs and assigns forever all and singular the above mentioned 1,000 acres of land so as aforesaid given and bequeathed by the said **John Colvill** unto the said **John West** and **Catharine** his wife, together with all and singular the rights members and appurtenances thereunto belonging and all houses buildings orchards meadows waters watercourses profits commodities emoluments and hereditaments whatsoever to the said 1,000 acres of land belonging or in any wise appertaining, which now are or formerly have been accepted reputed taken known used occupied or enjoyed to or with the same or as part parcel or member thereof or of any part thereof. To have and to hold the said 1,000 acres of land hereditaments and premises above mentioned and every part and parcel thereof with the appurtenances unto the said **John Hough** his heirs and assigns to the only proper use of him the said **John Hough** his heirs and assigns forever, **John West Jr.** and **Catharine West**. Sealed and delivered in the presence of **W. Ellzey, Francis Dade, Benja. Sebastian, James Donaldson, John Heryford**, and **Stephen Donaldson**. Proven on 8/11/1761. Lease and Release, Loudoun County Deed Book B, pp. 242-247

13. To all to whom these presents shall come. I **Thomas Colvill Gent.** of the County of Fairfax in the Colony and Dominion of Virginia, one of the executors of the last will and testament of **John Colvill Gent.** of the said County deceased, send greeting. Whereas the said **John Colvill** by his last will and testament bearing date the 6th day of May, 1755 among other things devised as followeth viz. I give and bequeath unto my daughter **Catharine** now the wife of **John West Jr.** and to the said **John West**, 1,000 acres of my **Catoctan Tract** of land to be laid off adjoining to **John Hough's** land which he bought of **Amos Janney** in such manner as my executors shall approve, and whereas the said **John West** and **Catharine** his wife have by deeds of lease and release for valuable consideration therein expressed sold and conveyed all their right title interest of in and to the said 1,000 acres of land sold them bequeathed by the said **John Colvill Gent. deceased**, unto the said **John Hough** his heirs and assigns as by the said deeds of lease and release duly proven enrolled and recorded in the Court of the County of Loudoun may more fully appear, and to the intent that the said 1,000 acres of land be laid off to the said **John Hough** the purchaser according to the intent and meaning of the said **John Colvill Gent. deceased** and the bounds thereof certified and made known. Know ye

that I the said **Thomas Colvill** executor aforesaid on the application of the said **John Hough** for the purposes aforesaid do approve of the manner the said 1,000 acres of land are laid off in plat and survey thereof made by **George West**, Surveyor of the said County of Loudoun, dated the 13th day of May, 1762, which plat and survey so made and signed by the said **George West** is hereunto annexed. And, I the said **Thomas Colvill** do hereby agree and approve of the manner and form in which the said 1,000 acres of land are laid off and bound believing it agreeable to the will and intention of the said testator, unless there shall be an error of the quantity of the number of acres in which case the line to include the said 1,000 acres is N 68° W from one outline to the other parallel to said **Hough's** lower line. In witness I the said **Thomas Colvill** have hereunto set my hand and affixed my seal this 11th day of May, 1762, **Thos. Colvill**. Sealed and delivered in the presence of **H. West, John West Jr.** (plat and survey), May 13th, 1762. At the request of **Mr. John Hough** I surveyed part of the above as follows viz. Beginning at A, a poplar near the **So. Fork of Catactian Creek** marked **FA JC** thence N 52-½° E 86 poles wanting 8 links to B near **Janney's** fence supposed to be in the line of **Janney's** land thence with the same N 14° E near a line of marked trees 326 poles and angled to C a white hickory on the side of the said **Catactian Creek** marked **JM JH** from thence **Mr. Hough** desired me to protract the other lines of the patent to include 1,000 acres exclusive of his 500 which is represented by black lines the letters D, E, F, G, H, and A, and also to protract the courses of his 500 acres which is represented by dotted lines and figures 1, 2, 3, 4, and the letter C, **George West**. Sworn C.C. (Chain Carriers), **Thos. Dodd** and **Levi Wells**. Proven on 6/8/1762. Loudoun County Deed Book C, Part 1, pp. 270-273

14. 1/7/766, The Right Honorable **Charles, Earl of Tankerville** of the one part to **Thomas Colvill** of the other part, Power of Attorney, Proven on 6/9/1766. Loudoun County Deed Book E, pp. 31-48.

15. To all persons whom it may concern. Know ye that I **Thomas Colvill**, Agent for the Rt. Honble. **Charles, Earl of Tankerville** in Virginia by virtue of a Power of Attorney duly recorded in the County Court of Loudoun, among other things empowering me to ask demand and recover from all persons who are indebted to the said **Earl** for rents and arrearages of rents or otherwise in the Colony, and further giving me full power to nominate and appoint any person I shall think fit to act in my stead in behalf of him the said **Earl of Tankerville**. Know ye that by virtue of the said power of attorney I do hereby appoint **George West** to demand and receive from all tenants of the said **Earl** seated in the said County of Loudoun their several rents and arrearages of rents now due from them at this present date, and I do empower him the said **George West** to give receipts and acquitances for the same under his hand, which shall be good and sufficient as if I myself had signed the same against the said **Lord Tankerville** and any other person or persons whatsoever. In witness whereof I have hereunto set my hand and seal the day and year first above written, **Thos. Colvill**. Sealed and delivered in the presence of **William Crawford**, and **William Templeman**. Proven on 8/11/1766. Power of Attorney, Loudoun County Deed Book E, pp. 115-116

John Mead's Tract from Catesby Cocke (circa 1731)

The section concerns the parceling of a certain tract of land containing about 703 acres, which was situated between the South Fork of Catoctin Creek and a draught of Limestone Run. It was originally secured by Catesby Cocke by a patent from out of the Proprietor's Office of the Northern Neck of Virginia bearing date 8/28/1731. Afterwards, it was conveyed under his hand and seal to John Mead by lease and release bearing date 11/20/1733. This same land it appears was referred to in Cocke and Mercer's partition survey dated in 1750 as having belonged to John Mead and Richard Averill.[1]

In 1742 John Mead sold a parcel of this tract containing 147 acres to David Griffeth (Griffith) for and in consideration of 12 pounds sterling. Nearly a year afterwards he sold another parcel containing 303 acres to Francis Hague for and in consideration of 30 pounds sterling, which explicitly consisted of the residual acreage. Presumably John Mead had already traded a parcel of the same tract consisting of the unaccounted acreage to Amos Janney as he was unambiguously in possession of the bordering parcel, but there is no surviving hardcopy deed or even a complete citation to show for it. It is noted that Cocke and Mercer's partition survey dated in 1750 had also made a reference to Amos's Branch.

It's not clear when Amos Janney would have bought his given land. Some have deduced it to have been around 1732-3, which is unlikely. He was described in deed records as a yeoman or free-holding farmer. More importantly Amos Janney was a surveyor with diverse real estate interests. It appears that Amos Janney applied his ways and means elsewhere in Loudoun Valley to a greater extent than here as is evidenced by the deed record, which excludes any definitive contemporary legal instrument for this site whereas there are ample other of his title documents.

By 1747 Amos Janney had died intestate. His heir at law, Mahlon Janney, was at that time a minor. In 1755 Amos Janney would sell a piece of such land it appears to trustees for the building and development of a Meetinghouse, Fairfax Monthly Meeting, Society of Friends (Waterford). There was a marker at that time for a boundary line such as MH. His widow, Mary Janney, lived out her days elsewhere in Loudoun County.

Francis Hague's given parcel of land was immediately northward of and bordering to Amos Janney's particular land. It was laid out and bounded with a relatively small more-or-less rectangular piece of ground cutout of its otherwise straight southernmost boundary line, which on the face of it was sited around the course of the South Fork of Catoctin Creek. While David Griffith's parcel of land was southeast of Amos Janney's land, but the courses of his boundary lines are perplexing.

This landscape is distinguished as a consequence of its cultural antiquity. The land was favored as to its suitability for the production of grain and the presence of potential mill-seat locations on the waters of Catoctin Creek. Mead's given tract was acquired very early and was parceled out in still relatively early

---

[1] Catesby Cocke and John Mercer, Partition Deed, Fairfax County Deed Book C, pp. 99-106

times. The monies paid for the given parcels of land in the backwoods made these relatively expensive lands, which indicates the presence thereon of improvements and or their comparative potential. In fact, the consideration monies paid by Francis Hague and David Griffith in specie no less was at a substantially higher rate than the monies paid nearly 20 years afterward for comparable real estate from the contiguous landholding at that time belonging to Catesby Cocke from Cocke & Mercer's survey and tract of land.

John Mead was not a real estate speculator per se; rather, he was a carpenter. He had possessed other landed interests as well under Catoctin Mountain. It's conceivable that John Mead had held the subject tract in the expectation of its being further implanted either contemporaneously or at some future time by some association of his fellow Quakers, which actually happened. Amos and Mary Janney were Quakers, lately arrived from Pennsylvania. Francis and Jane Yeardley Hague were Quakers, lately arrived from Pennsylvania. In fact, Jane was Amos's sister in law. It appears likely that David Griffith was Quaker too. Francis Hague's family was allied with the Mead family as well. His brother's last will and testament, John Hague's, was administered by his surviving wife Ann Hague, William Mead Sr., and William Mead Jr., dated 4/19/1767.

1. 8/28/1731, A certain tract or parcel of land containing 703 acres purchased from the Proprietor of the Northern Neck of Virginia by **Catesby Cocke Gent.**, and by him conveyed by lease and release to **John Mead** duly executed under his hand and seal bearing date 11/20/1733, and recorded in the Proprietor's Office in Libra B, Folio 187

2. 2/15 and 2/16/1742, **John Mead** of the County of Fairfax and Colony of Virginia, carpenter, of the one part to **David Griffeth** (David Griffith) of the same County, planter, of the other part. Whereas there is a certain tract or parcel of land lying and being in the County of Fairfax aforesaid bounded as followeth viz. Beginning at a small red oak sapling standing in the old line of the said **Mead's** land and running from thence South 11° East to a spanish oak on the north side of **Kittockton Mountain,** thence South West 70 poles to a large black oak, thence N 88° W 158 poles to a white oak in a branch, thence N 67° W until it strikes he dividing line of **Amos Janney's** land, from thence along the said **Janney's** line to the beginning red oak sapling containing 147 acres. And, whereas the same is part of 703 acres of land purchased of the Proprietor of the Northern neck of Virginia by **Catesby Cocke Gent**. of the County aforesaid and by him conveyed to the within named **John Mead** by lease and release duly had and executed under his hand and seal bearing date 11/20/1733 and recorded in Liber B, Folio 187, now this indenture witnesseth that the said **John Mead** for and in consideration of the sum of 12 pounds sterling to him in hand paid by the said **David Griffeth** the receipt whereof the said **John Mead** doth hereby acknowledge, hath granted bargained sold aliened released and confirmed and by these presents doth bargain sell alien release and confirm unto the said **David Griffeth** and to his heirs and assigns all and singular the said 147 acres of land situate bounded and being as is above set forth and described

together with all the houses barns buildings orchards gardens ways watercourses woods meadows cripples (sic) swamps fishings fowlings hawkings huntings rights liberties privileges improvements advantages hereditaments and appurtenances with the rents issues and profits thereof. To have and to hold the said 147 acres land hereditaments and premises hereby granted and released or mentioned and intended to be granted with the appurtenances unto the said **David Griffeth** his heirs and assigns forever, **John Mead** and **Mary Mead** sealed and delivered in the presence of **Saml. Mead, James** his O mark **Green, Jeremiah** his O mark **Farehurst** Proven on 2/17/1742. Lease and Release, Fairfax County Deed Book A, Part 1, pp 12-15

3.   3/19 and 3/20/1743, **John Mead** of the County of Fairfax and Colony of Virginia, carpenter, of the one part to **Francis Hague** of the same place, yeoman, of the other part. Whereas there is a certain tract or parcel of land situate lying and being in the County of Fairfax aforesaid and on the **South Fork of Kittockton** and bounded as followeth viz. Beginning at a white hickory standing by the southeast side of the **South Fork of Kittockton Creek** near the mouth of a small drain and extending thence S 53° E 184 poles to a black oak and white oak, thence S 12° E 264 poles to a small black oak corner to **David Griffith,** thence N 60° W 2 poles and 9 feet to a small white oak corner to **Amos Janney,** thence with his line N 61-½° W 215 poles to a stake, thence N 9° E 9 poles to a bush by a pond, thence N 63° W 12 poles to a small black oak on the west side of the **South Fork of Kittockton,** thence S 64° W 10 poles to a hickory sapling, thence N 61-½° W 71 poles to a small white oak on a hill the beginning corner of **Amos Janney's** tract, thence N 14° E to the first station containing 303 acres of land, being the remaining part of a tract of 703 acres which tract was confirmed to **Catesby Cocke Gent.** by a patent out of the Proprietor's Office duly executed bearing date 8/28/1731, and by him conveyed to the within named **John Mead** by lease and release duly had and executed under his hand and seal. Now this indenture witnesseth that the said **John Mead** for and in consideration of the sum of 30 pounds sterling to him in hand paid by the said **Francis Hague** the receipt whereof the said **John Mead** doth hereby acknowledge, hath granted bargained sold aliened released and confirmed and by these presents doth bargain sell release and confirm unto the said **Francis Hague** his heirs and assigns all and singular the said 303 acres of land be it more or less situate bounded and being as above set forth and described together with all and singular the houses edifices buildings orchards gardens ways watercourses woods meadows creeples swamps fishings fowlings hawkings huntings rights liberties privileges improvements advantages hereditaments and appurtenances with the rents issues and profits thereof. To have and to hold the said 303 acres of land hereditaments and premises hereby granted alienated released or confirmed or mentioned and intended to be granted and released with the appurtenances unto the said **Francis Hague** his heirs and assigns forever, **John Mead.** Sealed and delivered in the presence of **Amos Janney, Jacob Janney,** and **Jos.**

McGeath. Proven on 11/15/1744. Lease and Release, Fairfax County Deed Book A, Part 2, pp. 282-285

4.   3/5 and 3/6/1755, **Mahlon Janney** of the County of Fairfax and Colony of Virginia, planter, of the one part to **Francis Hague, Joseph Yates, John Hough, Edward Norton**, and **Mercer Brown,** of the other part. Witnesseth that the said **Mahlon Janney** for and in consideration of the sum of 20 shillings sterling to him in hand paid by the said **Francis Hague, Joseph Yates, John Hough, Edward Norton,** and **Mercer Brown,** the receipt whereof the said **Mahlon Janney** doth hereby acknowledge but more especially for the consideration hereinafter mentioned him thereunto moving, he the said **Mahlon Janney** hath granted bargained sold aliened released and confirmed and by these presents doth fully freely and absolutely grant bargain and sell alien release and confirm unto the said **Francis Hague, Joseph Yates, John Hough, Edward Norton,** and **Mercer Brown,** and to their hers and assigns forever all that piece or parcel of land situate lying and being in the said County of Fairfax containing 10 acres and bounded as followeth viz. Beginning at a black oak marked **M:H** standing on a hill in the line dividing the land of the said **Mahlon Janney** from the land of **Francis Hague** and extending thence S 9° W 32 poles to an hickory by a small branch on a hillside, thence S 76° – 30 minutes E 60 poles to a stake, thence N 9° E 18 poles to a white oak corner to the said **Janney's** and **Hague's** land, thence N 61° – 30 minutes W 60 poles to the beginning, together with all trees woods underwoods ways paths watercourses easements profits commodities advantages emoluments hereditaments rights members and appurtenances whatsoever to the same belonging or in any wise appertaining, excepting and always reserving unto the said **Mahlon Janney** his heirs and assigns full and free liberty to dig, raise and make such and so many dams, banks, ditches, trenches and drains in the said 10 acres of land or any part thereof as shall be necessary or convenient to convey water to the meadow or pasture ground of the said **Mahlon Janney** his heirs or assigns convenient and contiguous to the said 10 acres of land hereby granted, and the said dams, banks, ditches, trenches, and drains, from time to time to cleanse, scower, mend and keep in repair so as the said dams, banks, ditches, trenches and drains shall not prejudice any of the houses, buildings or other immediate conveniences to be erected and made upon the said 10 acres of land or any part thereof according to the true intent and meaning of these presents. To have and to hold the said 10 acres of land and every part and parcel thereof with the appurtenances except as before excepted unto the said **Francis Hague, Joseph Yates, John Hough, Edward Norton,** and **Mercer Brown,** and their heirs to the uses intents and purposes hereinafter mentioned limited and appointed and to and for no other use or uses, trusts, limitations or provisos whatsoever in any wise. That is to say in trust to suffer and permit such of the people called Quakers inhabiting within the said County of Fairfax to erect and build such and so many meetinghouses, schoolhouses and yards or places of burial as they shall from time to time forever think necessary and convenient for the worship of God, the

instruction of youth, and burial of the dead, together with all such necessary outhouses, gardens, orchards, and other conveniences as shall from time to time be thought necessary convenient or useful to and for such schoolhouses or schoolhouse, **Mahlon Janney**. Lease and Release, Fairfax County Deed Book D, Part 1, pp. 134-139

5. 6/14 and 6/15/1762, **Francis Hague** of the County of Loudoun and Colony of Virginia and **Jane** his wife of the one part to **Mahlon Janney** of the same County and Colony aforesaid of the other part. Witnesseth that the said **Francis Hague** for and in consideration of 12 acres of land the said **Mahlon Janney** conveyed to the said **Francis Hague** by deeds bearing date with these presents, and for other reasons him thereunto moving, he the said **Francis Hague** and **Jane** his wife hath granted bargained sold alienated released and confirmed and by these presents doth fully freely and absolutely grant bargain sell alien release and confirm unto the said **Mahlon Janney** and his heirs and assigns forever all that tract or parcel of land situate lying and being in the County of Loudoun aforesaid and bounded as followeth viz. Beginning at the edge of the **South Fork of Kittocton** just above the **mouth of the tailrace** of the said **Mahlon Janney's Mill** extending thence near the south side of the said **tailrace** and binding therewith S 56° E 23 poles, thence S 55° E 12 poles to a marked white oak, thence S 29° E 4 poles to a stone, thence S 13-½° E 7 poles to a stone, thence South 10 poles to a stone, thence S 5° E 9 poles to the division line between said **Hague** and **Janney's** land, thence with that line S 62-½° E 30 feet crossing **the head-race of said Janney's Mill,** thence with the east side of said **race** N 4° W 10 poles, thence N 3° E 8 poles, thence N 44 E 4-½ poles to a marked white oak by the north side of small drain, thence N 5 E 20 poles to a black oak, thence N 77 W 11 poles to **Kittocton Creek** aforesaid, thence up the said **Creek** binding therewith S 5 W 2 poles to the first station more or less within said boundaries, together with all members and appurtenances thereto belonging and the reversion and reversions, reminder and reminders, rents issues and profits thereof and all the estate right title interest claim and demand whatsoever both in law and equity of him the said **Francis Hague** and **Jane** his wife of in and to the said premises with the appurtenances unto the said **Mahlon Janney** his heirs and assigns forever. To have and to hold the said land with the appurtenances unto the said **Mahlon Janney** his heirs and assigns forever, **Francis Hague** and **Jane Hague**. Sealed and delivered in the presence of us **Thomas Dodd, John Hough, Joseph Janney,** and **Moses Cadwallader**. Proven on 8/10/1762. Lease and Release, Loudoun County Deed Book C, Part 1, pp. 367-372

6. 3/19 and 3/20/1773, **Francis Hague** of Loudoun County in Colony of Virginia, yeoman, of the one part to **Thomas Hague** of the same place, cordwainer, of the other part. Witnesseth that whereas there is a certain tract or parcel of land situate lying and being in the County of Loudoun aforesaid and on the **South Fork of Kittocton** and bounded as follows viz. Beginning at a white oak standing near the **road** corner to **Mahlon Janney's Mill Lot** and extending thence N 2-½° E 30 perches to a hickory on the hill, thence S

81° E 26 perches to a white oak bush, thence S 1-½° W 64 perches to a white oak bush by **Mahlon Janney's** fence, thence with **Mahlon Janney's** line N 65° W 29 perches to a small hickory by the **race**, thence down the **race** N 5° W 20 perches to a large white oak standing by the **race**, thence N 27° E 4 perches to the beginning containing 12 acres be the same more or less. Also, one other tract or parcel of land situate lying and being in Loudoun County aforesaid and bounded as follows viz. Beginning at a white oak standing near **the sawmill a corner to Mahlon Janney's Mill Lot** and extending thence up the **race** S 20° E 14 perches to a white oak standing on the **race** bank, thence up the **race** S 2° E 16 perches to a small gum bush by the **race** on **Mahlon Janney's** line, thence with said **Janney's** line N 65° W 22 perches, thence with said line N 12° E 9 perches, thence with said line N 66° W 12 perches to a black oak sapling on the west side of the **South Fork of Kittocton Creek** in the said line of **Mahlon Janney**, thence N 18° E 26 perches to a gum tree standing near the ford thence across the Creek and up **the tailrace** S 58° E 39 perches to the beginning containing 5 acres and three quarters be the same more or less, which two tract or parcel of land is part of a tract of land containing 303 acres, which tract was conveyed to **Francis Hague** by **John Mead** by lease and release duly had and executed under his hand and seal, which 303 acres is also part of a tract of 703 acres which tract was confirmed to **Catesby Cocke Gent.** by a patent out of the Proprietor's Office duly executed bearing date the 28th day of August, 1731 and by him conveyed to the above named **John Mead** by lease and release duly had and executed under his hand and seal. Now this indenture witnesseth that the said **Francis Hague** for and in consideration of the sum of 5 pounds sterling to him in hand paid by the said **Thomas Hague**, the receipt whereof the said **Francis Hague** doth hereby acknowledge, hath granted bargained sold aliened released and confirmed and by these presents doth bargain sell release and confirm unto the said **Thomas Hague** and his heirs and assigns all and singular the said two tracts or parcels of land aforesaid containing together 17-¾ acres more or less, situate lying and being as above set forth and described together with all and singular the houses edifices buildings ways water watercourses woods meadows swamps rights liberties privileges improvements advantages hereditaments and appurtenances with the rents issues and profits thereof. To have and to hold the said 17-¾ acres of land hereditaments and premises hereby granted, aliened and released or confirmed or mentioned and intended to be granted and released with the appurtenances unto the said **Thomas Hague** his heirs and assigns forever, **Francis Hague**. Sealed and delivered in the presence of **Saml. Canby, Amos Hough, John Hough Jr.** Proven on 3/22/1773. Lease and Release, Loudoun County Deed Book I, pp. 168-173

7. 5/1 and 5/2/1781, **Thomas Hague** of Loudoun County in Virginia and **Sarah** his wife of the one part to **Joseph Janney** of the same County of the other part. Witnesseth that for and in consideration of the sum of 200 pounds in gold and silver current money of Virginia to the said **Thomas Hague** and **Sarah** his wife in hand paid by the said **Joseph Janney** at or before the

sealing and delivery of these presents, the receipt whereof they do hereby acknowledge, have granted bargained sold aliened released and confirmed and by these presents doth grant bargain sell alien release and confirm unto the said **Joseph Janney** and his heirs all that tract or parcel of land situate in Loudoun County aforesaid joining **Mahlon Janney's Mill Lot** and further bounded as followeth viz. Beginning at a white oak standing near the **road** corner to **Mahlon Janney's Mill Lot** and extending thence N 2-½° E 30 poles to a hickory on a hill, then S 81° E 26 poles to a white oak bush, then S 1-½° W 64 poles to a white oak bush by **Mahlon Janney's** fence, then with said **Mahlon Janney's** line N 65° W 29 poles to a small hickory by the **millrace**, then down the race N 5° W 20 poles to a large white oak, then N 27° E 4 poles to the beginning containing 12 acres be the same more or less. Also, another tract or parcel of land joining the above bounded as followeth viz. Beginning at a white oak standing by **Mahlon Janney's Sawmill** corner to said **Janney's Mill Lot** extending thence up the west side of the said **race** S 20° E 14 poles to a white oak on the **race** bank, then continuing up the **race** S 2° E 9 poles, then with another of his lines N 66° W 12 poles to a black oak sapling the west side of **Kittockton Creek**, then N 18° E 26 poles to a gum tree standing near **the ford** then crossing the said Creek and up the **mill tailrace** S 58° E 39 poles to the beginning containing 5-¾ acres, which two parcels of land above described by buts and bounds are part of a larger tract containing 303 acres, which **Francis Hague** purchased of **John Mead** (and) the said **Francis Hague** conveyed the two small parcels above mentioned to the above named **Thomas Hague** his son by deeds bearing date the 19th and 20th days of March, 1773 and all houses buildings orchards ways water watercourses profits commodities hereditaments and appurtenances whatsoever to the said premises hereby granted or any part thereof belonging or in any wise appertaining. To have and to hold the lands hereby conveyed and all and singular other the premises hereby granted and released and every part and parcel thereof with their and every of their appurtenances unto the said **Joseph Janney** his heirs and assigns forever, **Thomas Hague** and **Sarah Hague**. Sealed and delivered in the presence of **Samuel Murrey, Patk. Cavan, William Taylor**, and **John Dodd**. Proven on 4/13/1784.

8. 6/17 and 6/18/1788, **Thomas Hague, Samuel Hague**, and **Israel Thompson** of Loudoun County in the State of Virginia, executors to the last will and testament of **Francis Hague** late of the aforesaid County, deceased, of the one part to **William Hough** of the said County of Loudoun of the other part. Witnesseth that for and in consideration of the sum of 900 pounds current money of Virginia to the said **Thomas Hague, Samuel Hague**, and **Israel Thompson** in hand paid by the said **William Hough** at or before the sealing and delivery of these presents the receipt whereof they do hereby acknowledge, and thereof doth release, acquit and discharge the said **William Hough** his executors and administrators by these presents they the said **Francis Hague, Samuel Hague**, and **Israel Thompson** executors aforesaid have granted bargained sold aliened released and confirmed and by these presents doth grant bargains sell alien release and confirm unto the said

William Hough and his heirs all that tract or parcel of land situate in Loudoun County aforesaid bounded as followeth viz. Beginning at a small poplar where the original white hickory stood by the southwest side of **Kittoctan Creek** corner to **John Hough** and being an original corner to **Cock** (sic) **and Mercer's** large survey extending thence with said **John Hough's** line N 27° E 60 poles to three small white oaks in a stony hill corner to **Andrew Brown**, then with said **Brown's** line S 54° E 260 poles to a heap of stones put together corner to said **Brown** and in a line of land **Mary McGeach** purchased of **John Mercer and Sons**, then with the said line S 14° W 150 poles to the line of the said **Francis Hague's** original survey purchased of **John Mead**, then with that line S 20-½° E 140 poles to where a black oak formerly stood in **James Balls** field, then N 60° W 2 poles and 9 feet to where a white oak stood an original corner to **Mahlon Janney**, then with said **Janney's** line N 64° W 169 poles to a corner made for **Thomas Hague** to land his father **Francis Hague** conveyed to him, then with the lines of that land North 58 poles to a small white oak, then N 82° W 24 poles to a hickory, then South 6 poles to a large black oak corner to **Mahlon Janney's Mill Lot,** then N 82° W 40 poles to a birch tree at **the mouth of his mill tailrace**, then crossing the **Kittoctan Creek** to a gum about two poles the west side of said Creek corner to the aforesaid **Thomas Hague's** land, then up the Creek with his line S 20° E 26 poles to a small black oak corner to **Mahlon Janney**, then with his lines S 55° W 8 poles to a white oak, then S 75-½° W 81 poles to a spanish oak and white oak, then N 10° E 285 poles to the first station containing 406 acres of land be the same more or less, within the aforesaid bounds being three several purchases made of **John Mead, Amos Janney,** and **John Mercer and Sons,** all which land the said **Francis Hague** by his last will and testament bearing date the 24th day of August, 1780 duly proven and recorded in Loudoun County Court, did therein devise order and direct the said **Thomas Hague, Samuel Hague,** and **Israel Thompson** to sell and convey the aforesaid lands for such price as might be had for uses and purposes in the said will specified, and all houses buildings orchards ways watercourses profits commodities hereditaments and appurtenances whatsoever to the said premises hereby granted, or any part thereof belonging or in any wise appertaining. To have and to hold the lands hereby conveyed and all and singular other the premises hereby granted and released and every part and parcel thereof, with their and every of their appurtenances unto the said **William Hough** his heirs and assigns forever, **Thomas Hague, Samuel Hague,** and **Israel Thompson.** Sealed and delivered in the presence of, Evidences for **Thomas Hague** and **Israel Thompson, James Moore, Thos. Moore Jr., Asa Moore,** and **John Hough 3rd**. Evidences for **Samuel Hague, John Hirst, John Butcher, Abel Janney,** and **Israel Janney**. Proven on 2/9/1789. It is to be remembered that **Francis Hague** did in his last will and testament above mentioned devise to the **Trustees of Fairfax Meetinghouse** a small slice of land adjoining said **House,** which is except in this deed and to be

thrown out of the above bounds according to the expressions of said will.
Release and Lease, Loudoun County Deed Book Z, pp. 80-86

Beginning at a white hickory standing by the south east side of the South Fork of Kittockton Creek near the mouth of a small drain and extending thence S° 53 E^t 184 poles to a black oak & white oak thence S° 12 E^t 264 poles to a small black oak corner to David Griffith thence N° 60 W^t 2 poles & nine feet to a small white oak corner to Amos Janney thence with his line N° 61½ W^t 215 poles to a stake thence N° 9 E^t 9 poles to a bush by a pond thence N° 63 W^t 12 poles to a small black oak on the west side of the South Fork of Kittockton thence S° 64 W^t 10 poles to a hickory saplin thence N° 61½ W^t 71 poles to a small white oak on a hill the beginning corner to Amos Janney's Tract thence N° 14 E^t to the first station

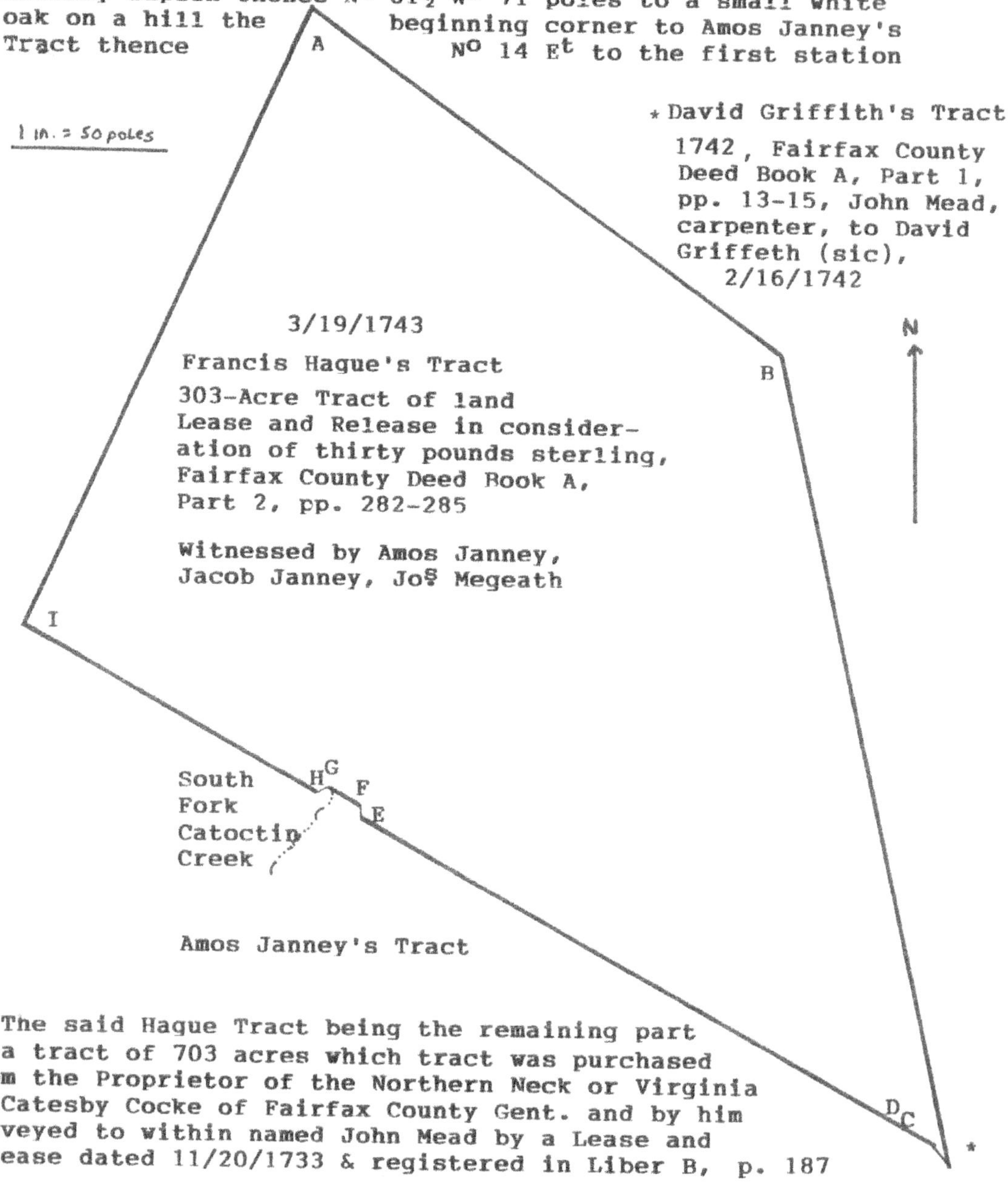

1 in. = 50 poles

*David Griffith's Tract
1742, Fairfax County Deed Book A, Part 1, pp. 13-15, John Mead, carpenter, to David Griffeth (sic), 2/16/1742

3/19/1743

Francis Hague's Tract

303-Acre Tract of land Lease and Release in consideration of thirty pounds sterling, Fairfax County Deed Book A, Part 2, pp. 282-285

Witnessed by Amos Janney, Jacob Janney, Jo^s Megeath

South Fork Catoctin Creek

Amos Janney's Tract

The said Hague Tract being the remaining part of a tract of 703 acres which tract was purchased from the Proprietor of the Northern Neck or Virginia by Catesby Cocke of Fairfax County Gent. and by him conveyed to within named John Mead by a Lease and Release dated 11/20/1733 & registered in Liber B, p. 187

...that is to say in trust to suffer and permit such of the people called Quakers inhabiting within the said County of Fairfax to erect & build such and so many meeting houses school houses and yards or places or burial, as they shall from time to time forever think necessary and convenient for the worship of God, the instruction of youth & burial of the dead, together with all such necessary out houses gardens orchards and other conveniences as shall from time to time thought necessary convenient or useful to and for such school houses...

Beginning at black oak marked M:H standing on a hill in the line dividing the land of Mahlon Janney from the land of Francis Hague and extending thence...

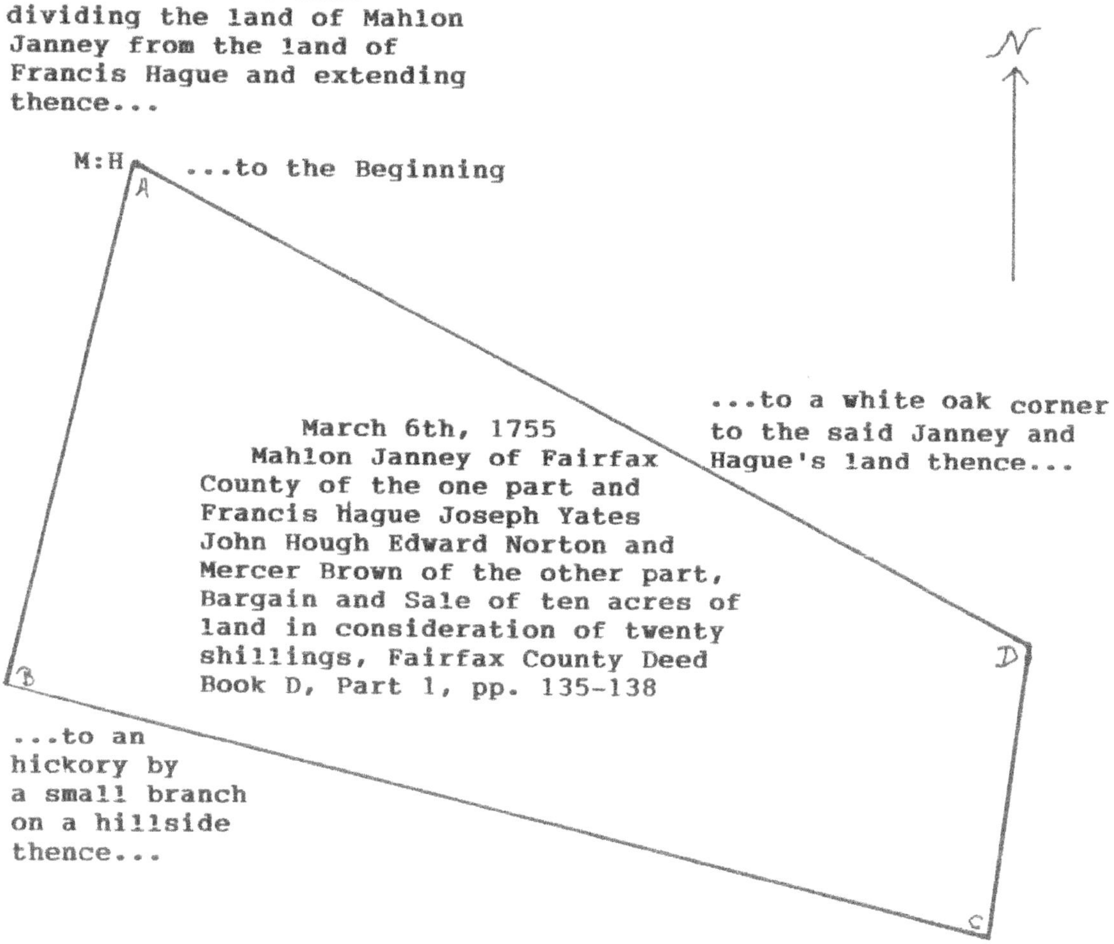

M:H ...to the Beginning

...to a white oak corner to the said Janney and Hague's land thence...

March 6th, 1755
Mahlon Janney of Fairfax County of the one part and Francis Hague Joseph Yates John Hough Edward Norton and Mercer Brown of the other part, Bargain and Sale of ten acres of land in consideration of twenty shillings, Fairfax County Deed Book D, Part 1, pp. 135-138

...to an hickory by a small branch on a hillside thence...

Loudoun County, Virginia

Scale: one inch = ten poles
       one pole = 16.5 feet

...to a stake thence...

Beginning at A at the edge of the Soth Fork of Kittocton Creek just above the Mouth of the tail-race of the said Mahlon Janney's Mill extending thence near the south side of the said tail-race and binding therewith to B thence to C a marked white oak thence to D a stone thence to E a stone thence to F a stone thence to G to the Division Line between said hague and Janney's Land thence with that line crossing the Head-race of said janney's Mill to H thence with the east side of the said race to I thence to J thence to K to a marked white oak by the north side of a small Drain thence to L to a black oak thence to M to the Kittocton Creek aforesaid thence up the said Creek and binding therewith to the beginning

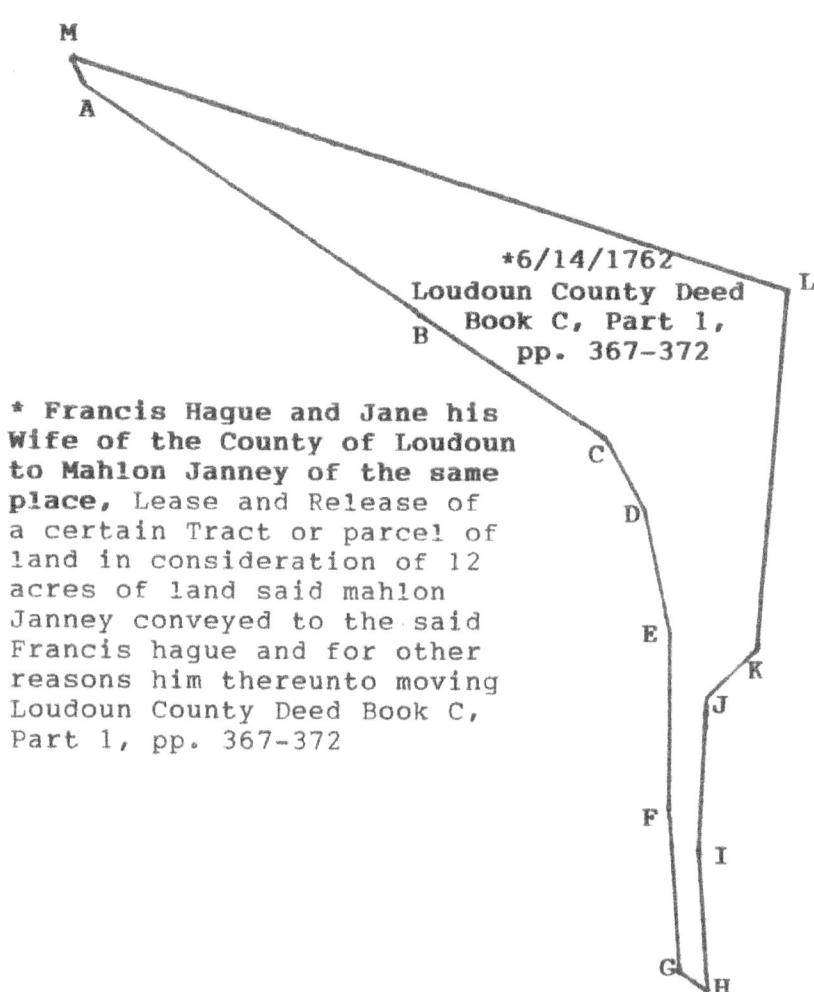

*6/14/1762
Loudoun County Deed
Book C, Part 1,
pp. 367-372

* Francis Hague and Jane his Wife of the County of Loudoun to Mahlon Janney of the same place, Lease and Release of a certain Tract or parcel of land in consideration of 12 acres of land said mahlon Janney conveyed to the said Francis hague and for other reasons him thereunto moving Loudoun County Deed Book C, Part 1, pp. 367-372

Scale: one inch = ten linear poles
       one poles = 16.5 linear feet

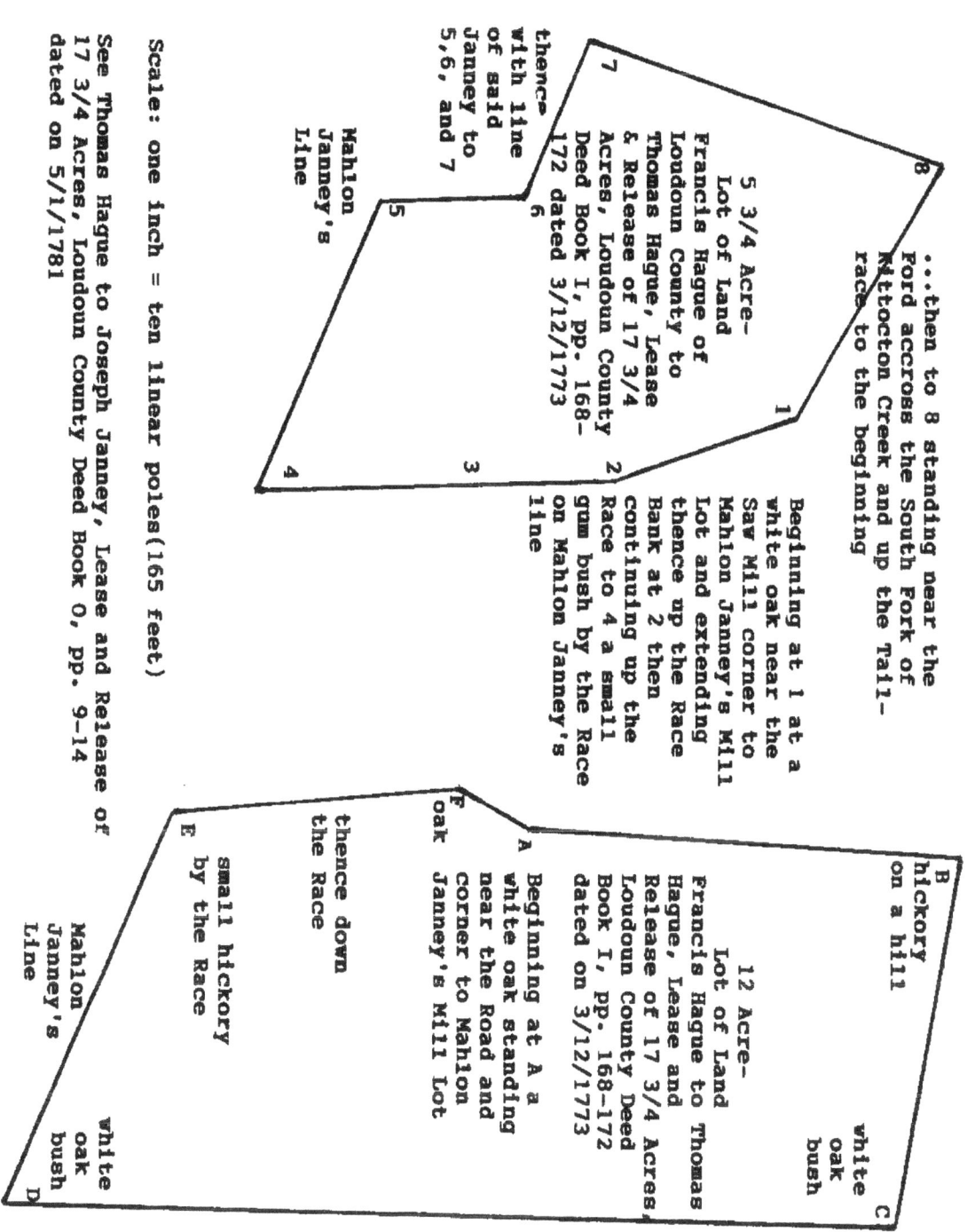

5 3/4 Acre- Lot of Land Francis Hague of Loudoun County to Thomas Hague, Lease & Release of 17 3/4 Acres, Loudoun County Deed Book I, pp. 168-172 dated 3/12/1773

Beginning at 1 at a white oak near the Saw Mill corner to Mahlon Janney's Mill Lot and extending thence up the Race Bank at 2 then continuing up the Race to 4 a small gum bush by the Race on Mahlon Janney's line

thence with line of of said Janney to 5,6, and 7

Mahlon Janney's Line

...then to 8 standing near the Ford accross the South Fork of Kittocton Creek and up the Tail-race to the beginning

12 Acre- Lot of Land Francis Hague to Thomas Hague, Lease and Release of 17 3/4 Acres, Loudoun County Deed Book I, pp. 168-172 dated on 3/12/1773

Beginning at A a white oak standing near the Road and corner to Mahlon Janney's Mill Lot

thence down the Race

small hickory by the Race

hickory on a hill

white oak bush

white oak bush

Mahlon Janney's Line

Scale: one inch = ten linear poles(165 feet)

See Thomas Hague to Joseph Janney, Lease and Release of 17 3/4 Acres, Loudoun County Deed Book O, pp. 9-14 dated on 5/1/1781

57

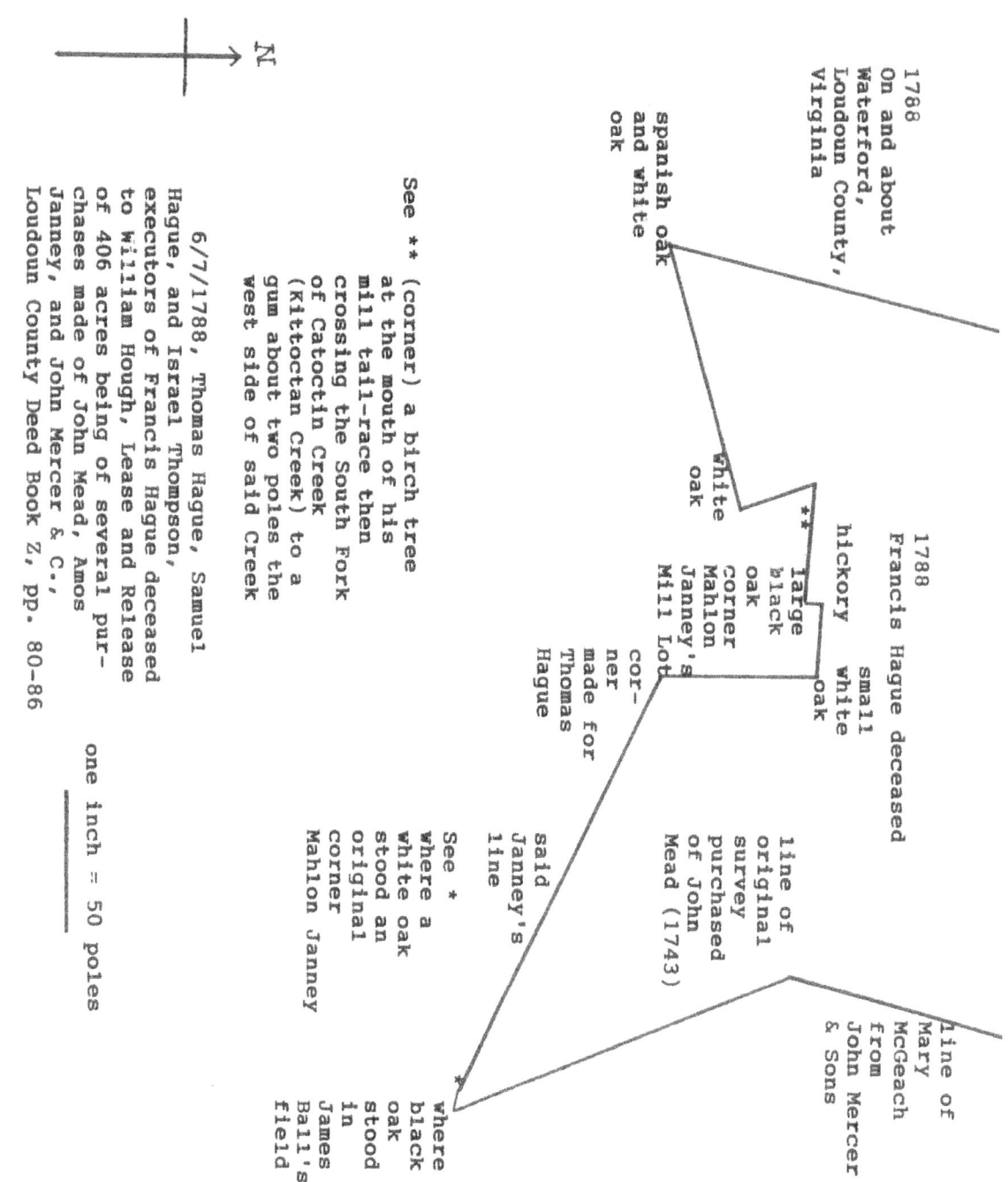

1788
On and about
Waterford,
Loudoun County,
Virginia

spanish oak
and white
oak

white
oak

large
black
oak
corner
Mahlon
Janney's
Mill Lot

small
hickory white
oak

1788
Francis Hague deceased

line of
original
survey
purchased
of John
Mead (1743)

cor-
ner
made for
Thomas
Hague

said
Janney's
line

See *
where a
white oak
stood an
original
corner
Mahlon Janney

See ** (corner) a birch tree
at the mouth of his
mill tail-race then
crossing the South Fork
of Catoctin Creek
(Kittoctan Creek) to a
gum about two poles the
west side of said Creek

where a
black
oak
stood
in
James
Ball's
field

line of
Mary
McGeach
from
John Mercer
& Sons

6/7/1788, Thomas Hague, Samuel
Hague, and Israel Thompson,
executors of Francis Hague deceased
to William Hough, Lease and Release
of 406 acres being of several purchases made of John Mead, Amos
Janney, and John Mercer & C.,
Loudoun County Deed Book Z, pp. 80-86

one inch = 50 poles

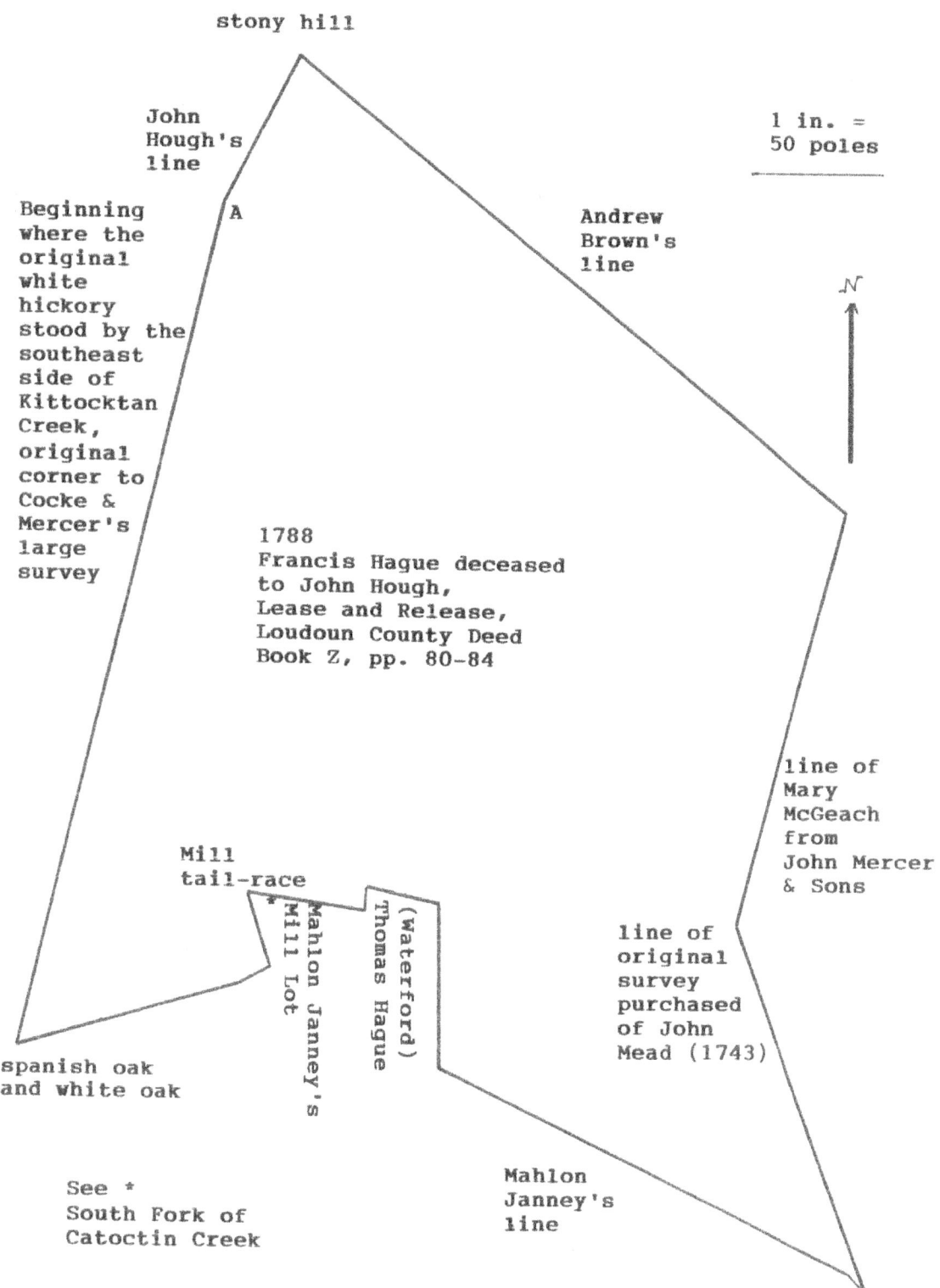

Richard Brown & Company on Catoctin Creek (c. 1741)

This section concerns the parceling of two bordering tracts of land on and about Catoctin Creek having belonged to Richard Brown, which land was bounded by John Colvill's Catoctin Tract, and Catesby Coke's lands. One such tract containing seemingly at least 435 acres was originally surveyed for one Samuel Maxberry (Mayberry, Marberry) before Richard Brown would acquire the same. The other tract containing about 600 acres of land was surveyed for Richard Brown and was confirmed to him by a patent out of the Proprietor's Office.

What is more, Richard Brown controlled still other real property in the area including a tract on a branch of the South Fork of Catoctin Creek containing 600 acres of land, which was held in the name of Edward Norton. It was immediately adjoining to a 200 acre parcel Richard Brown had released during his lifetime to William Dodd, planter, which was from still another sprawling tract the said Richard Brown had owned containing 634 acres of land. Lastly, Brown possessed a tract containing 505 acres of land on the Northwest Fork of Goose Creek. In summation, Richard Brown during his lifetime had controlled a total of at least 2,774 acres of land, which was later overlaid by the jurisdiction of Loudoun County.

There is lore surrounding the life and times of Richard Brown. Richard Brown was a descendent of William Brown of England who was an approved minister of the Society of Friends or Quakers.[1] His two sons William and James immigrated to Pennsylvania in early times. In 1702 William and his family moved into the backwoods as they settled in Nottingham. His brother James would follow him to the same locality. At the time Nottingham was deemed by their peers to be in Pennsylvania, but the site was actually situated on the border of Maryland, which led to conflict.

Richard Brown was a son of the aforesaid William Brown and his wife Ann Mercer Brown (born 1698). He was married in 1717 to Hannah Reynolds. They had at least four children. She died in 1726. Richard Brown was married for a second time in 1730-1 to Rachel Beeson. He was married for a third time in 1738 to Mary, the daughter of Edward Norton of County Armagh, Ireland. Apparently, during the early 1730's Richard Brown and his family had moved to Virginia. In the deed records of old Fairfax County he was described as a yeoman. The yeoman was a member of a class of free-holding farmers.

It seems Richard Brown's Tracts on Catoctin Creek were permanently settled by Richard Brown and Mary his wife; Henry Brown, and other children from his previous marriages; Edward Norton, his father in law; and Edmund Sands. By the time of his decease in 1745, Richard Brown's plantation would include a house, malthouse, mill, millhouse, saw, sawmill, brewhouse, and outhouses of all kinds, and

---

[1] Two interviews conducted by the author during the late 1990's with the late Howell Samuel Brown (b. 6/6/1908) and his wife the late Erma Brown (b. 2-11-11) of Purcellville, Virginia. Howell S. Brown presented the author as a guide a copy of, The Browns of Nottingham, The Historical Society of Pennsylvania, Presented by Gilbert Cope bearing date 6/1/1865. The aforesaid account was taken in writing in the year 1785 and was produced and read at the Monthly Meeting held at East Nottingham on 1/28/1786: Certified on the said Meeting's behalf by George Churchman.

sundry accessories. Apparently, these were the collective works of Richard Brown and company.

The late Richard Brown by his last will and testament dated in 1745 appointed his wife Mary and his son Henry Brown as his executors. The deceased left a one-half share of his 600-acre tract on or near Catoctin Creek or 300 acres unto his eldest son Henry Brown with specific instructions as to how it should be laid off and bounded. One part was to be taken off that tract whereon at that time Edmund Sands and Edward Norton had lived, and the other part was to be taken off that tract whereon the deceased had lately lived. The deceased left the remaining part of the 600-acre tract to his widow, Mary, together with the aforesaid improvements.

In 1749 Henry Brown, yeoman, and Esther his wife released a 304 acres of land joining on Catoctin Creek to Edmund Sands, cordwainer, for and in consideration of 20 pounds sterling, which at that time was bounded by Catesby Cocke's land. It was identified as being from a tract surveyed for Richard Brown during his lifetime containing 600 acres of land and confirmed to him by a patent out of the Proprietor's Office registered in Libra E, Folio 397.

Also, in 1749 Henry Brown, yeoman, and Esther his wife released a 100-acre parcel of land on the branches of Catoctin Creek to Edward Norton, weaver, for and in consideration of an agreement made and promise of a deed to him by the late Richard Brown. It was bounded on the line of a neighboring tract surveyed for one Saml. Maxberry or the like, which line was identified at that time as William Kirk's line. One of Norton's boundaries passed a tree marked for the dividing line between Henry Brown and Edmund Sands. Also, Norton's boundary lines joined Catesby Cocke's lines including a boundary marker for him as in CC. The deed indicates Norton's given 100 acres of land came from the aforesaid tract surveyed for Richard Brown during his lifetime and confirmed to him by a patent out of the Proprietor's Office registered in Book E, Folio 379 (graphical error?).

The said William Kirk was master of a gristmill on Catoctin Creek, which was on Mary's given land from her late husband. William Kirk had married Mary, who possessed title to the 300 acres of land. During the 18th Century this location was characterized for its economic vitality. Here was lively trade and industry. There was a public roadway here connecting Kirk's Mill with the Fairfax Meetinghouse, which is currently know as Loyalty Road, Rt. 665. Also, there was another public roadway connecting Kirk's Mill by extension with Leesburg (Road Cases File #38).[1]

Another important figure nearby was Richard Roach, a blacksmith by trade. He had acquired two adjacent parcels from Edmund Sands on land that Henry Brown had administered for Richard Brown deceased. Thereon he developed a smith's shop by 1754, which was followed in 1759 by the building of a gristmill on a branch of the Catoctin Creek. There was a public roadway here currently known as Featherbed Road (Rt. 673), which connected Roach's Mill in a westerly orientation by extension with Everheart's Mill and in an easterly orientation by extension with Leesburg (Road Cases File #38 and File # 39).[2]

---

[1] Loudoun County Circuit Court, Archives, Miscellaneous Road Cases 1758-1782, File No. 38
[2] Loudoun County Circuit Court, Archives, Miscellaneous Road Cases 1758-1782, File No. 38 and File No. 39

In 1762 Edward and Elizabeth Norton would release two tracts amounting to 500 acres of land including the aforesaid parcel containing 100 acres to Richard Williams, farmer, of Bucks County, Pennsylvania, for and in consideration of 220 pounds lawful money. Additionally, a little over a year later Henry Brown, farmer, and Hester (sic) his wife would release 76 acres land joining the aforementioned 100-acre parcel unto the said Williams at that time of Loudoun County, for and in consideration of 20 pounds current money.

It seems that the aforementioned Loyalty Road served at the time just as well as a boundary marker of sorts. The text of Edmund Sands (d. 1775) last will and testament includes a boundary description as follows. He had bequeathed to Joseph Sands all his lands, "from the Big Road, coming from Mercer Brown's Mill to the Meeting House, from Richard Roaches corner near the cross roads to the Mountain, all above the road from a corner of Henry Brown's on said road to a corner of Richard Roach at the cross road, both near the road making that the line".

As was stated the deceased left 300 acres unto his said widow Mary, which she in turn left unto their son Mercer Brown. In 1784 Mercer Brown and Sarah Brown his wife would release the same parcel to Thomas Taylor of Frederick County, Maryland, for and in consideration of 1,600 pounds current money of the State of Maryland. The deed explicitly included all houses, mills, buildings, orchards, ways, waters, watercourses and appurtenances whatsoever belonging to the said premises. This property at the time joined the lands of the Reverend William West, Richard Williams, Henry Brown, and the Earl of Tankerville and his brother, Henry Astley Bennett.

William Kirk's successor was Thomas Taylor, the master of Taylor's Mill. After the Revolutionary War he had acquired at least two bordering parcels containing 435 acres including 300 acres from Mercer Brown as above, and 135 acres more from the aforesaid Richard Williams. It is noted that Thomas Taylor's deed from Williams indicates that these 135 acres were adjacent to his other given land from Mercer Brown, formerly one Maxberry's land, which is to say the aforesaid mill-seat was spread over the surface of Maxberry's survey. Thomas Taylor would mark out and bound a proposed town nearby called "Milford" (Millford), which would later come to be called Taylor Town Farm or Taylor Town, and Taylorstown.

Lastly, Henry Brown deceased by his last will and testament left a tract of land containing 224 acres of land lying on Catoctin Creek to his son also named William Brown. This was the residual acreage of 300 acres of land, which the said Henry Brown had inherited from Richard Brown. The said William Brown and Hannah his wife in 1810 would convey the same to James Hamilton for monetary considerations. This land was marked at that time with a boundary marker for Henry Brown as in HB. Furthermore, the contemporary boundary description referred to the original line of Marberry's survey, which seems a spelling variation of Maxberry or Mayberry. This should account for a total of at least 1,004 acres on the Lower Catoctin Creek, which are somehow attributable to Richard Brown (d. 1745).

Lastly, it is further noted that seven years before the given sale to Hamilton on the motion of Adam Householder Junior, a writ of Adquod damnum was awarded him to condemn as much of the land of William Brown's as would be necessary for erecting an abutment or dam across Catoctin Creek where the said Householder intended to build a mill. The award turned out to be of 151 perches or about one acres of land for and in consideration of $ 85.00. This dam would come to be an essential element of Hamilton Mills.

1. Date unknown, **Samuel Maxberry (Mayberry, Marberry)**, survey of a tract of land, unknown registration.
2. 11/27/1741, The Office of the Proprietor of the Northern Neck of Virginia of the one part to **Richard Brown** of the other part, Patent for tract joining on **Kittocton Creek** containing 600 acres of land, Libra E, Folio 397 and or Libra E, Folio 379
3. Be it remembered that this third day of the second month called April in the year of our Lord one thousand seven hundred and forty five, I **Richard Brown** of Fairfax County in the Colony of Virginia, yeoman, being very weak and sick of body yet preserved (thro' mercy) in perfect sound mind and memory do make and ordain this my last will and testament in manner and form following (that is to say). Principally and first of all, I will that all my just debts and charges accruing at my death and burial may be well and truly and fully paid. And, I give and devise unto my eldest son **Henry Brown** and his heirs and assigns forever three hundred acres of land situate lying and being in the County aforesaid on or near **Kittockton Creek**, one part of which being a part of that tract whereon **Edmund Sands** and **Edward Norton** now liveth, and the other part to be taken off the tract whereon I now live lying most commodious to that before mentioned and least endangering the last mentioned tract. And, I give and devise unto my son **William Brown** and his heirs and assigns forever all that tract or parcel of land situate lying and being in the County aforesaid upon a branch of the **South Fork of Kittockton Creek** and joining to **Jacob Janney's** tract, containing four hundred and thirty four acres. And, I give and devise unto my sons **John Brown** and **Joseph Brown** and to their heirs and assigns forever all that tract or parcel of land situate lying and being in the County aforesaid on the **Northwest Fork of Goose Creek** containing five hundred and five acres, and to be equally divided between them to the best convenience of both. And, I give devise unto my son **Mercer Brown** and his heirs and assigns forever three hundred acres of land to be taken off that tract or parcel of land situate lying & being in the County aforesaid taken up and now held by the name of **Edward Norton** containing six hundred acres, and to be taken off in such manner as to make it as convenient as possible for a settlement with the least damage to the other part of the said tract and the residue or remaining part of the said tract and another tract containing two hundred acres. My will is that if my beloved wife **Mary** have issue in nine months after this date that then the said last mentioned lands be firmly conveyed and made over to such issue be it male or female and to their heirs and assigns forever. But if it so happens that no such issue be brought forth then I leave the

said lands to the discretion of my executors to dispose of the same as they shall see meet & divide it equally among my five sons above mentioned. And, I give and devise unto my beloved wife **Mary** and to her heirs and assigns forever all that remaining part of the tract or parcel of land whereon we now live together with the house, malthouse, mill, millhouse, saw, sawmill, brewhouse, outhouses of all kinds whatsoever and all the appurtenances to them belonging or in any wise appertaining to any of them. And, all my personal estate of what kind or nature whatsoever except to my son **Henry** the horse he now rides and one breeding mare, and to my son **William** one black horse branded with two esses (sic) across and one breeding mare, and to each of my other two sons, **Joseph** and **Mercer,** two young mares a piece and if it so happen that any of my sons aforementioned should decease before they arrive to the age of twenty one years, my will is that their estate both real and personal shall be equally divided among the survivors. And, I do hereby constitute ordain and appoint my son **Henry** and beloved wife **Mary** my sole executor & executrix of this my last will and testament investing in them with full power and authority to act and do in all aspects as they shall see meet and convenient, and I commit the care or doing and disposal of my two young children **Joseph** and **Mercer** unto the discretion of my said wife. And, (I) do nominate appoint my trusty friend **Jacob Janney** of the County aforesaid trustee and assistant to her in the affair. And, lastly, I hereby revoke annul & declare void all former and other will or wills by me at any time heretofore made declaring this and no other to be my last will and testament. In testimony whereof I have hereunto set my hand and seal the day and year fist above written. Signed, sealed published, pronounced & declared, by the said **Richard Brown** as his last will and testament in the presence of us, **Edward Norton, Danl. James, Jacob Janney**. At a Court held for Fairfax County May 21^{st,} 1745 this last will and testament of **Richard Brown deceased** was presented in Court by **Henry Brown** and **Mary Brown** executors therein named who made solemn affirmation of **Edward Norton** and **Jacob Janney** witnesses thereto is admitted to record and on motion of the said executors and their performing what is usual in such cases certificate is granted for obtaining a probate thereof in due form. Teste, **Catesby Cocke**, Clk. Ct. Last Will and Testament, Fairfax County Will Book A1, Part 1, p. 110-112

4.   1/6 and 1/7/1749, **Henry Brown** of Fairfax County in the Colony of Virginia, yeoman, and **Esther** his wife of the one part to **Edmund Sands** of the same place, cordwainer, of the other part. Whereas there is a certain tract or parcel of land situate lying and being in the County of Fairfax aforesaid and joining on **Kittocton Creek,** being part of a tract of land surveyed for **Richard Brown** containing 600 acres viz. Beginning at marked black oak standing in the middle of the fourth line of the original survey and extending thence up **Kittocton Creek** binding thereon S 16° E 14 poles, thence S 59° E 90 poles, thence South 68 poles, thence N 83° W 56 poles, thence S 24° W 38 poles, thence S 16° W 64 poles to a grove of pines in a line of **Catesby Cocke's,** thence with **Cocke's** line N 80° E 324 poles to three red oaks, thence N 49° E 92 poles to a great stone, thence N 20° W 53 poles to a forked white oak and two red oaks, thence N 71° W 222

poles to the beginning containing 304 acres, being part of the above said **Richard Brown's** tract which was confirmed to him by a patent out of the Proprietor' Office duly executed bearing date the 27th day of November, 1741 and registered in the Proprietor's Office in Libra E, Folio 397. Now this indenture witnesseth that the said **Henry Brown** and **Esther** his wife for and in consideration of the sum of 20 pounds sterling to him the said **Henry Brown** in hand paid by him the said **Edmund Sands** the receipt whereof the said **Henry Brown** doth hereby acknowledge, hath granted bargained sold aliened released and confirmed and by these presents doth bargain and sell release and confirm unto the said **Edmund Sands** and his heirs and assigns all and singular the said 304 acres of land situate bounded and being as is above set forth and described, together with the houses edifices buildings gardens orchards ways water watercourses woods meadows creeples swamps fishings fowlings hawkings huntings rights liberties privileges improvements advantages hereditaments and appurtenances with the rents issues and profits thereof. To have and to hold the said 304 acres of land hereditaments and premises hereby granted alienated released and confirmed or mentioned and intended to be granted and released with the appurtenances unto the said **Edmund Sands** his heirs and assigns forever, **Henry Brown** and **Esther** her E mark **Brown**. Sealed and delivered in the presence of **Francis Hague, John Hough, Richd. Roch,** and **Jacob Janney**. Proven on 6/26/1750. Lease and Release, Fairfax County Deed Book C, Part 1, pp. 32-35

5.   12/2 and 12/3/1749, **Henry Brown** of the County of Fairfax in the Colony of Virginia, yeoman, and **Esther** his wife of the one part to **Edward Norton** of the same place, weaver, of the other part. Whereas there is a certain tract or parcel of land situate lying and being in the County of Fairfax aforesaid on the branches of **Kittockton Creek** and bounded as followeth viz. Beginning at a white oak marked **CC** corner to **Catesby Cocke** about twenty poles from a line of a tract surveyed for **Saml. Maxberry** now belonging to **William Kirk**, extending thence parallel with **Kirk's** line S 60° W 85 poles to a small hickory on the west side of a branch of **Kittockton** and amongst a heap of rocks, thence S 18° W 199 poles to a black oak in a dividing line between **Edmund Sands** and the said **Henry Brown,** thence with the said dividing line S 71° E 113 poles to a spanish oak in a line of **Catesby Cocke's,** thence with **Cocke's** line N 20° W 253 poles to the beginning containing 100 acres of land. It being part of a tract that was surveyed for **Richard Brown** in his lifetime and confirmed to him by a good sufficient patent out of the Proprietor's Office for the Northern Neck dated the 27th day of November, 1741 and registered in the said Office in Book E, Folio 379 under certain rents reservations and exceptions in the said grant expressed by the said patent more fully and at large appears. Now this indenture witnesseth that the said **Henry Brown** and **Esther** his wife for and in consideration of an agreement made with the said **Edward Norton** and promise of a deed to him by **Richard Brown** late of said County and Colony aforesaid deceased, father of the said **Henry Brown**, which said **Henry Brown** and **Esther** his wife doth hereby acknowledge to be full satisfaction for them for the above mentioned land and is fully satisfied therewith, hath granted bargained sold aliened released and confirmed and by

these presents doth bargain and sell alien release and confirm unto the said **Edward Norton** and his heirs and assigns, all and singular the said 100 acres of land situate bounded and being as is above set forth and described together with all houses barns buildings orchards gardens ways waters watercourses woods meadows creeples swamps fishings fowlings hawkings huntings rights liberties privileges improvements advantages hereditaments and appurtenances with the rents issues and profits of the same. To have and to hold the said 100 acres of land hereditaments and premises hereby granted alienated released or confirmed or mentioned and intended to be granted and released with the appurtenances unto the said **Edward Norton** his heirs and assigns forever, **Henry Brown** and **Esther Brown**. Sealed and delivered in the presence of **John Hough**, **John Poultney**, **George Gregg**, and **William Kirk**. Proven on 6/26/1750. Lease and Release, Fairfax County Deed Book C, Part 1, pp. 35-38

6. 9/19 and 9/20/1750, **Edmund Sands** of Fairfax County in the Colony of Virginia, cordwainer, and **Rachel** his wife of the one part to **Richard Roach** of the County and Colony aforesaid, blacksmith, of the other part. Whereas there is a certain tract or parcel of land situate lying and being in the County aforesaid and bounded as followeth viz. Beginning at a white oak standing on the east side of **Kittocton Creek** nigh to said Creek and extending thence up said Creek with the several meanders thereof South 34 poles, thence N 83° W 56 poles, thence S 24° W 38 poles, thence S 16° W 64 poles to a grove of pines corner to **Catesby Cocke,** thence with **Cocke's** line N 80° E 209 poles to a large white oak, thence N 51° W 90 poles to several white oaks, thence N 1° E 9 poles to a white oak, thence N 51° W 36 poles to a white oak, thence N 69° W 30 poles to the beginning containing 100 acres of land, which land was confirmed to **Richard Brown** by a patent out of the Proprietor's Office of the Northern Neck of Virginia duly executed bearing date the 27th day of November, 1741 and registered in the Proprietor's Office in Libra E, Folio 397 and by his heirs conveyed to said **Sands** by good sufficient deed of lease and release duly executed according to law the said release bearing date the 2nd day of January, 1749. Now this indenture witnesseth that the said **Edmund Sands** and **Rachel** his wife for and in consideration of the sum of 20 pounds sterling to the said **Edmund Sands** in hand paid by the said **Richard Roach,** the receipt whereof the said **Edmund Sands** doth hereby acknowledge, hath granted bargained sold alienated released and confirmed and by these presents doth bargain sell release and confirm unto the said **Richard Roach** his heirs and assigns all and singular the said 100 acres of land situate bounded and being as is above set forth and described, together with all and singular the houses edifices buildings gardens orchards ways watercourses woods meadows creeples swamps fishings fowlings hawkings huntings rights liberties privileges improvements advantages hereditaments and appurtenances with the rents issues and profits thereof. To have and to hold the said 100 acres of land hereditaments and premises hereby granted alienated released and confirmed or intended to be granted and released with the appurtenances unto the said **Richard Roach** his heirs and assigns forever, **Edmund Sands** and **Rachel** her R mark **Sands**. Sealed and delivered in the presence of **Jno. Hough**, **Thomas** his T

mark **John**, **Isr. Thompson**, and **John Poultney**. Proven on 9/26/1750. Lease and Release, Fairfax County Deed Book C, Part 1, pp. 67-70

7. 8/11 and 8/12/1754, **Edmund Sands** of the County of Fairfax, planter, of the one part to **Richard Roach** of the same County, blacksmith, of the other part. Witnesseth that the said **Edmunds Sands** for and in consideration of the sum of 12 pounds current money of Virginia to him in hand paid by the said **Richard Roach** the receipt whereof the said **Edmund Sands** doth hereby acknowledge, hath granted bargained and sold aliened released and confirmed and by these presents doth fully freely and absolutely grant bargain and sell alien release and confirm unto the said **Richard Roach** and to his heirs and assigns forever all that piece or parcel of land situate lying and being in the said County of Fairfax containing 23 acres and bounded as followeth viz. Beginning at a white oak on the bank of **Kittocton Creek** and the east side thereof corner to said **Roach's** other land running from thence down the said **Creek** North 34 poles, thence N 59° E 20 poles to the mouth of a small branch which runs by the said **Roach's house,** thence up the said branch South 10 poles to four mulberry trees growing from one root, thence S 47° E 40 poles to a black oak sapling, thence S 51° E 136 poles to a stake and stone in a small valley in a line of said **Sands** and **Colo. Catesby Cocke's,** thence with that line S 80° W 35 poles to a white oak corner to the said **Roach's** other land, thence with the lines of that land N 51° W 90 poles to several small white oaks, thence N 1° E 9 poles to a white oak, thence N 51° W 36 poles to a white oak standing by the said **Roach's smith-shop,** thence N 69° W 30 poles to the beginning, together with all trees woods underwoods ways watercourses easements profits commodities advantages hereditaments rights members and appurtenances whatsoever to the same belonging or in any wise appertaining. To have and to hold the said 23 acres of land above mentioned and every part and parcel thereof with the appurtenances unto the said **Richard Roach** his executors administrators and assigns forever, **Edmund Sands**. Sealed and delivered in the presence of **Nich. Minor, Thos. Shepherd**, and **John McIlhaney**. Lease and Release, Fairfax County Deed Book C, Part 2, pp. 789-794

8. 11/15/1759, **Richard Roach** was granted leave to build a **mill** whereon he lived on **Kittocton Creek** by the Court of the County of Loudoun. Loudoun County Court Order Book A, p. 266, p. 308

9. 6/15 and 6/16/1762, **Edward Norton** of Loudoun County in the Colony of Virginia, farmer, and **Elizabeth** his wife of the one part to **Richard Williams** of Bucks County in the Province of Pennsylvania, farmer, of the other part. Witnesseth that the said **Edward Norton** and **Elizabeth** his wife for and in consideration of the sum of 220 pounds lawful money to him in hand paid by the said **Richard Williams** at and before the sealing and delivery of these presents the receipt whereof is hereby confessed and acknowledged, hath granted bargained and sold aliened released and confirmed and by these presents doth bargain and sell alien release and confirm unto the said **Richard Williams** his heirs and assigns forever two tract or parcel of land situate lying and being in Cameron Parish in the County of Loudoun formerly Fairfax. The first tract lying on the branches of **Kittocton Creek** containing 100 acres purchased by the said

Edward Norton from a certain **Henry Brown** by lease and release date the 2nd and 3rd days of December, 1749 and bounded as follows viz. Beginning at a white oak marked **CC** corner to **Catesby Cocke's** land almost twenty poles from a line of a tract surveyed for **Saml. Maxberry** then said to belong to **William Kirk**, thence parallel with **Kirk's** line S 60° W 85 poles to a small hickory on the west side of a branch of **Kittocton** amongst a heap of rocks, thence S 18° W 199 poles to a black oak in a dividing line between **Edmund Sands** and the said **Henry Brown**, thence with the said dividing line S 71° W 113 (S 71° E 113 ?) poles to a spanish oak in a line of **Catesby Cocke**, thence with **Cocke's** line N 20° W 253 poles to the beginning. The other tract lying on and about **Kittocton Mountain** containing 400 acres purchased by the said **Edward Norton** of **Aneas Campbell Gent**. attorney in fact for **Catesby Cocke** by lease and release dated the lease the 30th day of April, and the release the 1st day of May, 1760 and bounded as follows viz. Beginning at a white oak and two red oaks on the west side of said Mountain near the top thereof upwards of sixty poles above a corner of **Edmund Sands** land thence East 159 poles to a small gum in a gully near a marked chestnut oak on the east side of said Mountain, thence N 12° E 195 poles to two red oaks near a springhead, then N 63° – 30 minutes W 365 poles to a hickory and several red oak saplings by a poison field, thence S 20° E 320 poles to the beginning, and all houses buildings orchards meadows trees woods ways water watercourses easements profits advantages and hereditaments whatsoever to the said two tracts of land above mentioned belonging or in any wise appertaining. To have and to hold the said two tract of land and premises above mentioned and every part and parcel thereof with the appurtenances unto the said **Richard Williams** his heirs and assigns forever, **Edward Norton** and **Elizabeth Norton**. Sealed and delivered in the presence of **James Jones**, **William Jones**, and **John Steere**. Proven on July 13, 1762. Lease and Release, Loudoun County Deed Book, Part 1, pp. 314-319 (Note: The given tract or parcel of land containing 400 acres was originally patented to **Catesby Cocke** as part of a greater tract of land containing 591 acres of land from the Proprietor's Office of the Northern Neck of Virginia. See Lease and Release, Loudoun County Deed Book A, pp. 479-483.)

10. 8/10 and 8/11/1763, **Henry Brown** of Loudoun County in the Colony of Virginia, farmer, and **Hester** (sic) his wife of the one part to **Richard Williams** of the same County and Colony, farmer, of the other part. Witnesseth that the said **Henry Brown** and **Hester** his wife for and in consideration of the sum of 20 pounds current money to them in hand paid by the said **Richard Williams** at and before the sealing and delivery of these presents, the receipt whereof is hereby acknowledged, have granted bargained and sold aliened released and confirmed and by these presents do grant bargain and sell alien release and confirm unto the said **Richard Williams** and to his heirs and assigns forever all that tract or parcel of land with the appurtenances situate lying and being in the said County of Loudoun and bounded as follows viz. Beginning at a red oak corner to **West** and **Kirk** thence S 7-½° E 154 poles to a dogwood bush and heap of stones on the west side of a hill in **Cocke's** line, thence with said line N 63° W 158 poles to a white oak marked **CC**, thence S 60° W 83 poles to a hickory sapling in a heap of

stones in a valley, thence N 43° W 12 poles to a white oak in the east side of a hill near the bottom thereof in **William Kirk's** line, thence N 60° E to the beginning containing 76 acres and including the plantation whereon **Henry Pickerill** formerly lived, and all houses buildings orchards meadows trees woods waters watercourses easements profits and advantages whatsoever to the said tract of land belonging or in any wise appertaining. To have and to hold the said tract of land and all and singular the premises above mentioned with the appurtenances unto the said **Richard Williams** his heirs and assigns forever, **Henry Brown** and **Easter** (sic) her EB mark **Brown**. Sealed and delivered in the presence of **William Jones, James Jones**, and **Jenkin Williams**. Proven on 9/13/1763. Lease and Release, Loudoun County Deed Book C, Part 2, pp. 709-713

11.   5/27/1774 and 2/13/1775, Last will and testament of **Edmund Sands**, Loudoun County Will Book B, pp. 102-104

12.   6/10 and 6/11/1774, **Richard Williams** of Loudoun County in the Colony of Virginia, farmer, and **Margaret** his wife of the one part to **Joseph Sands** of the same County and Colony, farmer, of the other part. Witnesseth that the said **Richard Williams** and **Margaret** his wife for and in consideration of the sum of 20 pounds current money to them in hand paid by the said **Joseph Sands** at and before the sealing and delivery of these presents the receipt whereof is hereby acknowledged, have granted bargained and sold aliened released and confirmed and by these presents do grant bargain and sell alien release and confirm unto the said **Joseph Sands** and to his heirs and assigns forever all that tract or parcel of land with the appurtenances situate lying and being in the said County of Loudoun and bounded as follows viz. Beginning at a black oak in a line of **Edmund Sands** thence extending S 71° E 88 poles to a white oak marked **CC**, thence East 33 poles with a line of **Abraham Dawson's** to a black oak and hickory, thence N 10-½° E 109 poles to two dogwood saplings, thence N 79° W 79 poles to a white oak and hickory, thence N 70° W 20 poles to a rock on the south side of a branch, thence N 49-½° W 60 poles to a long stone on the east side of a hill, thence S 19° W 70 poles to the beginning corner containing 73 acres and including part of the plantation whereon **Jenkin Philips** formerly lived, and all houses buildings orchards meadows trees woods water watercourses easements profits and advantages whatsoever to the said tract of land belonging or in any wise appertaining. To have and to hold the said tract of land and all and singular the premises above mentioned with the appurtenances unto the said **Joseph Sands** his heirs and assigns, **Richard Williams** and **Margaret** her M mark **Williams**. Sealed and delivered in the presence of **Benjamin Sands, Isaac Sands**, and **James Roach**. Lease and Release, Loudoun County Deed Book K, pp. 267-272

13.   10/8 and 10/9/1784, **Mercer Brown** and his wife **Sarah Brown** of the County of Loudoun in Virginia of the one part to **Thomas Taylor** of the County of Frederick in Maryland of the other part. Witnesseth that for and in consideration of the sum of 1,600 pounds current money of the State of Maryland in hand paid by the said **Thomas Taylor** at or before the sealing and delivery of these presents, the said **Mercer Brown** and **Sarah** his wife hath granted bargained sold aliened released and confirmed and by these presents doth grant

bargain sell alien release and confirm unto the said **Thomas Taylor** and his heirs forever all that tract or parcel of land situate lying and being on **Kittockton Creek** in Loudoun County whereon we now live containing by estimation 300 acres more or less. It being a tract of land left by the will of **Richard Brown deceased** (dated in April, 1745) to his wife **Mary**, mother of the said **Mercer Brown,** and by her given to the said **Mercer**, joining the lands of the **Reverend William West**, **Richard Williams**, **Henry Brown**, and the **Honble. Bennett Esq**. of Great Britain, and all houses mills buildings orchards ways waters watercourses profits commodities hereditaments and appurtenances whatsoever to the said premises hereby granted or any part thereof belonging or in any wise appertaining. To have and to hold the said land and all and singular other the premises hereby granted and released and every part and parcel thereof with their every of their appurtenances unto the said **Thomas Taylor** his heirs and assigns forever, **Mercer Brown** and **Sarah Brown**. Proven on 10/11/1784. Lease and Release, Loudoun County Deed Book O, pp. 141-144.

14. 8/16 and 8/17/1785, **Joseph Sands** of the one part to **Jacob Sands** of the County of Loudoun and State of Virginia, blacksmith, of the other part. Whereas there is a certain tract or parcel of land situate lying and being in the County of Loudoun and State of Virginia aforesaid being on the east side of the **road leading from Thomas Taylor's Mill to Fairfax Meetinghouse**, and being part of a tract or parcel of land late the property of **Edmund Sands deceased** and willed to **Joseph Sands** containing 80 acres be it more or less. As also one tract or parcel of land laying and being on the north side of the before mentioned tract. Beginning at a black oak on a hill corner to **Richard Williams** standing in a line of the before mentioned tract extending thence with **Williams** line N 17° E 68 poles to a stone by a small marked white oak on the east side of a hill, thence S 50° E 58 poles to a black oak stump by a rock, thence S 73° E 12 poles to a heap of stones put together by a run, then leaving **Williams** line South 45 poles to several black oak saplings, thence S 28° E 80 poles to two hickories and a black oak sapling, thence S 65° W 11-½ poles to three hickory saplings, thence N 25° W 84 poles to a white oak and thence N 75-½° W 78 poles to the first station containing 22 acres. Now this indenture witnesseth that the said **Joseph Sands** for and in consideration of the sum of 100 pounds sterling to him the said **Joseph Sands** in hand paid him by the said **Jacob Sands** the receipt whereof the said **Joseph Sands** doth hereby acknowledge, hath granted bargained sold aliened released and confirmed and by these presents doth bargain sell release and confirm unto the said **Jacob Sands** and his heirs and assigns all and singular the said two tract or parcels of land one of 80 acres of land and the other of 22 acres of land, situate bounded and being as is above set forth and described together with all and singular the houses edifices buildings gardens orchards ways watercourses woods meadows creeples swamps fishing fowling hawking hunting rights liberties privileges improvements advantages hereditaments and appurtenances with the rents issues and profits thereof. To have and to hold the said two tract of land hereditaments and premises hereby granted alienated released and confirmed or mentioned and intended to be granted and released with

the appurtenances unto the said **Jacob Sands** his heirs and assigns forever, **Joseph Sands**. Sealed and delivered in the presence of **Richard Roach**, **Isaac Sands**, and **Jacob Harriss**. Proven on 9/11/1786. Lease and Release, Loudoun County Deed Book P, Part 2, pp. 375-378.

15. 8/14/1786, **Joseph Sands** of the one part to **Isaac Sands** of Loudoun County and State of Virginia of the other part. Witnesseth that the said **Joseph Sands** for and in consideration of 5 pounds lawful money of Virginia to him in hand paid by the said **Isaac Sands** the receipt whereof he doth hereby acknowledge, hath bargained and sold and by these presents doth bargain and sell unto the said **Isaac Sands** all and singular that tract of land situate lying and being in the County of Loudoun and State of Virginia being part of a tract or parcel of land the said **Joseph Sands** had conveyed him by **Richard Williams,** being the upper end of said land bounded by lands of **Richard Williams** and others containing 53 acres be it more or less, together with all and singular the houses edifices buildings orchards ways watercourses woods meadows creeples swamps fishings fowlings hawkings rights liberties privileges improvements advantages hereditaments and appurtenances with the rents issues and profits thereof. To have and to hold the said 53 acres of land hereditaments and premises hereby granted, alienated, released and confirmed or mentioned and intended to be granted and released with the appurtenances unto the said **Isaac Sands** his heirs and assigns forever, **Joseph Sands**. Signed, sealed and delivered in the presence of us, **Richard Roach, Jacob Sands,** and **Jacob Harriss**. Proven on 9/11/1786. Bargain and sale, Loudoun County Deed Book P, Part 2, pp. 378-380

16. 9/22 and 9/23/1793, **Richard Williams** of Loudoun County in the State of Virginia and **Margaret** his wife of the one part to **Thomas Taylor** of the said County of Loudoun of the other part. Witnesseth that for and in consideration of the sum of 189 pounds current money of Virginia to the said **Richard Williams** in hand paid by the said **Thomas Taylor** at or before the sealing and delivery of these presents, the receipt where he doth hereby acknowledge, have granted bargained sold aliened released and confirmed and by these presents do grant bargain sell alien release and confirm unto the said **Thomas Taylor** and his heirs all that parcel of land situate in Loudoun County aforesaid bounded as followeth viz. Beginning at a black oak standing in a line of **Thomas Taylor's** which he purchased of **Mercer Brown** formerly one **Maxberry's** land, extending thence with said line reversed S 57° W 115 poles to a small white oak by the **main road** corner to land **Enos Williams** lives on, then binding with his lines first along the said **road** S 1° E 61 poles to a heap of stones in the said **road** his corner, then with another of his lines S 70° E 92 poles to a heap of stones, then S 5° E 53 poles to a stump and stone, then S 74° E 182 poles to **James Shrieve's** line, then with said line N 6° E 45 poles to a small gum, then N 69° – 30 minutes W 156 poles to a stump and stone, then N 11° W 161 poles to the first station containing 135 acres be the same more or less, being parts of two tract of land taken up by one **Catesby Cocke** and **Richard Brown** the other, and all houses buildings orchards ways waters watercourses profits commodities hereditaments and appurtenances whatsoever to the said premises hereby granted or any part thereof belonging or in

any wise appertaining unto the said **Thomas Taylor** his heirs and assigns forever, **Richard Williams** and **Margaret** her M mark **Williams**. Sealed and delivered in the presence of **John Hough, Leonard** his L mark **Poston, A. Sutherland, Enos** his O mark **Williams, Joseph Williams**. Proven on 10/14/1793. Lease and Release, Loudoun County Deed Book V, pp. 138-142

17.   10/12/1796, **Thomas Taylor** and **Caleb** his wife of the County of Loudoun and Commonwealth of Virginia of the one part to **Joseph Taylor** of the same place of the other part. Witnesseth that the said **Thomas Taylor** and **Caleb** his wife for and in consideration of the sum of 5 pounds Virginia currency to the said **Thomas Taylor** in hand paid by the said **Joseph Taylor** before the sealing and delivery of these presents the receipt whereof is hereby acknowledged, have granted bargained and sold aliened and confirmed and by these presents doth grant bargain and sell alien and confirm unto the said **Joseph Taylor** all that lot or parcel of land situate lying and being in the said County of Loudoun in a town laid off by the said **Thomas Taylor** called **Milford (Millford)** and known by Lot Number 18, being part of a tract of land the said **Thomas Taylor** purchased of **Mercer Brown** and bounded as followeth viz. Beginning at a stone **Henry Taylor's** corner thence N 43° E 22 poles with **Henry Taylor's** line to a poplar his corner, then N 37° W 2 poles, then S 47° W 22 poles, then S 40° E 2 poles to the beginning containing one-quarter of an acre more or less, and all houses building ways waters watercourses profits commodities hereditaments and appurtenances whatsoever to the same belonging or in any wise appertaining. To have and to hold the land hereby conveyed and all and singular the premises hereby granted with the appurtenances unto the said **Joseph Taylor** and to his heirs and assigns forever and that free and clear of and from all former and other gifts grants bargain sale dower right and title of dower judgments executions title trouble and charges whatsoever, and the annual rent sum of 6 pounds sterling to be paid to the said **Thomas Taylor** his heirs and assigns by the said **Joseph Taylor** his heirs or assigns on or before the 25th day of December in every year. In witness whereof the said **Thomas Taylor** and **Caleb** his wife have hereunto set their hands and seals the day and year above written, **Thomas Taylor**. Signed, sealed and delivered in presence of, **Isaac Larowe, A. Sutherland**, and **Jacob Dehaven**. Proven on 9/14/1801. Assignment, Loudoun County Deed Book 2B, pp. 53-54

18.   11/11/1800, **Thomas Taylor** and **Benjamin Canby** executors of the last will and testament of **Thomas Taylor deceased** of the one part to **Joseph Taylor** of the other part. Witnesseth that the said **Thomas Taylor** and **Benjamin Canby** for and in consideration of the sum of 481 pounds and 10 shillings Virginia currency unto them in hand well and truly paid by the said **Joseph Taylor** at and before the sealing and delivery hereof the receipt whereof they do hereby acknowledge, have granted bargained sold aliened and by these presents do grant bargain sell alien release and confirm unto the said **Joseph Taylor** his heirs and assigns a certain tract or parcel of land situate lying and being on **Katocton Creek** in the County of Loudoun, being all the reminder and residue of a certain tract of land purchased by the said **Thomas Taylor deceased** from **Mercer Brown** after taking thereof 200 hundred acres at the lower end left by the will of

the said **Thomas Taylor** to his son **Henry Taylor**, and containing 107 acres be the same more or less together also with all and singular the rights members liberties privileges improvements hereditaments and appurtenances whatsoever thereunto belonging or in any wise appertaining. To have and to hold all and singular the premises hereby granted with the appurtenances unto the said **Joseph Taylor** his heirs and assigns forever, **Thomas Taylor** and **Benja. Canby**. Sealed and delivered in presence of **John Drean, Jacob Fadeley**, and **James Hamilton**. Proven 4/14/1801. Deed, Loudoun County Deed Book 2A, pp. 337-338

19.   5/1/1803, Memorandum of an agreement made between **Esther Brown**, widow, relict of **Henry Brown deceased, John Brown** and **William Brown**, executors of said **Henry Brown deceased**, and **Adam Householder Junior**, Writ of Adquod Damnum, Loudoun County Deed Book 2D, pp. 110-114.

20.   4/2/1810, **William Brown** and **Hannah** his wife of the County of Loudoun and State of Virginia of the one part to **John Hamilton** of the County and State aforesaid of the other part. Witnesseth that the said **William Brown** and **Hannah** his wife in consideration of the sum of $ 5,333.33 of lawful money of this Commonwealth to them in hand paid by the said **John Hamilton** at or before the ensealing and delivery of these presents the receipt whereof is hereby acknowledged, have bargained and sold and by these presents do each of them bargain and sell unto the said **John Hamilton** his heirs and assigns a certain tract of land situate lying and being on **Catoctin Creek** in the County of Loudoun. It being the tract of land left by the last will and testament of **Henry Brown deceased** to the said **William Brown** his son bounded follows viz. Beginning at a hickory amongst a parcel of rocks corner to **Eneas Williams** thence N 44° W 18 poles to a white oak in the original line of **Marberry's** survey, then with said line S 58-½° W 21-½ poles to a white oak in said line marked **HB**, thence 81-1/3° W 12 poles to a small sapling near the head of a hollow, thence N 37° W 14 poles to **Catoctin Creek** thence up the said Creek with the meanders thereof West 8 poles, (thence) N 60° W 30 poles, (thence) N 13° W 19 poles, (thence) N 51-½° W 60 poles, (thence) N 75° W 36 poles, (thence) S 40° W 11 poles, (thence) S 48° E 22 poles, (thence) S 22-½° E 50 poles, (thence) S 43° W 14 poles, (thence) S 7° W 30 poles, (thence) leaving the Creek S 66° E 11 poles to a large white oak corner to the original patent and to **Tankerville's** survey, thence with the original line of the patent S 51° E 127 poles, thence with another of the original lines N 56° E 78 poles to a pile of stones on the opposite side of **Catoctin Creek**, thence up the **Creek** with the meanders thereof S 38° E 12 poles, (thence) S 7° E 6 poles, (thence) S 35° W 30-¼ poles, (thence) S 28° W 45 poles, (thence) S 52° E 6 poles, (thence) S 76° E 45-½ poles, thence S 57° E 26 poles to a black oak corner, thence S 80° E 122 poles to a stone in **Sands** line and **Eneas Williams** corner, thence with **Williams's** line N 21° W 187-½ poles to the beginning containing 224 acres be the same more or less, together with all and singular the houses buildings yards pastures feedings commons woods water and watercourses, privileges profits and advantages, hereditaments and appurtenances whatsoever to the said tract of land belonging or in any wise appertaining, and the reversions and remainders, yearly and other rents, issues and profits thereof and of every part

and parcel thereof. To have and to hold the said tract of land with the appurtenances above mentioned and every part and parcel thereof with every of their members and appurtenances unto the said **John Hamilton** his heirs and assigns forever, **William Brown** and **Hannah Brown**. Signed sealed and delivered in the presence of **Timothy Hixon, Eneas** his X mark **Williams**, and **Amos Sinclair**. Proven on 12/10/1810. Deed, Loudoun County Deed Book 2O, pp. 321-324

21.   Know all men by these presents that whereas in and by one indenture of Deed of Trust bearing date the 26th day of July, 1819, and made between **Ann Taylor** and **Mary Taylor** of the County of Loudoun and State of Virginia, the said **Ann Taylor** and **Mary Taylor** for the consideration herein mentioned did grant bargain and sell unto the said **Benjamin Shreve** all the interest right and title of the said **Ann Taylor** and the said **Mary Taylor** of and into all that tract of land situate lying and being in the said County of Loudoun whereof **Henry Taylor** the husband of the said **Ann Taylor** and father of the said **Mary** died seized, and being the tract whereon the said **Henry Taylor** lived with all and singular the appurtenances upon their interest right and title of the said tract of land belonging or in any wise thereto appertaining. To have and to hold the said interest right and title of the said tract of land aforesaid unto me the said **Benjamin Shreve** my heirs and assigns forever for which said indenture me name was used in trust for **Abraham H. Collins**. Now know ye that I **Benjamin Shreve** in discharge of the trust in me reposed as aforesaid and at the special instance and request of the said **Abraham H. Collins**, have remised released surrendered assigned transferred and set over and by these presents do for me, my executors and administrators, fully and absolutely remise release surrender assign transfer and set over unto the said **Mary Taylor** her heirs and assigns all the estate right title interest benefit claim and demand whatsoever which I the said **Benjamin Shreve** have or claim of in or to the premises or of or in any sum or sums of money or other thing or matter whatsoever in the said deed of trust contained mentioned and expressed, so that neither I the said **Benjamin Shreve** my heirs executors administrators at any time hereafter shall or will claim challenge or demand and interest property benefit or other thing in any manner whatsoever by reason or means of the said indenture or any covenant therein contained thereof and therefrom and of any and all actions suits damages which I my heirs executors or administrators may have concerning the same shall be forever debarred by these presents. In witness whereof the said **Benjamin Shreve** have hereunto set my hand and seal this 10th day of February in the year of our Lord 1823, **Benj. Shreve**. Signed, sealed and delivered in the presence of **R. Braden, William Steer**, and **Jesse Gover**. Proven on 2/21/1823. Release, Loudoun County Deed Book 3F, pp. 279-280

22.   2/20/1823, **Mary A. Taylor** of **Waterford** in the County of Loudoun and State of Virginia of the one part to **John Hamilton** of the County and State aforesaid of the other part. Witnesseth that the said **Mary A. Taylor** in consideration of the sum of $ 1,500 lawful money to her in hand paid by the said **John Hamilton** at or before the ensealing and delivery of these presents the

receipt whereof she the said **Mary Taylor** do hereby acknowledge, hath sold and by these presents doth bargain and sell unto the said **John Hamilton** his heirs and assigns all her share of the undivided real estate of her father **Henry Taylor deceased** in the County of Loudoun. It being one seventh part of the tract and lots he possessed known by the name of **Taylor Town Farm**, also one seventh part of the tract or parcel of land which he the said **Henry Taylor** died possessed of on the west side of **Catoctin Creek** except what was sold and conveyed by **Mrs. Ann Taylor deceased** to **Levi Collins,** now in the possession of **Jacob Carnes**, together with all and singular the houses buildings orchards lands pastures woods ways water and watercourses privileges profits and advantages hereditaments and appurtenances whatsoever to the said lands belonging or appertaining or with the same used or enjoyed, or accepted, reputed, taken or known as part parcel or numbers thereof or as belonging to the same or any part thereof. To have and to hold the said one seventh part of the tract and premises above mentioned with the tenements hereditaments and all and singular other the premises herein before mentioned or intended to be bargained and sold and every part and parcel thereof with every of their rights members and appurtenances unto the said **John Hamilton** his heirs and assigns forever, **R. Braden**, and **Abriel Jenners** (?). Proven on 3/10/1823. Deed, Loudoun County Deed Book 3F, pp. 315-316

23.   2/9/1829, Survey and division of **Henry Taylor deceased's** estate in Loudoun County by virtue of an order of the worshipful Court of Loudoun County in Chancery sitting dated the 9th day of February, 1829 among his heirs and representatives. Lot No. 1 allotted to **Joshua Ratliff and Nancy** his wife and **Harriet** and **Sarah Taylor** jointly bounded as follows viz. Beginning at A, a stake on the south side of **Catocton Creek** about two poles north of a marked white oak a corner to **Stoutsenberger** thence with his line S 1° – 55 minutes W 22-½ poles to B, a stake between two rocks and near a forked dogwood, thence with another of **Stoutsenberger's** and **Potterfield's** line S 56° - 22 minutes W 171-¾ poles to C, a pile of stones in **Potterfield's** line and a corner to Lot No. 4, thence with the same and Lot No. 3, N 19-½° E 157 poles to D, a stake in the **road leading to the mill and across the Creek**, thence with said **road** N 65° W 24 poles to the east bank of the Creek at E, where said **road** crossed Creek, then down the Creek on the east side thereof with the several meanders thereof to the beginning containing 114 acres and 3 roods and 20 poles, together with the **dwelling house and barn.** And, also Lot No. 2 on the west side of **Catocton Creek** bounded as follows viz. Beginning at F, a planted stone on a hill in a line of **Stoutsenberger** and corner to **Jacob Carnes** thence with a line of the same S 48-½° E 25 poles and 15 links to G, on the west side of Creek, thence down the Creek with the meanders thereof N 26-½° E 20 poles, (thence) N 39-½° E 13 poles, (thence) N 35° E 8 poles, (thence) N 62-½° E 6 poles and 20 links to H, a pile of stones at the end of a ledge of rocks a corner to **Cordell**, thence with his line N 36-¼° W 41 poles to I, a white oak stump a corner to **Cordell** and **Stoutsenberger**, thence with **Stoutsenberger** S 22-¾° W 59 poles to the beginning containing 10 acres and 3 roods and 15 poles. Lot No. 3 allotted to **George W. Henry** for his three-sevenths share together with the **mill** and the

right of the water, **miller's house, lime-kiln, and the log house on the road occupied by Levi Collins,** bounded as follows viz. Beginning at M, the mouth the mouth of a small branch falling into **Catocton Creek** on the north side a corner to **Hamilton** and **Carnes** about 1-¾ poles from the edge of the Creek, thence with Carnes S 77° E 20 poles to N, a pile of stones a corner to **Carnes**, thence with his line S 45-¾° E 14-¾ poles to O, a large sycamore his corner, thence S 73° E 10 poles and 7 ½ links to P, a sycamore, thence N 24° E 12 poles and 9 links to Q, a pile of stones, N 31° E 8-½ poles and 9 links to R, a pile of stones, thence N 23-¾° E 15 poles to S, a pile of stones near a water birch, (thence) crossing the Creek S 65° E 4 poles to E, the east bank of the Creek and where the **road** crosses a corner to Lot No. 1, thence with two lines of the same S 65° E 24 poles to D, a stake in the **road** and corner to Lot No. 1, thence S 19-½° W 82 poles to J, a pile of stones by a locust a corner to Lot No. 4 in a line of Lot No. 1, thence with Lot No. 4 S 73° W 78-½ poles to K, a stake on the Creek at a short bind thereof a corner to Lot No. 4, thence down the Creek with the meanders thereof to L, opposite the mouth of the aforesaid branch, thence crossing the Creek N 5-½° E 7 poles to the beginning containing 51 acres and 2 roods and 24 poles. Lot No. 4 allotted to **Robt. Moffett** for one-seventh in right of his purchase from **Sampson Richards** and wife together with **the small house at the foot of the Mountain called the Schoolhouse** to be moved by said **Moffett** bounded as follows viz. Beginning at K, a stake a corner to Lot No. 3 on the Creek and a short bind thereof thence with Lot No. 3 N 73° E 78-½ poles to J, a pile of stones near a locust a corner to Lot No. 3 and in a line of Lot No. 1, thence with Lot No. 1 S 18-½° W 75 poles to C, a pile of stones in **Potterfield's** line, thence with **Potterfield** and **Williams** S 56° 22 W 72 poles to T, a pile of stones in **Williams** line a corner to **Hamilton,** a white oak, hickory, and black oak pointers, thence with **Hamilton** N 22° W 89 ¾ poles to U, a stone on the south bank of the Creek a corner to **Hamilton**, thence down the Creek with the meanders thereof to the beginning containing 41 acres and 2 roods and 3 poles, **Jno. G. Mathias**, L.S.C., **Jacob Carnes** and **Crumbaker**, S.C.C. (sworn chain carriers). Division of Henry Taylor's land, Loudoun County Deed Book 3T, pp. 109-109

...I give and devise unto my beloved wife Mary and her heirs and assigns forever all the remaining part of the Tract or parcel of land whereon we now live together with the house, malt-house, mill, mill-house, saw, saw-mill, brewer-house, outhouses of all kinds whatsoever and all the appurtenances to any of them belonging..., Last Will and Testament of Richard Brown of Fairfax County bearing date February 3rd, 1745, Fairfax County Will Book A, Part 1, p. 110

Witnessed by Edward Norton, Danꞏl James, Jacob Janney

At a Court held for Fairfax County on May 21, 1745, a certificate granted Henry Brown & Mary Brown, executors therein named for obtaining a probate thereof. The contents of his inventory of goods affirmed by Francis Hague, Edmund Sands, George Gregg

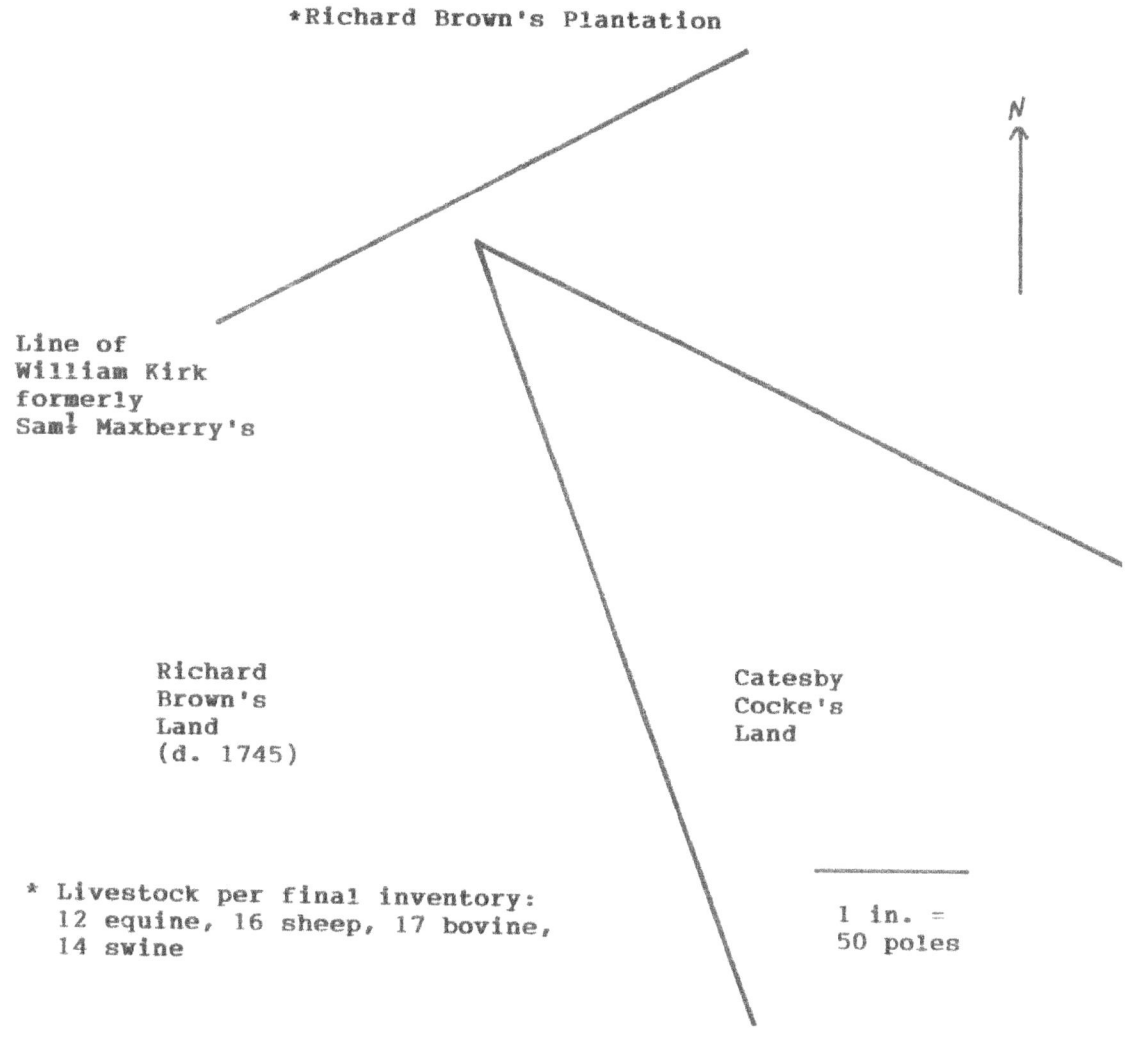

*Richard Brown's Plantation

Line of
William Kirk
formerly
Samꞏl Maxberry's

Richard
Brown's
Land
(d. 1745)

Catesby
Cocke's
Land

* Livestock per final inventory:
  12 equine, 16 sheep, 17 bovine,
  14 swine

1 in. =
50 poles

* This Indenture(s) made the second and third day of December, 1749, Henry Brown of Fairfax County, yeoman, to Edward Norton of the same place, weaver, Lease and Release, one hundred acres of land for and in consideration of an agreement with the said Edward Norton and promise of a Deed to him by Richard Brown deceased father of the said Henry Brown, Fairfax County Deed Book C, Part 1, pp. 35-38

Witnessed by John Hough, John Poultney, George Gregg, William Kirk

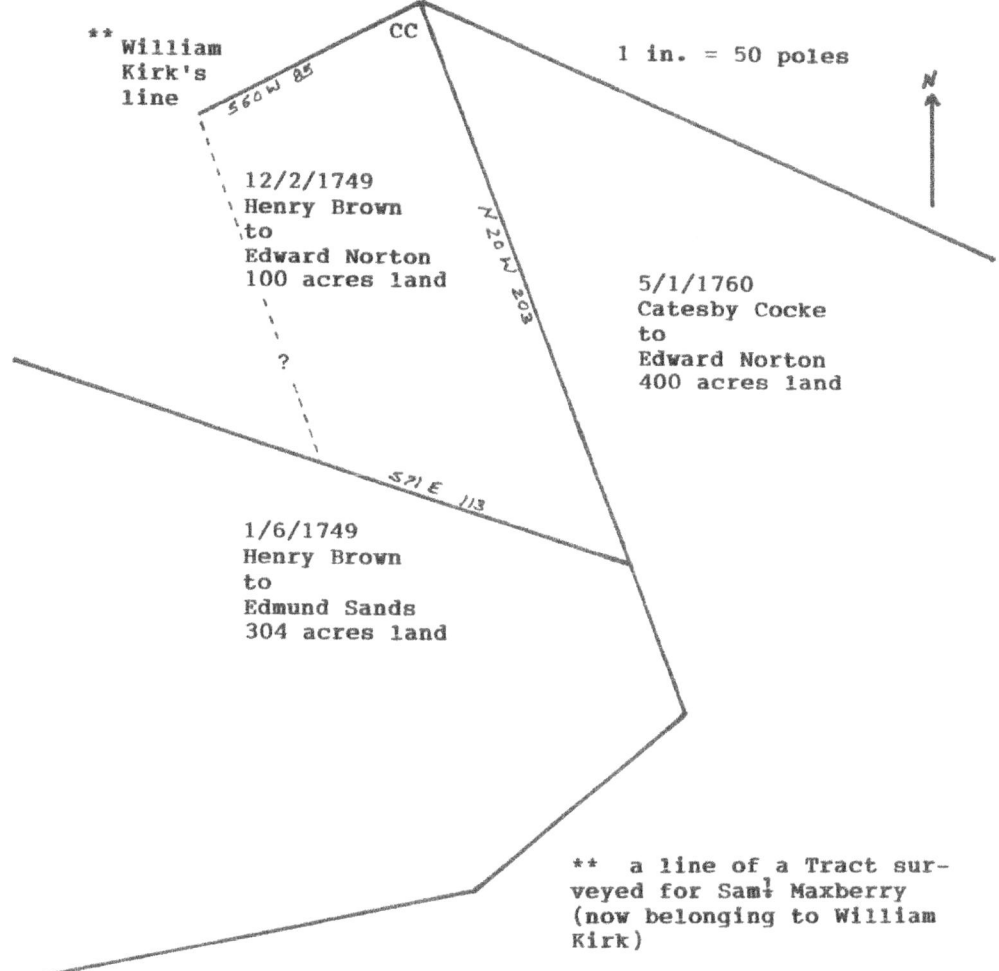

** William Kirk's line

12/2/1749
Henry Brown
to
Edward Norton
100 acres land

5/1/1760
Catesby Cocke
to
Edward Norton
400 acres land

1/6/1749
Henry Brown
to
Edmund Sands
304 acres land

** a line of a Tract surveyed for Saml Maxberry (now belonging to William Kirk)

* Being part of a Tract surveyed for Richard Brown and confirmed to him by patent, Proprietor's Office, 11/27/1741, Book E, Folio 379

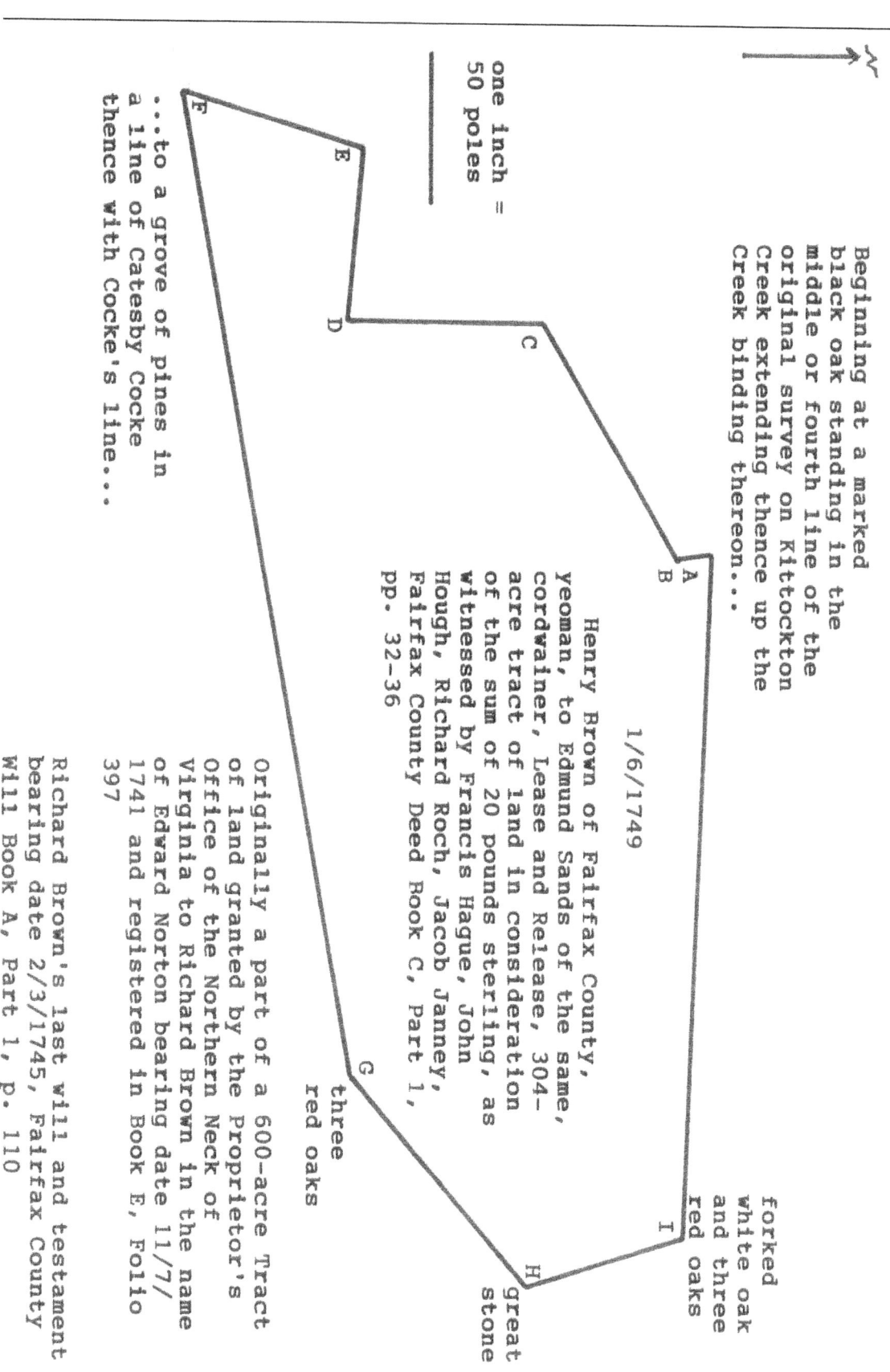

Beginning at a marked black oak standing in the middle or fourth line of the original survey on Kittockton Creek extending thence up the Creek binding thereon...

...to a grove of pines in a line of Catesby Cocke thence with Cocke's line....

one inch = 50 poles

1/6/1749

Henry Brown of Fairfax County, yeoman, to Edmund Sands of the same, cordwainer, Lease and Release, 304-acre tract of land in consideration of the sum of 20 pounds sterling, as witnessed by Francis Hague, John Hough, Richard Roch, Jacob Janney, Fairfax County Deed Book C, Part 1, pp. 32-36

Originally a part of a 600-acre Tract of land granted by the Proprietor's Office of the Northern Neck of Virginia to Richard Brown in the name of Edward Norton bearing date 11/7/1741 and registered in Book E, Folio 397

Richard Brown's last will and testament bearing date 2/3/1745, Fairfax County Will Book A, Part 1, p. 110

forked white oak and three red oaks

three red oaks

great stone

9/19/1750, Edmund Sands of Fairfax County, cordwainer, and Rachel his wife to Richard Roach of County aforesaid, blacksmith, Lease and Release, 100 acres land in consideration of the sum of 20 pounds sterling, witnessed by Jno Hough, Thomas his T mark John, Is^t Thompson, John Poultney, Fairfax County Deed Book C, Part 1, pp. 67-70

8/11/1754, Edmund Sands of Fairfax County, planter, to Richard Roach of the same County, blacksmith, Lease and Release, 23 acres land in consideration of the sum of 12 pounds current money of Virginia, witnessed by Thos Shepherd, John McIlhaney, Fairfax County Deed Book C, Part 2, pp. 789-792

Richard Roach's Petition for a road, Road Case File # 38 c. 1761: A Report of the Road from Jacob Everheart's Mill to Roach's Mill, Road Case File # 39 c. 1767: "...the road leading from Roches Mill to the German Settlement..." 4/9/1802, John A. Binns to Jonathan Cunnart, Bargain and Sale: "...the road leading from Roache's Mill to Leesburg..." 9/4/1785, Abraham Dawson to Richard Roach, Lease and Release, Loudoun County Deed Book O, pp. 407-11

11/15/1759: Richard Roach was granted leave to build a mill whereon he now lives on Kittocton, Loudoun County, Order Book A, p. 266, p. 308

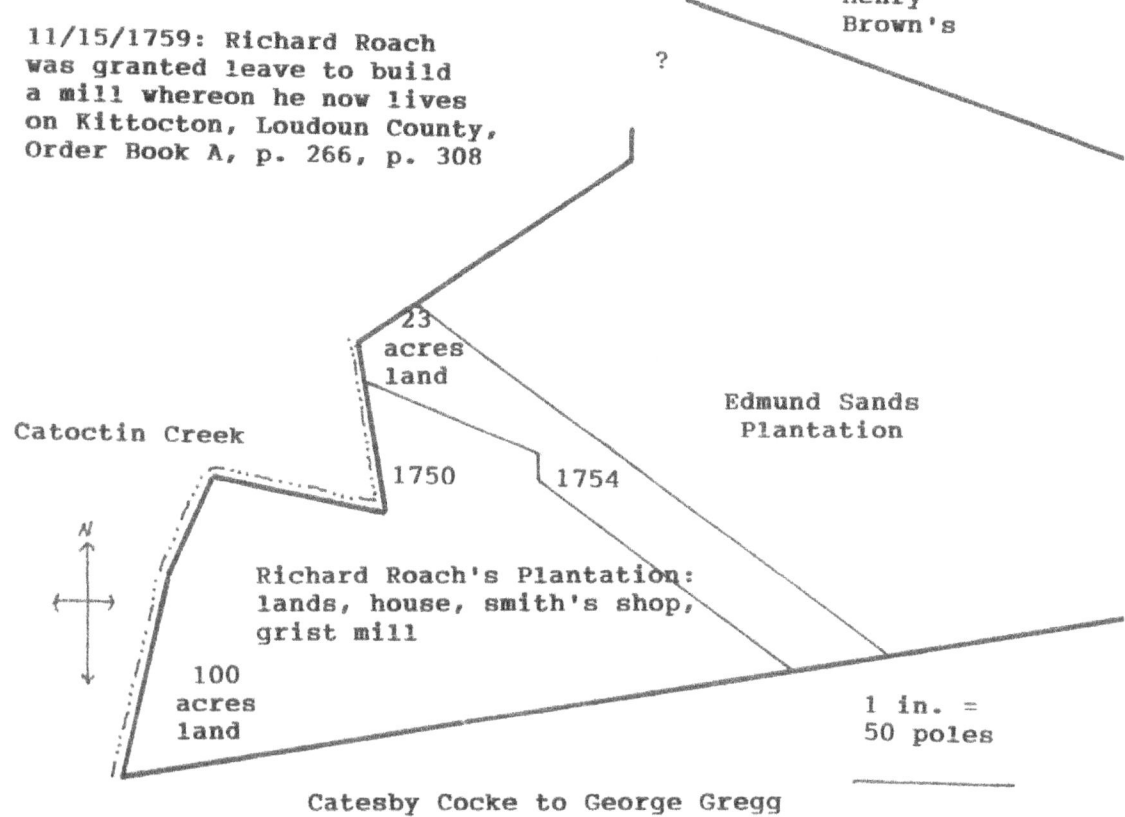

These Indentures made these fifteenth and sixteenth of June, 1762, Edward Norton of Loudoun County, farmer, to Richard Williams of Bucks County in the Province of Pennsylvania, farmer, Lease and Release, one Tract of land containing 400 acres of land and another separate Tract of land containing 100 acres of land for and in consideration of the sum of 220 pounds Pennsylvania currency, Loudoun County Deed Book C, Part 1, pp. 314-319

Witnessed by Lee Massey, James Jones, William Jones, John Steere

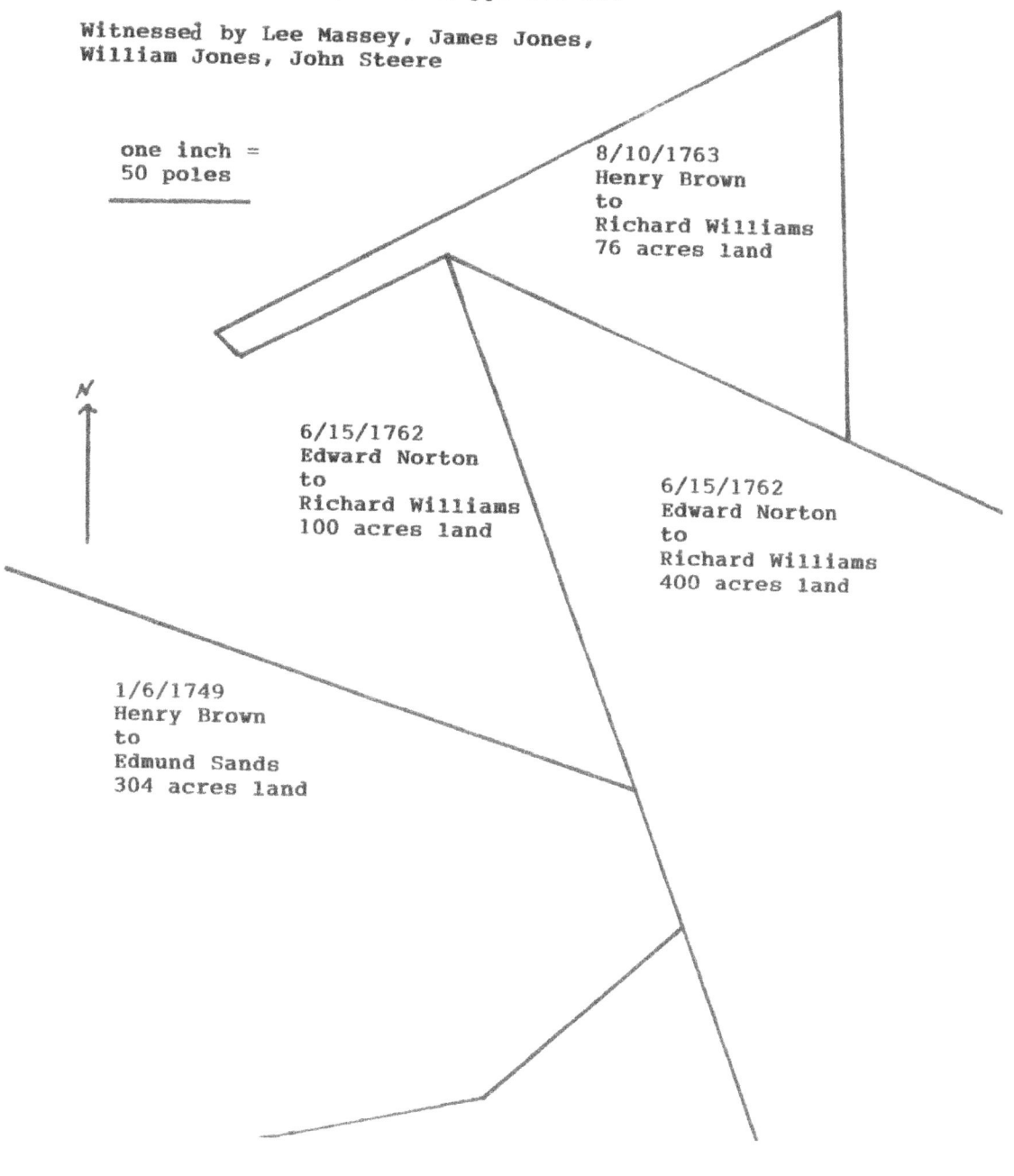

one inch = 50 poles

N

8/10/1763
Henry Brown
to
Richard Williams
76 acres land

6/15/1762
Edward Norton
to
Richard Williams
100 acres land

6/15/1762
Edward Norton
to
Richard Williams
400 acres land

1/6/1749
Henry Brown
to
Edmund Sands
304 acres land

These Indentures made these tenth and eleventh of August, 1763, Henry Brown of Loudoun County, farmer, and Hester his wife to Richard Williams of the same County, farmer, Lease and Release, all that Tract containing seventy six acres including the plantation whereon Henry Pickerill formerly lived in consideration of the sum twenty pounds current money, Loudoun County Deed Book C, Part 2, pp. 709-712

Witnessed by William Jones, James Jones, Jenkin Williams

one inch = 50 poles

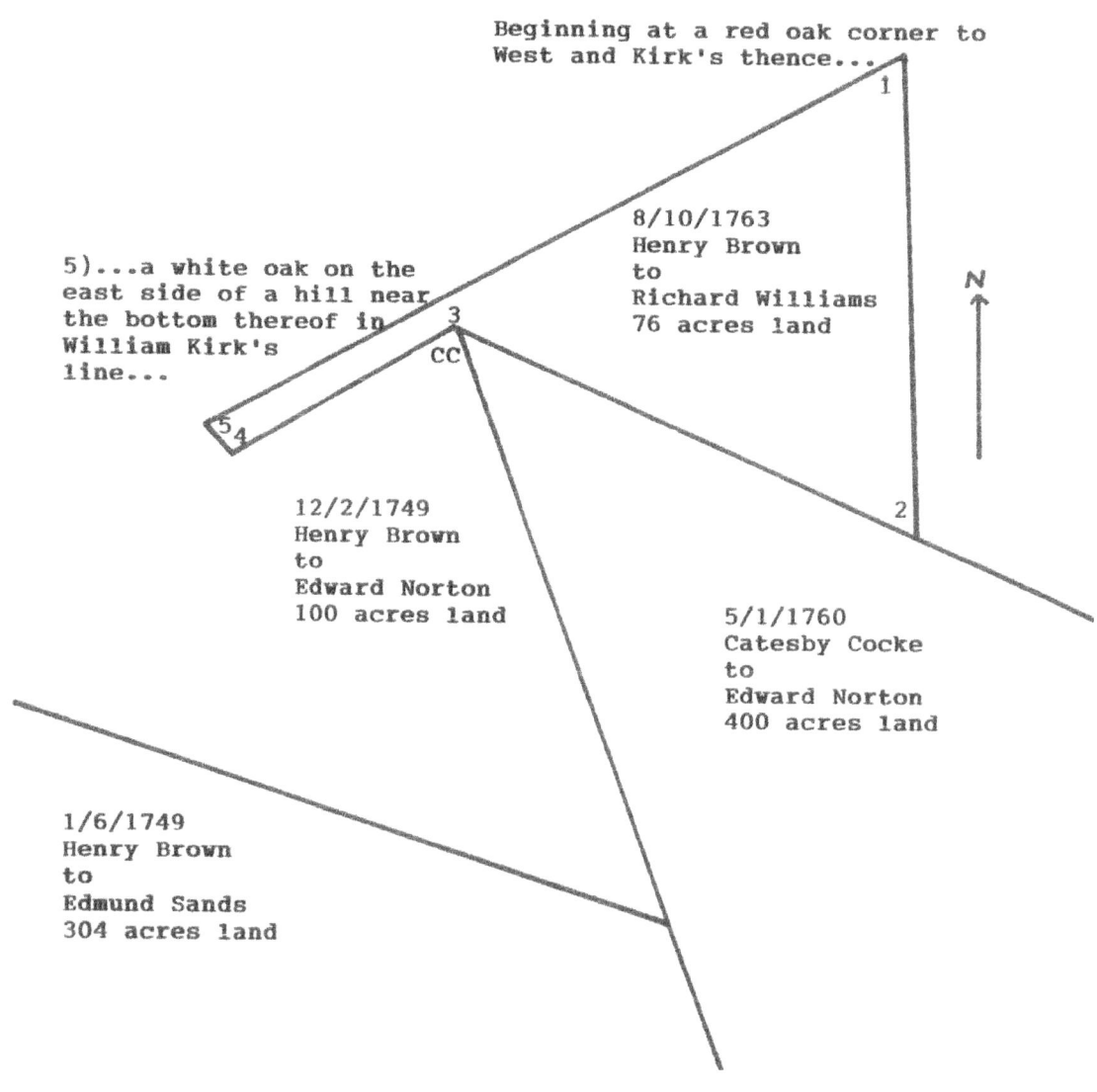

These Indentures made these tenth and eleventh days of June, 1774, Richard Williams of Loudoun County, farmer, and Margaret his wife to Joseph Sands of the same County, farmer, Lease and Release, seventy three acres of land and including part of the plantation whereon Jinkin Philips formerly lived for and in consideration of twenty pounds current money, Loudoun County Deed Book K, pp. 267-272

Witnessed by Benjamin Sands, Isaac Sands, James Roach

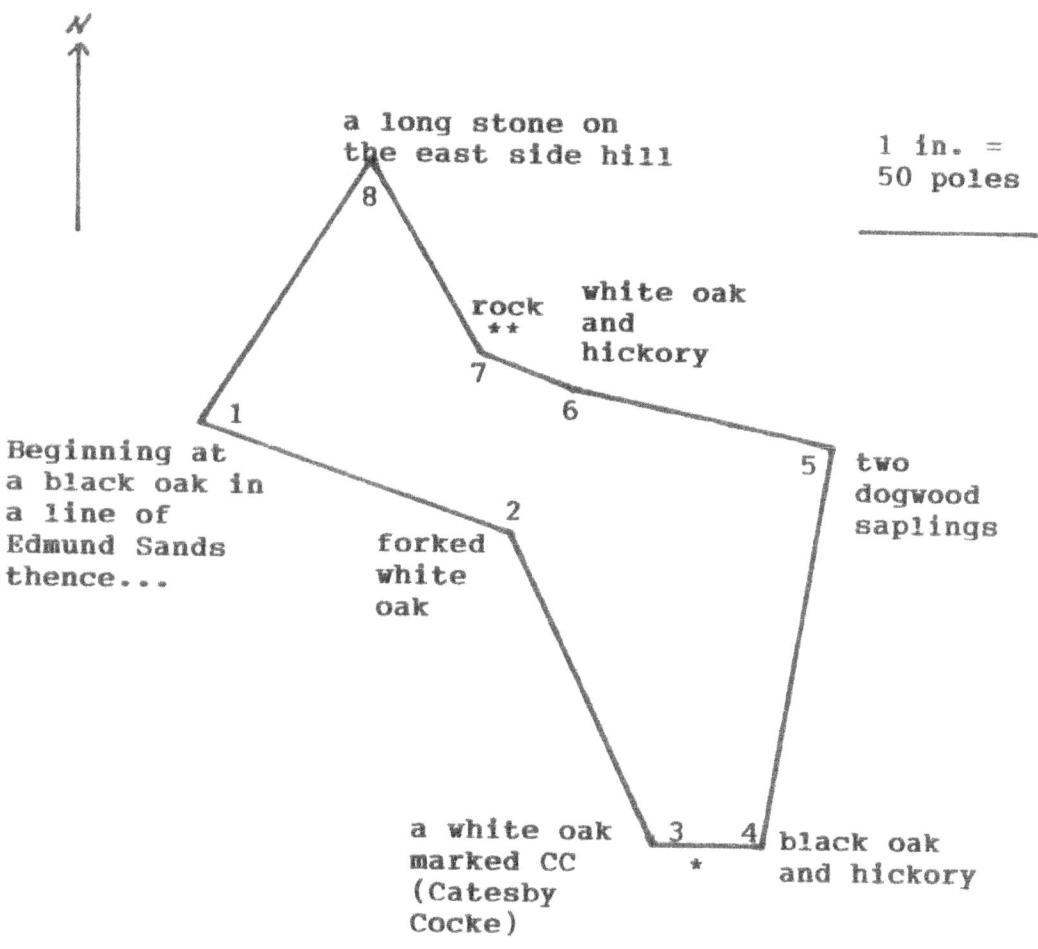

* Abraham Dawson's line

** on the south side of a branch

* Indenture made 8/15/1785 and 8/17/1785, Joseph Sands to Jacob Sands of Loudoun County, blacksmith, Lease and Release, a certain Tract or Parcel of land lying on the east side of the road leading from Thomas Taylor's Mill to Fairfax Meeting house being part of a tract or parcel of land late the property of Edmund Sands deceased and willed to Joseph Sands containing 80 acres more or less as also one Tract or Parcel of land laying and being on the north side of the before mentioned Tract, Fairfax County Deed Book , pp. 375-378

Witnessed by Richard Roach, Isaac Sands, Jacob Harriss

8/17/1786, Joseph Sands to Isaac Sands, Bargain and Sale, 53-acre Tract or Parcel of land, Loudoun County Deed Book S, pp. 378-381

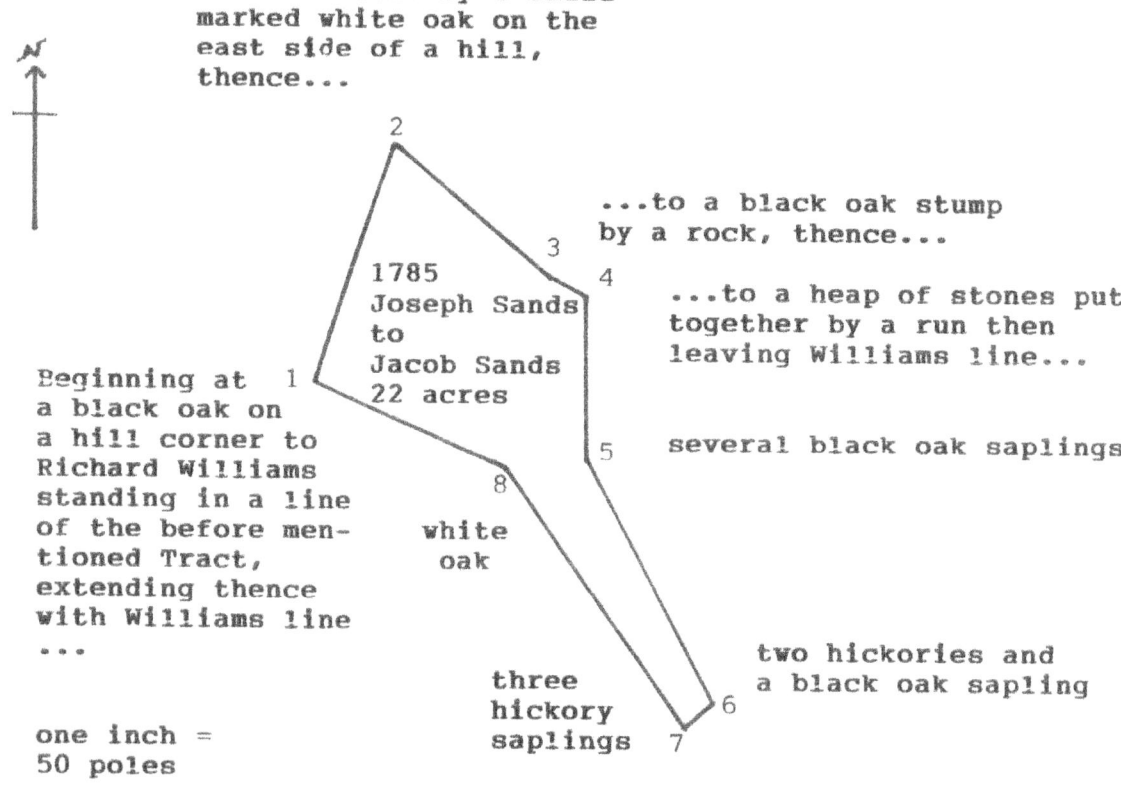

* Including two tract or parcel of land in consideration of 100 pounds sterling

This Indenture made the twenty third day of September, 1793, Richard Williams of Loudoun County and Margaret his wife to Thomas Taylor of the said County of Loudoun, Release, one hundred and thirty five acres being parts of two Tracts of land taken up by Catesby Cocke the one and Richard Brown the other for and in consideration of the sum of 189 pounds current money of Virginia, Loudoun County Deed Book V, pp. 138-142

Witnessed by John Hough, Leonard his L mark Poston, A. Sutherland, Enos his O mark Williams, Joseph Williams

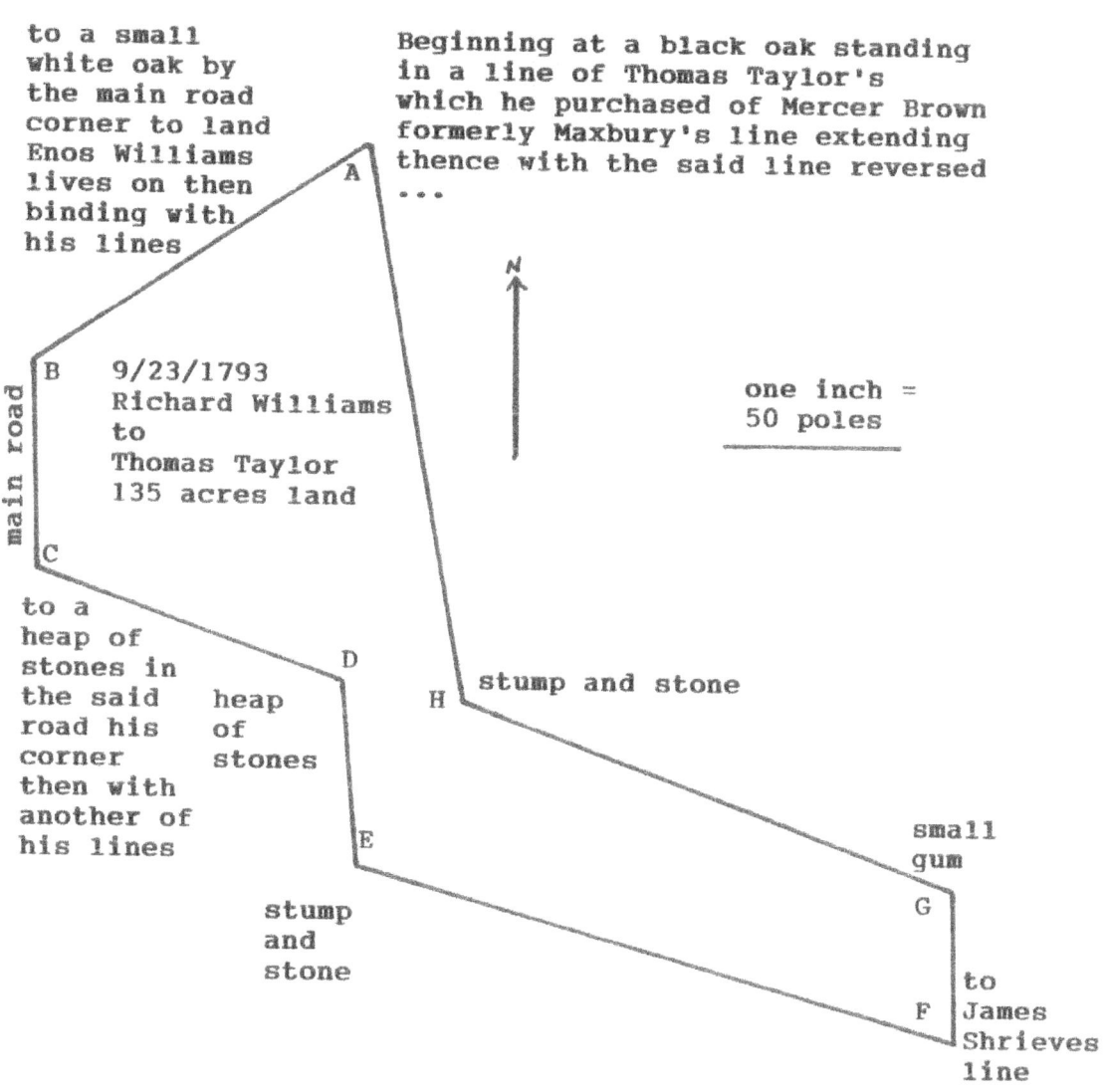

Memorandum of an Agreement made 5/11/1803 between **Esther Brown, Widow, relict of Henry Brown dec. John Brown and William Brown Executors of the said Henry Brown deceased.**

The Commonwealth of Virginia to the Sheriff of Loudoun County
We I Command you that by the Oath's of 12 able and discreet freeholders of you bailiwick they also being of the vicinage and no ways related to either party by whom the truth may be better known. That they appear and meet upon the lands of William Brown where Adam Householder Junior intends to erect an abutment or dam across the catoctin Creek and build a Water Grist Mill, and diligently inquire what damages it will be to the said William Brown if the dam is erected as aforesaid, and that they have the Inquisition thereupon openly made under your seal and seal of those by whom it shall be made together with this Writ before the Justice of our said County Court at the Court House thereof on the second Monday in February next Witness **Charles Binns Clerk of Court**

Editor's Note: A portion of the later **William Brown to John Hamilton, 4/2/1810, Book 20, pp. 321-323**

...thence down the Creek with the several meanders thereof and binding therewith to the beginning...

Beginning at A maple and ash on the East Bank of Catoctin Creek thence N 81¼ E three poles to B dogwood and white oak on hill side

Catoctin Creek

1 Acre of Land 5/11/1803 **Writ of Adquod damnum Awarded to Adam Householder Junior to Condemn Land of William Brown,** 151 perches (one acre) in consideration of $ 85.00 Loudoun County Deed Book 2D, pp. 110-114 (Issued to access damages for land seized for public use) Recorded on 9/13/1803

hickory

Scale: 1 in. = 4 poles
1 pole or rod = 16.5 ft.
(5.03 meters)

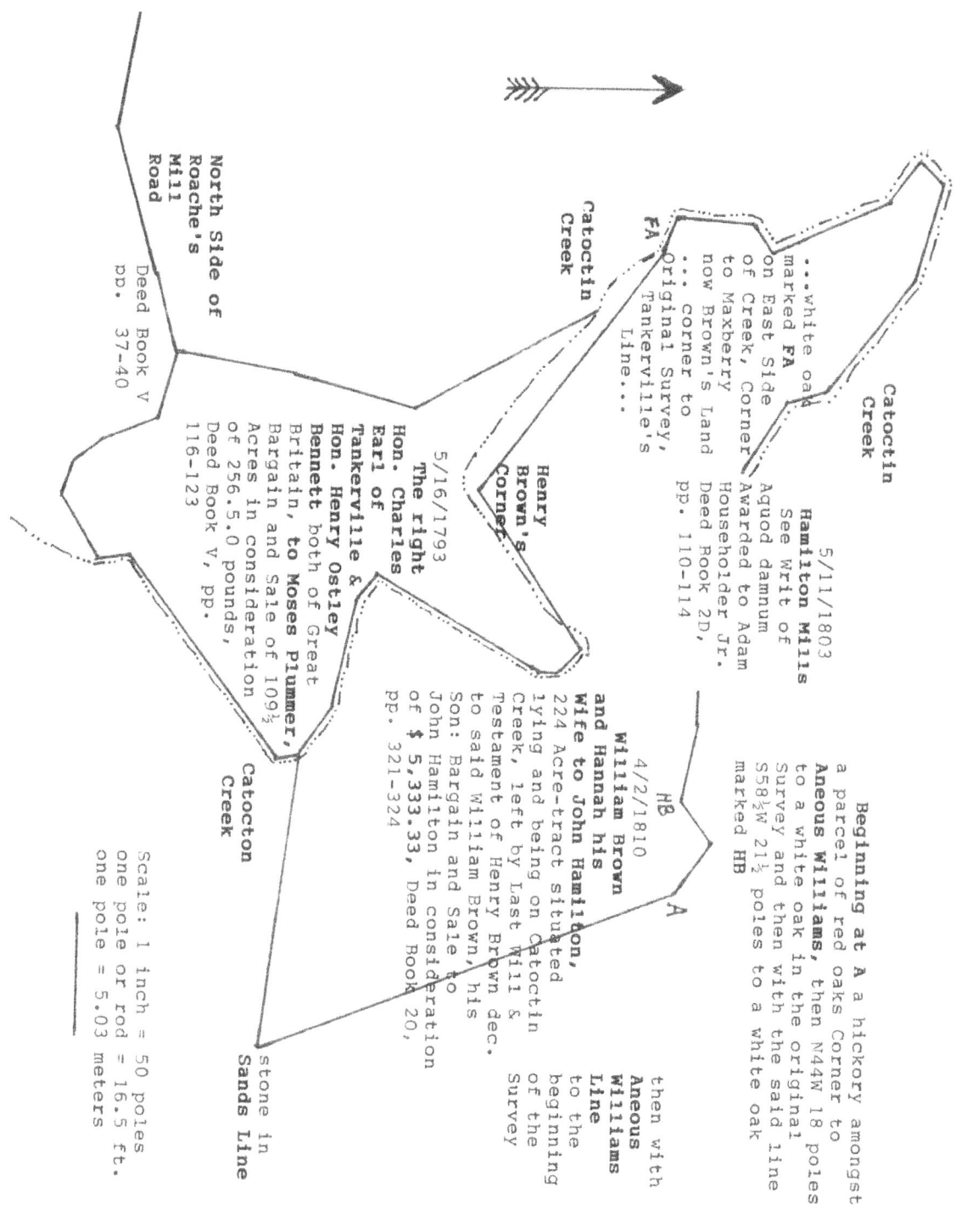

Catoctin Creek

Catoctin Creek

FA

...white oak marked **FA** on East Side of Creek, Aquod damnum Householder now Brown's Land ... corner to Original Survey, Tankerville's Line....

5/11/1803
Hamilton Mills
See Writ of Aquod damnum Awarded to Adam Maxberry Householder Jr. Deed Book 2D, pp. 110-114

Henry Brown's Corner

5/16/1793
The right Hon. Charles Earl of Tankerville & Hon. Henry Ostley Bennett both of Great Britain, **to Moses Plummer,** Bargain and Sale of 109½ Acres in consideration of 256.5.0 pounds, Deed Book V, pp. 116-123

North Side of Roache's Mill Road

Deed Book V pp. 37-40

Catocton Creek

Sands Line

4/2/1810
William Brown and Hannah his Wife to John Hamilton, 224 Acre-tract situated lying and being on Catoctin Creek, left by Last Will & Testament of Henry Brown dec. to said William Brown, his Son: Bargain and Sale to John Hamilton in consideration of $5,333.33, Deed Book 20, pp. 321-324

HB

A

Beginning at A a hickory amongst a parcel of red oaks Corner to **Aneous Williams**, then N4W 18 poles to a white oak in the original Survey and then with the said line S58½W 21½ poles to a white oak marked HB then with **Aneous Williams Line** to the beginning of the Survey

Scale: 1 inch = 50 poles
one pole or rod = 16.5 ft.
one pole = 5.03 meters

87

Division of Henry Taylor's Land

Survey and Division of Henry Taylor dec. Estate in Loudoun County by virtue of an order of worshipful Court of Loudoun County in Chancery sitting dated the 9th day of February, 1829, among his heirs and representatives. Loudoun County Deed Book 3T, pp. 107 - 109

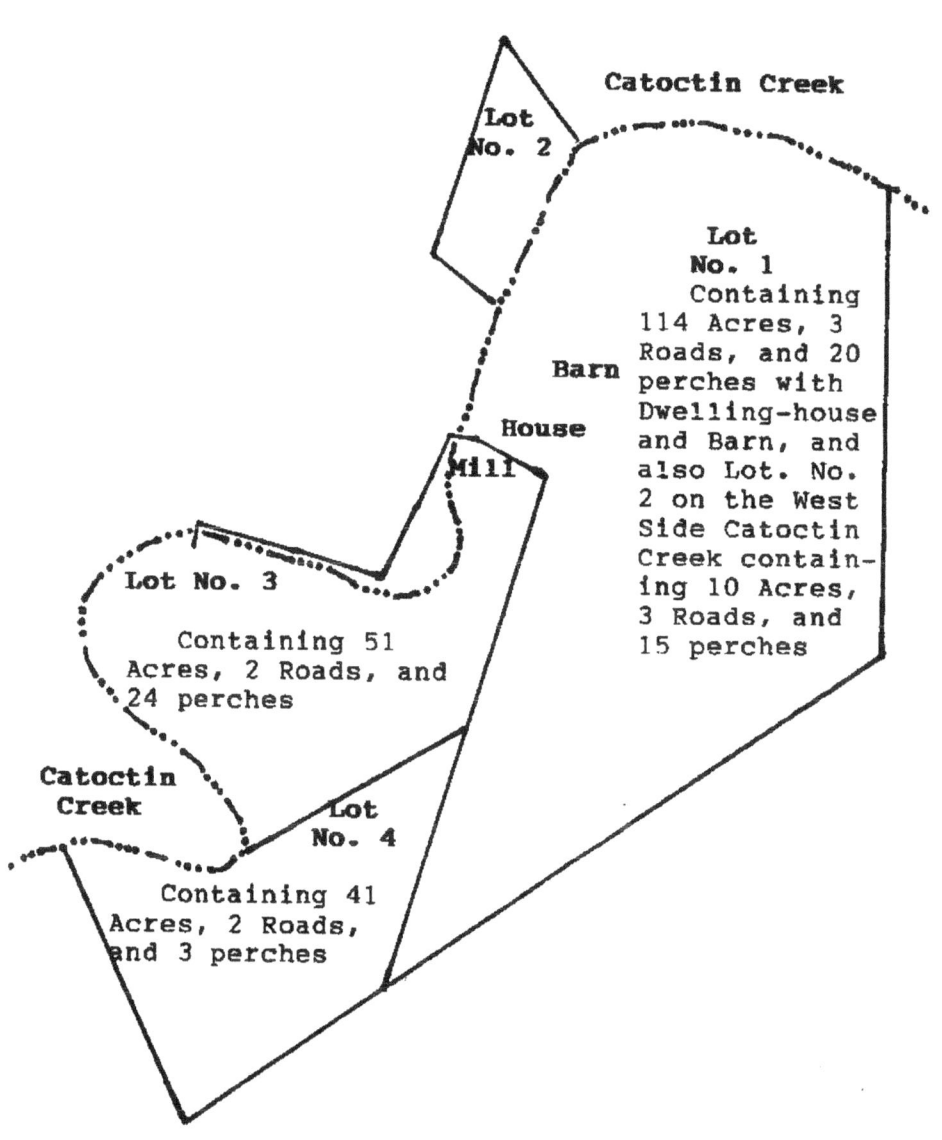

Scale: 1 inch = 50 poles

107

Division of
H Taylor's
Land

Survey and Division of Henry Taylor decd Estate in [...]
Lot. No 1 allotted to Joshua Ratliff & Nancy his wife [...]
& Sarah Taylor Jointly Beginning at **A** a stake on the [...]
of Catocton Creek, about 2 poles North of a marked [...]
a corner to Stoutsenberger thence with his line S° 55 W [...]
po. to **B** a stake between two rocks, & near a forked [...]
thence with another of Stoutsenberger & Potterfield [...]
S 56. 22 W 171½ po. to **c** a pile of stones in Potterfield's [...]
Corner to No 4 thence with the same and No 3, N 49 [...]
po. to **D** a stake in the road leading to the Mill and a [...]
Creek, thence with said road, N 65 W 24 poles to the east [...]
of the Creek, at **E**, where said road crosses said Creek, thence [...]
the Creek on the east side thereof with the several meanders [...]
thereof to the Beginning Containing 114. 8. 3. R. 8. 20 B [...]
with the dwelling house and Barn. And also Lot No [...]
West Side of Catocton Creek bounded as follows, Beg[inning]
at **F** a planted stone on a hill in a line of Stoutsenberger [...]
[...] to Jacob Carner thence with a line of the same [...]

89

John Hough's Catoctin Lands (c. 1747)

This section concerns the parceling of John Hough's lands, which were on or about the Catoctin Creek (died 1797). John Hough's expanse of private property was to be found running up and down Catoctin Creek and the bodies of water thereof from in close proximity to Broad Run or Milltown Creek up to the vicinity of Waterford. Originally, the great bulk of such landholdings comprising over 1,700 acres were acquired by the said John Hough as follows. Firstly, about 250 acres of such land was obtained through descent of a parcel of land from John Hough, blacksmith. Secondly, about 250 acres more was purchased from George Gregg. Thirdly, about 1,000 acres more was obtain through acquisition of the release of a tract of land from John West Jr. and Catharine his wife. All of the aforesaid lands had originally been connected in some way to John Colvill's Catoctin Tract. Otherwise, John Hough acquired two neighboring parcels of land including about 200 acres from Eleanor Poultney, widow, and from John Plummer and Eleanor his wife, lately Eleanor Poultney, which were originally from George William Fairfax's Piedmont Tract or Piedmont Manor. Moreover, John Hough owned other landholdings encompassing thousands of acres more. Many of which are covered in separate sections of this publication.

1. 10/7/1747, **John Colvill, Gent.** of Fairfax County and Colony of Virginia of the one part to **John Hough** of Fairfax County, blacksmith, of the County and Colony aforesaid of the other part. Whereas there is a certain tract or parcel of land situate lying and being in the County of Fairfax aforesaid on the **North and South Forks of Kittocton** viz. Beginning at a white hickory corner to **John Mead** extending thence N 27° E 300 poles to a stake, thence N 68° W 225 poles to a hickory or stake, thence S 19° W 403 poles to a stake on a hill, thence S 70° E 196 poles to a stake in a bog, thence N 14° E 100 poles to the first station containing 500 acres of land, and whereas the same is part of a tract that was granted to the said **John Colvill** his heirs and assigns forever by a good sufficient deed from the Proprietor of the Northern Neck of Virginia by virtue of a warrant and survey and promise of a deed to **Francis Awbrey** containing 4,403 acres the said patent bearing date the 18th day of May, 1739 and registered in the said Proprietor's Office in Book E, Folio 49 and 53, under certain rents reservations and exceptions in the said grant expressed as by the said patent more fully and at large appears. Now this indenture witnesseth that the said **John Colvill** for and in consideration of a **Reserve** of the late **Francis Awbrey** made with the said **John Colvill** agreed to by the said **Colvill,** whereof the said **John Colvill** doth hereby acknowledge full satisfaction thereof and for every part thereof, doth acquit and discharge the said **John Hough** his heirs and assigns by these presents hath granted bargained sold alienated released and confirmed and by these presents doth bargain sell alien release and confirm unto the said **John Hough** and his heirs and assigns all and singular the 500 acres of land situate bounded and being as is above set forth and described, together with all the houses barns buildings orchards gardens ways waters watercourses woods meadows swamps fishings fowlings hawkings huntings rights liberties

privileges improvements advantages hereditaments and appurtenances with the rents issues profits of the same. To have and to hold the said 500 acres of land hereditaments and premises hereby granted alienated released or confirmed or mentioned or intended to be granted and release with the appurtenances unto the said **John Hough** his heirs and assigns forever, **John Colvill**. Sealed and delivered in the presence of us, **Hugh West Jr., Francis Hague,** and **Saml. Mead**. Proven on 11/17/1747. Lease and Release, Fairfax County Deed Book B, Part 1, pp. 280-282

2. 10/17 and 18/1748, **John Hough** of Fairfax County in the Colony of Virginia, blacksmith, and **Sarah** his wife of the one part to **George Gregg** of the same place, yeoman, of the other part. Whereas there is a certain tract or parcel of land situate lying and being in the County of Fairfax aforesaid on and near **Kittockton Creek** viz. Beginning at a white oak and stake near the **Lower Beaver Dam Branch of Kittockton** extending thence S 19° W 187 poles to a stake and black oak, thence S 68° E 202 poles to a stake and white oak, thence N 27° E 186 poles to a stake, thence N 68° W 225 poles to the first station containing by estimation 250 acres being the half part of a tract said to contain 500 acres of land conveyed to the above said **John Hough** by **John Colvill Gent**. by lease and release bearing date the 7th day of October, 1747 recorded in Libra B, Folio 281. And, whereas the said 500 acres is part of a tract that was granted to the said **John Colvill** his heirs and assigns forever by good sufficient deed from the Proprietor of the Northern Neck in Virginia by virtue of a warrant of a survey and promise of a deed to **Francis Awbrey** containing 4,403 acres the said patent bearing date the 18th of May, 1739 and registered in the said Proprietor's Office in Book E, Folio 49 and 53, under certain rents reservations and exceptions in the said grant expressed as by the said patent more fully and at large appears, now this indenture witnesseth that the said **John Hough** and **Sarah** his wife for and in consideration of a settlement and satisfaction made to the administrators of **Amos Janney** late of the County of aforesaid deceased by the said **George Gregg** whereof the said **John Hough** doth hereby acknowledge as full satisfaction and therewith fully satisfied contented and paid, hath granted bargained and sold alienated released and confirmed and by the presents doth bargain sell alien release and confirm unto the said **George Gregg** and his heirs and assigns all and singular the said 250 acres of land more or less situate lying and being as is above set forth and described, together with all and singular the barns buildings orchards gardens ways waters watercourses woods meadows swamps fishings fowlings hawkings huntings rights liberties privileges improvements advantages hereditaments and appurtenances with the rents issues and profits of the same. To have and to hold the said 250 acres of land hereditaments and premises hereby granted alienated released or confirmed or mentioned or intended to be granted and released with the appurtenances unto the said **George Gregg** his heirs and assign forever, **John Hough** and **Sarah Hough**. Sealed and delivered in the presence of **Francis Hague, John Hanbey,** and **Martha Harris**. Proven on

11/15/1748. Lease and Release, Fairfax County Deed Book B, Part 1, pp. 413-416.

3. 3/10 and 3/11/1760, **George Gregg** of the County of Loudoun and Colony of Virginia and **Elizabeth** his wife of the one part to **John Hough** of the said County of the other part. Witnesseth that the said **George Gregg** and **Elizabeth** his wife for and in consideration of the sum of 66 pounds and three shillings current money of Virginia the receipt whereof the said **George Gregg** and **Elizabeth** his wife doth hereby acknowledge, hath granted bargained sold aliened released and confirmed and by these presents doth fully freely and absolutely grant bargain sell alien release and confirm unto the said **John Hough** and to his heirs and assigns forever, all that tract or parcel of land containing 250 acres of land situate lying and being in the County of Loudoun aforesaid on the **Kittocton Creek** including the main fork thereof and bounded as followeth viz. Beginning at a stake near a marked hickory sapling and a spanish oak on hill corner to the said **John Hough's** land above his lane and extending thence N 19° E 190 poles to a hickory and red oak, thence S 68° E 225 poles to a stake in a line of **John Mercer** crossing the said Creek, thence with said **Mercer's** line S 27° W 188 poles to a white oak and red oak on hillside corner to said **Hough,** thence with his line N 68° W 200 poles to the first station crossing the said Creek below the said **Hough's** meadow, together with all members and appurtenances thereunto belonging and the reversion and reversions, remainder and remainders, rents issues and profits thereof and all the estate right title interest claim and demand whatsoever both in law and equity to him the said **George Gregg** and **Elizabeth** of in and to the said premises above mentioned with the appurtenances. To have and to hold the said 250 acres of land with the appurtenances unto the said **John Hough** his heirs and assigns forever, **George Gregg** and **Elizabeth Gregg**. Proven on 5/13/1760. Lease and Release, Loudoun County Deed Book A, pp. 406-410

4. These indenture made these 20th and 21st days of July, in the year of our Lord Christ 1761, and first year of the reign of our **Sovereign Lord, George the Third,** by the grace of God of Great Britain, France and Ireland, King, Defender of the Faith and so forth, between, **John West, Gent**. of the County of Fairfax in the Colony and Dominion of Virginia, and **Catharine** his wife of the one part to **John Hough, Gent**. of the County of Loudoun in the Colony and Dominion of Virginia aforesaid of the other part. Whereas **John Colvill Gent**. late of the County of Fairfax aforesaid, deceased, by his last will and testament bearing date the 6th day of May, 1755 amongst other things therein contained did give and bequeath unto his daughter the wife of the said **John West** and their heirs forever, 1,000 acres of land part of his **Catactan Tract** to be laid off adjoining to **John Hough's** land which he bought of **Amos Janney,** in such manner as his executors in the said will mentioned should appear as by the said last will and testament duly proven recorded and enrolled in the Court of the County of Fairfax by inspection may at large appear. And, whereas the said executors nominated and appointed in and by the said will hath not laid off unto the said **John West**

and **Catharine** his wife the said 1,000 acres of land nor marked the same with particular metes and bounds, but it still remains to be done according to the above bequest. Now this indenture witnesseth that they the said **John West** and **Catharine** his wife for and in consideration of the sum of 327 pounds and 10 shillings current money of Virginia to them in hand paid by the said **John Hough** the receipt whereof they the said **John West** and **Catharine** his wife do hereby confess and acknowledge and for diverse other good causes and consideration them thereunto moving, they the said **John West** and **Catharine** his wife have granted bargained and sold aliened released and confirmed and by these presents do grant bargain and sell alien release and confirm unto the said **John Hough** and to his heirs and assigns forever, all and singular the above mentioned 1,000 acres of land so as aforesaid given and bequeathed by the said **John Colvill** unto the said **John West** and **Catharine** his wife, together with all and singular the rights members and appurtenances thereunto belonging and all houses buildings orchards meadows waters watercourses profits commodities emoluments and hereditaments whatsoever to the said 1,000 acres of land belonging or in any wise appertaining, which now are or formerly have been accepted reputed taken known used occupied or enjoyed to or with the same or as part parcel or member thereof or of any part thereof. To have and to hold the said 1,000 acres of land hereditaments and premises above mentioned and every part and parcel thereof with the appurtenances unto the said **John Hough** his heirs and assigns to the only proper use of him the said **John Hough** his heirs and assigns forever, **John West Jr.** and **Catharine West**. Sealed and delivered in the presence of **W. Ellzey, Francis Dade, Benja. Sebastian, James Donaldson, John Heryford**, and **Stephen Donaldson**. Proven on 8/11/1761. Lease and Release, Loudoun County Deed Book B, pp. 242-247

5. To all to whom these presents shall come. I **Thomas Colvill Gent**. of the County of Fairfax in the Colony and Dominion of Virginia, one of the executors of the last will and testament of **John Colvill Gent**. of the said County deceased, send greeting. Whereas the said **John Colvill** by his last will and testament bearing date the 6th day of May, 1755 among other things devised as followeth viz. I give and bequeath unto my daughter **Catharine** now the wife of **John West Jr**. and to the said **John West**, 1,000 acres of my **Catoctan Tract** of land to be laid off adjoining to **John Hough's** land which he bought of **Amos Janney** in such manner as my executors shall approve, and whereas the said **John West** and **Catharine** his wife have by deeds of lease and release for valuable consideration therein expressed sold and conveyed all their right title interest of in and to the said 1,000 acres of land sold them bequeathed by the said **John Colvill Gent. deceased**, unto the said **John Hough** his heirs and assigns as by the said deeds of lease and release duly proven enrolled and recorded in the Court of the County of Loudoun may more fully appear, and to the intent that the said 1,000 acres of land be laid off to the said **John Hough** the purchaser according to the intent and meaning of the said **John Colvill Gent. deceased** and the bounds thereof certified and made known. Know ye that I the said **Thomas Colvill**

executor aforesaid on the application of the said **John Hough** for the purposes aforesaid do approve of the manner the said 1,000 acres of land are laid off in plat and survey thereof made by **George West**, Surveyor of the said County of Loudoun dated the 13th day of May, 1762, which plat and survey so made and signed by the said **George West** is hereunto annexed. And, I the said **Thomas Colvill** do hereby agree and approve of the manner and form in which the said 1,000 acres of land are laid off and bound believing it agreeable to the will and intention of the said testator, unless there shall be an error of the quantity of the number of acres in which case the line to include the said 1,000 acres is N 68° W from one outline to the other parallel to said **Hough's** lower line. In witness I the said **Thomas Colvill** have hereunto set my hand and affixed my seal this 11th day of May, 1762, **Thos. Colvill**. Sealed and delivered in the presence of **H. West, John West Jr.** (plat and survey). May 13th, 1762. At the request of **Mr. John Hough** I surveyed part of the above as follows viz. Beginning at A, a poplar near the **So. Fork of Catactian Creek** marked **FA JC** thence N 52-½° E 86 poles wanting 8 links to B, near **Janney's** fence supposed to be in the line of **Janney's** land, thence with the same N 14° E near a line of marked trees 326 poles and angled to C, a white hickory on the side of the said **Catactian Creek** marked **JM JH**, from thence **Mr. Hough** desired me to protract the other lines of the patent to include 1,000 acres exclusive of his 500 which is represented by black lines the letters D, E, F, G, H, and A, and also to protract the courses of his 500 acres, which is represented by dotted lines and figures 1, 2, 3, 4, and the letter C, **George West**. Sworn C.C. (Chain Carriers), **Thos. Dodd** and **Levi Wells**. Proven on 6/8/1762. Loudoun County Deed Book C, Part 1, pp. 270-273

6. 5/9 and 10/1770, **John Hough** of the County of Loudoun Colony and Dominion of Virginia and **Sarah** his wife of the one part to **Mahlon Janney** of the said County of the other part. Witnesseth that for and in consideration of the sum of 150 pounds current money of Virginia to the said **John Hough** in hand paid by the said **Mahlon Janney** at or before the sealing and delivery of these presents the receipt whereof he doth hereby acknowledge, hath granted bargained sold aliened released and confirmed and by these presents doth grant bargain sell alien release and confirm unto the said **Mahlon Janney** and his heirs all that tract or parcel of land situate in the said County of Loudoun on the **South Fork of Kittocton Creek** bounded as followeth viz. Beginning at a poplar in the bottom on **So. Fork of said Creek** about his **mill dam** running thence N 47° W 215 poles to a black oak on the point of a hill, thence N 84° E 260 poles to a spanish and white oak in a line of **Francis Hague's** on a hill seven poles from the **road** the north side thereof, thence S 11° W 130 poles to a bush by said **Janney's** field fence near his **mill dam** then up said **South Fork** S 61° W 86 poles to the beginning containing 155 acres of land, and all houses buildings orchards ways waters watercourses profits commodities hereditaments and appurtenances whatsoever to the said premises hereby granted or any part thereof belonging or in any wise appertaining. To have and to hold the lands

hereby conveyed and all and singular the premises hereby granted released and every part and parcel thereof with their and every of their appurtenances unto the said **Mahlon Janney** his heirs and assigns, **John Hough** and **Sarah Hough**. Proven on 12/10/1770. Lease and Release, Loudoun County Deed Book H, pp. 33-36 (Note: The above tract or parcel of land would have been located in the southeast corner of the aforesaid tract of 1,000 acres of land conveyed by John West Jr. and Catharine his wife unto John Hough, which was surveyed and laid on paper by George West)

7. 5/9 & 10/1770, **Mahlon Janney** of the County of Loudoun Colony and Dominion of Virginia and **Sarah** his wife of the one part to **John Hough** of the said County of the other part. Witnesseth that for and in consideration of the sum of 150 pounds current money of Virginia to the said **Mahlon Janney** in hand paid by the said **John Hough** at or before the sealing and delivery of these presents the receipt whereof he doth hereby acknowledge, and thereof doth release acquit and discharge the said **John Hough** his executors and administrators. By these presents he the said **Mahlon Janney** and **Sarah** his wife hath granted bargained sold aliened released and confirmed and by these presents doth grant bargain sell alien release and confirm unto the said **John Hough** and his heirs all that tract or parcel of land situate in the County of Loudoun on the **North Fork of Kittocton Creek** bounded as followeth viz. Beginning at six white oaks standing by the north side of the said **Fork of Kittockton Creek** marked JC FA at a mouth of a small branch at the head of the said **Hough's mill dam** corner to land formerly **John Colvill's** extending thence N 14° W 56 poles to a white oak near the head of a small branch and marked **FA JC,** then N 13° E 58 poles to a red oak in a field, then S 59° W 175 poles to several saplings, then S 24° - 30 minutes E 195 poles to a double bodied white oak by a ledge of rocks the north side of the said Creek, then S 68° E 70 poles to a white oak, then North 160 poles to the first station containing 155 acres of land and all houses buildings orchards ways waters watercourses profits commodities hereditaments and appurtenances whatsoever to the said premises hereby granted or any part thereof belonging or in any wise appertaining, and the reversion and reversions, remainder and remainders rents issues and profits thereof and also all the estate right title interest use trust property claim and demand whatsoever of them the said **Mahlon Janney** and **Sarah** his wife of in and to the premises, and all deeds evidences and writings touching or in any wise concerning the same. To have and to hold the lands hereby conveyed and all and singular other the premises hereby granted and released and every part and parcel thereof with their and every of their appurtenances unto the said **John Hough** his heirs and assigns forever, **Mahlon Janney** and **Sarah Janney**. Proven on 12/10/1770. Lease and Release, Loudoun County Deed Book H, pp. 29-33 (Note: This tract of land at that time was situated on a boundary line of Ellen Poultney's from John Poultney deceased. See Thomas Plummer and Ellen his wife to John Hough, Loudoun County Deed Book B, pp. 238-241.)

8. 5/6 and 5/7/1790, **John Hough** of Loudoun County in the State of Virginia of the one part to **William Hough** son of the said **John Hough** of the other part. Witnesseth that for and in consideration of the sum of 20 pounds current money of Virginia to the said **John Hough** in hand paid by the said **William Hough** before the sealing and delivery of these presents but more especially for the love and affection he beareth unto his said son **William,** and thereof doth release acquit and discharge the said **William Hough** his executors and administrators. By these presents he the said **John Hough** hath granted bargained sold aliened released and confirmed and by these presents doth grant bargain sell alien release and confirm unto the said **William Hough** and his heirs all that tract or parcel of land situate in Loudoun County in and about the **Beaver Dam Branch of Kittocton** bounded as followeth viz. Beginning at a black oak and white oak saplings by the west side of a spring branch about ten poles below **Ball's Road** and the southwest corner of **Joseph Wilkinson's** lot extending thence down the branch and crossing the **Beaver Dam Branch** N 77° W 106 poles to a white oak on a hill in a line of **John Hough Junior deceased's** land, then with his lines South 70 poles to a white oak and hickory on a hillside **John Hough Junior's** corner, (then) with his lines West 120 poles to a leaning white oak by a spring head his corner still with his lines South 70 poles to a black oak on a stony hill his corner, then S 70° W 112 poles to a white and black oak by a small branch corner to **Nicholas France's** lot, then with his line West 84 poles to two red oak saplings, then South 145 poles to a small white oak, then East 140 poles to a white oak marked **JH** corner to **Hannah Cadwallader** now **Benjamin Steer's** lot, then North 10 poles to a white oak marked **WH**, then N 61° E 92 poles to a box white oak by a **road**, then N 80° E 40 poles to three small white oaks, then S 77° E 20 poles to a small white oak on a knoll, then N 73° E 80 poles to three white oaks the east side of a gully, then N 5° E 37 poles to a red oak by said **William Hough's** fence, then along the fence N 43° E 102 poles to a white oak bush by the **main road**, then S 40° W 76 poles to a black by west side of a gully thence to the beginning about 30 poles containing about 415 acres be the same more or less according to the true intent and meaning of these presents, and all houses buildings orchards ways waters watercourses profits commodities hereditaments and appurtenances whatsoever to the said premises hereby granted or any part thereof belonging or in any wise appertaining unto the said **William Hough** his heirs and assigns forever. To have and to hold the lands hereby conveyed and all and singular other the premises hereby granted and released and every part and parcel thereof with their every of their appurtenances unto the said **William Hough** his heirs and assigns forever, **John Hough**. Sealed and delivered in the presence of **William Paxson, James Ratekin,** and **William Moxley**. Proven on 5/10/1790. Lease and release, Loudoun County Deed Book S, pp. 55-61 (Note: The eastern part of this tract overlaid John Hough's land from John West Jr. and Catharine his wife whereas the western part of this tract overlaid John

Hough's land from Eleanor Poultney bearing dates 12/10 and 12/11/1759, Loudoun County Deed Book A, pp. 347-351.)

9. 11/15/1791, The Honorable **Henry Astley Bennett Esq.** of the Kingdom of Great Britain of the one part to **Nathan Ball** of the County of Loudoun in the State of Virginia of the other part. Now this indenture witnesseth that the said **Henry Astley Bennett Esq.** for and in consideration of the sum of 439 pounds and 13 shillings current money of Virginia to him in hand paid by the said **Nathan Ball** at or before the sealing and delivery of these presents the receipt whereof they do hereby acknowledge, hath given granted bargained sold aliened confirmed and by these presents doth give grant bargain sell alien and confirm unto the said **Nathan Ball** his heirs and assigns forever, all that piece or parcel of land lying and being in the County of Loudoun aforesaid and bounded as followeth viz. Beginning at a red oak marked **JH** in the line of **Colville's** including patent on the right hand of the **main road leading from Farling Ball's Mill to John Hough's Mill** and near the **fence and house** in the lot of land whereon **John Reed** now lives running thence S 9-¾° W 100 poles with the line of **Hough's** deed from **John West** to a stump and stake in the said line, thence S 69-¾° E 378 poles to a white oak and a poplar corner to **Hickson's** land in the line of **Colville's** patent, thence N 22° – 50 minutes E 98 poles to a red oak marked **JH** in the line of **Colville's** patent, thence N 69-¾° W 402 poles to the beginning containing 244-¼ acres and being the land conveyed by **John Hough** to **Henry A. Bennett** aforesaid as by deed of the 14th of January, 1790 will appear on record, and all houses buildings gardens orchards meadows trees underwoods waters watercourses, profits commodities hereditaments and appurtenances whatsoever to the said to the said premises belonging or in any wise appertaining, and the reversion and reversions, remainder and remainders, rents issues profits thereof and every part and parcel thereof. To have and to hold the said tract of land hereditaments and all and singular the premises hereby granted, with their and every of their appurtenances unto the said **Nathan Ball** his heirs and assigns forever, **Henry A. Bennett**. Sealed and delivered in the presence of **Patrick Cavan, Farling Ball, George Muir,** and **John Davis**. Proven on 2/14/1792. Bargain and Sale, Loudoun County Deed Book T, pp. 242-245

10. 3/8 and 3/9/1793, **John Hough** of Loudoun County in the State of Virginia of the one part to **Anthony Connard** of the said State and County of the other part. Witnesseth that for and in consideration of the sum of 200 pounds current money of Virginia to the said **John Hough** in hand paid by the said **Anthony Cunnard** at or before the sealing and delivery of these presents the receipt whereof he doth hereby acknowledge, hath granted bargained sold aliened released and confirmed and by these presents doth grant bargain sell alien release and confirm unto the said **Anthony Cunnard** and his heirs all that parcel of land situate in Loudoun County aforesaid and bounded as followeth viz. Beginning at a small walnut tree on the south side of the **North Fork of Kittoctan Creek** below a small spring branch then up said Creek S 34° W 29 poles to a stake by the upper rack (?) and on the south

side of the said Creek, then crossing the Creek twice N 68° W 32 poles to a small hickory ten poles southwest of or from the **mill dam,** then S 67° W 57 poles to a white oak on a hill, then S 23° E 55 poles to a white oak, then S 25° W 30 poles to a red oak by a **road,** S 40° E 64 poles by the **road,** then S 46° E 24 poles to a hickory by the **road,** then S 55° E 20 poles to a hickory by the **road,** then N 51° E 90 poles to a stake in a field, then with a straight line to the beginning containing 100 acres of land be the same more or less, and all houses buildings orchards ways waters watercourses profits commodities hereditaments and appurtenances whatsoever to the said premises hereby granted or any part thereof belonging or in any wise appertaining, and the reversion and reversions, remainder and remainders, rents issues and profits thereof. To have and to hold the lands hereby conveyed and all and singular the premises, and all deeds evidences hereby granted and released and every part and parcel thereof with their and every of their appurtenances unto the said **Anthony Cunnard** his heirs and assigns forever, **John Hough**. Sealed and delivered in the presence of **William Paxson, John Martin,** and **Thomas Gillingham**. Proven on 9/9/1798. Lease and Release, Loudoun County Deed Book 2A, pp. 233-237

11. 1/27 and 1/28/1794, **John Hough** of Loudoun County in the State of Virginia of the one part to **Jacob Wine** of the said County of the other part. Witnesseth that for and in consideration of the sum of 480 pounds current money of Virginia to the said **John Hough** in hand paid by the said **Jacob Wine** at or before the sealing and delivery of these presents the receipt whereof he doth hereby acknowledge, hath granted bargained sold aliened released and confirmed and by these presents doth grant bargain sell alien release and confirm unto the said **Jacob Wine** and his heirs all that parcel of land situate in Loudoun County aforesaid bounded as followeth viz. Beginning at a small black oak and planted stone the west side of a springhead in **William Hough's** line and near his fence running thence down the spring branch S 17° E 56 poles to a spanish oak on a hill, then S 25° W 54 poles to a black oak on a hillside, then S 10° E 45 poles to a white oak by the north side of the **North Fork of Kittoctan Creek** above a **ford and road,** then crossing the Creek S 30° E 28 poles to a small hickory on a stony hillside corner to **Anthony Connard,** then S 14° W 74 poles to a white oak by a bottom or swamp corner to **Patterson Wright,** then with his line S 60° W 40 poles to a black oak on a stony point his corner, then N 24° W 130 poles across the Creek to a white oak on a stony knoll, then S 75° W 112 poles to a black oak in **Benjamin Steer's** line, then with said line N 2° W 112 poles to a white oak corner to **William Hough,** then with his lines N 61° E 92 poles to a box white oak, S 80° E 40 poles to two white oaks, S 71° E 20 poles to a white oak, thence about N 70° E 70 poles to the beginning, and all houses buildings orchards ways waters watercourses profits commodities hereditaments and appurtenance whatsoever to the said premises hereby granted, or any part thereof belonging or in any wise appertaining unto the said **Jacob Wine** his heirs and assigns forever. To have and to hold the lands hereby conveyed and all and singular other the premises hereby granted and

released and every part and parcel thereof belonging and with their and every of their appurtenances unto the said **Jacob Wine** his heirs and assigns forever, **John Hough**. Sealed and delivered in the presence of **Jeremiah Purdom, Peter Calrik**, and **John** his X mark **Wineburg**. Proven on 5/12/1794. Lease and Release, Loudoun County Deed Book V, pp. 263-266

12. 1/30/1794, **Jacob Wine** of Loudoun County in the State of Virginia of the one part to **John Hough** of the said County of the other part. It is to be remembered that 150 pounds part of the within mentioned sum of 480 pounds was paid before the signing and sealing of the within mortgage, **John Hough**, 1/20/1794. Signed, sealed and delivered in the presence of **Jeremiah Purdom, Peter Calrick**, and **John** his X mark **Wineburg**. This indenture of mortgage and the receipt thereon endorsed were acknowledged by **Jacob Wine** party thereof and ordered to be recorded on 5/12/1794. Mortgage, Loudoun County Deed Book V, pp. 267-269

13. 1/7 and 1/8/1795, **John Hough** of Loudoun County in the State of Virginia of the one part to **Patterson Wright** of the said County of the other part. Witnesseth that for and in consideration of the sum of 250 pounds current money of Virginia to the said **John Hough** in hand paid by the said **Anthony Wright** at or before the sealing and delivery of these presents the receipt whereof he doth hereby acknowledge, hath granted bargained aliened released and confirmed and by these presents doth grant bargain sell alien release and confirm unto the said **Patterson Wright** and his heirs that parcel of land situate in Loudoun County bounded as followeth viz. Beginning at a small black oak marked **MJ** corner to land conveyed to **Mahlon Janney** now **John Janney's,** and in a line of **George William Fairfax Manor**, extending thence with said line S 50-½° W 116 poles, then N 74° E 56 poles to a black oak on a stony point corner to **Jacob Wine,** then with his line N 68° E 41 poles to a white oak his corner, then S 14° E 75 poles to a small hickory corner to said **Wine** and to **Anthony Connard**, then with **Connard's** lines S 40° E 64 poles to a black oak, then S 46° E 24 poles, then S 55° E 20 poles to a hickory **Connard's** corner and corner to **William Paxton**, then with his line S 32° E 90 poles to the line of the said **Mahlon Janney**, then binding therewith S 81-½° W 149 poles to the beginning containing 117 acres of land and all houses buildings orchards ways waters watercourses profits commodities hereditaments and appurtenances whatsoever to the said premises hereby granted or any part thereof belonging or in any wise appertaining. To have and to hold the lands hereby conveyed and all and singular other the premises hereby granted and released and every part and parcel thereof, with their every of their appurtenances unto the said **Patterson Wright** heirs and assigns forever, **John Hough**. Proven on 1/12/1795. Lease and Release, Loudoun County Deed Book V, pp. 478-481

14. 4/8/1799, **Patterson Wright** of the County of Loudoun and Commonwealth of Virginia and **Nancy** his wife of the one part to **Anthony Wright** of the same place of the other part. Witnesseth that the said **Patterson Wright** and **Nancy** his wife for and in consideration of the sum of 30 pounds Virginia currency to the said **Patterson Wright** in hand the

receipt whereof is hereby acknowledged, have granted bargained and sold aliened and confirmed and by these presents do grant bargain and sell alien and confirm unto the said **Anthony Wright** and to his heirs and assigns a certain piece or parcel of land situate lying and being in the County aforesaid being part of a larger tract of land sold and transferred by **John Hough** to the said **Patterson Wright** by deed bearing date the (blank space) day of (blank space) in the year one thousand seven hundred and ninety (blank space) duly recorded in the County Court of Loudoun, reference hereunto being had will more fully appear bounded as follows viz. Beginning at a hickory corner to **William Paxton** in a line of **John Janney** then with **Janney's** line the course corrected S 82° W 53 poles to a stone near a black oak and hickory sapling, thence N 52° W 14 poles to a stone near a marked white oak, thence N 29-¼° E 13 poles to a hickory, then N 52° E 42 poles to a white oak sapling in a line of **William Packson**, then with said line S 32° E 46-¼ poles to the beginning containing 10 acres of land, together with all houses buildings ways waters watercourses profits commodities hereditaments and appurtenances whatsoever to the said premises belonging or in any wise appertaining. To have and to hold the land hereby conveyed and all and singular the premises hereby granted with the appurtenances unto the said **Anthony Wright** and to his heirs and assigns forever, **Patterson Wright** and **Nancy Wright.** Signed, sealed and delivered in presence of **Asa Harriss, Christian** his X mark **Clymore,** and **Isaac Larrowe.** Proven on 4/8/1799. Bargain and Sale, Loudoun County Deed Book Z, pp. 154-155

15. 4/8/1799, **Mahlon Janney** of the County of Loudoun and State of Virginia and **Sarah** his wife of the one part to **James Moore** of the County aforesaid of the other part. Witnesseth that for and in consideration of the sum of 745 pounds and 10 shillings current money of Virginia to the said **Mahlon Janney** in hand paid by the said **James Moore** at or before the sealing and delivery of these presents the receipt whereof he doth hereby acknowledge, have granted bargained and sold to the said **James Moore** and by these presents doth grant sell alien and confirm unto the said **James Moore** his heirs and assigns forever all that tract or parcel of land lying and being on the waters of **Kittoctan Creek** in the County aforesaid bounded as by a survey thereon made by **Israel Janney** as follows viz. Beginning at a poplar standing on the north side of **Kittoctan Creek** running N 50° - 53 minutes W 209-¼ poles to a black oak on the point of a hill marked **MJ & W**, extending thence N 82° E 251-¼ poles to a white oak standing about six poles north of the **road leading from Mahlon Janney's Mill to Jonah Thompson's Mill** marked **MJ,** thence S 9° W 119-¼ poles to a planted stone in **Mahlon Janney's** line, thence S 53-¾ W 82-¾ poles to the beginning containing 142 acres and 13 perches of land, and all houses buildings orchards waters watercourses profits hereditaments and appurtenances whatsoever to the said premises hereby granted or any part thereof belonging or in any wise appertaining. To have and to hold the lands hereby granted and all and singular the premises hereby granted and every part thereof with every of their appurtenances unto the said **James Moore** his heirs and

assigns forever, **Mahlon Janney** and **Sarah Janney**. Proven on 4/8/1799. Deed, Loudoun County Deed Book Z, pp. 160-192

16. 5/1/1802, **William Hough, Samuel Hough**, and **Mahlon Hough** of Loudoun County executors of **John Hough deceased** of the one part to **Asa Moore** of the County and State aforesaid of the other part. Witnesseth that the said executors for and in consideration of the sum of 426 pounds current money of Virginia unto them in hand well and truly paid by the said **Asa Moore** at and before the sealing and delivery hereof the receipt whereof they do hereby acknowledge, have granted bargained sold aliened released and confirmed and by these presents doth grant bargain sell alien release and confirm unto the said **Asa Moore** his heirs and assigns forever all that part of a tract of land situate in the County of Loudoun aforesaid on both sides of **Kittocton Creek** and bounded as followeth viz. Beginning between a white oak and black oak saplings corner to **Jacob Shibeley** in a line of the land sold by the aforesaid executors to **Ebenezer Grubb** extending thence with his line S 69° – 45 minutes W 36 poles and 12 links to a stone heap between three chestnut oak saplings corner to said **Grubb** and in a line of **John Hough's** original tract, then with that line and **Cunard Verts** N 21° E 178 poles crossing **Kittocton Creek** to a poplar cornered by **Hooe and Little** as a boundary for the said **John Hough,** then with the line they made N 70° W 124 poles to a black oak in **The Narrows** in a thicket of laurels near a **road** corner to the aforesaid **Grubb,** (then) with his lines S 30-½° W 18 poles, then up the **Kittocton Creek** near the bank thereof S 10° W 30 poles, (then) S 3-½° W 12 poles to an ash corner to said **Grubb** and **Israel Shibeley,** then with **Shibeley's** line about S 16° E 139 poles to the first station containing 104-¾ acres be the same more or less as surveyed by **Joshua Daniel**, together with all and singular the rights members liberties privileges improvements hereditaments and appurtenances whatsoever thereunto belonging or in any wise appertaining unto the said **Asa Moore** his heirs and assigns forever, **Wm. Hough** and **Samuel Hough**. Sealed and delivered in the presence of **James Moore** and **Daniel Stone, Thos. Phillips**, and **Jonah Hough** as to **William Hough** and **Samuel Hough**. Proven on 9/12/1802. Bargain and Sale, Loudoun County Deed Book 2C, pp. 28-30

17. 5/21/1802, **William Hough, Samuel Hough**, and **Mahlon Hough** of the County of Loudoun and State of Virginia executors of **John Hough deceased** of the one part to **Isaac Steer** of the County aforesaid of the other part. Witnesseth that the said executors for and in consideration of the sum of 1,775 pounds current money of Virginia to them in hand paid by the said **Isaac Steer** the receipt whereof they do hereby acknowledge, have granted bargained sold aliened released and confirmed and by these presents doth grant bargain sell alien release and confirm unto the said **Isaac Steer** his heirs assigns forever a certain tract or parcel of land being in the County aforesaid belonging to the estate of the said **John Hough deceased** being that part of the land whereon the said deceased lived, and bounded as followeth viz. Beginning at a marked spanish oak corner to land sold to **Ebenezer Grubb** by said executor and corner to **William Hough** standing

by **the road leading to the German Settlement** extending thence with the said **Hough's** line S 46° W 103 poles to a red oak stump his corner, (then) with another of his lines S 3-½° W 32 poles to a heap of stones, (then) with another of his lines S 74-½° W 21 poles to a planted stone in said line and corner to **Jacob Wine,** thence with **Wine's** lines S 22° E 54 poles to a spanish oak on a hill his corner, (then) S 24° W 52 poles to a black oak his corner, (then) S 10° E 43 poles to a white oak, (then) S 31° E 28 poles crossing the **North Fork of Kittocton Creek** to a hickory sapling corner to said **Wine** and **Anthony Cunard,** (then) with **Cunard's** line N 24° E 30-½ poles to a white oak, (then) N 21-½° W 36 poles to leaning white oak, (then) N 68° E 57-½ poles to a hickory stump in the bottom, (then) S 69° E 51 poles crossing the Creek twice to a planted stone on the south side of said Creek, then N 34° E 28-½ poles to a walnut, (then) S 16-½° E 34 poles to a stone in said **Cunard's** line corner to **William Paxson's** land which he purchased of the said **John Hough**, (then) with **Paxson's** lines N 40° E 72-½ poles to a wild cherry tree, (then) N 51-½° E 82 poles crossing the **South Fork of Kittocton Creek** to an ash near said Creek, (then) S 89° E 47 poles to several white oak saplings in the original line corner to **William Paxson, William Hough,** and **Jesse Taylor,** (then) with the lines of said **Taylor** and **Cunard Virtz** N 21° E 113 poles to a black oak on a stony knoll in the said original line corner to the land sold to **Ebenezer Grubb,** (then) with his lines N 79° W 122 poles to a hickory on a small ridge, (then) S 72° W 49 poles crossing the main **Kittocton** a small distance below the Fork to a large white oak near the foot of a hill, (then) S 43° W 31 poles to a planted stone near the aforesaid **road,** (then) up said **road** N 65° W 70 poles to the beginning containing 325 acres be the same more or less agreeable to a survey made thereon near five years past. Together with all and singular the rights members' liberties privileges improvements hereditaments and appurtenances whatsoever thereunto belonging or in any wise appertaining unto the said **Isaac Steer** his heirs and assigns forever. To have and to hold all and singular the premises hereby granted with the appurtenances unto the said **Isaac Steer** his heirs and assigns forever, **Wm. Hough** and **Samuel Hough**. Sealed and delivered in the presence of **James Moore, Asa Moore, Jonah Hough**, and **Thomas Phillips** for **Samuel Hough**. Bargain and Sale, Loudoun County Deed Book 2C, pp. 125-128

18. 6/24/1803, **William Hough, Samuel Hough,** and **Mahlon Hough** executors of the least will and testament of **John Hough deceased** of the one part to **Ebenezer Grubb** of the other part, all of the County of Loudoun and Commonwealth of Virginia. Whereas **John Hough** departed this life on or about the day of (blank space) in the year 1797 having first made his last will and testament and therein appointed the aforesaid **William, Samuel,** and **Mahlon** his executors with full powers to sell and dispose of certain lands on the waters of **Kittocton Creek** whereon the said **John Hough** then resided of which said tract this is part. Now this indenture witnesseth that the said executors for and in consideration of the sum of 1,050 pounds current money of Virginia to them in hand paid by the aforesaid **Ebenezer Grubb** the

receipt whereof they do hereby acknowledge, have granted bargained sold aliened released and confirmed and by these presents do grant bargain sell alien release and confirm unto the said **Ebenezer Grubb** his heirs executors administrators and assigns forever all that tract or parcel of land lying and being in the County of Loudoun and Commonwealth aforesaid on the waters of **Kittocton Creek** and bounded as follows viz. Beginning at a spanish oak corner to **Wm. Hough Jr.** by the corner of his field extending thence along his field N 45° W 68 poles to a white oak sapling near the corner of said field corner to **William Hough** and **Thomas Hough,** thence with **Thomas Hough's** line N 52° E 122 poles to a sassafras his corner, thence N 7° E 125 poles to a white oak and spanish oak in **Arnold's** line corner to the said **Thomas Hough,** thence S 70° E 42 poles to several maples on the bank of **Beaverdam** corner to **Arnold,** thence N 19-½° E 26-½ poles to **Arnold's** corner, (then) S 70° E 118 poles to a black oak in line run by **Hooe and Little** on a high bank called **The Narrows,** thence S 30-½° W 17 poles, then up the meanders of **Kittocton** S 18° E 30 poles, (then) S 3-½° W 12 poles to an ash on the bank of **Kittocton Creek** corner to **Jacob Shively,** thence with his line N 82° W 40 poles to a stake by a marked hickory his corner, then with another of his lines S 17° W 108 poles to a hickory his corner, then with another of his lines S 69° E 98 poles crossing **Kittocton Creek** to a white and black oak sapling his corner and the same course continued 36 poles further to the line of **Howell's** land, then with that line S 21° W 32 poles to a black oak in said line, then leaving said line N 79° W 122 poles to a hickory on small ridge, then S 72° W 49 poles crossing said **Kittocton Creek** to a large white oak, then S 43° W 31 poles to a stone in the edge of the land leading from **J. Hough's Mill** to **Ball's Mill** up the **road** N 65° W 70 poles to the first station containing 267 acres, together with all houses, buildings orchards trees ways woods water watercourses profits commodities hereditaments and appurtenances to the same belonging or in any wise appertaining. To have and to hold the aforesaid tract or parcel of land and premises with the appurtenances unto the said **Ebenezer Grubb** his heirs executors administrators and assigns forever, **Wm. Hough, Samuel Hough,** and **Mahlon Hough**. Signed, sealed and delivered in the presence of **Walker Reid, G. W. Blincoe,** and **Saml. Blincoe** as to **Saml. Hough. Mahlon Roach, Edward Cunnard Sr.,** and **Thos. Hough** as to **Mahlon Hough. Thomas Phillips, David Potts,** and **Bayn Smallwood** as to **William Hough**. Proven on 12/112/1803. Deed, Loudoun County Deed Book 2G, pp. 18-20 (Note: corrections noted to boundary description on bottom of Book 2G, p. 19)

19. 4/1/1806, **William Hough, Samuel Hough,** and **Mahlon Hough** executors of **John Hough deceased** all of the County of Loudoun and State of Virginia of the one part to **William Paxon** of the same County and State of the other part. Witnesseth that the said **William Hough, Samuel Hough,** and **Mahlon Hough** executors of the said **John Hough deceased** for and in consideration of the sum of 2,050 pound(s) unto them in hand well and truly paid by the said **William Paxon** at and before the sealing and delivery

hereof, hath granted bargained sold aliened released and confirmed and by these presents doth bargain sell alien release and confirm unto the said **William Paxon** his heirs and assigns a certain tract of land situate on the waters of **Kittoctin Creek** in the County aforesaid and bounded as followeth viz. Beginning at a white oak on a hill in a line of **Tankerville** and near **Edward Stone's house** and running S 81° W 106-½ poles to a hickory corner to **Anthony Wright,** then with **Anthony** and **Patterson Wright's** line N 32-¼ W 89 poles to a hickory corner to **Patterson Wright** and **Moore & Phillips,** thence with their line N 50-½° E 90 poles to a stone in **William Paxon's** field corner to **Anthony Cunard,** then with his line N 15-½° W 78-¼ poles to a stone near **a gate corner to Conard and Isaac Steer,** then with **Steer's** line N 45° E 73 poles to a wild cherry tree corner to said **Steer,** thence with his line N 54° E 81-¾ poles to a crooked ash on the east bank of **Kittoctin Creek** corner to **Steer,** then with another of his lines S 89° E 47 poles to two white oaks and a hickory on a hill corner to said **Steer, Jesse Taylor,** and **William Hough,** then with **Hough's** line S 22-½° W 60 poles to an ash stump and lime tree corner to said **Hough,** thence with his line S 9° W 239-½ poles to the beginning containing 208 acres be the same more or less. Together also with all and singular the rights members liberties privileges improvements hereditaments and appurtenances whatsoever thereunto belonging or in any way appertaining unto the said **William Paxon** his heirs and assigns forever, **Wm. Hough, Samuel Hough,** and **Mahlon Hough.** Signed, sealed, and delivered in the presence of **Daniel Stone, W. S. Neale, Edward Stone, David Goodwin, Timothy Hixon, Nathan Ball,** and **Edwd. Dorsey**. Proven on 5/12/1806. Deed, Loudoun County Deed Book 2G, pp. 261-263

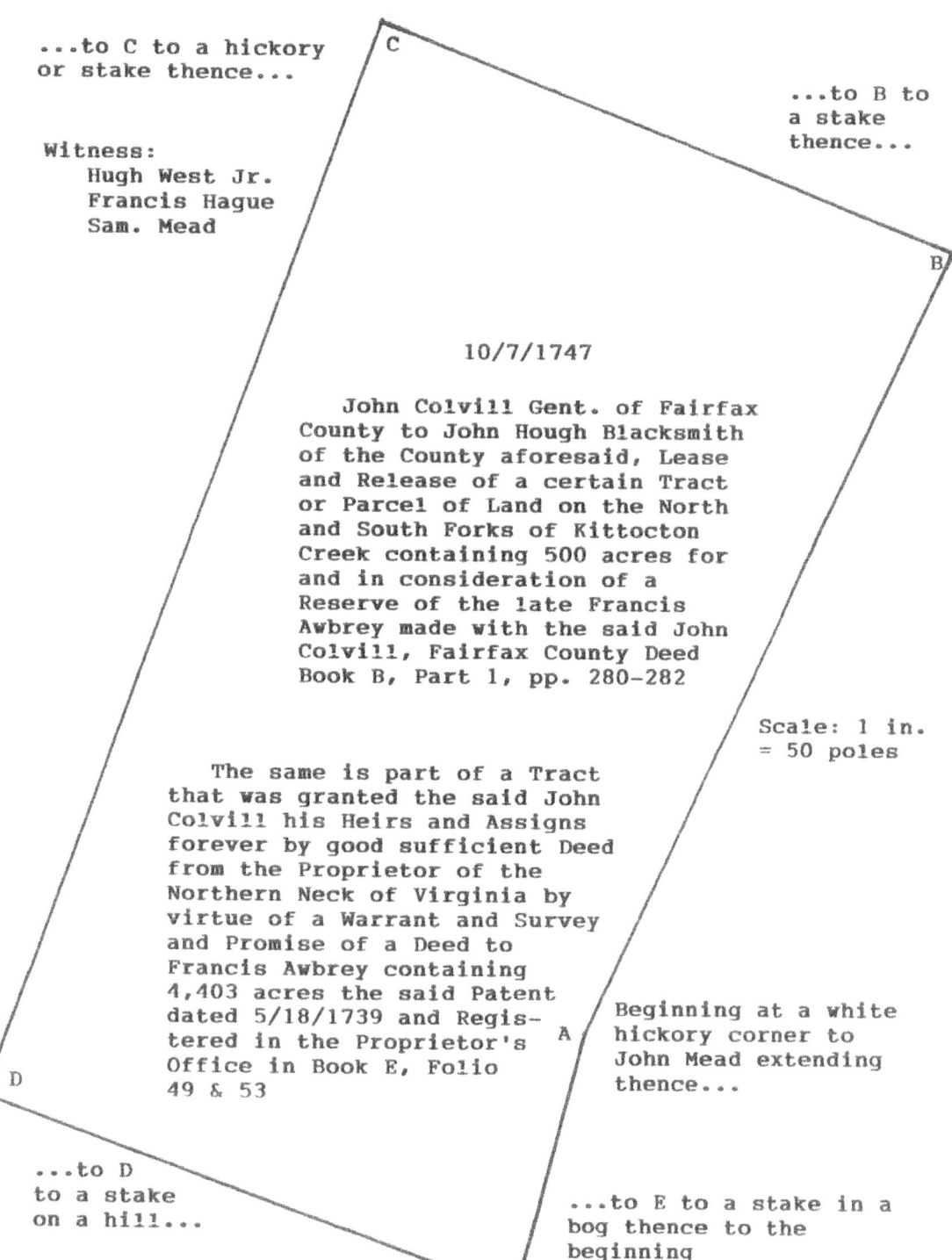

...to C to a hickory or stake thence...

...to B to a stake thence...

Witness:
   Hugh West Jr.
   Francis Hague
   Sam. Mead

10/7/1747

John Colvill Gent. of Fairfax County to John Hough Blacksmith of the County aforesaid, Lease and Release of a certain Tract or Parcel of Land on the North and South Forks of Kittocton Creek containing 500 acres for and in consideration of a Reserve of the late Francis Awbrey made with the said John Colvill, Fairfax County Deed Book B, Part 1, pp. 280-282

Scale: 1 in. = 50 poles

The same is part of a Tract that was granted the said John Colvill his Heirs and Assigns forever by good sufficient Deed from the Proprietor of the Northern Neck of Virginia by virtue of a Warrant and Survey and Promise of a Deed to Francis Awbrey containing 4,403 acres the said Patent dated 5/18/1739 and Registered in the Proprietor's Office in Book E, Folio 49 & 53

Beginning at a white hickory corner to John Mead extending thence...

...to D to a stake on a hill...

...to E to a stake in a bog thence to the beginning

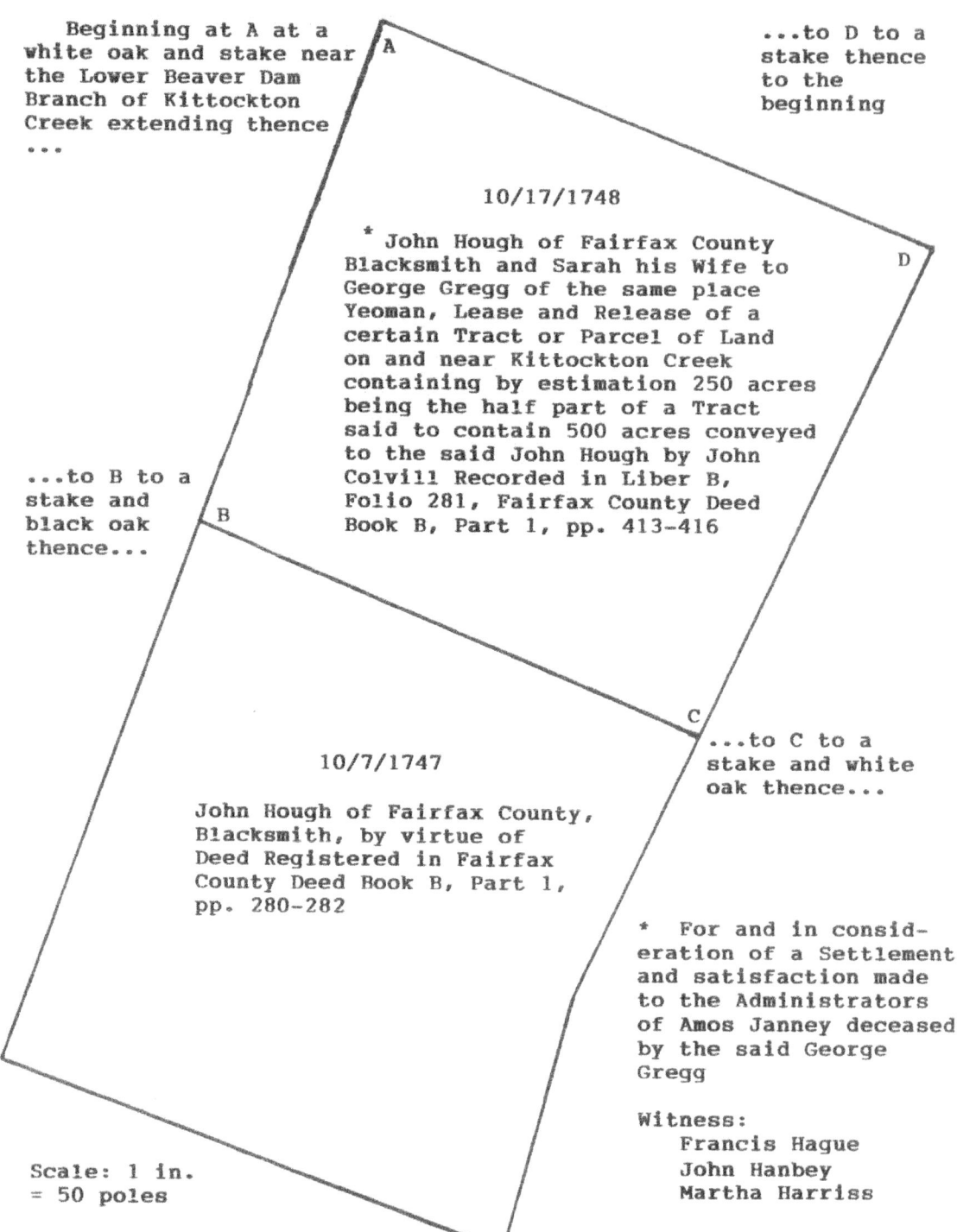

Beginning at A at a white oak and stake near the Lower Beaver Dam Branch of Kittockton Creek extending thence ...

...to D to a stake thence to the beginning

10/17/1748

* John Hough of Fairfax County Blacksmith and Sarah his Wife to George Gregg of the same place Yeoman, Lease and Release of a certain Tract or Parcel of Land on and near Kittockton Creek containing by estimation 250 acres being the half part of a Tract said to contain 500 acres conveyed to the said John Hough by John Colvill Recorded in Liber B, Folio 281, Fairfax County Deed Book B, Part 1, pp. 413-416

...to B to a stake and black oak thence...

...to C to a stake and white oak thence...

10/7/1747

John Hough of Fairfax County, Blacksmith, by virtue of Deed Registered in Fairfax County Deed Book B, Part 1, pp. 280-282

* For and in consideration of a Settlement and satisfaction made to the Administrators of Amos Janney deceased by the said George Gregg

Witness:
  Francis Hague
  John Hanbey
  Martha Harriss

Scale: 1 in. = 50 poles

Beginning at a stake near a marked hickory saplin and spanish oak on hill corner to the said John Hough his land above his lane end and extending thence to a hickory and red oak thence to a stake in a line of John Mercer crossing the said Creek thence with said Mercer line to a white and red oak on hillside corner to the said Hough thence with his line to the first station crossing the said Creek below the said Hough's meadow containing two hundred and fifty acres of land

...On the Kittocton Creek including the main fork thereof...

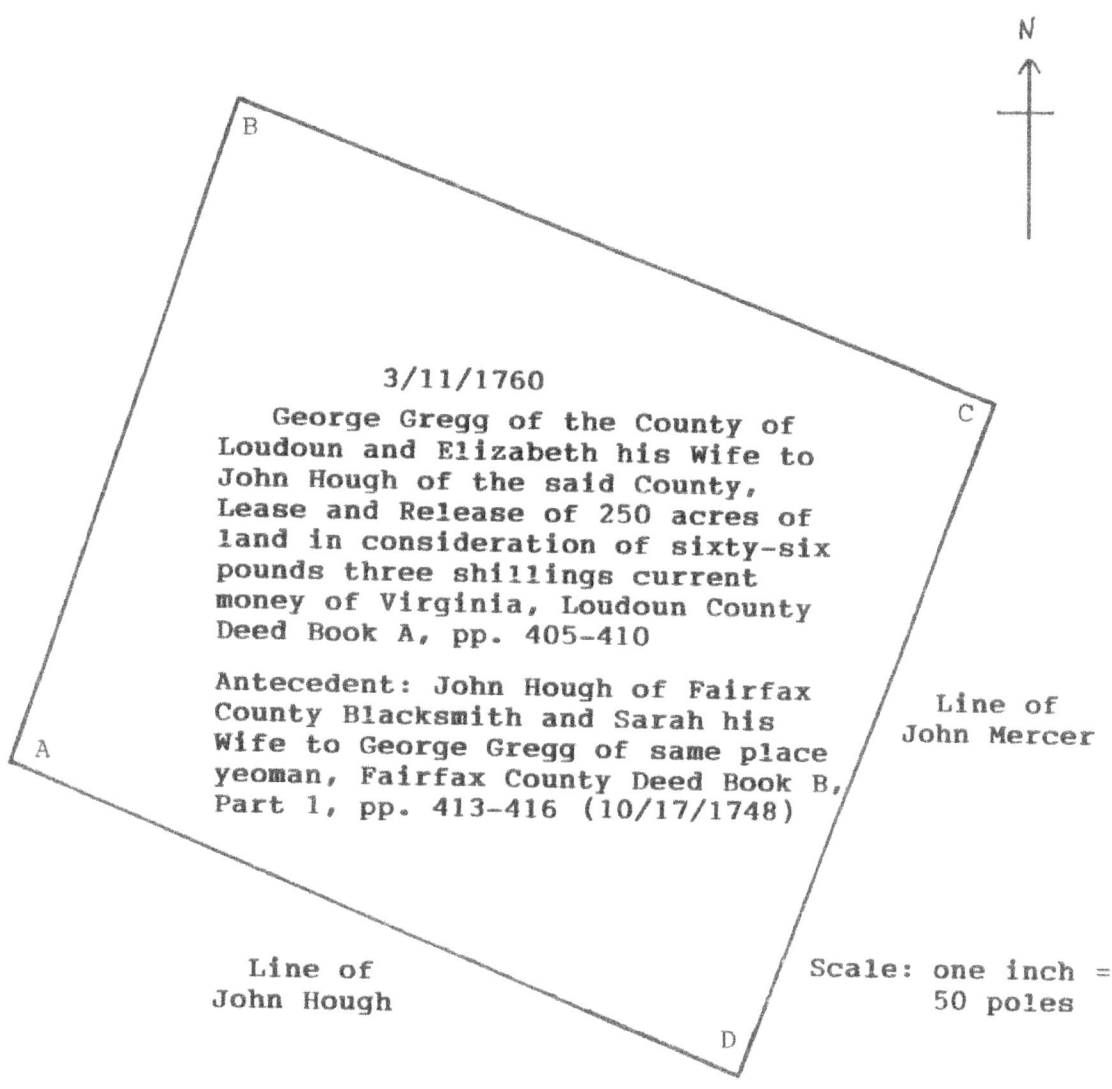

3/11/1760

George Gregg of the County of Loudoun and Elizabeth his Wife to John Hough of the said County, Lease and Release of 250 acres of land in consideration of sixty-six pounds three shillings current money of Virginia, Loudoun County Deed Book A, pp. 405-410

Antecedent: John Hough of Fairfax County Blacksmith and Sarah his Wife to George Gregg of same place yeoman, Fairfax County Deed Book B, Part 1, pp. 413-416 (10/17/1748)

Line of John Mercer

Line of John Hough

Scale: one inch = 50 poles

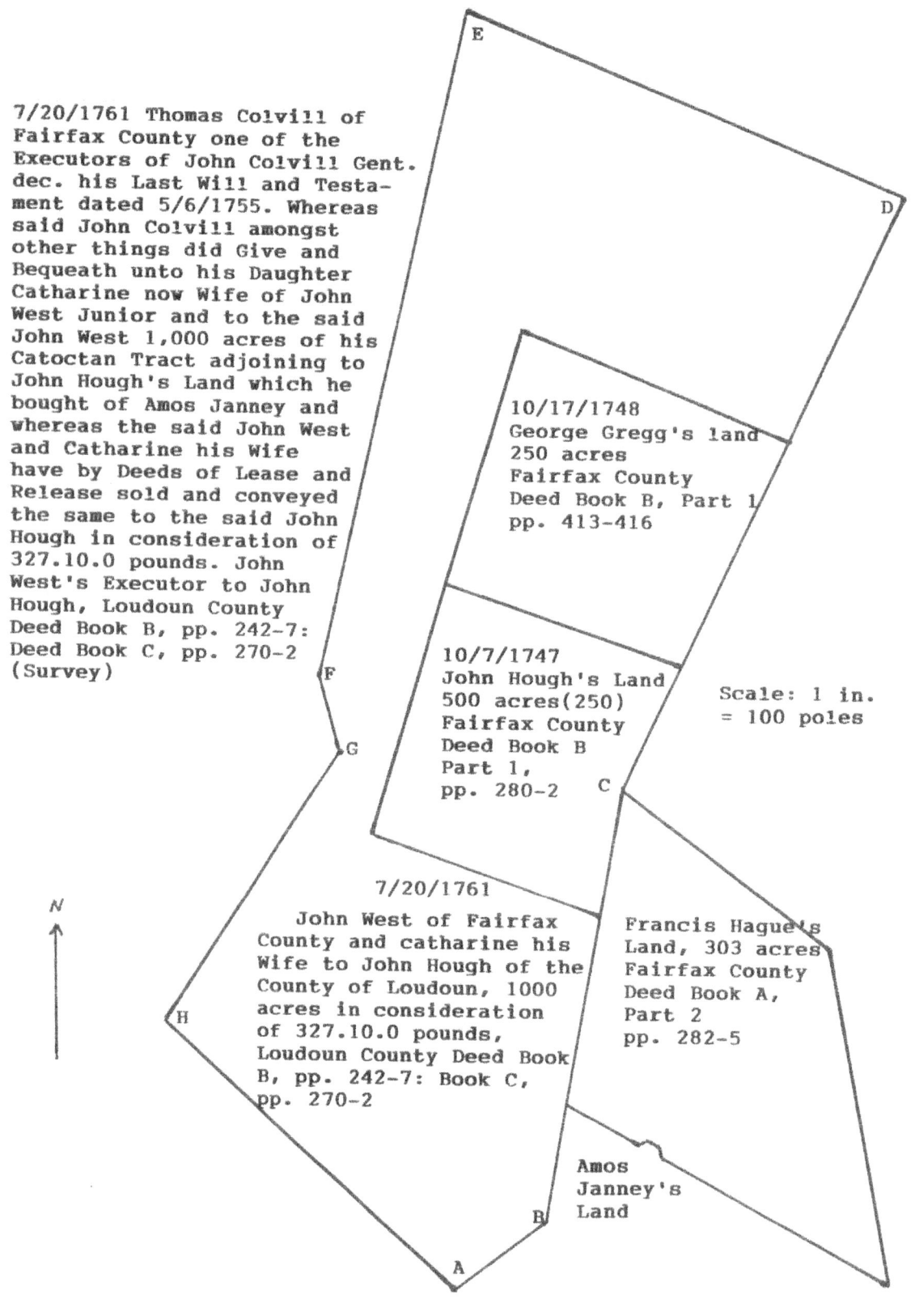

7/20/1761 Thomas Colvill of Fairfax County one of the Executors of John Colvill Gent. dec. his Last Will and Testament dated 5/6/1755. Whereas said John Colvill amongst other things did Give and Bequeath unto his Daughter Catharine now Wife of John West Junior and to the said John West 1,000 acres of his Catoctan Tract adjoining to John Hough's Land which he bought of Amos Janney and whereas the said John West and Catharine his Wife have by Deeds of Lease and Release sold and conveyed the same to the said John Hough in consideration of 327.10.0 pounds. John West's Executor to John Hough, Loudoun County Deed Book B, pp. 242-7: Deed Book C, pp. 270-2 (Survey)

10/17/1748
George Gregg's land
250 acres
Fairfax County
Deed Book B, Part 1
pp. 413-416

10/7/1747
John Hough's Land
500 acres (250)
Fairfax County
Deed Book B
Part 1,
pp. 280-2

Scale: 1 in. = 100 poles

7/20/1761
John West of Fairfax County and catharine his Wife to John Hough of the County of Loudoun, 1000 acres in consideration of 327.10.0 pounds, Loudoun County Deed Book B, pp. 242-7: Book C, pp. 270-2

Francis Hague's Land, 303 acres
Fairfax County
Deed Book A,
Part 2
pp. 282-5

Amos Janney's Land

Beginning at A a poplar near the S⁰. Fork of Catoctian Creek marked F thence to B near Janney's fence supposed to be line of Janney's Land thence with the same to C a white hickory on the side of Catoctian Creek marked JM from thence Mr. Hough desired me to protract the other lines of the Patent to include areas exclusive of his 500 which is represented by black lines & the letters DEFGH and protract the courses of his 500 Acres which is represented by black lines and figures 1234 and the Letter C

Survey by George West

Sworn C.C.(chain carriers) Thos. Dodd & Levi Wells

June 8th, 1762
Loudoun County
Deed Book C,
pp. 270-272

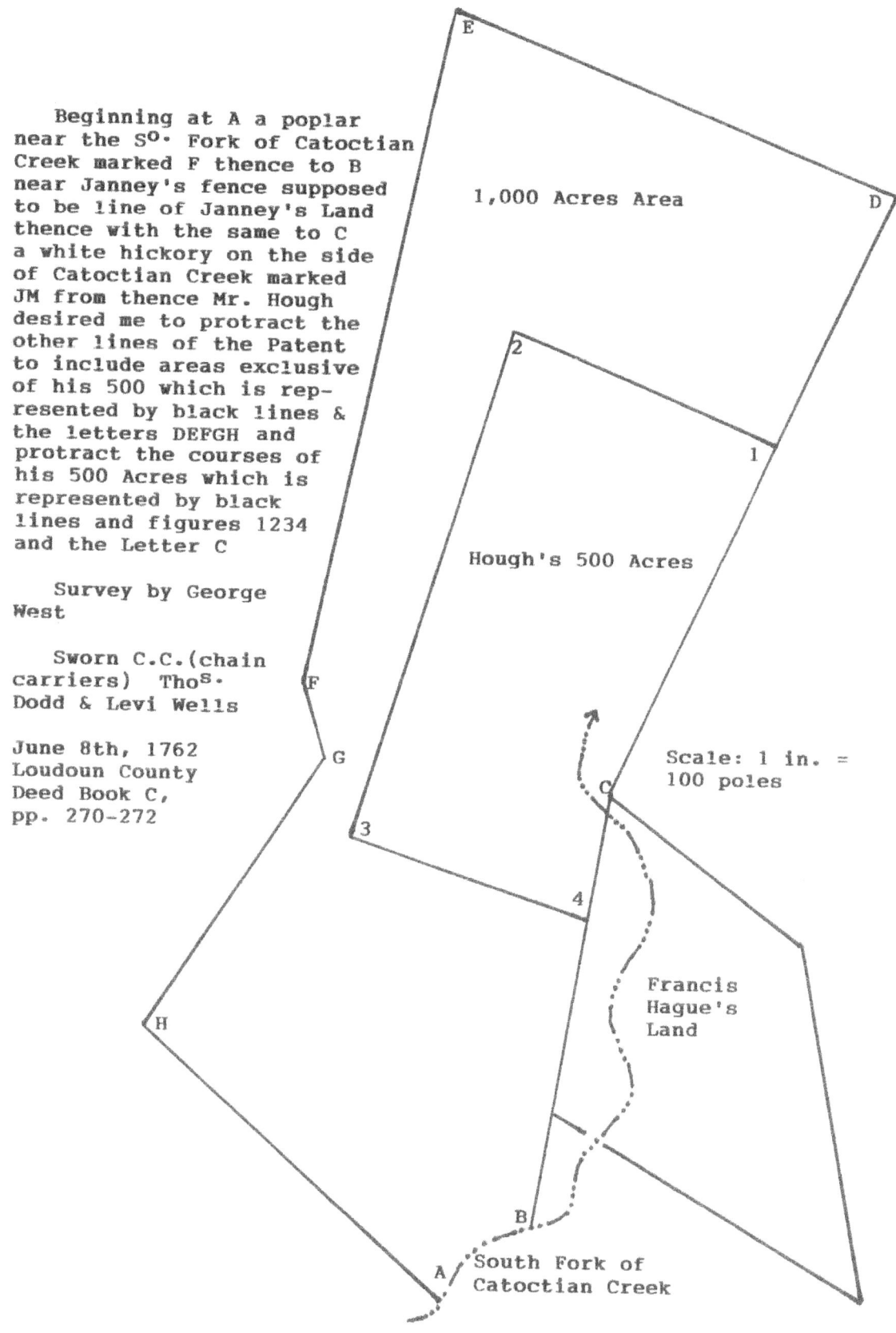

1,000 Acres Area

Hough's 500 Acres

Scale: 1 in. = 100 poles

Francis Hague's Land

South Fork of Catoctian Creek

May one thousand seven hundred and Sixty two which Plat and Survey so made and signed by the said George West is hereunto annexed and the said Thomas Colvill do hereby agree and approve of the manner and form in which the said one thousand Acres of Land are laid off & Bounded as believing it agreeable to the Will and intention of the said Testator unless there shall be an Error in the Quantity of the number of Acres in which Case the line to include the said Thousand Acres is to be N68.10E from one out line to the other parralel to said Hough's lower line   Jn° Wilney

I the said Thomas Colvill have hereunto set my hand and affixed my Seal this 17th day of May 1762.

Sealed and Delivered
In presence of
J. West, John West Jun.r   Thos Colvill (LS)

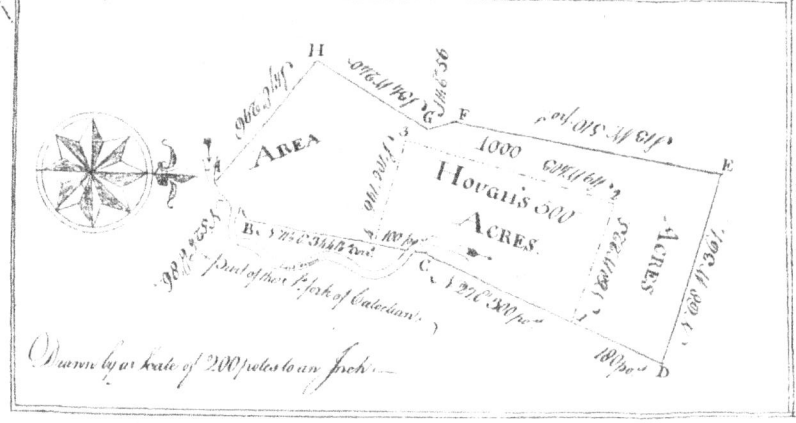

Drawn by a Scale of 200 poles to an Inch

May 13th 1762   At the Request of Mr John Hough I Surveyed part of the above as follows Beginning at A a Poplar near the E. fork of Goleclian Creek mark'd F.A.IC Thence S.52°E 686 poles wanting 8 links to B near Janney's fence Supposed to be in the Line of Janney's Land thence with the same N.W.E near a line of mark'd Trees 326 poles and angles to a white Hickory on the side of the said Goleclian Creek marked IN.III. from thence Mr Hough desired me to Protract the other Lines of the Patent to include 1000 Acres exclusive of his 500 which is Represented by black lines & the letters D.E.F.G.H.A and also the

This Indenture made 5/9/1770 between Mahlon Janney of Loudoun County of the one part and John Hough of the same, 150 Acre-lot, Lease and Release in consideration 150 pounds current money of Virginia, Loudoun County Deed Book H, pp. 29-33

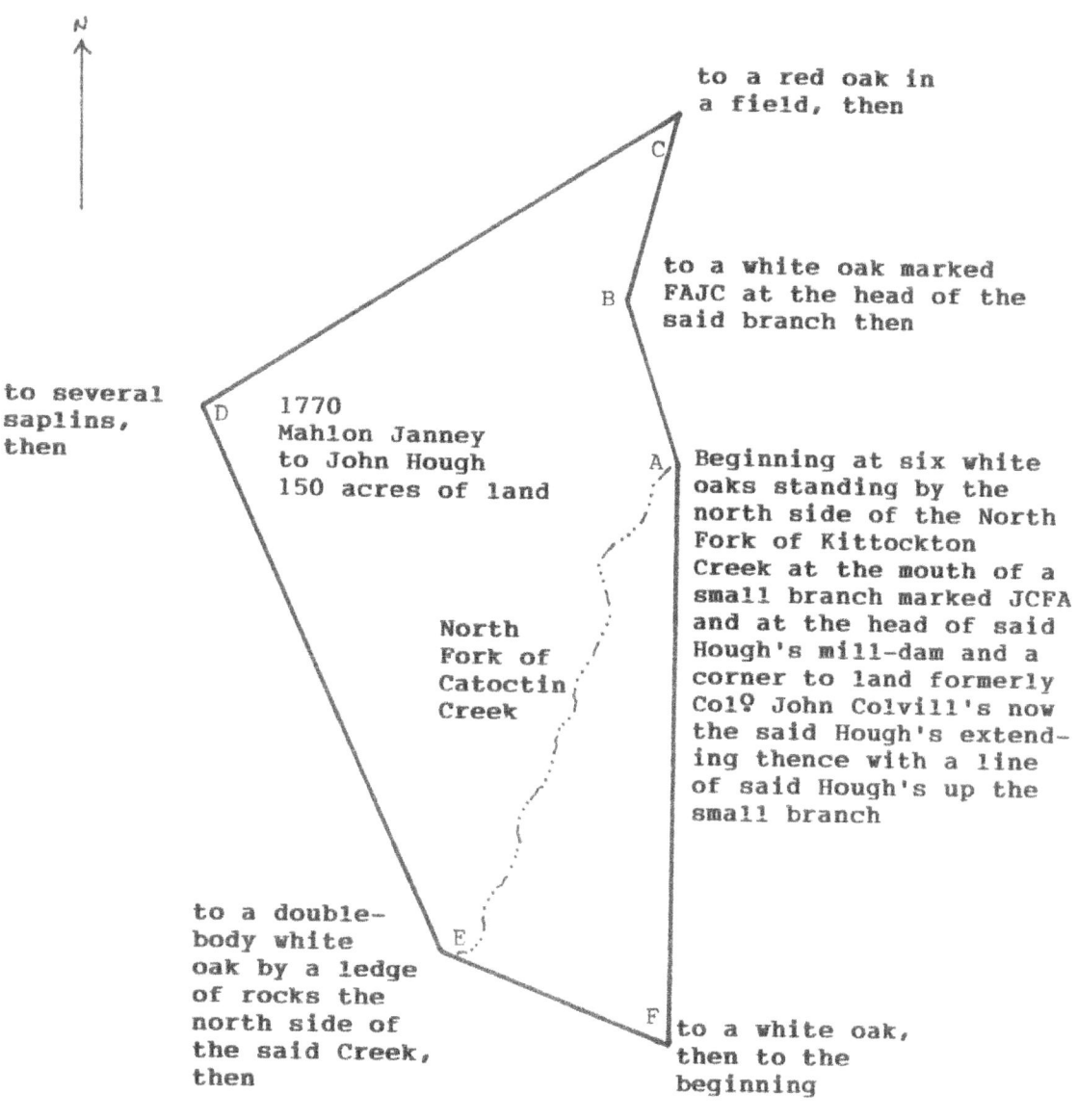

N

to a red oak in a field, then

to a white oak marked FAJC at the head of the said branch then

to several saplins, then

1770 Mahlon Janney to John Hough 150 acres of land

Beginning at six white oaks standing by the north side of the North Fork of Kittockton Creek at the mouth of a small branch marked JCFA and at the head of said Hough's mill-dam and a corner to land formerly Col? John Colvill's now the said Hough's extending thence with a line of said Hough's up the small branch

North Fork of Catoctin Creek

to a double-body white oak by a ledge of rocks the north side of the said Creek, then

to a white oak, then to the beginning

one inch = 50 poles

5/9 and 5/10/1770, John Hough and Sarah his wife of the one part to Mahlon Janney of the other part, Lease and Release of 155 acres of land for and in consideration of 150 pounds current money of Virginia, Loudoun County Deed Book H, pp. 33-36

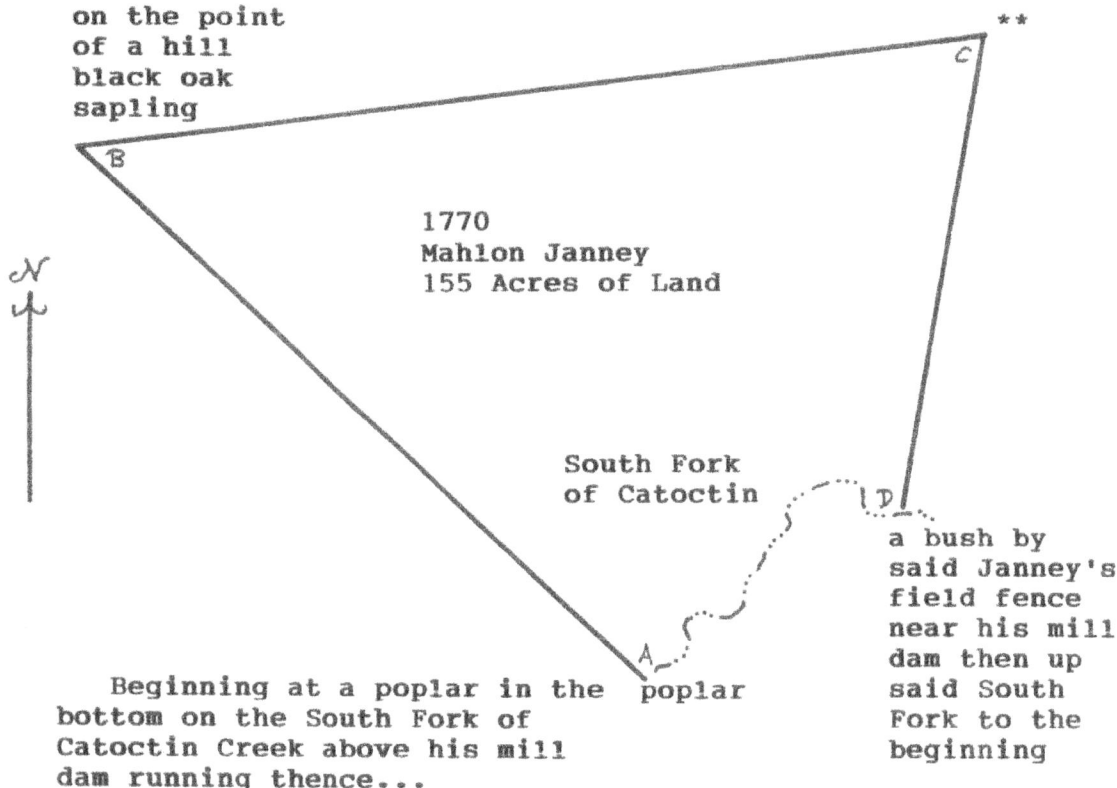

on the point of a hill black oak sapling

1770
Mahlon Janney
155 Acres of Land

South Fork of Catoctin

a bush by said Janney's field fence near his mill dam then up said South Fork to the beginning

Beginning at a poplar in the bottom on the South Fork of Catoctin Creek above his mill dam running thence...

See ** a spanish and white oak
in a line of Francis Hague's
on a hill seven poles from
the road the north side thereof

one inch = 50 poles

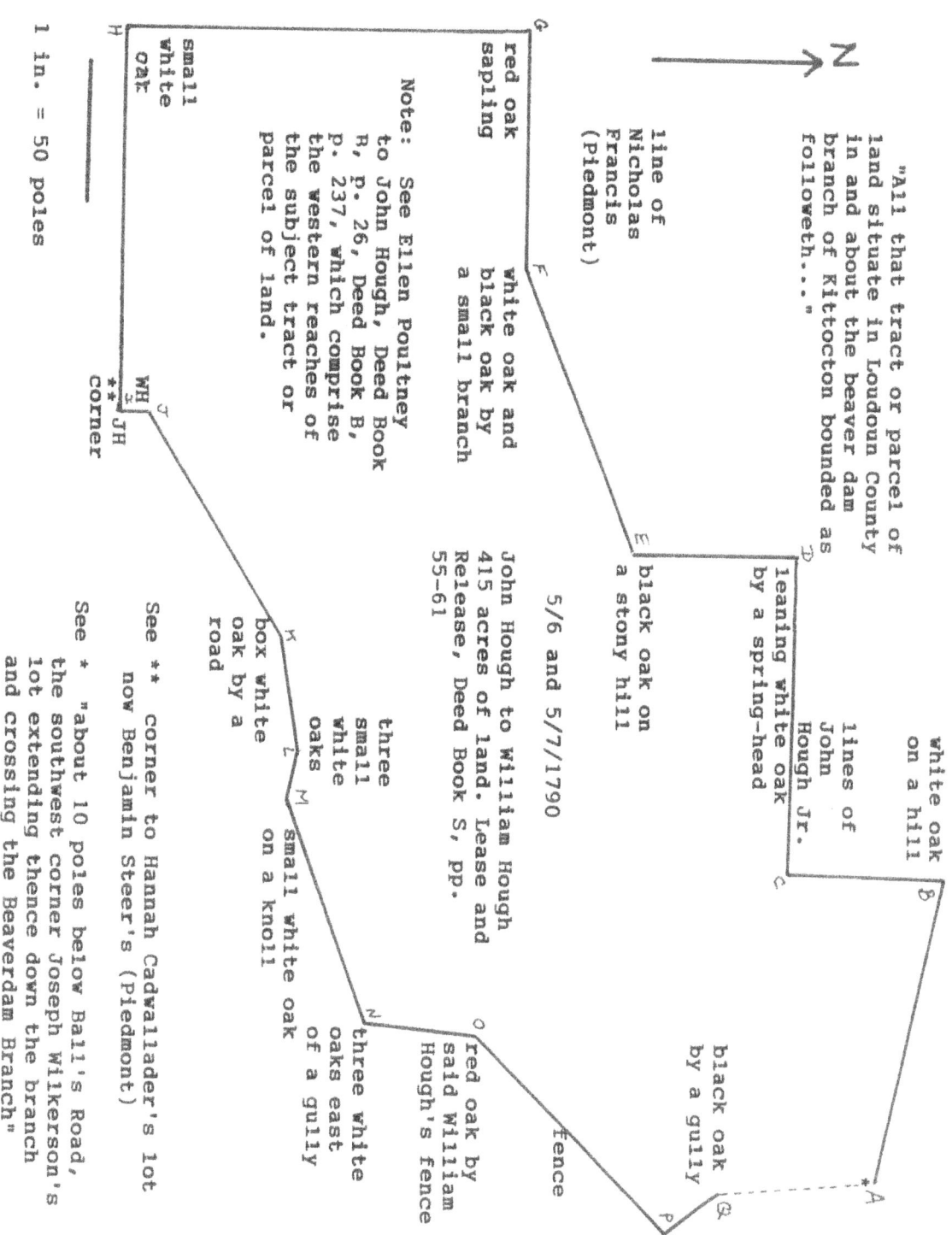

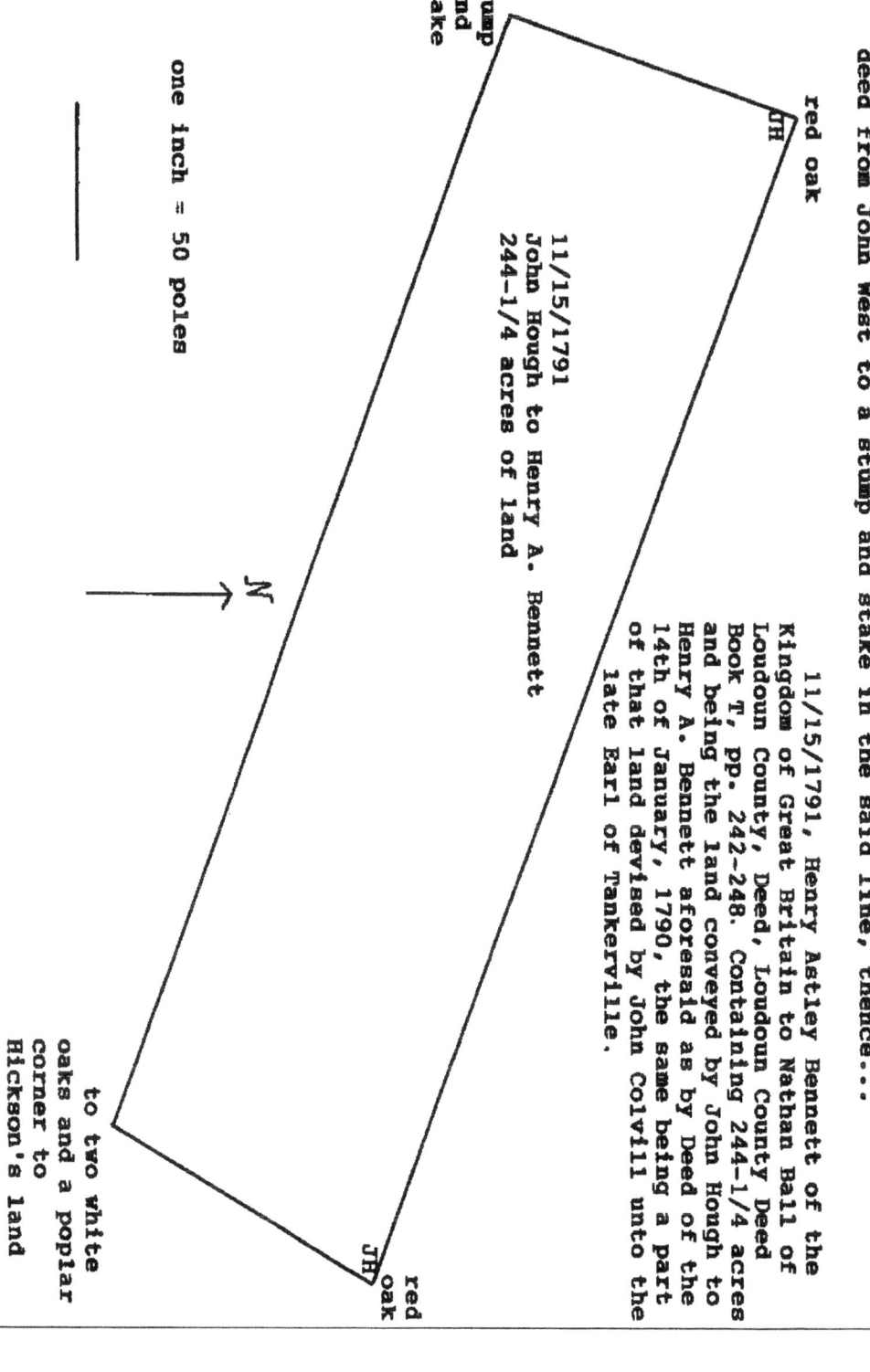

Beginning at a red oak marked JH in the line of Colvill's including patent on the right hand side of the main road leading from Farling Ball's Mill to John Hough's Mill and near the fence and house in the lot of land whereon John Reed now lives running thence S 9-3/4 W 100 poles with the line of Hough's deed from John West to a stump and stake in the said line, thence...

11/15/1791, Henry Astley Bennett of the Kingdom of Great Britain to Nathan Ball of Loudoun County, Deed, Loudoun County Deed Book T, pp. 242-248. Containing 244-1/4 acres and being the land conveyed by John Hough to Henry A. Bennett aforesaid as by Deed of the 14th of January, 1790, the same being a part of that land devised by John Colvill unto the late Earl of Tankerville.

11/15/1791
John Hough to Henry A. Bennett
244-1/4 acres of land

one inch = 50 poles

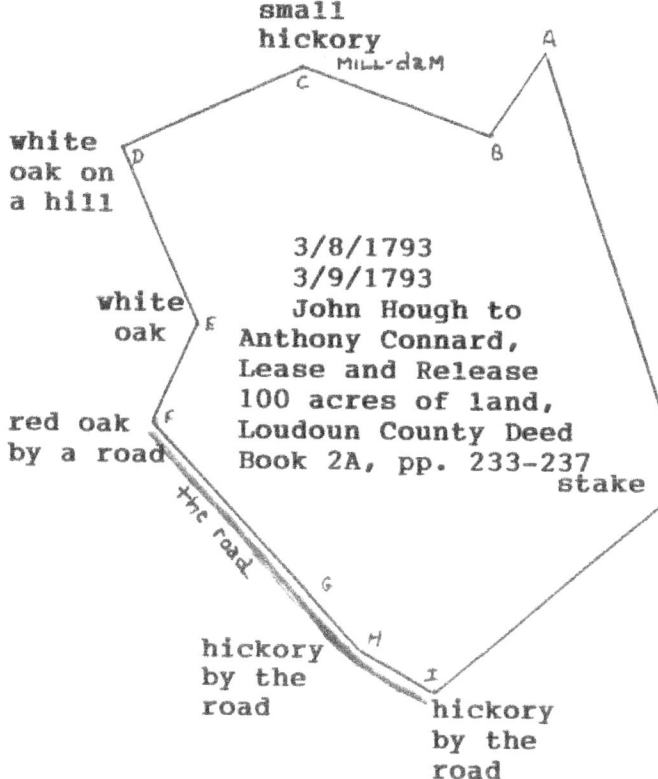

Beginning at a small walnut tree on the south side of the North Fork of Kittoctan Creek below a small spring branch extending thence up the said Creek S 34 W 29 poles by the upper ash and on the south side of the Creek, then crossing the Creek twice N 68 W 32 poles to a small hickory 10 poles S^o W^t of Mill-dam thence...

one inch = 50 poles

Loudoun County, Virginia

one inch = 50 poles

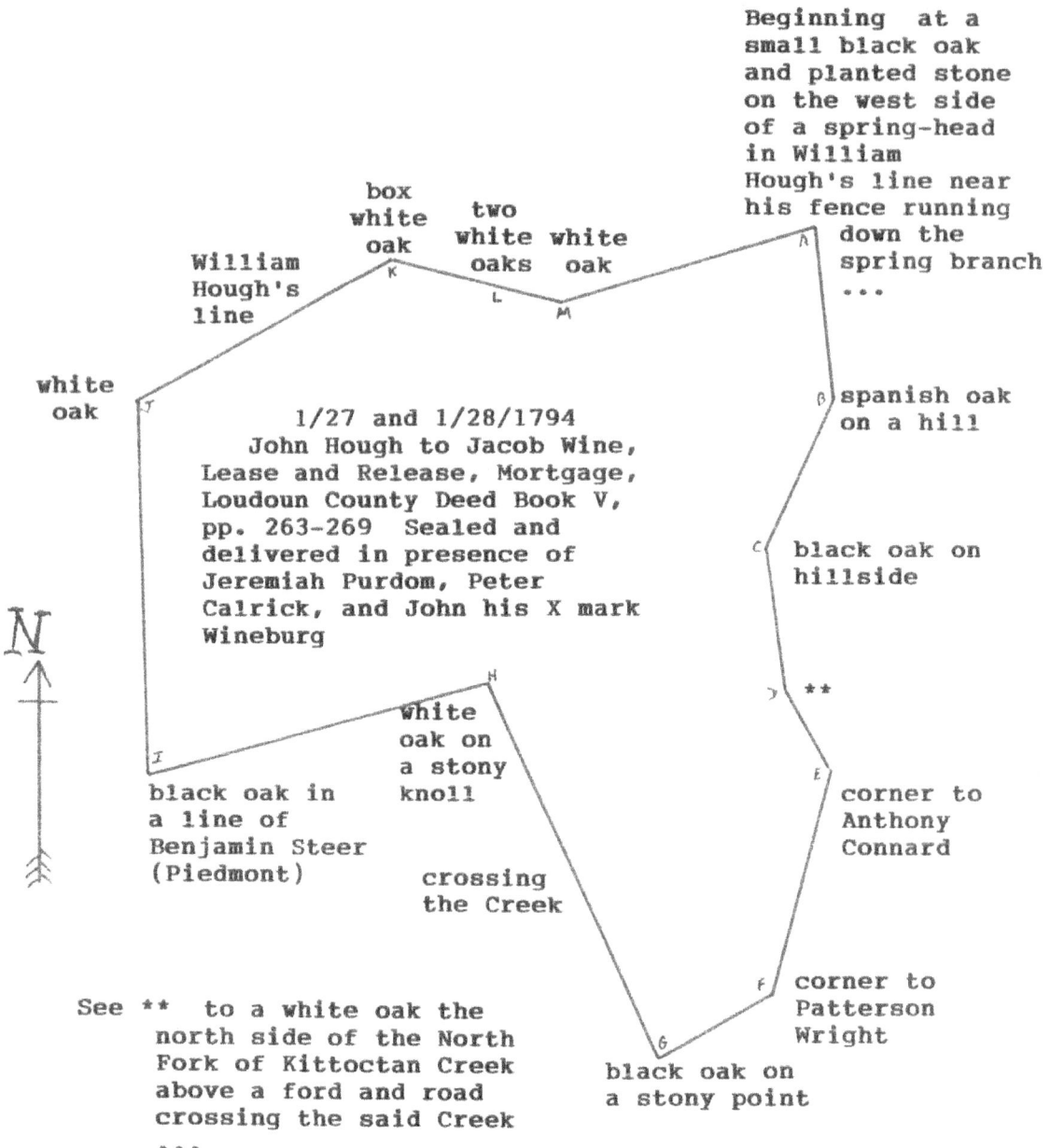

1/7/1795, John Hough of Loudoun County to Patterson Wright of same, 117 Acre-lot, Lease and Release in consideration of 250 pounds Virginia currency, Loudoun County Deed Book V, pp. 478-481, and, 4/7/1803, Ferdinando Fairfax of Jefferson County to Patterson Wright of Loudoun County, 83 3/4 Acre-lot, Bargain and Sale in consideration of $ 1,675, Loudoun County Deed Book 2C, pp. 302-303

*4/8/1799, Patterson Wright of Loudoun County to Anthony Wright of same, 10 Acre-lot, Bill of Sale in consideration of $ 30, Loudoun County Deed Book Z, pp. 154-156

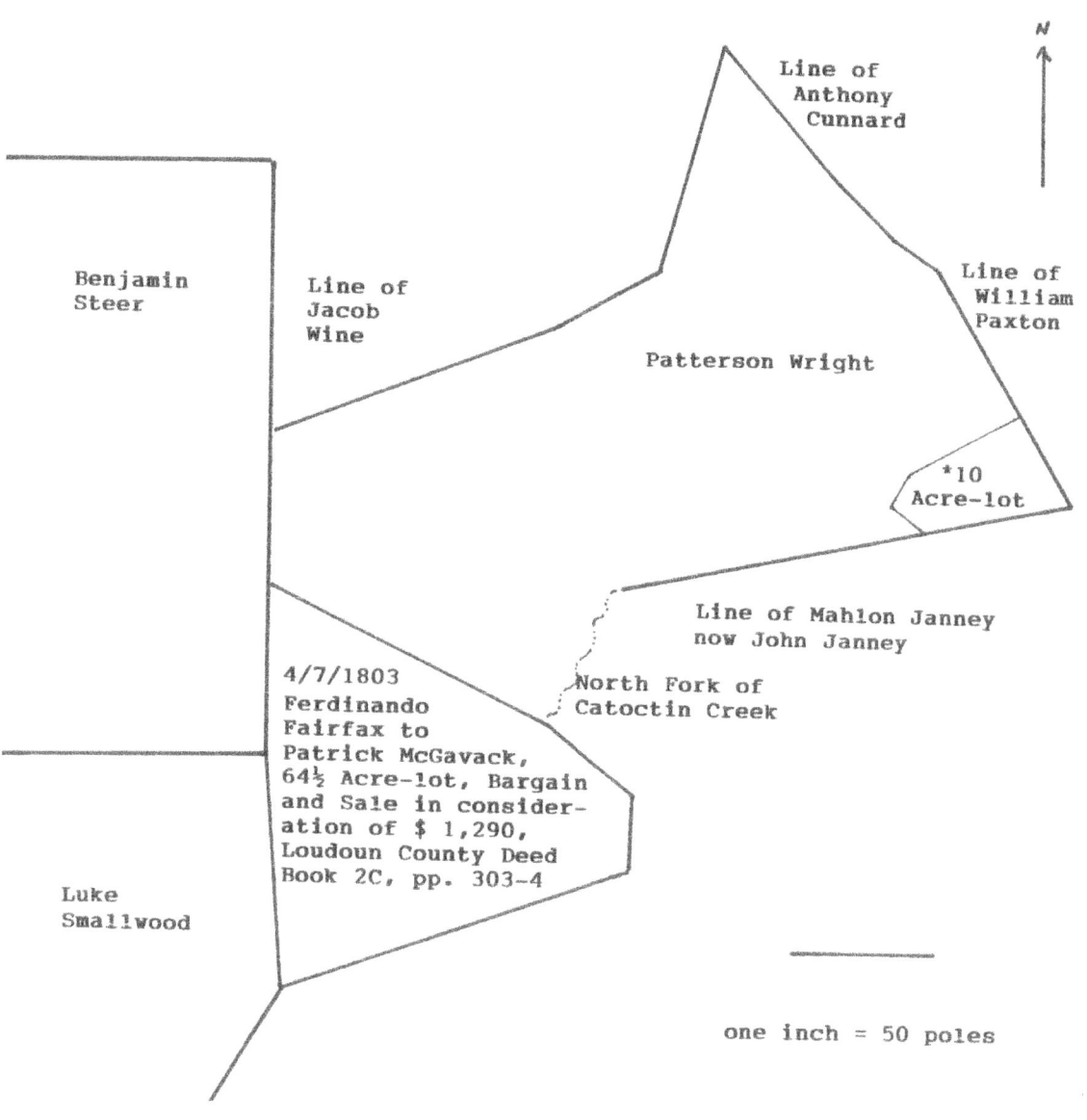

one inch = 50 poles

All that tract or parcel of land lying and being on the waters of Kittoctan Creek bounded as by a survey thereon made by Israel Janney as follows, and containing 142 acres and 13 perches of land

one inch = 50 poles

on the point of a hill, a black oak marked MJ & W extending thence...

black oak

4/8/1799
Mahlon Janney and Sarah his wife to James Moore, Deed, Deed Book Z, pp. 160-2

N ↑

a planted stone in Mahlon Janney's line thence to the beginning

Beginning at a poplar standing on the north side of Kittoctan Creek (South Fork of Catoctin Creek)

poplar

See ** a white oak standing about six poles north of the road leading from Mahlon Janney's Mill to Jonah Thompson's Mill marked MJ

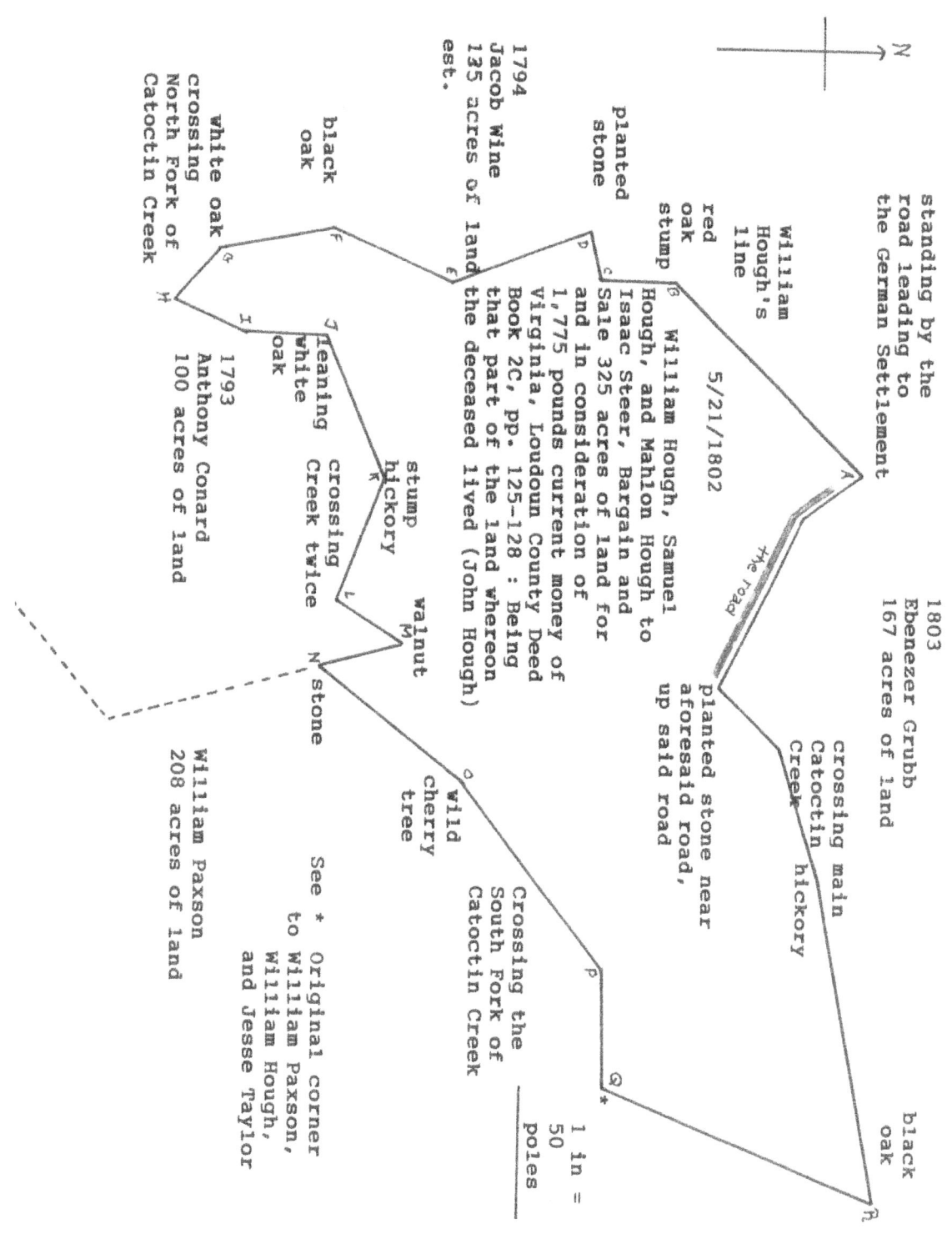

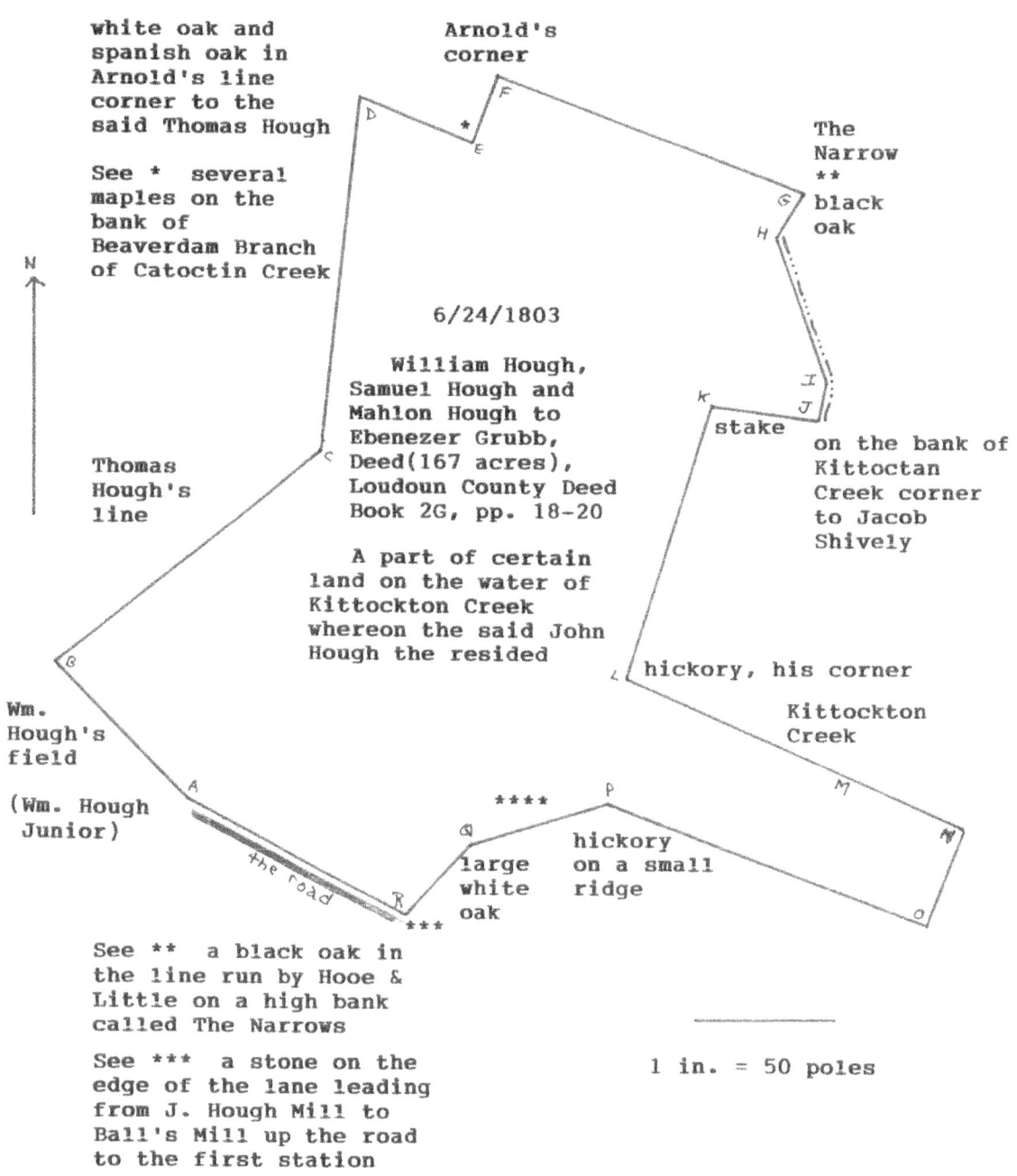

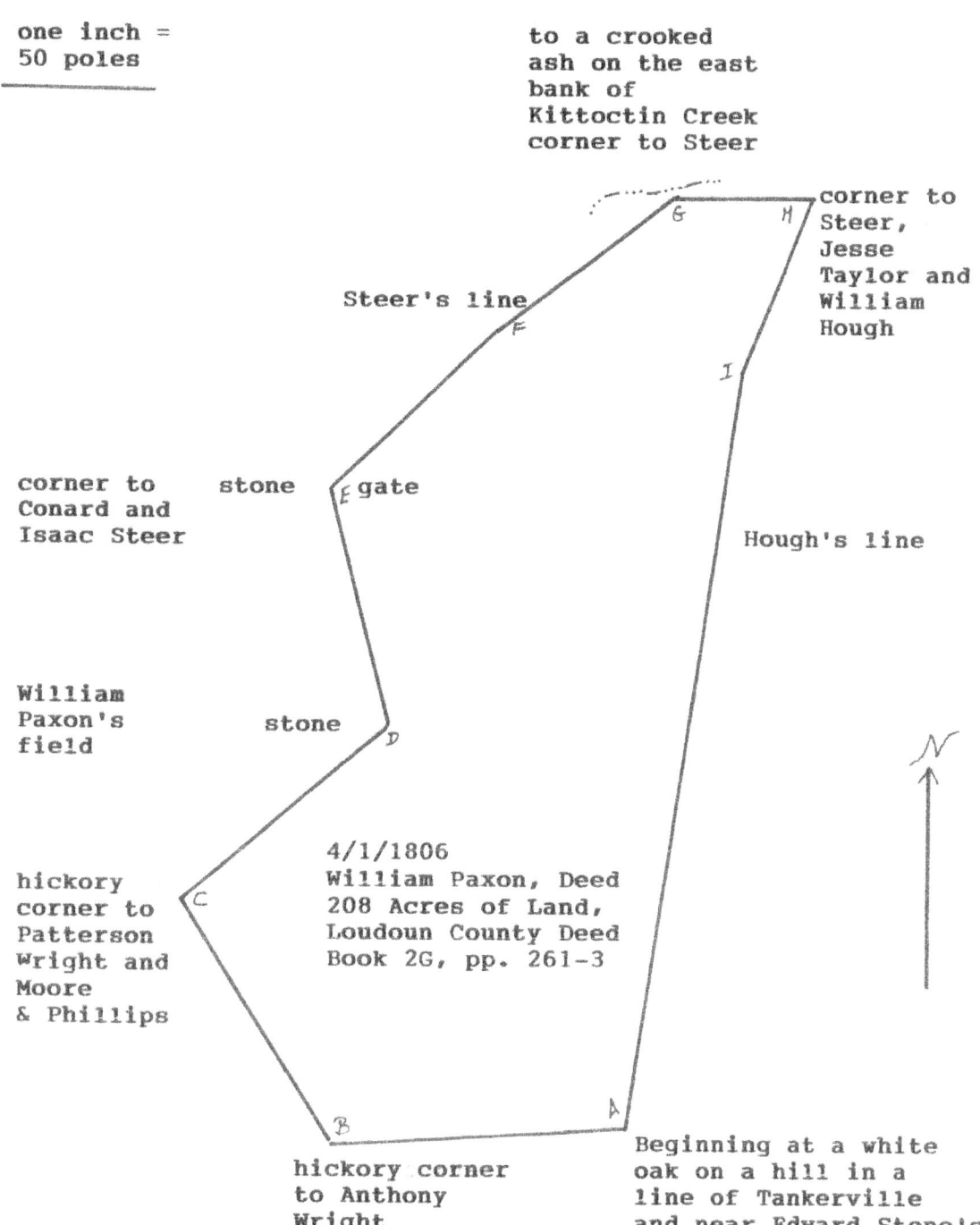

The Earl of Tankerville's Catoctin Manor (circa 1759)

There is a large quantity of land on or about the waters of the Potomac River and the Catoctin Creek up to the Quarter Branch, and Dutchmans Run, which has come to be associated with its one time proprietor in the name of the Earl of Tankerville. Originally, he was being one Charles Bennett, Earl of Tankerville of Newcastle on the River Tyne, Kingdom of Great Britain (d. circa 1762). He had been the principal creditor of John Colvill and as such he would come to possess a large and valuable estate of land and personal property in Virginia including the aforementioned land, which at that time was said to contain about 16,000 acres of land.

In 1759 the Earl nominated and appointed one John Patterson as his attorney in fact over his given lands and personal estate, and thereby lawfully empowered him to transact and execute certain contracts and to enter into and upon, and take possession of all maters and things belonging to John Colvill deceased. Thereafter John Colvill's former Catoctin Tract was transformed into the Catoctin Manor with lots of land for ready lease to farm. These were for the most part unimproved lands situated in remote locations. Most of the bulk of Catoctin Manor was to be found from a point near the Potomac River at Catoctin Creek in a westerly orientation up to the western side of "Little Dutchmans Run," and as far back as Tom's Cabin Branch of the Catoctin Creek. Still another separate section of the rambling Catoctin Manor was situated on or about the South Fork of Catoctin Creek downstream from modern Route 9, which was the site of its Backline.

In his authority as the agent for the Earl of Tankerville, John Patterson traded indentures of lease for lives for land to varied freeholders. There were a total of 14 such lots on or about the waters of Catoctin Creek leased from the Earl of Tankerville by John Patterson amounting to about 1,472 acres of land, which were entered into the records of Loudoun County. Patterson also traded another indenture of lease for lives for a lot on Difficult Run, which at that time was in the jurisdiction of Loudoun County (Fairfax County).

Two of such lots on or about Catoctin Creek leased to William Grant and James Ferguson respectively, were marked with like boundary markers for John Colvill as in JC. Another lot for Adam Count was marked with a marker for the line between Francis Awbrey and John Colvill as in FA & JC, and a marker for Francis Awbrey as in FA. Samuel Coombs's lot was marked with a marker for William Henry Fairfax as in WFX and a marker for Samuel himself as in SC. A neighboring lot of James Hamilton's was marked with a marker for Samuel Coombs as in SC and a marker seemingly for William Fairfax as in WF.

Around the same time, Charles, Earl of Tankerville, died. Bearing date 8/13/1762 the deceased devised unto his two sons, Charles, Earl of Tankerville and Henry Astley Bennett, both of the Kingdom of Great Britain, the aforementioned lands as by the said will of record did more filly appear in the Dumfries District Court. Within a few years after varied difficulties the aforesaid John Patterson was replaced in 1766 by Thomas Colvill of Fairfax County as the attorney, steward and agent for the proprietor. Shortly thereafter the apparently ailing Thomas Colvill (d. 1766) assigned such authority over to George West. Afterwards, formal transactional activities and the use of the appellation Catoctin Manor was brought to an end.

Beginning in the second half of the 1780's, formal transactions of real property resumed at a high rate of frequency on the Catoctin Tract as the records of Loudoun County are replete with deeds and other legal instruments in the names of Henry Astley Bennett Esq. and or Charles, Earl of Tankerville. And, whereas the said Charles, Earl of Tankerville and Henry Astley Bennett mutually agreed to sell the aforesaid lands, they by their letter of attorney dated December 22, 1789 did constitute and appoint Robert Townshend Hooe & Charles Little, their attorneys for them and each of them, to dispose of and convey the lands and estate to which John Colvill deceased had or might have had any right, title or claim. The author has identified a total of about 45 more lease transactions, 75 bargain and sale transactions, 33 mortgage transactions and 3 re-mortgage transactions as above. As a result, the Catoctin Tract was systematically liquidated piece by piece to diverse freeholders.

1. 5/6/1755, **John Colvill** (John Colville), Last Will and Testament, Fairfax County Will Book B, p. 97: Inventory, Fairfax County Will Book B, p. 135, p. 141: Estate Account, Fairfax County Will Book B, p. 395, p. 442, Fairfax County Will Book E, p. 334, p. 280, p. 282

2. 3/5/1759 The Right Honorable **Charles, Earl of Tankerville** of the one part to **John Patterson** of the other part. Power of Attorney, Loudoun County Deed Book C, Part 1, pp. 98-109

3. June 12, 1760, Maryland Gazette, No. 788: **John Patterson**, agent, at Fairfax County, Virginia, has land for rent, property of **Charles, Earl of Tankerville**, lying on **Potomack River and Kittockton Creek**, in Loudoun County, Virginia. Apply to **Patterson** at **William Kirk's** on **Kittockton Creek** or **Andrew Adams**, merchant, in **Leesburg**

4. This indenture made this 24th day of June, in the 34th year of the reign of our sovereign **Lord, George the Second,** by the grace of God of Great Britain, France, and Ireland, King, Defender of the Faith & c., 1760, between **John Patterson Gent**. of Loudoun County in the Colony of Virginia and attorney in fact for Right Honorable **Charles, Earl of Tankerville** of Great Britain of the one part to **William Grant** of the aforesaid County and Colony of Virginia of the other part. Witnesseth that the said **John Patterson** in consideration of the rents and covenants hereinafter reserved and expressed on the part of **William Grant** to be paid and performed, hath demised set and to farm let unto the said **William Grant** his heirs executors and administrators one messuage tenement tract or parcel of land situate lying and being in the said County of Loudoun being part of that tract or parcel of land called and known by the name of **Catocton Manour** and bounded as follows viz. Beginning at a white oak and hickory on the side of the **South Fork of Catoctian Creek** thence S 50° E 215 poles to a white oak on a hill marked **JC,** thence N 50° E 70 poles to the **main road,** thence with the several courses of the said **road** as follows N 22-½° W 46 poles, (thence) N 43° – 15 minutes W 32 poles, (thence) N 62° – 45 minutes 160 poles to the **Backline,** then to the beginning containing 113-½ acres, together with all houses orchards meadows pastures ways woods water and watercourses, and all and singular the liberties profits commodities easements and emoluments thereto belonging or in any wise appertaining except as hereafter is excepted. To have and to hold the

said messuage and tenement of 113-½ acres of land with the appurtenances thereunto belonging or in any wise appertaining all mines minerals and quarries excepted unto the said **William Grant** for and during the natural life of him the said **William Grant** aged 32 years, and for and during the natural life of his wife aged 26 years, and for and during the natural life of his son **John Grant** aged 1 year, to them and every of them longest living from the date hereof, **John Patterson**, Agent. Sealed and delivered in the presence of **John Hough, Flemg. Patterson, Andrew Adam**, and **Evan Williams**. Proven on 9/9/1761. Lease for Lives, Loudoun County Deed Book B, pp. 342-346

5. This indenture made this 24th day of June, in the 34th year of the reign of our sovereign **Lord, George the Second,** by the grace of God of Great Britain, France, and Ireland, King, Defender of the Faith & c., 1760, between **John Patterson Gent.** of Loudoun County in the Colony of Virginia and attorney in fact for the Right Honorable **Charles, Earl of Tankerville** of Great Britain of the one part to **Samuel Coombs (Combs)** of the aforesaid County and Colony of Virginia, farmer, of the other part. Witnesseth that the said **John Patterson** in consideration of the rents and covenants hereinafter reserved and expressed on the part of the said **Samuel Coombs** to be paid and performed hath demised set and farm let unto the said **Samuel Coombs** his heirs executors administrators one messuage tenement tract or parcel of land situate lying and being in the County of Loudoun aforesaid, being part of that tract or parcel of land called and known by the name of **Catoctian Manour** and bounded as followeth viz. Beginning at a stake in the **Backline** of **Catoctian Creek** lower corner to the said **John Patterson's Reserve** thence S 56° E 206 poles to two white oaks marked **WFX,** thence N 50° E 99 poles to a stake near a white oak marked **SC**, thence N 56° W 240 poles to a small hickory in the **Backline**, thence with the said back line to the beginning containing 150 acres, together with all houses orchards meadows pastures ways woods water and watercourses, and all and singular the liberties profits commodities easements and emoluments thereto belonging or in any wise appertaining except as hereafter is excepted. To have and to hold the said messuage and tenement of 150 acres of land with the appurtenances thereunto belonging or in any wise appertaining all mines minerals and quarries excepted unto the said **Samuel Coombs** for and during the natural life of **Samuel Coombs** aged 32 years, and for and during the natural life of his wife **Mary Coombs** aged 27 years, and for and during the natural life of his son **Samuel** aged 1 year, to them and every of them longest living from date hereof, **John Patterson**, Agent. Sealed and delivered in the presence of **George West, James Ferguson, Samuel Schooley**, and **Fleming Patterson**. Proven on 9/9/1761. Lease for Lives, Loudoun County Deed Book B, pp. 346-350.

6. This indenture made the 20th day of November, in the 34th year of the reign of our sovereign **Lord, George the Second,** by the grace of God of Great Britain, France and Ireland, King, Defender of the Faith & c., 1760, between **John Patterson** Gent. of Loudoun County in the Colony of Virginia and attorney in fact for the Right Honorable **Charles, Earl of Tankerville** of Great Britain of the one part to **William Braddock** of the aforesaid County and Colony of Virginia, farmer, of the other part. Witnesseth that the said **John Patterson** in

consideration of the rents and covenants hereinafter reserved and expressed on the part of the said **William Braddock** to be paid and performed hath demised set and to farm let unto the said **William Braddock** his heirs executors and administrators one messuage tenement tract or parcel of land situate lying and being in the County of Loudoun aforesaid, being part of that tract or parcel of land situate lying and being in the County of Loudoun aforesaid being part of that tract of parcel of land called and known by the name of **Catoctian Manour** and bounded as followeth viz. Beginning at a white oak and dogwood corner to **Ralph Braddock** thence S 31° W 140 poles to a hickory and red oak, thence N 59° W 114 poles to a stake near a red and white oak, thence N 31° E 140 poles to two red oaks and a white oak sapling, thence to the beginning containing 100 acres of land, together with all houses orchards meadows pastures ways woods water and watercourses, and all and singular the liberties profits commodities and emoluments thereto belonging or in any wise appertaining except as hereafter excepted. To have and to hold the said messuage and tenement of 100 acres of land with the appurtenances thereunto belonging or in any wise appertaining all mines minerals and quarries excepted unto the said **William Braddock** for and during the natural life of him the said **William Braddock** aged 25 years, and for and during the natural life of his wife **Mary Braddock** aged 30 years, and for and during the natural life of his daughter **Prudence Braddock** aged 1 year, to them and every of them longest living from the date hereof, **John Patterson**, Agent. Sealed and delivered in the presence of **John Hough**, **Fleming Patterson**, **Andrew Adam**, and **Evan Williams**. Proven on 9/9/1761. Lease for Lives, Loudoun County Deed Book B, pp. 350-355

7. This indenture made this 24th day of April, in the first year of the reign of our sovereign **Lord, George the Third,** by the grace of God of Great Britain, France and Ireland, King, Defender of the Faith & c., 1761, between **John Patterson Gent**. of Loudoun County and Colony of Virginia and attorney in fact for the Right Honorable **Charles, Earl of Tankerville** of Great Britain of the one part to **James Ferguson** of the aforesaid County and Colony of Virginia, farmer, of the other part. Witnesseth that the said **John Patterson** in consideration of the rents and covenants hereinafter reserved and expressed on the part of the said **James Ferguson** to be paid and performed hath demised set and to farm let unto the said **James Ferguson** his heirs executors and administrators one messuage tenement tract or parcel of land situate lying and being in the County of Loudoun aforesaid, being part of that tract or parcel of land called and known by the name of **Catoctian Manour** and bounded as followeth viz. Beginning at a stake on the north side of **Broad Run** thence N 20-½° E 82 poles to two small red oaks marked **JC,** thence N 16° W 102 poles to a white oak, thence East 104 poles to two red oaks and hickory on a stony hill, thence South 164 poles to a red oak on the said **Broad Run,** thence the several meanders thereof to the beginning containing 100 acres, together with all houses orchards meadows pastures ways woods water and watercourses, and all and singular the liberties profits commodities easements and emoluments thereunto belonging or in any wise appertaining except as hereafter excepted. To have and to hold the said messuage and tenement of 100 acres of land with the appurtenances thereunto belonging or

in any wise appertaining all mines minerals and quarries excepted unto the said **James Ferguson** for and during the natural life of him the said **James Ferguson** aged 32 years, and for and during the natural life of his wife **Margaret Ferguson** aged 28 years, and for and during the natural life of his daughter **Auzabah Ferguson** aged 7 years, to them and every of them longest living from the date hereof, **John Patterson**, Agent. Sealed and delivered in the presence of **George West, Samuel Schooley, Flemg. Patterson** and **Saml. Coombs**. Proven on 9/9/1761. Lease for Lives, Loudoun County Deed Book B, pp. 355-359

8.   This indenture made this 24th day of April, in the first year of the reign of our sovereign **Lord, George the Third,** by the grace of God of Great Britain, France, and Ireland, King, Defender of the Faith & c., between **John Patterson, Gent**. of Loudoun County in the Colony of Virginia and attorney in fact for the Right Honorable **Charles, Earl of Tankerville** of Great Britain of the one part to **Samuel Schooley** of the aforesaid County in the Colony of Virginia, farmer, of the other part. Witnesseth that the said **John Patterson** in consideration of the rents and covenants hereinafter expressed on the part of the said **Samuel Schooley** to be paid and performed hath demised set and to farm let unto the said **Samuel Schooley** his heirs executors and administrators one messuage tenement tract or parcel of land situate lying and being in the County of Loudoun aforesaid, being part of that tract or parcel of land called and known by the name **Catactian Manour** and bounded as followeth viz. Beginning at a thorn bush on the side of **Broad Run** thence North 173 poles to a red oak sapling, thence East 88 poles to a black oak on the side of a hill, thence South 60 poles, thence S 70° E 11 poles to a white oak on the side of the said Run, thence up the several meanders thereof to the beginning containing by estimation 100 acres, together with all houses orchards meadows pastures ways woods water and watercourses, and all and singular the liberties profits commodities easements and emoluments thereunto belonging except as hereafter excepted. To have and to hold the said messuage and tenement of 100 acres of land with the appurtenances thereunto belonging or in any wise appertaining all mines quarries and minerals excepted unto the said **Samuel Schooley** for and during the natural life of **Garret Albertson** aged 24 years, and for and during the natural life of **William Schooley** aged 5 years, and for and during the natural life of **Nicholas Schooley** aged 1 year, and for and during the life of the longest liver of them from the date hereof, **John Patterson**, Agent. Sealed and delivered in the presence of **Fleming Patterson, George West, James Ferguson**, and **Samuel Coombs**. Proven on 9/9/1761. Lease for Lives, Loudoun County Deed Book C, pp. 5-10

9.   This indenture made this 24th day of April, in the first year of the reign of our sovereign **Lord, George the Third,** by the grace of God of Great Britain, France, and Ireland, King, Defender of the Faith & c., between **John Patterson, Gent**. of Loudoun County in the Colony of Virginia and attorney in fact for the Right Honorable **Charles, Earl of Tankerville** of Great Britain of the one part to **Samuel Schooley** of the aforesaid County and Colony of Virginia, farmer, of the other part. Witnesseth that the said **John Patterson** in consideration of the rents and covenants hereinafter reserved and expressed on the part of the said **Samuel Schooley** to be paid and performed hath demised set and to farm let unto the said

Samuel Schooley his heirs executors and administrators one messuage tenement tract or parcel of land situate lying and being in the County of Loudoun aforesaid being part of that tract or parcel of land called and known by the name **Catactian Manour** and bounded as followeth viz. Beginning at a red oak on **Broad Run** lower corner to **James Ferguson** thence North 164 poles to two red oaks a white oak and hickory, thence East 97 poles to a black oak sapling, thence South 173 poles to a thorn bush on the side of the said Run, thence up the meanders thereof to the beginning containing 100 acres, together with all houses orchards meadows pastures ways woods waters and watercourses, and all and singular the liberties profits commodities easements and emoluments thereunto belonging or in any wise appertaining except as hereafter excepted. To have and to hold the said messuage and tenement of 100 acres of land with the appurtenances thereunto belonging or in any wise appertaining all mines quarries and minerals excepted unto the said **Samuel Schooley** for and during the natural life of him the said **Samuel Schooley** aged 32 years, and for and during the natural life of his wife **Dorothy Schooley** aged 24, and for and during the natural life of his son **Garret Schooley** aged 3 years, to them and every of them longest living from the date hereof, **John Patterson**, Agent. Sealed and delivered in the presence of **George West, Samuel Coombs, James Ferguson,** and **Fleming Patterson**. Proven on 9/9/1761. Lease for Lives, Loudoun County Deed Book C, pp. 10-14

10. This indenture made this 8th day of April, in the second year of the reign of our sovereign **Lord, George the Third,** by the grace of God of Great Britain, France and Ireland, King, Defender of the Faith & c., 1762, between **John Patterson Gent**. of Loudoun County in the Colony of Virginia and attorney in fact for the Right Honorable **Charles, Earl of Tankerville** of Great Britain of the one part to **David Foxal** of the aforesaid County and Colony of Virginia, farmer, of the other part. Witnesseth that the said **John Patterson** in consideration of the rents and covenants hereinafter reserved and expressed on the part of the said **David Foxal** to be paid and performed hath demised set and to farm let unto the said **David Foxal** his heirs executors and administrator one messuage tenement tract or parcel of land situate lying and being in the County of Loudoun aforesaid, being part of that tract or parcel of land called and known by the name of **Catoctain Manour** and bounded as followeth viz. Beginning at A, a corner to **Adam Counts** lot thence S 31° E 106 poles to O, two white oaks in a drain, thence N 53-½° E 158 poles to P, two white oaks in a glade, thence N 37° W 106 poles to E, also a corner to **Adam Counts lot**, thence with his line S 53-½° W 149 poles to the beginning containing 100 acres of land, together with all houses orchards meadows pastures ways woods water and watercourses, and all and singular the liberties profits commodities easements and emoluments thereunto belonging or in any wise appertaining except as hereafter excepted. To have and to hold the said messuage and tenement of 100 acres of land with the appurtenances thereunto belonging or in any wise appertaining all mines minerals and quarries excepted unto the said **David Foxal** for and during the natural life of him the said **David Foxal** aged 27 years, and for and during the natural life of his wife **Elizabeth Foxal** aged 24 years, and for and during the natural life of **Catharine Foxal** their daughter aged 4 years, to them and every of them longest

living from the date hereof, **John Patterson**, Agent. Sealed and delivered in the presence of **Henry Graham, M. Armstrong, Saml. Mead** and **Archd. Crawford**. Proven on 6/8/1762. Lease for Lives, Loudoun County Deed Book C, Part 1, pp. 297-302.

11. This indenture made this 8th day of April, in the second year of the reign of our sovereign **Lord, George the Third,** by the grace of God of Great Britain, France and Ireland, King, Defender of the Faith & c., 1762, between **John Patterson, Gent.** of Loudoun County and the Colony of Virginia and attorney in fact for the Right Honorable **Charles, Earl of Tankerville** of Great Britain of the one part to **Joseph Teel** of the aforesaid County and Colony of Virginia, farmer, of the other part. Witnesseth that the said **John Patterson** in consideration of the rents and covenants hereinafter reserved and expressed on the part of the said **Joseph Teel** to be paid and performed hath demised set and to farm let unto the said **Joseph Teel** his heirs executors and administrators one messuage tenement tract or parcel of land situate lying and being in the County of Loudoun aforesaid, being part of that tract or parcel of land called and known by the name of **Catoctain Manour** and bounded as followeth viz. Beginning at K, two white oaks thence N 46° W 16 poles to J, several saplings, thence N 53-½° E 175 poles to three white oaks in a small drain, thence S 37° E 88 poles to G, a corner to **Joseph Teel Junior's lot**, thence with his line S 53-½° W 197 poles to F, also a corner to **Joseph Teel Junior's lot**, thence N 35° W 27 poles to L, eight white oaks and a gum, thence N 11° W 40 poles to the beginning containing 100 acres of land, together with all houses orchards meadows pastures ways woods water and watercourses, and all and singular the liberties profits commodities easements and emoluments thereunto belonging or in any wise appertaining all mines minerals and quarries excepted unto the said **Joseph Teel** for and during the natural life of him the said **Joseph Teel** aged 62 years, and for and during the natural life of his son **Henry Teel** aged 13 years, and for and during the natural life of his daughter **Mary Teel** aged 16 years, to them and every of them longest living from the date hereof, **John Patterson**, Agent. Sealed and delivered in the presence of **Archd. Crawford, Henry Graham, M. Armstrong,** and **Saml. Mead**. Proven on 6/8/1762. Lease for Lives, Loudoun County Deed Book C, Part 1, pp. 302-307

12. This indenture made this 8th day of April, 1762 in the second year of the reign of our sovereign **Lord, George the Third,** by the grace of God of Great Britain, France and Ireland, King, Defender of the Faith & c., 1762, between **John Patterson Gent.** of Loudoun County and Colony of Virginia and attorney in fact for **Charles, Earl of Tankerville** of Great Britain of the one part to **Joseph Teel Jr.** of Loudoun County of the other part. Witnesseth that the said **John Patterson** in consideration of the rents and covenants hereinafter reserved and expressed on the part of the said **Joseph Teel Jr.** to be paid and performed hath demised set and to farm let unto the said **Joseph Teel Jr.** his heirs executors and administrators one messuage tenement tract or parcel of land situate lying and being in the County of Loudoun aforesaid, being part of that tract or parcel of land called and known by the name of **Catoctain Manour** and bounded as followeth viz. Beginning at C, a corner to **Adam Counts** lot thence N 35° W 80 poles to F,

a stake and several sapling, thence N 53-½° E 200 poles to G, a stake and several saplings, thence S 37° E 80 poles to D, also corner to **Adam Counts**, thence S 53-½° W 200 poles to the beginning containing 100 acres of land, together with all houses orchards meadows pastures ways woods water and watercourses, and all and singular the liberties profits commodities easements ad emoluments thereunto belonging or in any wise appertaining except as hereafter excepted. To have and to hold the said messuage and tenement of 100 acres of land with the appurtenances thereunto belonging or in any wise appertaining all mines minerals and quarries excepted unto the said **Joseph Teel Jr.** aged 28, and for and during the natural life of **Peter Teel** his brother aged 14, and for and during the natural life of **George** his brother aged 5 years, to them and every of them longest living from the date hereof, **John Patterson**, Agent. Sealed and delivered in the presence of **Archd. Crawford, Henry Graham, M. Armstrong**, and **Saml. Mead**. Proven on 6/8/1762. Lease for Lives, Loudoun County Deed Book C, Part 1, pp. 307-312

13. This indenture made this 13th day of May, in the second year of the reign of our **Lord, George the Third,** by the grace of God of Great Britain, France and Ireland, King, Defender if the Faith & c., 1762, between **John Patterson Gent**. of Loudoun County and the Colony of Virginia and attorney in fact for the Right Honorable **Charles, Earl of Tankerville** of Great Britain of the one part to **Henry O'Daniel** of the County aforesaid and the Colony of Virginia, farmer, of the other part. Witnesseth that the said **John Patterson** in consideration of the rents and covenants hereinafter reserved and expressed on the part of the said **Henry O'Daniel** to be paid and performed hath demised set and to farm let unto the said **Henry O'Daniel** his heirs executors and administrators one messuage tenement tract or parcel of land situate lying and being in the County of Loudoun aforesaid, being part of that tract or parcel of land called and known by the name of **Catoctian Manour** and bounded as followeth viz. Beginning on the line of the patent between the **South Fork** and the **North Fork of Catoctin Creek** at A, a white oak standing in a drain near a branch, thence S 42° W 160 poles to B, a stake standing between two red oaks, thence S 48° E 100 poles to C, a hickory and red oak sapling, thence S 42° W 160 poles to D, two hickory saplings and one red oak standing in the line of the patent, thence along said line N 4-½° W 100 poles to the beginning containing 100 acres of land, together with all houses orchards meadows pastures, ways, woods, water and watercourses, and all and singular the liberties profits commodities easements and emoluments thereunto belonging or in any wise appertaining except as hereafter excepted. To have and to hold the said messuage and tenement of 100 acres of land with the appurtenances thereunto belonging or in any wise appertaining all mines minerals and quarries excepted unto the said **Henry O'Daniel** for and during the natural life of him the said **Henry O'Daniel** aged 48 years, and for and during the natural life of his wife **Mary** aged 34, and for and during the natural life of his son **Charles** aged 8 years, to them and every of them longest living from the date hereof, John Patterson, Agent. Sealed and delivered in the presence of **Henry Graham, F.Ellzey, Abraham Dawson, John Urquhart**. Proven on 6/8/1762. Lease for Lives, Loudoun County Deed Book C, Part 1, pp. 287-292

14. This indenture made this 24th day of May in the second year of the reign of our sovereign **Lord, George the Third,** by the grace of God of Great Britain, France and Ireland, King, Defender of the Faith & c., 1762, between **John Patterson Gent.** of Loudoun County and the Colony of Virginia, and attorney in fact for the Right Honorable **Charles, Earl of Tankerville** of Great Britain of the one part to **James Hamilton** of the County aforesaid and the Colony of Virginia, framer, of the other part. Witnesseth that the said **John Patterson** in consideration of the rents and covenants hereinafter reserved and expressed on the part of the said **James Hamilton** to be paid and performed hath demised set and to farm let unto the said **James Hamilton** his heirs executors and administrators one messuage tenement tract or parcel of land situate lying and being in the County of Loudoun aforesaid, being part of that tract or parcel of land situate lying and being in the County of Loudoun aforesaid being part of that tract or parcel of land called and known by the name of **Catoctain Manour** and bounded as followeth viz. Beginning at A, a stake near two black oaks corner to **William Henderson's** lot, thence S 47° - 15 minutes W 90 poles to B, a stake near several saplings, thence S 43° E 151 poles to C, a stake near **Samuel Combs** corner white oak marked **SC**, thence the lines and binding therewith S 50° W 104 poles to D, two white oaks marked **WF**, thence N 65° E 109 poles to F, a stake near an ash and black oak near a branch standing in the line of the patent, thence N 47° – 15 minutes E 90 poles to F, a stake between two white oaks also in the line of the patent, thence N 43° E 178 poles to the beginning containing 109 acres and 13 perches of land, together with all houses orchards meadows pastures ways water and watercourses, and all and singular the liberties profits commodities easements and emoluments thereunto belonging or in any wise appertaining except as hereafter excepted. To have and to hold the said messuage and tenement of 109 acres and 13 perches of land with the appurtenances thereunto belonging unto the said **James Hamilton** for and during the natural life of the said **James Hamilton** aged 42, and for and during the natural life of his wife **Priscilla** aged 49, and for and during the natural life of **Aneas Campbell Jr.** aged 4 years, to them and every of them the longest living from the date hereof, **John Patterson**, Agent. Sealed and delivered in the presence of **Henry Graham, F. Ellzey, Henry O'Daniel**, and **Joseph Colvill** (?). Proven on 6/8/1762. Lease for Lives, Loudoun County Deed Book C, Part 1, pp. 277-282

15. This indenture made this 4th day of June in the second year of the reign of our sovereign **Lord, George the Third,** by the grace of God of Great Britain, France and Ireland, King, Defender of the Faith & c., 1762, between **John Patterson Gent.** of Loudoun County and the Colony of Virginia and attorney in fact for **Charles, Earl of Tankerville** of Great Britain of the one part to **Adam Count (Counts)** of the aforesaid County and Colony of Virginia, farmer, of the other part. Witnesseth that the said **John Patterson** in consideration of the rents and covenants hereinafter reserved and expressed on the part of the said **Adam Count** to be paid and performed hath demised set and to farm let unto the said **Adam Count** his heirs executors and administrators one messuage tenement tract or parcel of land situate lying and being in the County of Loudoun aforesaid, being part of that tract or parcel of land called and known as **Catoctain Manour**

and bounded as followeth viz. Beginning at A, a white oak marked **FA** and **JC** thence S 86° W 64 poles to B, a black oak marked **FA**, thence N 35° W 50 poles to C, a stake, thence N 53-¼° E 200 poles to D, two white oaks, thence S 37° E 83 poles to E, a black oak, thence S 53-½° W 149 poles to the beginning containing 100 acres of land, together with all houses orchards meadows pastures ways woods water and watercourses, and all and singular the liberties profits commodities and emoluments thereto belonging or in any wise appertaining except as hereafter excepted. To have and to hold the said messuage and tenement of 100 acres of land with the appurtenances thereunto belonging or in any wise appertaining mines minerals and quarries excepted unto the said **Adam Count** for and during the natural life of him the said **Adam Count** aged 20 years, and for and during the life of his wife **Mary Count** aged 20 years, and for and during the natural life of his son **David Count** aged one year, and every of them the longest living from date hereof, **John Patterson**, Agent. Sealed and delivered in the presence of **M. Armstrong, Samuel Mead, Henry Graham**, and **Archd. Crawford**. Lease for Lives, Loudoun County Deed Book C, pp. 272-276

16.   This indenture made this 4th day of June, in the second year of the reign of our sovereign **Lord, George the Third,** by the grace of God of Great Britain, France and Ireland, King, Defender of the Faith & c., 1762, between **John Patterson Gent**. of Loudoun County and the Colony of Virginia and attorney in fact for the Right Honorable **Charles, Earl of Tankerville** of Great Britain of the one part to **Henry Count (Counts)** of the County aforesaid and the Colony of Virginia, farmer, of the other part. Witnesseth that the said **John Patterson** in consideration of the rents and covenants hereinafter reserved and expressed on the part of the said **Henry Count** to be paid and performed hath demised set and to farm let unto the said **Henry Count** his heirs executors and administrators one messuage tenement tract or parcel of land situate lying and being in the County of Loudoun aforesaid, being part of that tract or parcel of land called and known by the name of **Catoctain Manour** and bounded as followeth viz. Beginning at J, a corner to **Joseph Teil's lot** thence N 53-½° E 175 poles to H, also corner to **Joseph Teil**, thence N 37° W 105 poles to M, a stake, thence S 43-½° W 190 poles to N, two white oaks, thence S 46° E 88 poles to the beginning containing 100 acres of land, together with all houses, orchards, meadows, pastures, ways, woods, water and watercourses, and all and singular the liberties profits commodities easements and emoluments thereunto belonging or in any wise appertaining except as hereafter excepted. To have and to hold the said messuage and tenement of 100 acres of land with the appurtenances thereunto belonging or in any wise appertaining unto the said **Henry Count** for and during the life of the said **Henry Count** aged 27, and for and during the natural life of **Kathrine** his wife aged 20, and for and during the natural life of **Salamy Count** their daughter aged 3 years, to them and every of them longest living from the date hereof, **John Patterson**, Agent. Sealed and delivered in the presence of **Martin Armstrong, Samuel Mead, Henry Graham**, and **Archd. Crawford**. Proven on 6/8/1762. Loudoun County, farmer, of the other part, a certain 100 acres lot of land, Lease for Lives, Loudoun County Deed Book C, pp. 282-287

17.	This indenture made this 4th day of June, in the second year of the reign of our **Lord, George the Third,** by the grace of God of Great Britain, France and Ireland, King, Defender of the Faith & c., 1762, between **John Patterson Gent.** of Loudoun County and the Colony of Virginia and attorney in fact for the Right Honorable **Charles, Earl of Tankerville** of Great Britain of the one part to **William Henderson** of the aforesaid County and Colony of Virginia, farmer, of the other part. Witnesseth that the said **John Patterson** in consideration of the rents and covenants hereinafter reserved and expressed on the part of the said **William Henderson** to be paid and performed hath demised set and to farm let unto the said **William Henderson** his heirs executors administrators one messuage tenement tract or parcel of land situate lying and being in the County of Loudoun aforesaid, being part of that tract or parcel of land called and known by the name of **Catoctain Manour** and bounded as followeth viz. Beginning at O, a hickory (and) red oak corner to **McFarlan's** lot thence S 47° – 15 minutes W 53 poles to P, a stake near two black oaks, thence S 43° E 178 poles to G, a stake between two white oaks in the line of the patent, thence with the said line N 47° 15 minutes E 144 poles to H, a red oak stump, thence N 43° W 70 poles to W, a red oak, thence S 47° - 15 minutes W 91 poles to X, a red oak, thence N 43° W 102 poles to the beginning containing 100 acres of land, and all and singular the liberties profits commodities easements and emoluments thereunto belonging or in any wise appertaining except as hereafter excepted. To have and to hold the said messuage and tenement of 100 acres of land with the appurtenances thereunto belonging or in any wise appertaining all mines minerals and quarries excepted unto the said **William Henderson** for and during the natural life of him the said **William Henderson** aged 26 years, and **Kathrine** his wife aged 21 years, and **Mathew** their daughter aged 1 year, and every of them longest living from the date hereof, **John Patterson**, Agent. Proven on 6/8/1762. Lease for Lives, Loudoun County Deed Book C, Part 1, pp. 292-297.

18.	1/7/1766, The Right Honorable **Charles, Earl of Tankerville** of the one part to **Thomas Colvill** of the other part, Power of Attorney, Proven on 6/9/1766. Loudoun County Deed Book E, pp. 31-48

19.	To all persons whom it may concern. Know ye that I **Thomas Colvill**, Agent for the Rt. Honble. **Charles, Earl of Tankerville** in Virginia by virtue of a Power of Attorney duly recorded in the County Court of Loudoun, among other things empowering me to ask demand and recover from all persons who are indebted to the said **Earl** for rents and arrearages of rents or otherwise in the Colony, and further giving me full power to nominate and appoint any person I shall think fit to act in my stead in behalf of him the said **Earl of Tankerville**. Know ye that by virtue of the said power of attorney I do hereby appoint **George West** to demand and receive from all tenants of the said **Earl** seated in the said County of Loudoun their several rents and arrearages of rents now due from them at this present date, and I do empower him the said **George West** to give receipts and acquitances for the same under his hand, which shall be good and sufficient as if I myself had signed the same against the said **Lord Tankerville** and any other person or persons whatsoever. In witness whereof I have hereunto set my hand and seal the day and year first above written, **Thos. Colvill**. Sealed and delivered in the presence of **William Crawford**, and **William Templeman**. Proven on 8/11/1766. Power of Attorney, Loudoun County Deed Book E, pp. 115-116

20. 10/8/1766, **Thomas Colville (Thomas Colvill)**, Last Will and Testament, Fairfax County Will Book B, p. 424: Inventory, Fairfax County Will Book C, p. 144: Estate Account, Fairfax County Will Book E, p. 338 and p. 376, Fairfax County Will Book F, p. 278 and pp. 283-284, Fairfax County Will Book G, p. 118

21. 3/7/1785, **Adam Counce** of the County of Loudoun and Commonwealth of Virginia of the one part to **Adam Axline** of the County and Commonwealth aforesaid of the other part. One tract or parcel of land situate in the County of Loudoun aforesaid beginning at a white oak and further bounded as more fully and at large appears. Assignment for and in consideration of the sum of 120 pounds, **Adam Counce**. Sealed and delivered in the presence of **Adam Shover**, **Simon Shover**, and **Nicholas Border**. Assignment, Loudoun County Deed Book O, pp. 371-372

22. 10/11/1785, **Samuel Combs** of the County of Loudoun and Commonwealth of Virginia of the one part to **Joseph Braden** of the County and Commonwealth aforesaid of the other part. The following tract or parcel of land with its appurtenances situate lying and being in the said County of Loudoun and Parish of Cameron now Shelburne as follows viz. Beginning at a stake in the **Backline** of **Kittockton Creek** lower corner to said **John Patterson's Reserve**, thence S 56° E 206 poles to a white oak marked **WFX,** thence N 50° E 99 poles to a stake near a white oak marked **SC,** thence N 56° W 240 poles to a small hickory in that Backline, thence with said **Backline** to the beginning containing 150 acres of land. Assignment for an in consideration of the sum of 70 pounds, **Saml. Combs**. Proven on 10/10/1785. Assignment, Loudoun County Deed Book O, pp. 429-431

Agreement made November 20th, 1760, Between John Patterson of Loudoun County Gent. and Attorney in fact for the Right Honorable Charles Earl of Tankerville of Great Britain and William Braddock of Loudoun County of the other part, Lease for Lives of a 100 Acre-lot during the natural lives of the said William Braddock aged 25 years, his Wife Mary aged 30 years and his Daughter Prudence aged one year, and the longest liver of them to have and to hold a certain Tract or parcel of land known by the name of Catoctian Manour and bounded as follows...

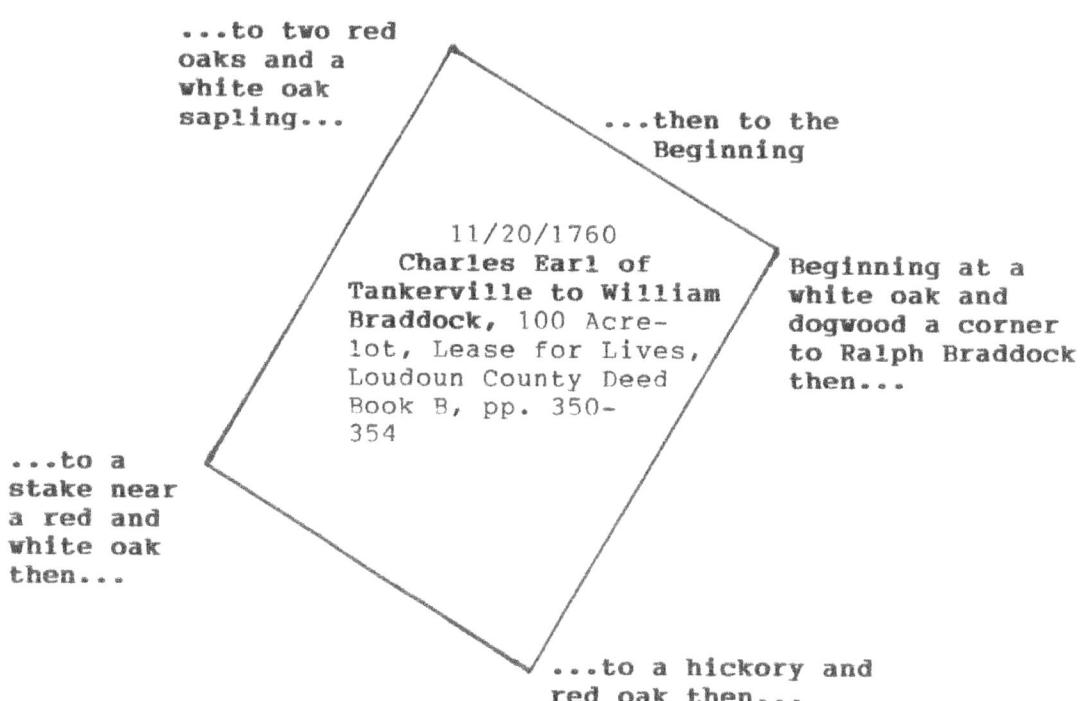

Scale: 1 inch = 50 poles

Loudoun County, Virginia

These are two Indentures made between John Patterson of Loudoun County in the Colony of Virginia Gent. and Attorney in fact for the Right Honorable Charles Earl of Tankerville of Great Britain of the one part and Samuel Schooley of the aforesaid County in the Colony of Virginia, Farmer, of the other part, Witnesseth that the said John Patterson in consideration of the rents and covenants expressed on the part of the said Samuel Schooley to be paid and performed hath dimised set and to farm let unto the said Samuel Schooley his Heirs Executors and Administrators one Messuage Tenement Tract or Parcel of Land situate lying and being in the County of Loudoun aforesaid being part of that Tract or Parcel of Land called and known by the name of Catoctian Manour and bounded as followeth...

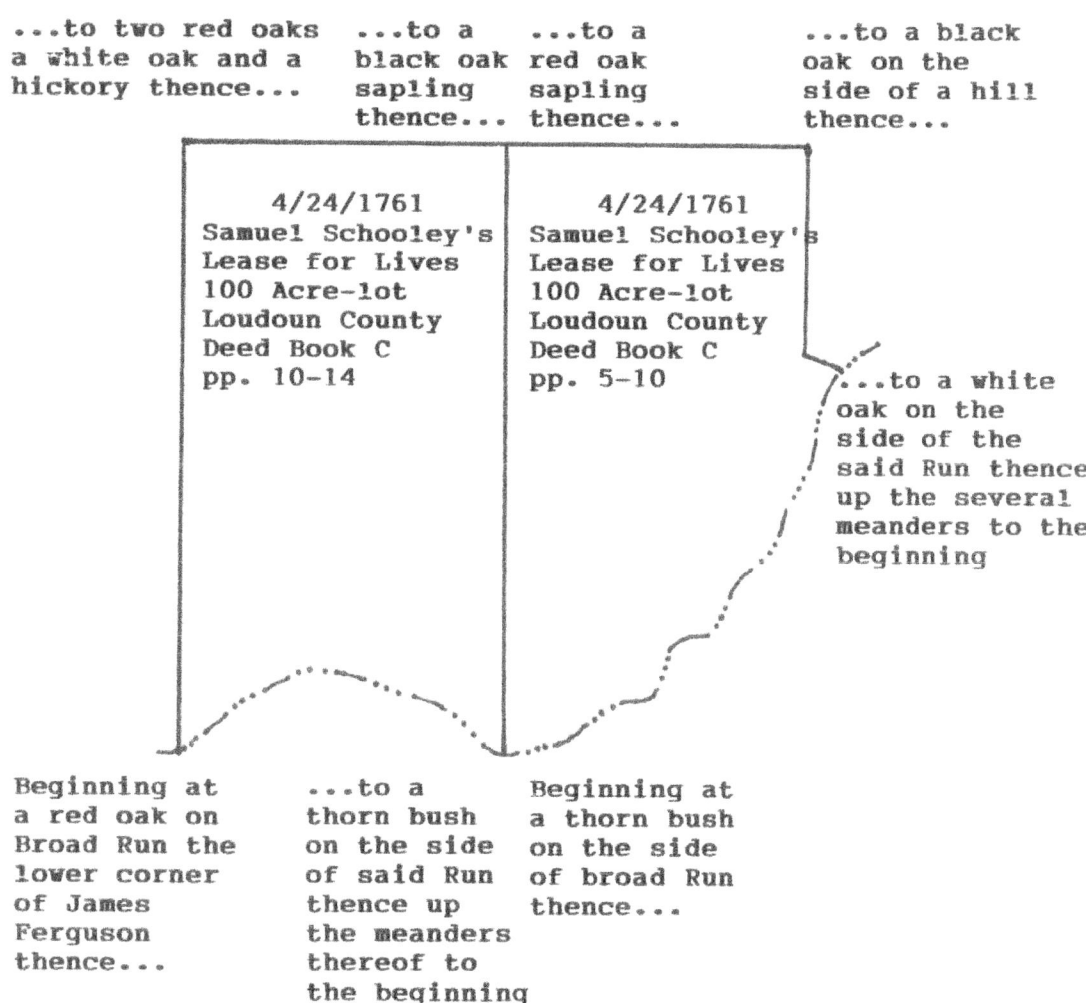

Agreement between John Patterson of Loudoun County Gent and Attorney in fact for the Right Honorable Charles Earl of Tankerville of Great Britain and James Ferguson of Loudoun County, Lease for Lives of a 100 Acre-lot for and during the natural lives of the said James Ferguson aged 32 and Margaret his Wife aged 28, and Auzabah his Daughter aged 7 years and the longest liver of them...Catoctin Manor...

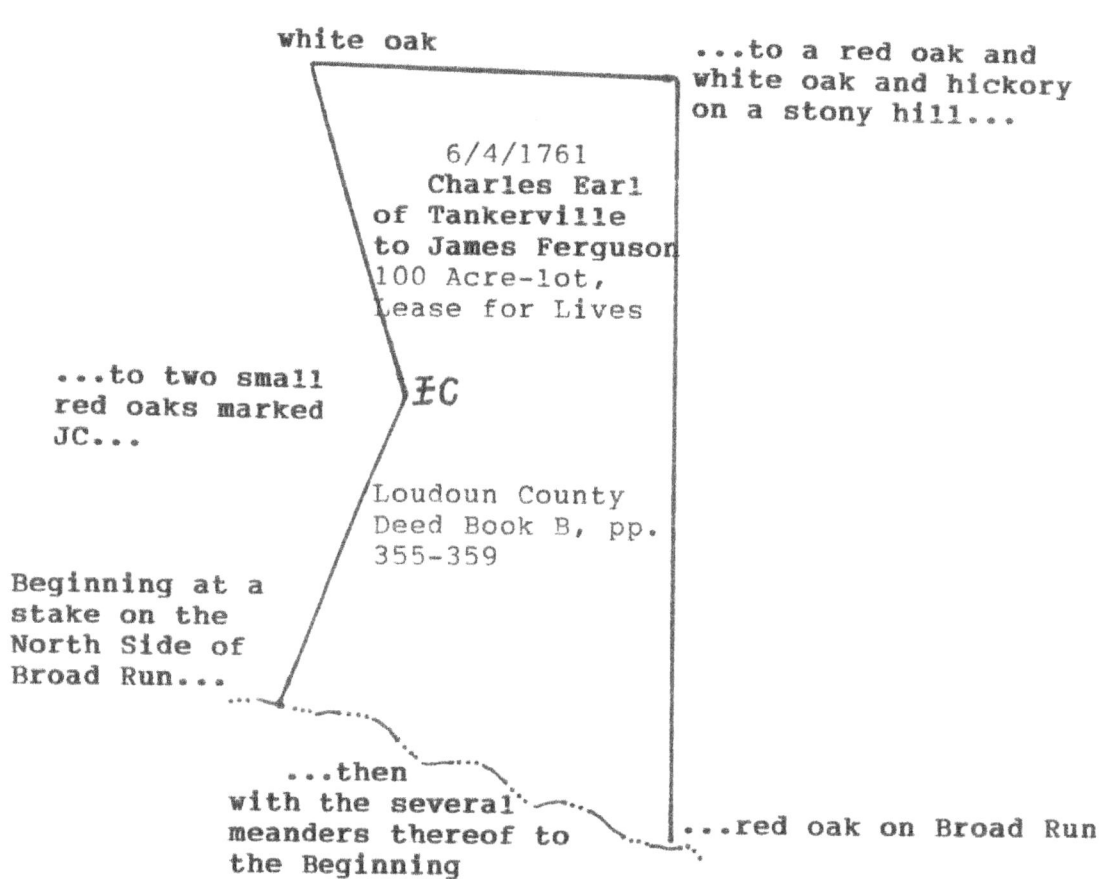

Scale: one inch = 50 poles

Beginning at A at three white oaks and a black oak in a line of the Earl of Tankerville and corner to James Ferguson's Lot and extending thence with Tankerville's line to B a white oak corner to Henry Adington's Lot thence with his line to C a black oak and hickory corner to Michael Custord's Lot thence to D a spanish oak corner to said Ferguson and thence with his line to the beginning containing sixty Acres of Land

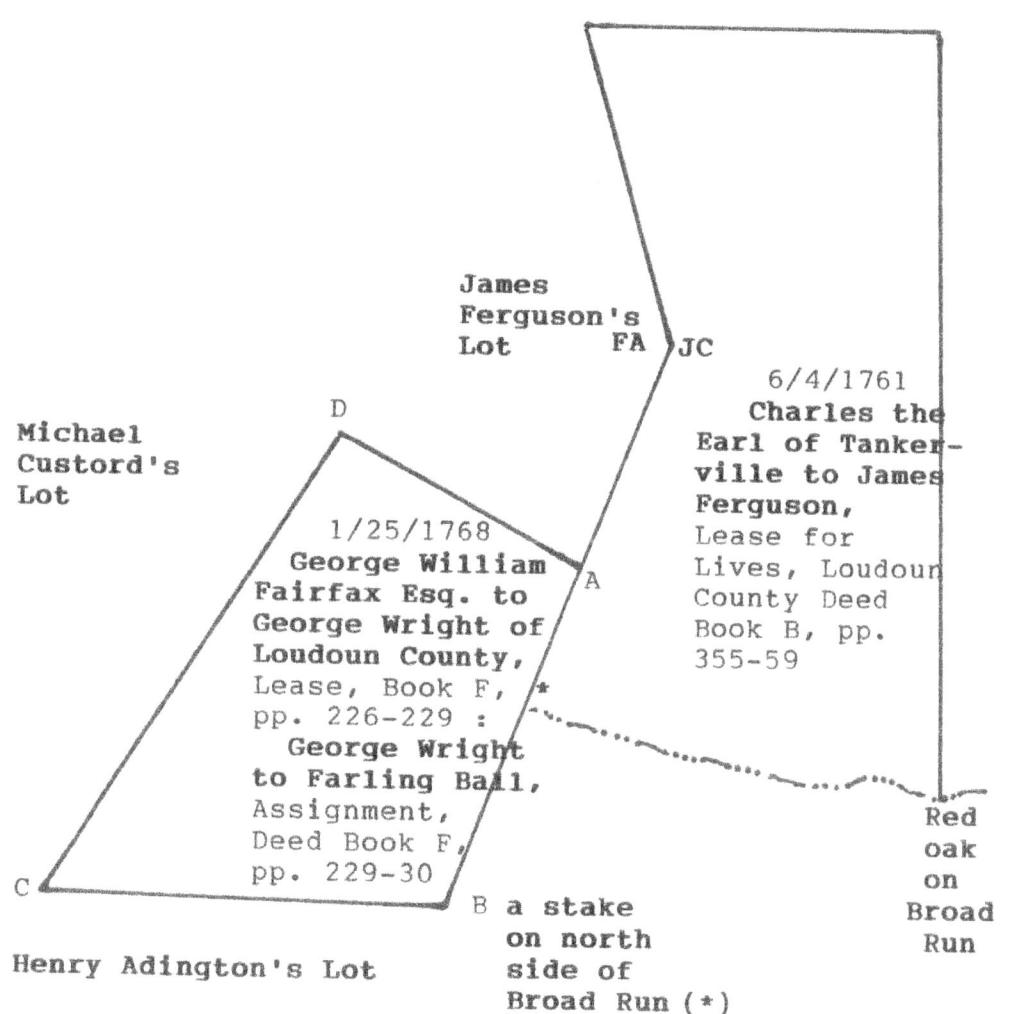

Loudoun County, Colony of Virginia   Scale: 1 in. = 50 poles

Indenture made June 24, 1761, between John Patterson of Loudoun County Gent. and Attorney in fact for the Right Honorable Charles Earl of Tankerville of Great Britain and William Grant, Farmer, of Loudoun County of the other part, Lease for Lives, 113½ Acre-lot, during the natural lives of the said William Grant aged 32 and his Wife aged 26, and his Son John aged one year old and the longest liver of them to have and to hold a certain Tract or Lot of land in Catoctian Manour and bounded as follows...

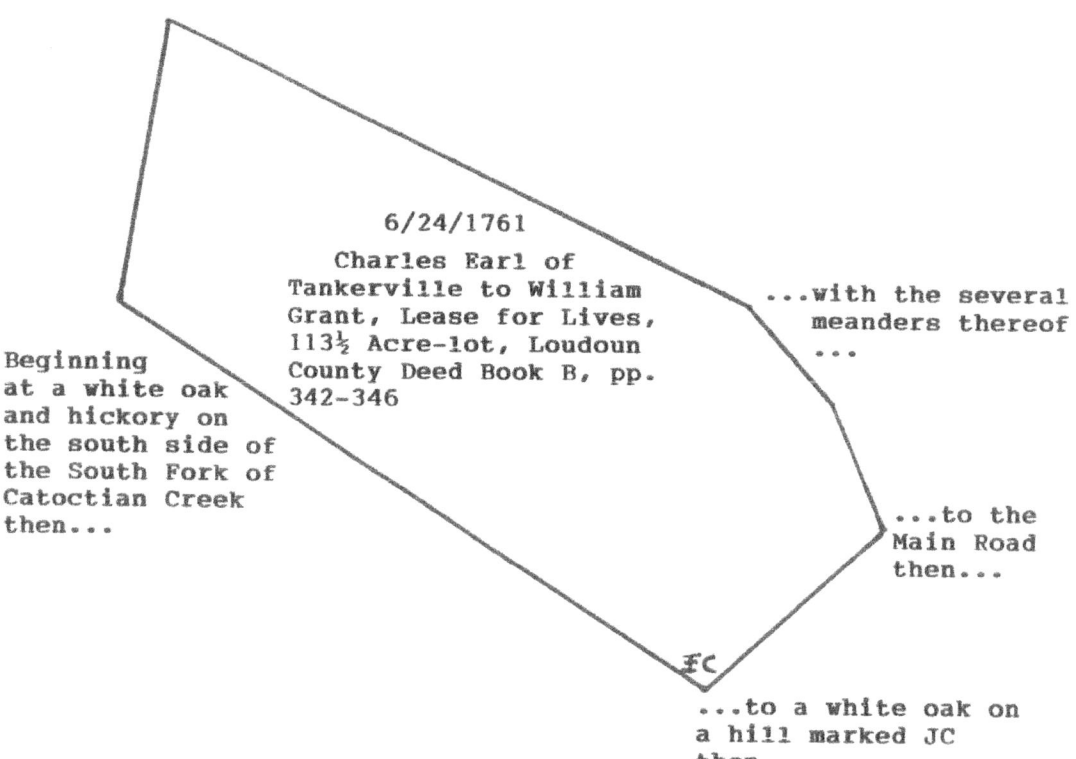

Scale: one inch = 50 linear poles

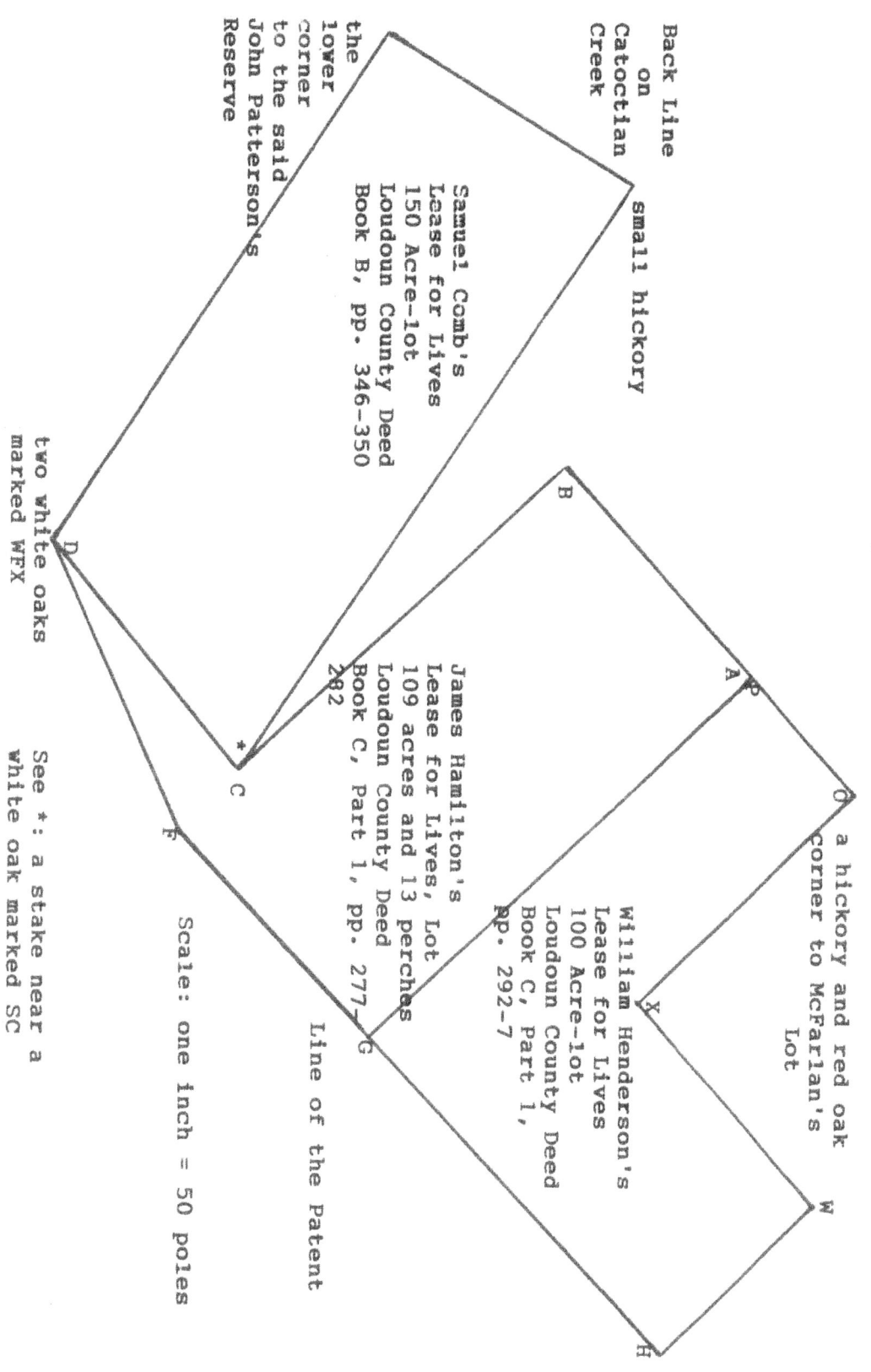

Indentures made by John Patterson of Loudoun County Gent. and Attorney in fact for the Right Honorable Charles Earl of Tankerville, Catoctian Manour, Lease for Lives Agreements, Loudoun County, Colony of Virginia

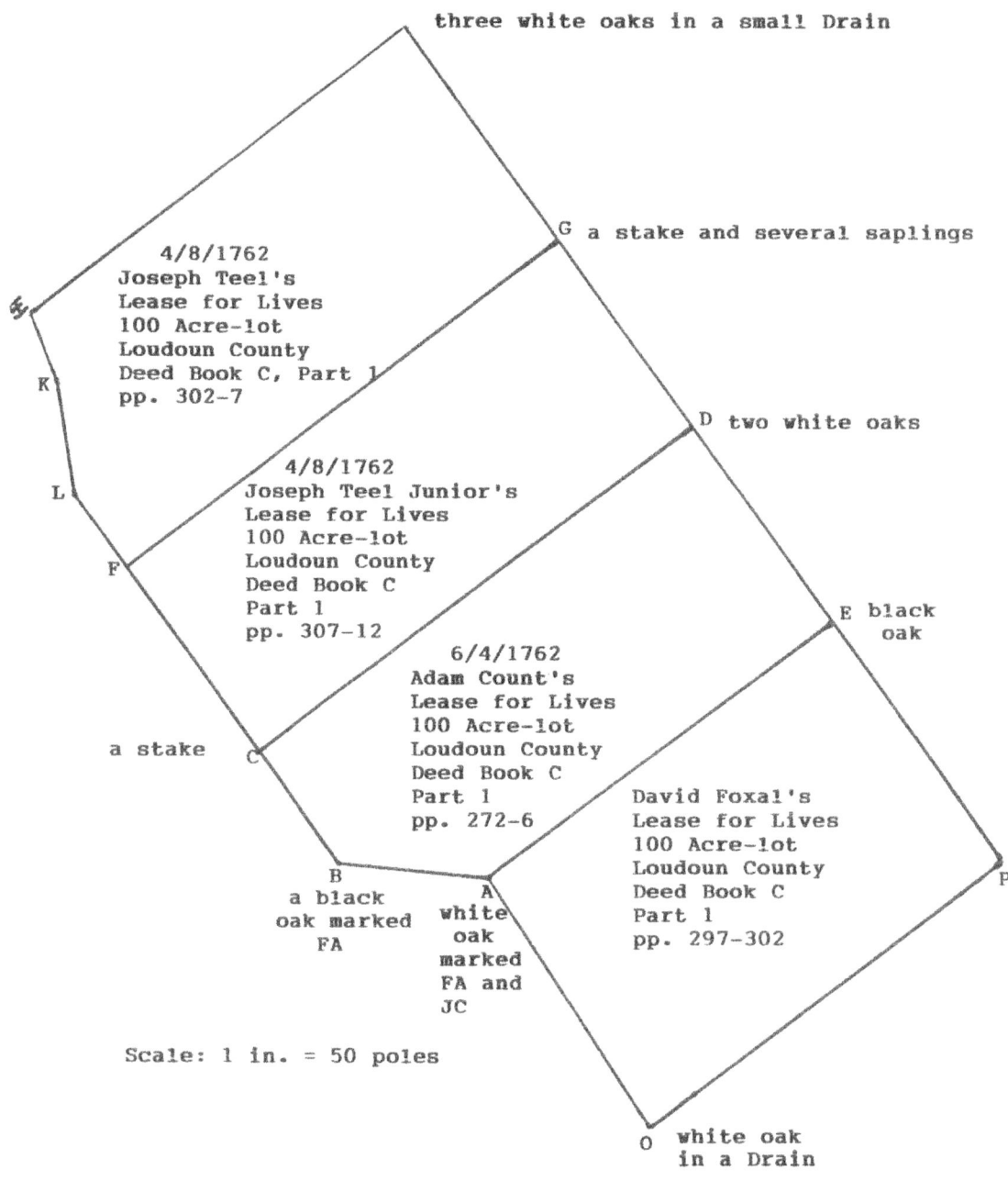

Agreement made June 4th, 1762, Between John Patterson of Loudoun County Gent. and Attorney in fact for the Right Honorable Charles earl of Tankerville of Great Britain and Henry Count of Loudoun County, Farmer, of the other part, Lease for Lives of a one hundred Acre-lot during the natural lives of the said Henry Count aged 27, his Wife Mary aged 20 and his Daughter Salamy aged three years old, and the longest liver of them to have and to hold a certain tract or parcel of land known by the name of catoctian Manour and bounded as followeth...

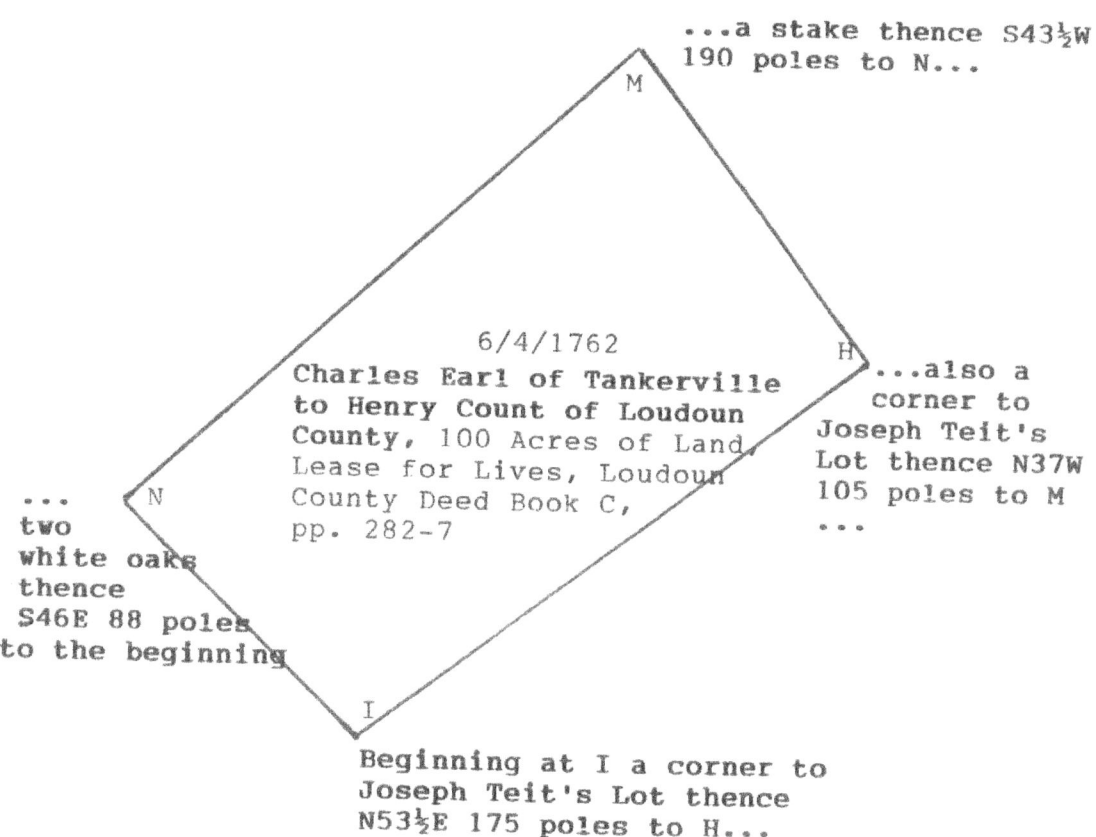

...a stake thence S43½W 190 poles to N...

6/4/1762
Charles Earl of Tankerville to Henry Count of Loudoun County, 100 Acres of Land, Lease for Lives, Loudoun County Deed Book C, pp. 282-7

...also a corner to Joseph Teit's Lot thence N37W 105 poles to M...

...two white oaks thence S46E 88 poles to the beginning

Beginning at I a corner to Joseph Teit's Lot thence N53½E 175 poles to H...

Scale: one inch = 50 linear poles or 825 feet

Agreement made June 24th, 1760, Between John Patterson of Loudoun County Gent. and Attorney in fact for the Right Honorable Charles Earl of Tankerville of Great Britain and Samuel Combs of Loudoun County, Lease for Lives of 150 Acre-lot during the natural lives of said Samuel Coombs aged 32, Mary his Wife aged 27, Samuel his Son aged one, and the longest liver of them to have and to hold a certain tract or parcel of land bounded as followeth...Loudoun County Deed Book B, pp. 346-350

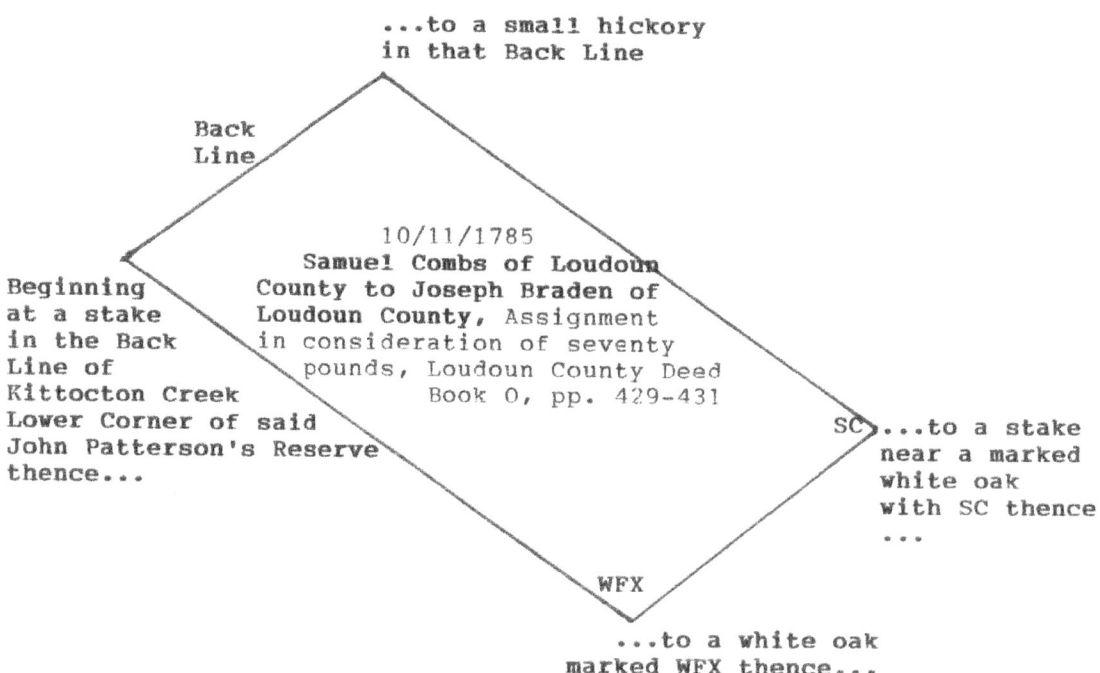

1 inch = 50 poles

Catesby Cocke's 591-Acre Tract of Land (c. 1745)

The parceling of a certain tract of land containing 591 acres granted solely to Catesby Cocke by a patent out of the Proprietor's Office of the Northern Neck of Virginia. This property was situated on and about the west side of Catoctin Mountain down to the drains of Clark's Run. During the Colonial Period it was marked with two forms of markers apparently for Catesby Cocke as in CC; and CC 1745. It would eventually be divided into two parcels of land, which were traded in 1760 by Aneas Campbell for Catesby Cocke to Edward Norton, and John Trammell respectively.

1. Date unknown, The Office of the Proprietor of the Northern Neck of Virginia to **Catesby Cocke**, a certain tract containing 591 (590) acres of land granted to the said **Catesby Cocke** by a patent
2. 12/18/1759, **Catesby Cocke** of the County of Fairfax of the one part to **Aneas Campbell** of the County of Loudoun of the other part and recorded in Loudoun County, Letters of Attorney
3. 4/30 and 5/1/1760, **Catesby Cocke Esq**. of the County of Fairfax and Colony of Virginia by his attorney in fact **Aneas Campbell Gent**. of the County of Loudoun and Colony aforesaid of the one part to **Edward Norton** of the County and Colony aforesaid of the other part. Whereas there is a certain tract or parcel of land situate lying and being in the County of Loudoun aforesaid on and about the **Kittocton Mountain** being part of a tract of land containing 591 acres granted to **Catesby Cocke** by a patent from the Proprietor's Office and bounded as followeth viz. Beginning at a white oak and two red oaks on the west side of the said mountaintop thereof upward of 60 poles above corner of **Edmund Sands** land, extending thence East 159 poles to a small gum in a gully near a marked chestnut standing on the east side of said mountain, thence N 12° E 195 poles to two red oaks near a springhead, thence N 63° - 30 minutes W 365 poles to a hickory and several red oak saplings by a poison field, thence S 20 E 320 poles to the first station containing 400 acres of land. Now this indenture witnesseth that the said **Catesby Cocke** by his attorney in fact **Aneas Campbell** who by virtue of a letter of attorney given him the said **Aneas Campbell** by the said **Catesby Cocke** dated the 18th day of December, 1759 and recorded in Loudoun County Office, for and in consideration of the sum of 60 pounds current money of Virginia to him the said **Catesby Cocke** in hand paid by the said **Edward Norton**, the receipt whereof the said **Catesby Cocke** by his attorney in fact **Aneas Campbell** doth hereby acknowledge and himself fully paid and satisfied thereof and every part thereof, hath granted bargained sold alienated released and confirm and by these presents doth bargain and sell release and confirm unto the said **Edward Norton** and his heirs all and singular the said 400 acres of land situate bounded and being as is above set forth and described, together with all houses barns buildings orchards ways water watercourses woods meadows swamps rights liberties improvements hereditaments and appurtenances with the rents issues and profits of the same.

To have and to hold the said 400 acres of land and premises hereby granted alienated released and confirmed or mentioned and intended to be granted with the appurtenances unto the said **Edward Norton** his heirs and assigns forever, **Catesby Cocke**. Sealed and delivered in the presence of **Jas. Hamilton, John Hough,** and **Francis Hague**. Proven on 6/20/1760. Lease and Release, Loudoun County Deed Book A, pp. 479-483

4. 8/11 and 8/12/1760, **Catesby Cocke Esq.** of the County of Fairfax by his attorney in fact **Aneas Campbell Gent.** of the County of Loudoun of the one part to **John Trammell Gent.** of the County of Loudoun of the other part. Whereas there is a certain tract or parcel of land situate lying and being in the County of Loudoun aforesaid on the south side **Kittocton Mountain** on the drains of **Clark's Run**, being part of a tract patented to the said **Catesby Cocke** and containing in the whole 590 acres and bounded as followeth viz. Beginning at a spanish oak on a point in a fork of **Clark's Run** extending thence S 25° W 78 poles to a small spanish oak marked **CC 1745** near a branch, thence S 60° W 30 poles to two red oaks and hickory marked **CC 1745,** thence West 186 poles to a small gum in a gully by a marked double bodied chestnut oak being made for **Edward Norton** in a division of said tract, thence with said dividing line N 12° E 195 poles to two red oaks near a springhead corner to said **Norton,** thence S 63-½° E 232 poles to the beginning containing 191 acres be the same more or less. Now this indenture witnesseth that the said **Catesby Cocke** by virtue of a power of attorney by him given to the said **Aneas Campbell** bearing date the (blank space) day of December in the year of our Lord 1759, for and in consideration of the sum 40 pounds current money of Virginia to him the said **Catesby Cocke** in hand paid by the said **John Trammell,** the receipt whereof the said **Catesby Cocke** by his attorney in fact **Aneas Campbell** doth hereby acknowledge and himself fully paid and satisfied thereof and every part thereof, hath granted bargained sold alienated released and confirmed and by these presents doth bargain and sell alien release and confirm unto the said **John Trammell** and his heirs and assigns all and singular the said 191 acres of land situate bounded and being as is above set forth and described together with all houses barns buildings orchards ways waters watercourses woods meadows swamps rights liberties improvements hereditaments and appurtenances with the rents issues and profits of the same. To have and to hold the said 191 acres of land and premises hereby granted and released and confirmed or mentioned and intended to be granted and released with the appurtenances unto the said **John Trammell** his heirs or assigns forever, **Catesby Cocke**. Proven on 8/12/1760. Lease and Release, Loudoun County Deed Book B, pp. 20-24

5. 8/10/1761, **John Trammell** of Loudoun County, planter, of the one part to **William Jones** of Loudoun County, farmer, of the other part. Three tracts or parcels of land in the said County of Loudoun viz. The first tract containing 425 acres, being the same formerly granted to **David Richardson** by Proprietor's Deed dated 12/8/1742, and by the said **David Richardson** and **Mary** his wife sold and conveyed unto the said **John Trammell** by deeds of lease and release bearing date the 11th and 12th of September, 1758. The

second tract being a parcel of a tract surveyed for **Margaret Halling** now **Sinclair** containing 150 acres. It being the same formerly sold and conveyed by the said **Margaret Sinclair** to the said **Mary Richardson** wife of the said **David Richardson** by deeds of lease and release dated the 18th and 19th of July 1744, and by the said **David Richardson** and **Mary** his wife sold and conveyed unto the said **John Trammell** by deeds of lease and release bearing date the 13th and 14th of September 1758. The third tract containing 190 acres, being the parcel of a greater tract granted by the Proprietor's deed to **Catesby Cocke** and by the said **Catesby Cocke by Aneas Campbell** his attorney in fact sold and conveyed unto the said **John Trammell** by deeds of lease and release bearing date the 11th and 12th of August 1760. Lease and Release in consideration of the sum of 675 pounds current money of Pennsylvania, Loudoun County Deed Book B, pp. 206-212

6. 6/15 and 6/16/1762, **Edward Norton** of Loudoun County in the Colony of Virginia, farmer, and **Elizabeth** his wife of the one part to **Richard Williams** of Bucks County in the Province of Pennsylvania, farmer, of the other part. Witnesseth that the said **Edward Norton** and **Elizabeth** his wife for and in consideration of the sum of 220 pounds lawful money to him in hand paid by the said **Richard Williams** at and before the sealing and delivery of these presents the receipt whereof is hereby confessed and acknowledged, hath granted bargained and sold aliened released and confirmed and by these presents doth bargain and sell alien release and confirm unto the said **Richard Williams** his heirs and assigns forever two tracts or parcels of land situate lying and being in Cameron Parish in the County of Loudoun formerly Fairfax. The first tract lying on the branches of **Kittocton Creek** containing 100 acres purchased by the said **Edward Norton** from a certain **Henry Brown** by lease and release date the 2nd and 3rd days of December, 1749 and bounded as follows viz. Beginning at a white oak marked **CC** corner to **Catesby Cocke's** land almost twenty poles from a line of a tract surveyed for **Saml. Maxberry** then said to belong to **William Kirk**, thence parallel with **Kirk's** line S 60° W 85 poles to a small hickory on the west side of a branch of **Kittocton** amongst a heap of rocks, thence S 18° W 199 poles to a black oak in a dividing line between **Edmund Sands** and the said **Henry Brown**, thence with the said dividing line S 71° W 113 (S 71° E 113 ?) poles to a spanish oak in a line of **Catesby Cocke**, thence with **Cocke's** line N 20° W 253 poles to the beginning. The other tract lying on and about **Kittocton Mountain** containing 400 acres purchased by the said **Edward Norton** of **Aneas Campbell Gent.** attorney in fact for **Catesby Cocke** by lease and release dated the lease the 30th day of April, and the release the 1st day of May, 1760 and bounded as follows viz. Beginning at a white oak and two red oaks on the west side of said mountain near the top thereof upwards of sixty poles above a corner of **Edmund Sands** land thence East 159 poles to a small gum in a gully near a marked chestnut oak on the east side of said mountain, thence N 12° E 195 poles to two red oaks near a springhead, then N 63° – 30 minutes W 365 poles to a hickory and several red oak saplings by a poison field, thence S 20° E 320 poles to the beginning containing 400 acres, and all

houses buildings orchards meadows trees woods ways water watercourses easements profits advantages and hereditaments whatsoever to the said two tracts of land above mentioned belonging or in any wise appertaining. To have and to hold the said two tract of land and premises above mentioned and every part and parcel thereof with the appurtenances unto the said **Richard Williams** his heirs and assigns forever, **Edward Norton** and **Elizabeth Norton**. Sealed and delivered in the presence of **James Jones, William Jones**, and **John Steere**. Proven on July 13, 1762. Lease and Release, Loudoun County Deed Book, Part 1, pp. 314-319 (Note: These were adjoining parcels of land but only the later one originally had been a part of the subject tract of land, which was originally granted to Catesby Cocke.)

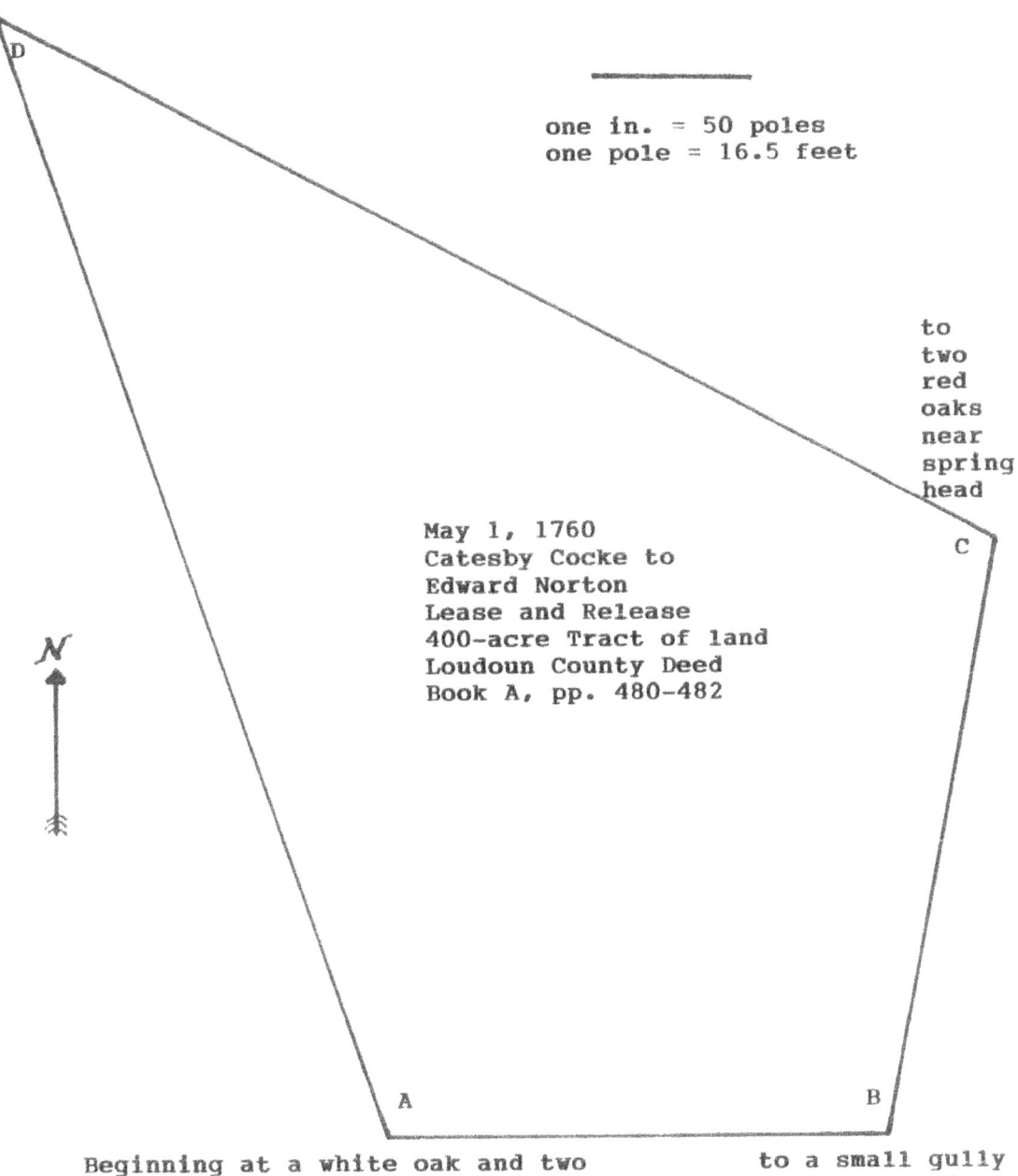

Whereas there is a certain tract or parcel of land lying and being on the south side of Kittocton Mountain on the drains of Clark's Run, being part of a tract patented to Catesby Cocke containing in the whole 591 acres and bounded as followeth viz.

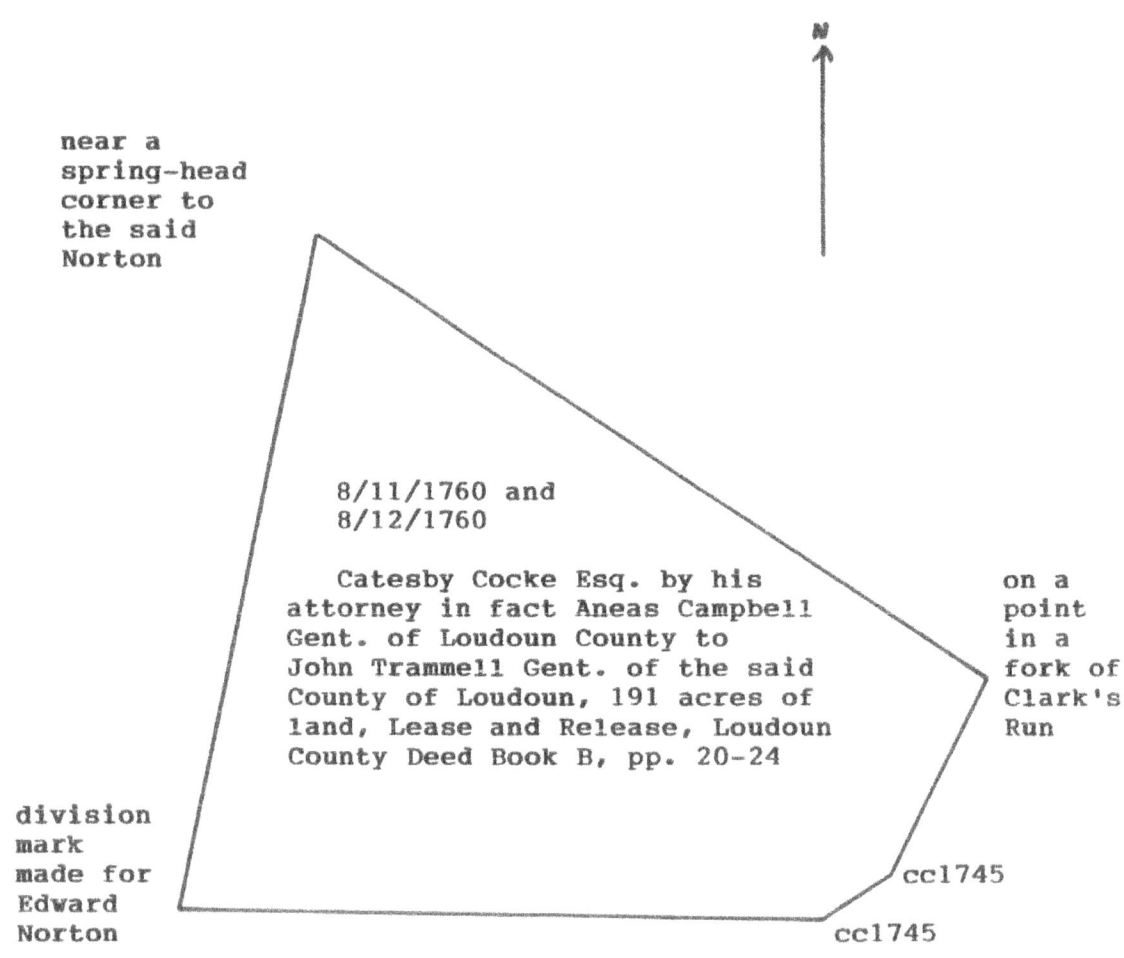

8/11/1760 and 8/12/1760

Catesby Cocke Esq. by his attorney in fact Aneas Campbell Gent. of Loudoun County to John Trammell Gent. of the said County of Loudoun, 191 acres of land, Lease and Release, Loudoun County Deed Book B, pp. 20-24

1 in. = 50 poles

Catesby Cocke's 2,672-Acre Tract of Land (c. 1741)

This section concerns the parceling of an expanse of land containing about 2,672 acres, which was situated on and about the east side of Catoctin Mountain. Apparently, Catesby Cocke had owned this tract of land previous to him having acquired other nearby lands in partnership with John Mercer as in Cocke & Mercer's survey and tract of land. It might have come in whole or in part to Catesby Cocke from one Patrick Lynch based on John Warner's survey and boundary description dated 1750 for Cocke & Mercer's given contiguous landholding.[1]

In time such land would come to be traded by Aneas Campbell by virtue of letter of attorney given him dated December 18, 1759. Cocke's subject landholding was also adjacent to his otherwise mentioned 591-acre tract of land from the Proprietor's Office of the Northern Neck of Virginia. This particular tract was divided into at least two large parcels of land, which were traded by Aneas Campbell to John Hough, and George Gregg respectfully. It appears these were largely unimproved lands as they sold cheaply counting total earnings of only 305 pounds of revenues against about 2,672 acres of land.

One of the two parcels of land was situated under Catoctin Mountain on a draught of Limestone Run containing about 1,537 acres of land, which was traded to John Hough. It was adjacent to a 323-acre tract of land on the branches of Limestone Run belonging at that time to Thomson Mason called and known by the name of Rasberry Plain (see Loudoun County Deed Book A, pp. 467-472). The boundaries of John Hough's given land in those times were marked with markers for on the face of it Catesby Cocke as in CC 1745, and 1745; Cocke & Mercer as in CM; Coke & Mercer and Francis Awbrey as in CM & FA.

The other parcel of land was situated over the Catoctin Mountain on the drains of Catoctin Creek containing about 1,100 acres of land, which was traded to George Gregg. There was a saw-mill here, which belonged to George Gregg near Joseph Hough's boundary line (Deed Book E, pp. 77-81). His land was traversed by a road leading from William Kirk's Mill to Mahlon Janney's Mill, and another road from Roache's Mill to Leesburg. The boundaries of George Gregg's given land in those times were marked with markers for on the face of it Catesby Cocke as in 1745, and another unknown marker as in JA (Averill?).

1. 4/7 and 4/8/1760, **Catesby Cocke Esq**. of the County of Fairfax and Colony of Virginia by his attorney in fact **Aneas Campbell Gent**. of the County of Loudoun and Colony of Virginia of the one part to **John Hough** of the said County of Loudoun and Colony aforesaid of the other part. Whereas there is a certain tract or parcel of land situate lying and being in the County of Loudoun aforesaid the southeast side of **Kittocton Mountain** and on the draught of **Limestone Run** and bounded as followeth viz. Beginning at a red oak and chestnut marked **CM** standing on one of the broken hillsides about a chain from a **road that crosses said mountain** running thence S 49° E 92 poles to a large hickory marked **CM** near a pond, then N 75° E 50 poles to a double spanish oak marked **CM** on a gravely point near a branch, then S 29° E 40 poles to a box oak marked **CM,** then S 58-½° E 88 poles to a red oak and two white oaks marked

---

[1] Catesby Cocke and John Mercer, Deed of Partition, Fairfax County Deed Book C, pp. 99-106

CM & FA standing by a branch corner to **Thomson Mason's** land, thence N 47° E 92 poles to three red oak saplings on the edge of a poison field near a limestone rock, thence N 8° - 30 minutes E 336 poles to a box oak marked **CC 1745** near a branch, thence N 52° W 46 poles to a marked white oak **1745** near a large white oak not marked, thence N 8° W 172 poles to a hickory and spanish oak in a thicket, (thence) N 58° 30 minutes W 76 poles to a box white oak on a ridge between two drains, thence N 1° E 98 poles to a hickory in the fork of a branch alias white oak and chestnut, thence N 31° E 96 poles to a white oak by a sunken hole marked **1745,** thence N 31° W 82 poles to a red and white oak, thence S 70° W 384 poles to a red oak alias hickory on a level, thence S 14° E 590 poles to the beginning containing 1,537 acres more or less. Now this indenture witnesseth that the said **Catesby Cocke Esq.** by his attorney in fact **Aneas Campbell** who by virtue of a letter of attorney given the said **Aneas Campbell** by the said **Cocke** bearing date the 18th day of December, 1759 and recorded in Loudoun County Office, for and in consideration of the sum of 125 pounds current money of Virginia to him the said **Catesby Cocke** in hand paid by the said **John Hough** the receipt whereof the said **Catesby Cocke** by his attorney in fact **Aneas Campbell** doth hereby acknowledge and himself fully paid and satisfied thereof and every part thereof, hath granted bargained sold aliened released and confirmed and by these presents doth bargain and sell alien release and confirm unto the said **John Hough** and his heirs and assigns all and singular the said 1,537 acres of land more or less situate bounded and being as is above set forth and described together with all houses barns buildings orchards ways waters watercourses woods meadows swamps rights liberties improvements hereditaments and appurtenances with the rents issues and profits of the same. To have and to hold the said 1,537 acres of land be the same more or less and premises hereby granted alienated released and conformed or mentioned and intended to be granted and released with the appurtenances unto the said **John Hough** his heirs and assign forever, **Catesby Cocke.** Sealed and delivered in the presence of **Josias Clapham, Nich. Minor, Craven Peyton, John Moss Jr., Jos. McGeach.** Proven on 5/13/1760. Lease and Release, Loudoun County Deed Book A, pp. 410-416

2. 4/30 and 5/1/1760, **Catesby Cocke Esq.** of the County of Fairfax and Colony of Virginia by his attorney in fact **Aneas Campbell Gent.** of the County of Loudoun and Colony aforesaid of the one part to **George Gregg** of the said County of Loudoun of the other part. Whereas there is a certain tract or parcel of land situate lying and being in the County of Loudoun aforesaid joining the west side of **Kittocton Mountain** on the drains of **Kittocton Creek** (and bounded as followeth viz.) Beginning at a white oak by a grove of pines the south side of **Kittocton Creek** extending thence S 20° E 440 poles to a black oak, thence N 58° E 104 poles to three black oaks, thence S 41° E 122 poles to a hickory, thence S 65° E 106 poles to a white oak, thence East 47 poles to a white oak, thence N 1° E 540 poles to a white oak, thence West 74 poles to a white and red oak marked **1745** being corner to that tract **Edward Norton** purchased, thence with the line of that tract N 20° W 31 poles to a white and red oak, thence S 80° W 390 poles to the first station containing 1,135 acres. Now this indenture witnesseth that the said

Catesby Cocke Esq. by his attorney in fact **Aneas Campbell Gent**. who by virtue of a letter of attorney given the said **Aneas Campbell** by the said **Catesby Cocke** bearing date 12/18/1759 and recorded in Loudoun County Office, for and in consideration of the sum of 180 pounds current money of Virginia to him the said **Catesby Cocke** in hand paid by the said **George Gregg** the receipt whereof the said **Catesby Cocke** by his attorney in fact **Aneas Campbell** doth hereby acknowledge and himself fully paid and satisfied and every part thereof, hath granted bargained sold alienated released and confirmed and by these presents doth bargain and sell alien release and confirm unto the said **George Gregg** and his heirs and assigns all and singular the said 1,100 acres of land more or less situate lying and being as is above set forth and described together with all houses barns buildings orchards ways waters watercourses woods meadows swamps rights liberties improvements hereditaments and appurtenances with the rents issues and profits of the same. To have and to hold the said 1,100 acres of land more or less and premises hereby granted alienated released and confirmed or mentioned and intended to be granted and released with the appurtenances unto the said **George Gregg** his heirs and assigns forever, **Catesby Cocke**. Sealed and delivered in the presence of **Jas. Hamilton, Francis Hague, Jos. McGeach**, and **John Hough**. Proven on 5/13/1760. Lease and Release, Loudoun County Deed Book A, pp. 437-443

3. 4/30 and 5/1/1760, **George Gregg** of the County of Loudoun and **Elizabeth** his wife of the one part to **Farlin Ball (Farling Ball)** of the same County of the other part. Whereas there is a certain tract or parcel of land situate lying and being in the County of Loudoun aforesaid and bounded as followeth viz. Beginning at a white oak the south side of **Kittocton Creek** by a grove of pines corner to **Richard Roach** extending thence N 20° E 239 poles to a small hickory by a **road,** thence N 74° E 174 poles to a small black oak, thence N 20° W 142 poles to two small white oaks by a meadow and by a small branch, thence up the branch N 74° E 110 poles to a forked white oak on the mountainside, thence N 20° W 75 poles to two box white oaks on a hill in a line of **Edmund Sands,** thence with **Sands** and **Roach's** line S 80° W 287 poles to the first station containing 302 acres. The same being part of a tract granted to the said **Gregg** by **Catesby Cocke** by his attorney in fact **Aneas Campbell**. Now this indenture witnesseth that the said **George Gregg** and **Elizabeth** his wife for and in consideration of the sum of 100 pounds current money of Virginia to him in hand paid by the said **Farlin Ball** the receipt whereof the said **George Gregg** and **Elizabeth** his wife doth hereby acknowledge and themselves fully paid and satisfied thereof and every part thereof, hath granted bargained sold alienated released and confirmed and by these presents doth bargain sell alien release and confirm unto the said **Farlin Ball** and his heirs and assigns all and singular the said 302 acres of land situate bounded and being as is above set forth and described together with all houses barns buildings orchards gardens ways waters watercourses woods meadows swamps rights liberties improvements hereditaments and appurtenances with the rents issues and profits of the same. To have and to hold the said 302 acres of land and premises hereby granted alienated released and confirmed or mentioned and intended to be granted and released with

the appurtenances unto the said **Farlin Ball** his heirs and assigns forever, **George Gregg** and **Elizabeth Gregg**. Sealed and delivered in the presence of **John Hough, Aneas Campbell, James Hamilton**, and **Craven Peyton**. Proven on 5/13/1760. Lease and Release, Loudoun County Deed Book A, pp. 432-437

4. 6/10 and 6/11/1760, **John Hough** of the County of Loudoun and Colony of Virginia of the one part to **James Stephens** of the County of Loudoun of the other part. Whereas there is a certain tract of land situate lying and being in the County of Loudoun aforesaid being part of a tract purchased of **Catesby Cocke** by his attorney in fact **Aneas Campbell** to the said **John Hough,** and bounded as followeth viz. Beginning at a chestnut tree beginning tree of the original tract and extending thence with the lines of the original S 49° E 92 poles to a hickory near a pond, thence N 75° E 50 poles to a double bodies spanish oak, thence S 29° E 42 poles to a box oak, thence S 58-½° E 101 poles to a red oak and two white oaks marked **CM & FA** by a branch corner to **Thomson Mason,** thence N 47° E 26 poles to a red oak sapling, thence N 63° W 326 poles to the given line of the original survey, thence with the said line S 16° E 66 poles to the first station, laid out for 75 acres more or less according to the above boundaries. Now this indenture witnesseth that the said **John Hough** for and in consideration of the sum of 17 pounds and 10 shillings current money of Virginia to him the said **John Hough** in hand paid by the said **James Stephens**, the receipt whereof the said **John Hough** doth hereby acknowledge and himself fully paid and satisfied thereof and every part thereof, hath granted bargained sold alienated released and confirmed and by the presents doth bargain and sell alien release and confirm unto the said **James Stephens** and his heirs and assigns all and singular the said 75 acres of land situate lying and being as is above set forth and described, together with all houses barns buildings orchards ways water watercourses woods meadows swamps rights liberties improvements hereditaments and appurtenances with the rents issues and profits of the same. To have and to hold the said 75 acres of land and premises hereby granted and released or mentioned and intended to be granted and released, with the appurtenances unto the said **James Stephens** his heirs and assigns, to the only proper use and behoove of him the said **James Stephens** his heirs and assigns forever, **John Hough**. Sealed and delivered in the presence of **Robert Wilson, Fleming Patterson, John Walton**, and **Andrew Adam**. Proven on 11/12/1760. Lease and Release, Loudoun County Deed Book B, pp. 62-66

5. 8/7 and 8/8/1760, **George Gregg** of the County of Loudoun and **Elizabeth** his wife of the one part to **John Hanby** of the same County of the other part. Whereas there is a certain tract or parcel of land situate lying and being in the County of Loudoun aforesaid and bounded as followeth viz. Beginning at two black oaks one marked **JA** and corner to **Thomas John** extending thence N 2 E 188 poles to a small red oak corner to **Farlin Ball (Farling Ball)**, thence with his line S 74 W 174 poles to a small hickory corner to said **Ball** in a line of **John Mercer's** land, thence with **Mercer's** line S 20 E 200 poles, thence N 58 E 104 poles to the first station containing 150 acres of land. It being part of a tract granted to **Catesby Cocke Gent.** and by him transferred to the said **George Gregg** by **Aneas Campbell** attorney in fact for the said **Catesby Cocke**. Now this

indenture witnesseth that the said **George Gregg** and **Elizabeth** his wife for and in consideration of the sum of 50 pounds current money of Virginia to him the said **George Gregg** in hand paid by the said **John Hanby** the receipt whereof the said **George Gregg** doth hereby acknowledge and himself fully paid and satisfied, hath granted bargained sold alienated released and confirmed by these presents doth bargain and sell alien release and confirm unto the said **John Hanby** and his heirs and assigns all and singular the said 150 acres of land and premises hereby granted and released or mentioned and intended to be granted and released with the appurtenances unto the said **John Hanby** his heirs and assigns forever. To have and to hold the said 150 acres of land and premises hereby granted and released or mentioned and intended to be granted and released with the appurtenances unto the said **John Hanby** his heirs and assigns forever, **George Gregg** and **Elizabeth Gregg**. Sealed and delivered in the presence of **Farling Ball** and **James Steere**. Lease and Release, Loudoun County Deed Book B, pp. 26-29

6. 8/12/1760, **George Scott** of the County of Loudoun and Colony of Virginia of the one part to **John Scott** of the same County of the other part. Witnesseth that the said **George Gregg** for and in consideration of the rents and covenants hereinafter mentioned hath demised granted and to farm let unto the said **John Scott** his heirs and assigns a certain messuage tenement or parcel of land containing 150 acres bounded as followeth viz. Beginning at a small red oak corner to **Farlin** (Farling) **Ball's** land and to **John Hanby** and to **John Walton's** lot extending thence with **Ball's** line N 20° W 130 poles to a small white oak in a line of **William Himming's** lot, thence N 74° E 112 poles to a double bodied white oak, thence N 24° W 65 poles to a line of **Edmund Sands**, thence N 80° E 70 poles to a red oak, thence S 57° E 194 poles to two black oaks near a drain, thence S 74° W 130 poles to the first station, together with all profits commodities and appurtenances to the same belonging or in any wise appertaining, excepting and reserving unto the said **George Gregg** his heirs and assigns all mines minerals quarries and the use of them with free ingress egress and regress into and from said demised premises, and also the privilege of hunting and fowling upon any part thereof. To have and to hold the said messuage tenement or parcel of land with the appurtenances except as before excepted, unto the said **John Scott** his heirs and assigns from the date hereof for and during the natural lives of him the said **John Scott**, his wife **Mary**, and son **Daniel**, and the longest liver of them, **George Gregg**. Sealed and delivered in presence of **Hugh Black, Richard Roach**, and **John Hanby**. Proven on 8/12/1760. Lease for Lives, Loudoun County Deed Book B, pp. 33-36

7. 6/8 and 6/9/1761, **Thomas John** of the County of Loudoun and Colony of Virginia of the one part to **John Hanby** of the same County and Colony of the other part. Whereas there is a certain parcel of land situate lying and being in the County of Loudoun aforesaid containing 16 acres of land being part of a parcel of land granted to said **Thomas John** by **George Gregg**. The said 16 acres bounded as followeth viz. Beginning at a white oak in a line of a tract said **Hanby** purchased of **George Gregg** formerly in possession of **Catesby Cocke Esq**. and also being a dividing corner between said **Thomas John** and said **George Gregg**,

extending thence with said dividing line S 25° E 81 poles to a spanish oak in a thicket crossing a branch at forty poles, thence N 50° E 40 poles to three small gums near two small marked white oaks by the east side of a swamp, thence N 33° W 75 poles to two small red oaks in aforesaid original line, thence with said line S 55° W 29 poles to the beginning laid out for 16 acres. Now this indenture witnesseth that the said **Thomas John** for and in consideration of the sum of 9 pounds current money of Virginia to him the said **Thomas John** in hand paid by the said **John Hanby** the receipt whereof the said **Thomas John** doth hereby acknowledge and himself fully paid thereof and every part thereof, hath granted bargained sold alienated released and confirmed and by these presents doth bargain and sell alien release and confirmed unto the said **John Hanby** and his heirs and assigns all and singular the said 16 acres situate bounded and being as is above set forth and described together with all houses barns buildings orchards ways watercourses woods meadows swamps rights liberties improvements hereditaments and appurtenances with the rents issues and profits of the same. To have and to hold the said 16 acres of land and premises hereby granted released or confirmed or intended to be granted and released with the appurtenances unto the said **John Hanby** his heirs and assigns forever, **Thomas** his T mark **John**. Sealed and delivered in the presence of **Samuel Harriss Jr.**, **Farling Ball**, and **Edward** his E mark **Harden**. Proven on 6/9/1761. Lease and Release, Loudoun County Deed Book B, pp. 113-117.

8. 4/16 and 4/17/1769, **Abraham Dawson** of the County of Loudoun and Colony of Virginia of the one part to **Farlen Ball (Farling Ball)** of the said County of the other part. Witnesseth that for and in consideration of the sum 6 pounds current money of Virginia to the said **Abraham Dawson** in hand paid by the said **Farlen Ball** at or before the sealing and delivery of these presents the receipt whereof he doth hereby acknowledge, hath granted bargained sold aliened and confirmed and by these presents doth grant bargain sell alien and confirm unto the said **Farlin Ball (Farling Ball)** and his heirs all that parcel of land situate in the County of Loudoun aforesaid and bounded as followeth viz. Beginning at a stone set up by the **road leading from William Kirk's Mill to Mahlon Janney's Mill** and extending in the line of the said **Farlin Ball's** land and extending thence with the same N 21° W 27 poles to three white oaks corner to said **Ball**, thence N 70° E 34 poles to a stone set up by said **road**, then binding with said **road** S 13° W 5 poles to a stone near a branch, thence S 35° W 26 poles to a white oak by said **road**, then S 23° W 12 poles to the beginning containing 3 acres more or less, being part of a tract of land the said **Abraham Dawson** purchased of **George Gregg**, and all houses buildings orchards ways waters watercourses profits commodities hereditaments and appurtenances whatsoever to the said premises hereby granted or any part thereof belonging or in any wise appertaining. To have and to hold the lands hereby conveyed and all and singular the premises hereby bargained and sold and every part and parcel thereof with their and every of their appurtenances unto the said **Farlen Ball** his heirs and assigns forever, **Abraham Dawson**. Sealed and delivered in the presence of **Thomas Mathews, Ephraim Bonham, Charles Saxton Jr., and Nathanial**

Saxton. Proven on 4/17/1769. Lease and Release, Loudoun County Deed Book G, pp. 175-178

9. 11/24 and 11/25/1772, **Farling Ball** of the County of Loudoun and Colony and Dominion of Virginia and **Mary** his wife of the one part to **Thomas Mifflin** of the City of Philadelphia, merchant, of the other part. Witnesseth that for and in consideration of the sum of 822 pounds current money of Pennsylvania to the said **Farling Ball** and **Mary** his wife in hand paid by the said **Thomas Mifflin** at or before the sealing and delivery of these presents the receipt whereof they do hereby acknowledge, have granted bargained sold aliened released and confirmed and by these presents do grant bargain sell alien release and confirm unto the said **Thomas Mifflin** and his heirs all that tract or parcel of land situate lying and being in the County of Loudoun and Colony aforesaid on a small branch of **Kittocton Creek**, being a tract the said **Farling Ball** purchased of **George Gregg** containing 303 acres bounded by the lines of **Mathew Hickson, Richard Roach, Edmund Sands, Abraham Dawson, William Gregg,** and **John Hanby,** and according to the courses and expressions in the deeds of conveyance from the said **Gregg** to the said **Ball**, which deeds are recorded in Loudoun County Court. Also another small parcel of land lying contiguous and adjoining the above described land, which the said **Farling Ball** purchased of **Abraham Dawson** containing 3 acres as by the deeds of conveyance will more fully (and at large) appear. The whole being part of a larger tract granted to **Catesby Cocke Esq**. by a patent from the Proprietor's Office and by the said **Cocke** transferred to the above named **George Gregg,** and all houses buildings orchards ways water watercourses profits commodities hereditaments and appurtenances whatsoever to the said premises hereby granted or any part thereof belonging or in any wise appertaining. To have and to hold the lands hereby conveyed and all and singular other the premises hereby granted and released, and every part and parcel thereof with their and every of their appurtenances unto the said **Thomas Mifflin** and to his heirs and assigns forever, **Farling Ball** and **Mary Ball**. Sealed and delivered in the presence of **H. Neilson, John Gunnell,** and **Wm. Johnston**. Proven on 11/25/1772. Lease and Release, Loudoun County Deed Book I, pp. 114-118.

10. 9/8 and 9/9/1785, **Abraham Dawson** of the County of Loudoun and **Ann** his wife of the one part to **Richard Roach** of the County of Loudoun of the other part. Witnesseth that for and in consideration of the sum of 45 pounds current money of Virginia to the said **Abraham Dawson** and **Ann** his wife in hand paid by the said **Richard Roach** at or before the sealing and delivery of these presents the receipt whereof he doth hereby acknowledge, have granted sold aliened released and confirmed and by these presents doth grant bargain sell alien release and confirm unto the said **Richard Roach** and heirs one moiety of part of a tract or parcel of land situate lying and being in the County of Loudoun and State of Virginia. It being part of a larger tract granted to **Catesby Cocke** by patent from the Proprietor's Office and by the said **Catesby Cocke** transferred to **George Gregg** by **Aneas Campbell** attorney in fact for the said **Catesby Cocke**, and the said **Gregg** conveyed the same to **Abraham Dawson** by deed of lease and release (blank space). The land intended to be granted bounded as follows viz. Beginning at a black oak on the northwest side of **Kittockton Mountain** near the **Bald Hill**

in a line of **Richard Williams** and a line of the original tract extending thence with the original line S 52° - 30 minutes E 102 poles to three spanish oak saplings near the **road leading from Roache's Mill to Leesburg**, then with said **road** N 64-½° W 22 poles to a hickory, then N 82° W 42 poles to between a marked black oak and walnut, then N 56° W 47 poles to a black oak on the north side of the aforesaid **road**, then N 30° W 65 poles to a white oak a former corner to **Richard Williams** and then with his line N 87° E 70 poles to the first station containing 45 acres of land, and all houses buildings orchards ways waters watercourses profits commodities hereditaments and appurtenances whatsoever to the said premises hereby granted or any part thereof belonging or in any way appertaining. To have and to hold the lands hereby conveyed and all and singular other the premises hereby granted and released and every part and parcel thereof with their and every of their appurtenances unto the said **Richard Roach** his heirs and assigns forever, **Abraham. Dawson** and **Ann Dawson**. Sealed and delivered in the presence of **Wm. Hough, Mahlon Hough**, and **William Woollard**. Proven on 9/12/1785. Lease and Release, Loudoun County Deed Book O, pp. 407-411

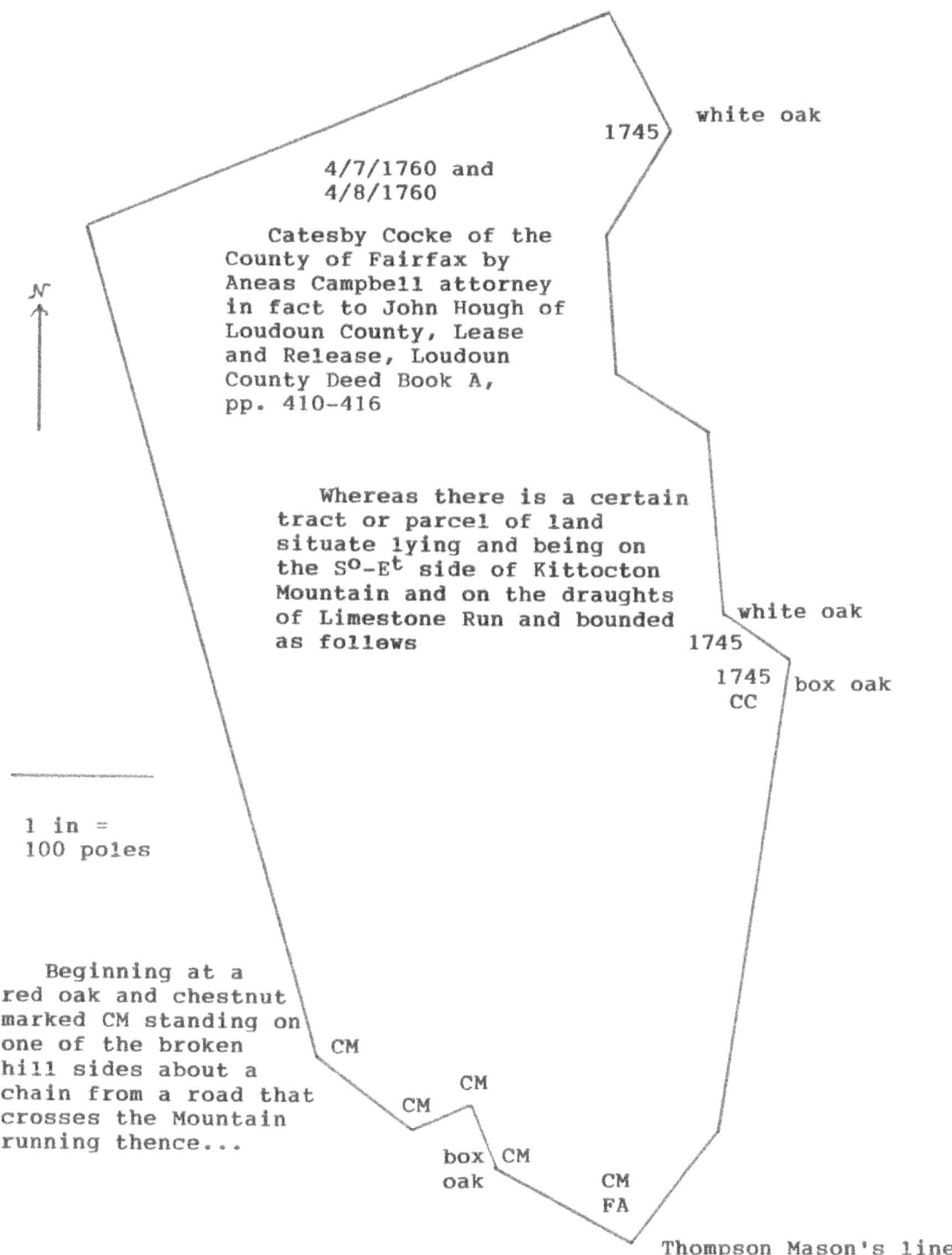

Beginning at a white oak by a grove of pines on the south side of Kittockton Creek extending thence...joining (at A, again) on the west side of Kittockton Mountain on the Drains of Kittockton Creek

* ...to a white and red oak marked 1745 being corner to the tract Edward Norton purchased thence with the said line of that tract...

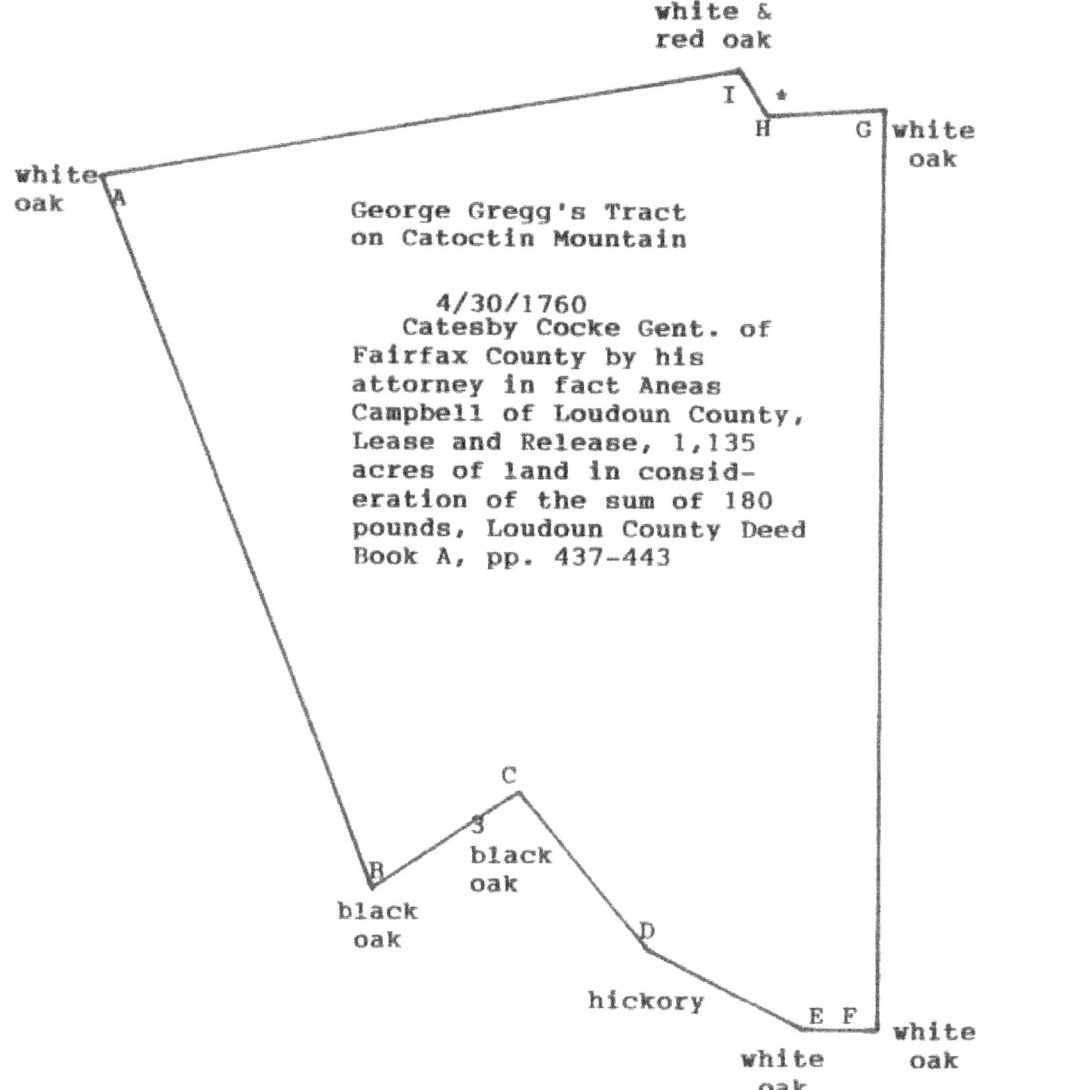

George Gregg's Tract on Catoctin Mountain

4/30/1760
Catesby Cocke Gent. of Fairfax County by his attorney in fact Aneas Campbell of Loudoun County, Lease and Release, 1,135 acres of land in consideration of the sum of 180 pounds, Loudoun County Deed Book A, pp. 437-443

Scale: one inch = one hundred poles
       one inch = 1,650 feet

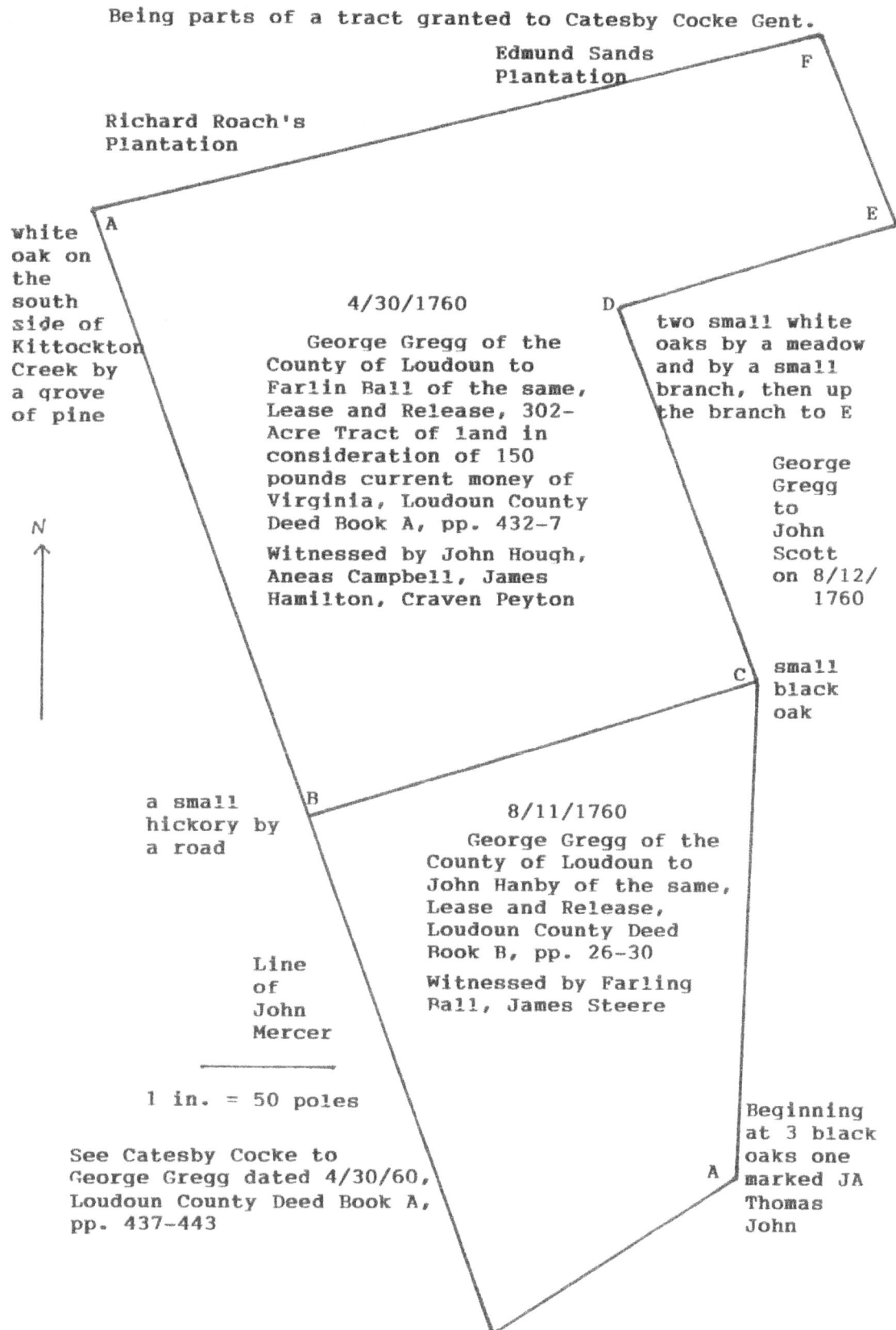

4/16/1769 and 4/17/1769, Abraham Dawson of the County of Loudoun and Colony of Virginia of the one part to Farlen (Farling) Ball of the same County of the other part, Lease and Release of 3 acres of land, Loudoun County Deed Book G, pp. 175-178

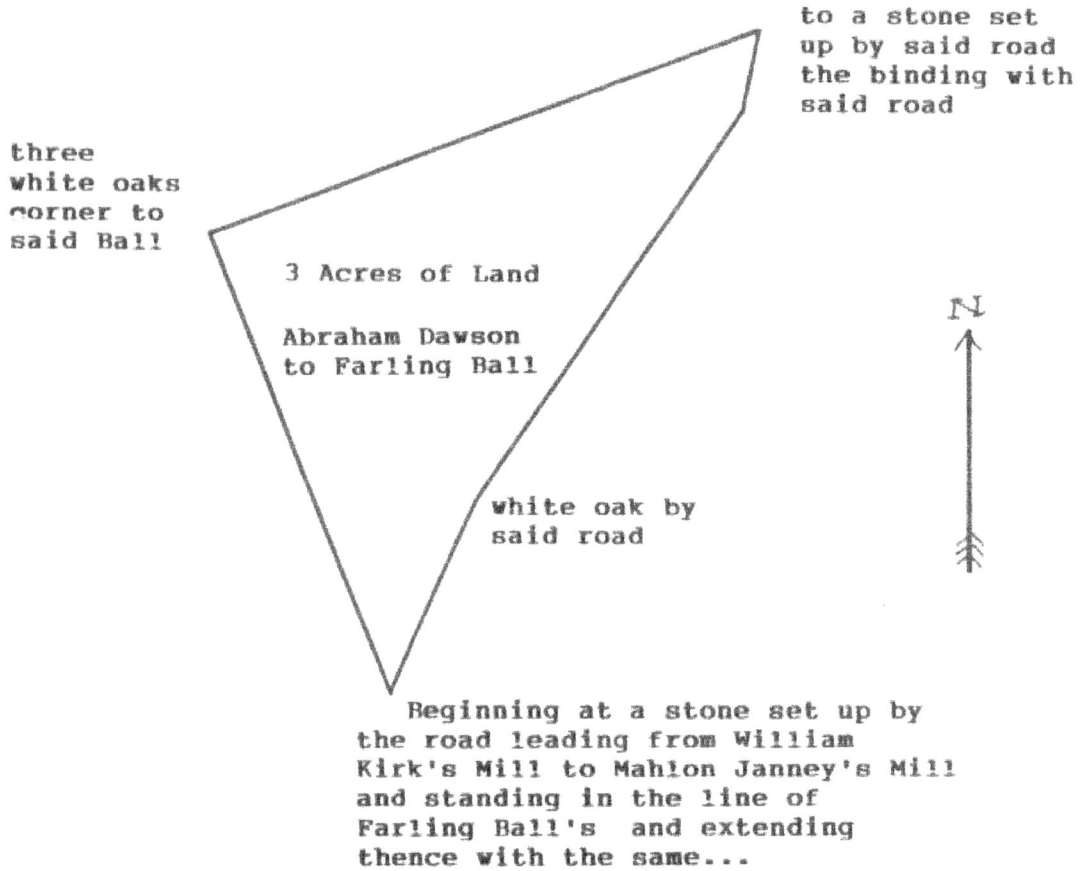

Being part of a tract of land the said Abraham Dawson purchase of George Gregg

to a stone set up by said road the binding with said road

three white oaks corner to said Ball

3 Acres of Land

Abraham Dawson to Farling Ball

white oak by said road

N

Beginning at a stone set up by the road leading from William Kirk's Mill to Mahlon Janney's Mill and standing in the line of Farling Ball's and extending thence with the same...

one inch = 10 poles

Catesby Cocke's Partition from Cocke & Mercer's Tract (circa 1742)

The parceling of part of a tract of land said to contain 5,985 acres that was situated on or about the Catoctin Creek and Catoctin Mountain, which Catesby Cocke and John Mercer had jointly obtained from Thomas, Lord Fairfax and Baron Cameron, the Proprietor of the Northern Neck of Virginia, dated 4/13/1742. Afterwards, John Mercer would relinquish a portion of it to Catesby Cocke in a division made thereof by a Deed of Partition recorded in the County of Fairfax bearing date 12/31/1750. In turn, Catesby Cocke would come to appoint Aneas Campbell as his true and lawful attorney in fact over his share of the land by virtue of letter(s) of attorney given him bearing date 12/18/1759, and recorded in the County of Loudoun.

According to the plan and draft of the said 5,985 acres of land and the division and partition thereof annexed into four lots numbered 1, 2, 3, and 4. The first lot contained 1,361 acres and 1 rood and 6 perches; the second lot contained 1,532 acres and 2 roods and 38 perches; the third lot contained 1,801 acres and 1 rood and 12 perches; the fourth lot contained 1,431 acres and 3 roods and 12 perches. The second and third of which contiguous lots were allotted to the said Catesby Cocke and his heirs and assigns, and the first and fourth separate lots were allotted to John Mercer and his heirs and assigns upon this division or partition between them.

Catesby Cocke's partition spread from the locality of the later town of Waterford down to Thomson Mason's boundary lines apparently for Rasberry Plain. The boundaries were marked at the time with markers for Cocke & Mercer as in CM; William Henry Fairfax and Cocke & Mercer as in WFX CM; Richard Wood as in RW; and Cocke & Mercer and Francis Awbrey as in CM FA. It appears that Cocke's partition was laid off and bounded through John Hough into several parcels of land by Aneas Campbell. It seems that most of this land was cheaply sold by Aneas Campbell for Catesby Cocke. During this period of time the author counted revenues of 200 pounds from such sales against about 2,632 acres of land.

It is noted that Aneas Campbell sold a parcel of land as above containing 410 acres of land to Francis Hague dated in 1760. It overlaid a certain parcel of land containing 303 acres, which Hague at that time retained by conveyance from John Mead dated in 1743. This suggests that Hague's original deed was less than perfect or, instead, that he was actually confirming a resurvey of the same while simultaneously adding acreage to it. In fact, the additional 80 to 85 acres actually came from the contiguous John Mercer & Sons Partition (Deed Book L, pp. 401-406).

It's evident that James Kennedy was an important early figure in this neighborhood. He was recognized as a weaver and was a contemporary of Mahlon Janney. In fact, his land had neighbored Mahlon Janney's property. Kennedy's dwelling house was one of only a few such buildings, which were identified in the early deed records. Presumably, it was of durable construction. Nevertheless, the heretofore published historical interpretations of Waterford and environs make nary a mention of him.

In 1760 William Henry Fairfax deceased's lines and boundary marker were recognized adjacent to Mahlon Janney's fence, and on the lines of a certain parcel of land belonging to James Hamilton containing 240 acres, which pursuant to litigation was subsequently conveyed to James Kennedy. It appears Kennedy had resided on the site in "Canady's House" since at least 1760. In turn, Kennedy would convey 140 acres of the same to Joseph Janney and Mahlon Taylor dated in 1772, which joined a tract of land they had already purchased from John Griffith. These parcels would make up a larger parcel they packaged for conveyance to one Jonathan Myers dated in 1773. Later, Kennedy's current lines and house as in "Kenady's house" were referred to again in a deed of conveyance to Patrick McHolland dated in 1786.

1. 12/31/1750, **Catesby Cocke** Gent. of the Parish of Truro in the County of Fairfax of the one part to **John Mercer** Gent. of Marlborough in the County of Stafford of the other part. Whereas the **Rt. Hon. Thomas, Lord Fairfax and Baron Cameron**, in that part of Great Britain called Scotland, Proprietor of the Northern Neck of Virginia by his deed bearing date 4/13/1742 did give grant and confirm unto **Catesby Cocke and John Mercer** one certain tract or parcel of land in the County of Prince William and bounded according to a survey thereof by **John Warner** as followeth. Beginning at A, a white hickory marked **PL** and **JM** on the south side of **Kittockton Run** by the mouth of a drain and is corner of a tract granted unto **John Mead and Richard Averill**, also corner of **Colo. John Colvill's** land, and running thence with the lines of the said **Mead and Averill** S 53° E 202 poles and found B, the corner a spanish oak 4 poles on the left from B, (thence) S 16° E 390 poles to C, a spanish oak on an hill the corner, also another spanish oak marked **CM**, thence S 22° – 30' W 74 poles to D, a large red oak on an hill another corner marked **CM**, thence N 88° W 114 poles to E, a white oak in the line of the said **Mead and Averill** and corner to the land of **Colo. John Colvill,** and also corner to the land surveyed for **Cornelius Eltinge** now belonging to **William Fairfax Esquire,** which tree is marked **WFx** and **CM**, then along the lines of that tract S 34° E 106 poles to F, an hickory and white oak in the fork of a branch of Kittockton called **Amos's Branch** marked **WFx** and **CM**, (thence) S 1° E 578 poles and found G, the corner two white oaks in the line of the land of **Capt. Benjamin Grayson** nine poles on the left and standing on the side of a mountain near one of the head drains of **Limestone Run** and marked CM, from the said two white oaks running along the lines of **Grayson** N 19° E 26 poles to H, four small and one large spanish oak (marked) **CM** on the head of a drain of the said **Limestone**, (thence) East 310 poles to I, three beeches standing on the NW side of the said **Limestone Run** six poles above a fork of the said run and in an island of the same between the broken hills or mountains and is marked **CM**, (thence) S 34° E 114 poles to K, two small white oaks on a drain of the said **Limestone** and on the south side of the top of an hill or mountain and marked **CM**, then with the given line of the said **Grayson's** land S 11° W 424 poles to L, a white oak on the side of the broken hills or mountains and the end of the dividing line of two tracts of the said **Grayson's** (marked) **CM**, then with the given line of the said tract of the said **Grayson's** S 11° W 94 poles to M, a white oak on the north side of the **North Fork of Tuskarora Run** and in the line of the said **Grayson** and in the line of the land of **John Richardson** and marked **CM**, then with **Richardson's** line N 29° E 15 poles to N, a white oak and red oak both dying marked **FA** and corner to the said **Richardson's** land and the land of

Francis Awbrey now **Mrs. Mason's**, there (are) two large white oaks near marked **CM** and is near a pond of water, then with the said **Awbrey's** or **Mason's** lines N 17° E 280 poles and found O, the corner three black oaks on an hill marked **CM** on the north side of a branch of **Cool Spring** 18 poles on the left from O, their three black oaks run(ning) N 36° E 82 poles to P, a large white oak and small hickory and poplar (marked) **CM** in a branch of the **Cool Spring**, (thence) N 25° E 150 poles to Q, a black oak on a stony point, thence N 20° E 184 poles to R, a black gum and poplar on the south side of the **South Fork of Limestone** near a point of rocks the end of piney mountain marked **CM**, (thence) N 25° E 186 poles to S, three red oaks at the head of a valley, (thence) N 19° E 148 poles to T, the line of the land of **Joseph Dixon** then with the lines of the said **Dixon's** land N 14° W 53 poles to U, a dead red oak marked, a chestnut oak, a red oak and white oak (marked) **CM**, then with another of **Dixon's** lines N 34° E 102 poles to W, a large white oak, (thence) N 63° E 44 poles to X, a white oak under the hill two poles on the left, (thence) N 30° E 48 poles to Y, a red oak on the side of one of the broken hills or mountains and corner of the said **Dixon** and **Awbrey** now **Mason's**, thence S 72° – 30' E 234 poles to Z, a red oak and three white oaks corner of **Francis Awbrey** or **Mason's** and **Patrick Lynch's** 1,537 acre tract now the said **Cocke's** six poles on the left marked **FA** and **CM**, standing on a branch of **Limestone** then with the lines of the said **Cocke's** tract N 58° – 30' W 102 poles to &, a white oak marked **CM**, (thence) N 29° W 44 poles to a, two spanish oaks growing from one root (marked) **CM**, (thence) S 75° – 30' W 52 poles to b, an hickory (marked) **CM**, (thence) N 49° W 96 poles to c, a chestnut and red oak on the top of one of the broken hills or mountains the beginning tree of the land marked **CM**, thence with the given line of the said tract N 14° W 452 poles to d, the said **Cocke's** 1,488 acre tract, then with that line N 80° W 104 poles to e, the given line of the land formerly **Richard Wood's**, then with that line S 27° W 192 poles to f, a red oak the old corner of **Wood's** marked **CM**, also found a white oak near marked **CM**, from the old corner red oak went along **Wood's** line West 42 poles to g, a white oak the corner of **Wood's** marked **RW**, (thence) N 45° W 199 poles to h, a red oak the old corner on the side of the said hill or mountain N 17° W 188 poles to i, a small hickory and two black oaks on an hill by a broken white oak the old corner near a branch, (thence) N 57° E 134 poles to k, a black oak in the line of the said **Wood** and also in the line of the said tract of the said **Cocke's** 1,488 acre tract then with the line of that tract N 20° W 429 poles to l, a white oak and two black oaks by the north side of **Kittockton Run** near a grove of small pines corner to said **Cocke** and also corner to piece of land of **Colo. Colvill's** then with said **Colvill's** line N 30° W 126 poles to m, two small black oaks in a line of **Colo. Colvill's Kittockton Creek Tract**. Finally, with a line of that tract S 27° W 701 poles to the beginning crossing **Kittockton Creek** at 89 poles, 125 poles, 259 poles, 309 poles, 369 poles and twice more just by the beginning containing 5,985 acres. Together with all rights members and appurtenances thereunto belonging royal mines excepted and a full third part of all lead copper tin coals iron mines and iron ore that should be found thereon. To have and to hold the said 5,985 acres of land together with all rights profits and benefits to the same belonging or in any wise appertaining except before excepted to them the said **Cocke and John Mercer** their heirs and assigns forever. They the said **Catesby Cocke and John Mercer** their heirs and assigns therefore yielding and paying to the said proprietor his heirs and assigns or to his certain attorney or attorneys, agent or agents, or to the certain attorney or attorneys of his heirs and assigns proprietors of the said Northern Neck yearly and every year on the Feast of St. Michael the Archangel the fee rent of one shilling sterling money for every fifty acres of land thereby granted and so proportionably for a greater or lesser quantity as by the said deed relation being thereunto had may fully appear. And, whereas the said **Catesby Cocke and John Mercer** have entered unto the said 5,985 acres of land and premises and now stand seized thereof to them and their heirs forever, and have made and agreed upon a full and complete partition and division of the said land and premises with the appurtenances so that they the said **Catesby Cocke and John Mercer** and their heirs may for the future severally and respectively have hold occupy possess and enjoy their several and respective parts and portions of the said lands and premises with the appurtenances separately and divided from the other. Now this indenture witnesseth that the said **Catesby Coke and John Mercer** have made and by these presents do with one assent and consent for themselves and their heirs make a full and complete division of the said 5,985 acres of land and premises with the appurtenances in manner and form following. That is to say **Catesby Cocke** his heirs and assigns shall and may from hence forth have hold occupy and enjoy to the said **Catesby Cocke** his heirs and assigns forever all that part or parcel of the said 5,985 acres of land and premises with the appurtenances bounded as followeth. Beginning at T in the line of the land of **Joseph Dixon** and thence running the several courses and distances herein before mentioned to the letters U, W, X, Y, Z, &, a, b, c, d, e, f, g, h, then N 17° W 68 poles, then S 59° W 300 poles to the line of **Mead and Averill,** then S 16° E 272 poles to one of their corners at C, and thence running the several courses and distances herein before mentioned to the letters D, E, F, then S 1° E 232 poles, then N 87° E 660 poles to the beginning at T, in the line of **Dixon** aforesaid. And, that the said **John Mercer** his heirs and assigns shall and may from henceforth have hold occupy and enjoy to the said **John Mercer** his heirs and assigns all the rest and residue of the said 5,985 acres of land and premises with the appurtenances lying in two several pieces or parcels on each side of the part or parcel of the said **Catesby Cocke** herein before described. One piece or parcel thereof being bounded as followeth that is to say. Beginning at the said **Catesby Cocke's** corner in the line from the letter h, before mentioned and running thence N 17° W 120 poles to i, a small hickory and two black oaks on a hill by broken white oak the old corner near a branch herein before mentioned and thence running the several courses and distances herein before also mentioned to the letters k, l, m, A, B, a corner spanish oak of **Mead and Averill,** then with their line S 16° E 118 poles to the said **Catesby Cocke's** corner in the said line, then along the line before mentioned dividing this parcel from the said **Catesby Cocke's** land N 59° E 300 poles to the beginning in the line from h, to i, aforesaid. The other part or parcel assigned or allotted to the said **John Mercer** being bounded as followeth that is to say. Beginning at the said **Catesby Cocke's** corner in the line from the letter F, before mentioned and running thence S 1° E 346 poles, nine poles on the right of g, two white oaks in the line of the land of **Benjamin Grayson** herein before mentioned and thence running the several courses and distances herein before mentioned to the letters H, I, K, L, M, N, O, P, Q, R, S, T, and thence S 87° W 660 poles along the line of the line before mentioned dividing this parcel from the said **Catesby Cocke's** land. In witness whereof the parties to these presents have hereunto set their hands and seals the day and year first before written, **Catesby Cocke, J. Mercer**. Sealed and delivered in the presence of us **Chas. Green, Richd. Parker, George Mercer**. Proven on 3/26/1751. Deed of Partition, Fairfax County Deed Book C, pp. 99- 106

2.   12/18/1759, **Catesby Cocke** of the County of Fairfax of the one part to **Aneas Campbell** of the County of Loudoun of the other part and recorded in Loudoun County, Letters of Attorney

3.   4/30 and 5/1/1760, **Catesby Cocke Esq**. of the County of Fairfax and Colony of Virginia by his attorney in fact **Aneas Campbell Gent**. of the County of Loudoun and Colony aforesaid of the one part to **Francis Hague** of the said County of Loudoun of the other part. Whereas there is a certain tract or parcel of land situate lying and being in the County of Loudoun aforesaid and in the **Kittocton Mountain** being part of one certain tract of land granted to the said **Catesby Cocke and John Mercer** by patent from the Proprietor's Office and relinquished by the said **Mercer** to the said **Cocke** by a division made, the said parcel of land bounded as followeth viz. Beginning at two hickories the southwest corner of **Patrick Holland's** late purchase extending thence S 12° W 208 poles to a dividing line of said **Cocke and Mercer,** thence with the said dividing line N 87° E 200 poles to a red oak and white oak on a hillside corner to **William Schooley's** mountain lot, thence with his line N 40° E 160 poles to three red oak saplings on point of hill the east side of a small branch of **Limestone Run** corner to said **Schooley,** thence with his line N 10° W 250 poles to a black oak in gully corner to said **Patrick Holland,** thence with his line West 108 poles to a chestnut and two red oaks on a point corner to said **Holland,** then with another of his lines S 16° E 116 poles to red (oak) on a hill by a **path** corner to **Holland,** thence S 73° W 154 poles to the first station containing 410 acres more or less. Now this indenture witnesseth that the said **Catesby Cocke** by his attorney in fact **Aneas Campbell** who by virtue of letters of attorney to him given by the said **Catesby Cocke** bearing date the 18th day of December, 1759 and recorded in Loudoun County Office, for and in consideration of the sum of 15 pounds current money of Virginia to him the said **Catesby Cocke** in hand paid by the said **Francis Hague** the receipt whereof the said **Catesby Cocke** by his attorney in fact **Aneas Campbell** doth hereby acknowledge and himself fully paid and satisfied, hath granted bargained sold aliened release and confirmed and by these presents doth bargain and sell alien release and confirm unto the said **Francis Hague** and his heirs all and singular the said 410 acres of land situate bounded and being as is above set forth and described, together with all houses barns buildings orchards ways waters watercourses woods meadows swamps rights liberties improvements hereditaments and appurtenances with the rents issues and profits thereof. To have and to hold the said 410 acres of land more or less and premises hereby granted

alienated released and confirmed or mentioned and intended to be granted and released with the appurtenances unto the said **Francis Hague** his heirs and assigns forever, **Catesby Cocke**. Sealed and delivered in the presence of **John Hough**, **Jas. Hamilton**, and **Nich. Minor**. Lease and Release, Loudoun County Deed Book A, pp. 473-478

4. 4/30 and 5/1/1760, **Catesby Cocke Esq**. of the County of Fairfax and Colony of Virginia by his attorney in fact **Aneas Campbell Gent**. of the County of Loudoun and Colony aforesaid of the one part to **John Ball** of the County of Loudoun and Colony aforesaid of the other part. Whereas there is a certain tract or parcel of land situate lying and being in the County of Loudoun aforesaid being part of a tract granted to the said **Catesby Cocke and John Mercer** by a patent from the Proprietor's Office, and relinquished by the said **John Mercer** to the said **Catesby Cocke** by a division made. The said parcel of land bounded as followeth viz. Beginning at a white oak in a valley in a line of **Francis Hague** and the original survey of said **Cocke and Mercer** and corner to **William Schooley's** purchase extending thence with **Schooley's** line N 73° E 140 poles to two small white oaks in a poison field corner to said **Schooley**, thence S 16° E 195 poles to a white oak the east side of a branch corner to **Joseph Caldwell** in a line of **Patrick Holland**, thence with his line S 73° W 50 poles to a crooked white oak on a hill corner to **Holland**, thence with another of his lines S 4° W 171 poles to two hickories corner to **Holland** and the beginning corner of **Francis Hague's** late purchase, thence with said **Hague's** line S 12° W 208 poles to the dividing line of said **Cocke and Mercer**, then with that line S 87° W 12 poles to a corner of **James Canady's (Kennedy)**, then with his line N 1° W 187 poles to two hickory bushes on a hillside above said **Canady's house**, thence with **Canady's** lines N 5° W 121 poles to a small oak and hickory corner to **Canady**, thence N 88° W 52 poles to a dead red oak on a hill corner to the said original and to **Mahlon Janney**, then with **Janney's** and the lines of the original N 22-½° E 74 poles to a spanish and white oak on a hill, thence N 16° W 176 poles to the first station containing and laid out for 290 acres more or less. Now this indenture witnesseth that the said **Catesby Cocke** by his attorney in fact **Aneas Campbell** who by virtue of letters of attorney to him given by the said **Catesby Cocke** bearing date the 18th day of December, 1759 and recorded in Loudoun County Office, for and in consideration of the sum of 50 pounds current money of Virginia to him the said **Catesby Cocke** in hand paid by the said **John Ball**, the receipt whereof the said **Catesby Cocke** by his attorney in fact **Aneas Campbell** doth hereby acknowledge and himself fully satisfied thereof and every part thereof, hath granted bargained sold alienated released and confirmed and by these presents doth bargain and sell alien release and confirm unto the said **John Ball** and his heirs all and singular the said 290 acres of land situate bounded and being as is above set forth and described together with all houses barns buildings orchards ways watercourses woods meadows swamps rights liberties improvements hereditaments and appurtenances with the rents issues and profits thereof. To have and to hold the said 290 acres of land more or less and premises hereby granted alienated released and confirmed or mentioned and intended to be granted and released with the appurtenances unto the said **John Ball** his heirs and

assigns forever, **Catesby Cocke**. Sealed and delivered in the presence of **Craven Peyton**, **John Hough**, and **Jas. Hamilton**. Proven in 6/10/1760. Lease and Release, Loudoun County Deed Book A, pp. 484-490

5.   4/30 and 5/1/1760, **Catesby Cocke Esq**. of the County of Fairfax and Colony of Virginia by his attorney in fact **Aneas Campbell Gent**. of the County of Loudoun and Colony aforesaid of the one part to **Joseph McGeach** of the said County of Loudoun aforesaid of the other part. Whereas there is a certain tract or parcel of land situate lying and being in the County of Loudoun aforesaid joining the **Kittocton Mountain** and being part of a large tract granted to the said **Catesby Cocke and John Mercer** by a patent from the Proprietor's Office and relinquished by the said **Mercer** to the said **Cocke** by a division made. The said parcel of land bounded as followeth viz. Beginning at a black oak on a hill by his field corner to his patent land and to the original survey of the said **Cocke and Mercer** extending thence N 17° W 68 poles to a hickory dividing corner between said **Cocke** and **Mercer**, thence with the said dividing line S 59° W 100 poles to two red oak saplings corner to **William Schooley's** purchase, thence with his line S 47° E 284 poles to a red oak corner to **Joseph Caldwell**, thence with his line N 61° E 10 poles to a white oak and red oak his corner, thence with another of his lines S 47° E 132 poles to a white oak and red oak his corner, thence with another of his lines S 63° E 290 poles to a chestnut tree on the southeast side of said mountain the beginning corner of **John Hough's** late purchase being another tract and corner to said **Caldwell**, thence with the given line of the said **Hough's** land N 14° W 452 poles to a white oak corner to **Gregg's** late purchase being another tract, thence N 80° W 104 poles to the given line of one **Richard Wood's** survey now **Thomas John's**, thence with that line S 27° W 192 poles to a red oak marked **CM**, thence said **Wood's** line West 42 poles to a white oak marked **RW**, thence N 45° W 199 poles to the first station containing and laid out for 600 acres of land more or less. Now this indenture witnesseth that the said **Catesby Cocke** by his attorney in fact **Aneas Campbell** who by virtue of letters of attorney given him by the said **Catesby Cocke** bearing date the 18th day of December, 1759 and recorded in Loudoun County Office, for and in consideration of the sum of 30 pounds current money of Virginias to him the said **Catesby Cocke** in hand paid by the said **Joseph McGeach**, the receipt whereof the said **Catesby Cocke** by his attorney in fact **Aneas Campbell** doth hereby acknowledge and himself fully paid and satisfied thereof and every part thereof, hath granted bargained sold aliened released and confirmed and by these presents doth bargain and sell alien release and confirm unto the said **Joseph McGeach** and his heirs all and singular the said 600 acres of land situate bounded and being as is above set forth and described together with all houses barns buildings orchards ways water watercourses woods meadows swamps rights liberties improvements hereditaments and appurtenances with the rents issues and profits thereof. To have and to hold the said 600 acres of land more or less and premises hereby granted alienated released and confirmed or mentioned and intended to be granted and released with the appurtenances unto the said **Joseph McGeach** his heirs and assigns forever, **Catesby Cocke**. Sealed and delivered in the presence of **Nich. Minor**, **Jas. Hamilton**, and **John Moss Jr**.

Proven on 6/10/1760. Lease and Release, Loudoun County Deed Book A, pp. 496-502

6. 4/30 and 5/1/1760, **Catesby Cocke Esq.** of Fairfax County by his attorney in fact **Aneas Campbell Gent.** of the County of Loudoun of the one part to **William Schooley** of the County of Loudoun of the other part. Whereas there is a certain tract or parcel of land situate lying and being in the County of Loudoun, being part of one certain tract of land granted to the said **Catesby Cocke and John Mercer** by a patent out of the Proprietor's Office and relinquished by the said **Mercer** to the said **Cocke** by a division made. The said parcel of land bounded as followeth viz. Beginning at a white oak in a valley in a line of **Francis Hague** near the **Meetinghouse** the beginning corner of **John Ball's** land extending thence with the said **Ball's** line N 73° E 140 poles to two small white oaks in a poison field **Ball's** corner, thence S 16° E 61 poles to a hickory by a **road** corner to **Joseph Caldwell**, thence with his line N 61° E 152 poles to a line of **Joseph McGeach's,** thence with his line N 47° W 190 poles to two red oak saplings in one of the dividing lines of said **Cocke** and **Mercer** and corner to said **McGeach,** thence with said dividing line S 50° W 195 poles to a heap of stones by a marked white oak in the said **Hague's** line and in the line of the original survey of **Cocke and Mercer,** thence with said line N 16° E 87 poles to the first station. And, whereas there is another parcel of land within the bounds of the above said original survey of **Cocke and Mercer** bounded as followeth viz. Beginning at three red oak saplings on a point of a hill east side of a small drain of **Limestone Run** being the southeast corner of **Francis Hague's** lot being on the **Kittocton Mountain** extending thence with **Hague's** line N 10° W 110 poles to a red oak on a hill corner to **Patrick Holland,** thence with his line N 75° E 175 poles to a red and white oak corner to **Joseph Caldwell** and a **Reserve** of the said **Aneas Campbell,** thence with his line S 13° W 270 poles to a dividing line of said **Cocke and Mercer,** thence with that line S 87° W 200 poles to a red and white oak on a hillside corner to said **Hague,** thence N 40° E 160 poles to the first station containing 210 acres of land more or less according to the above boundaries. Now this indenture witnesseth that the said **Catesby Cocke** by his attorney in fact **Aneas Campbell** who by virtue of letters of attorney to him given by the said **Catesby Cocke** bearing date the 18th day of December, 1759 and recorded in Loudoun County Office, for and in consideration of the sum of 30 pounds current money of Virginia to him the said **Catesby Cocke** in hand paid by the said **William Schooley,** the receipt whereof the said **Catesby Cocke** by his attorney in fact **Aneas Campbell** doth hereby acknowledge and himself fully paid and satisfied thereof and every part thereof, hath granted bargained sold alienated released and confirmed and by these presents doth bargain and sell alien release and confirm unto the said **William Schooley** and his heirs all and singular the said two tract of land both containing and laid out for 411 acres situate bounded and being as is above set forth and described together with all houses barns buildings orchards ways water watercourses woods meadows swamps rights liberties improvements hereditaments and appurtenances with the rents issue and rights thereof. To have and to hold the said land and premises hereby granted alienated released or confirmed or mentioned and intended to be granted or

released with the appurtenances unto the said **William Schooley** his heirs and assigns forever, **Catesby Cocke**. Sealed and delivered in the presence of **Craven Peyton, John Hough**, and **Jas. Hamilton**. Proven on 6/10/1760. Lease and Release, Loudoun County Deed Book pp. 490-496

7. 4/30 and 5/1/1760, **Catesby Cocke Esq**. of the County of Fairfax and Colony of Virginia by his attorney in fact **Aneas Campbell Gent**. of the County of Loudoun and Colony aforesaid of the one part to **Joseph Caldwell** of the said County of the other part. Whereas there is a certain tract or parcel of land situate lying and being in the County of Loudoun aforesaid on and about the **Kittocton Mountain** being part of a certain tract of land granted to said **Catesby Cocke and John Mercer Gent**. by patent from the Proprietor's Office and relinquished by the said **Mercer** to the said **Cocke** by a division made the said parcel of land bounded as followeth viz. Beginning at a hickory by a **road from John Ball's to Joseph McGeach's corner to William Schooley in a line of John Ball's,** extending thence with **Ball's** line S 16° E 140 poles to a white oak the east side of a branch corner to **Ball** in a line of **Patrick Holland's** late purchase, thence with his line N 73° E 192 poles to a red oak on hillside corner to **Holland,** thence with another of his lines S 51° E 215 poles to a red oak **Holland's** corner and corner to said **Schooley's** mountain lot and corner to **Aneas Campbell's Reserve,** thence with said **Campbell's** line S 72° - 30 minutes E 183 poles to a red oak corner to the original **Cocke and Mercer's** survey and to **Thomson Mason's** land, the same course continued 234 poles to a large red oak and two white oaks corner to said original and said **Mason** and to **John Hough's** late purchase, then with said **Hough's** lines N 58-½° W 102 poles to a white oak, thence N 29° W 44 poles to two spanish oaks growing from one root, thence S 75° - 30 minutes W 52 poles to a hickory, thence N 49° W 96 poles to a chestnut tree on the mountainside by a **road** the beginning tree of said **Hough's** land and corner to **Joseph McGeach's** late purchase, thence with **McGeach's** line N 63° W 290 poles to a red oak his corner, thence with another of his lines N 47° W 132 poles to a white and red oak, thence S 61° W 10 poles to a white and red oak, thence N 47° W 92 poles to a red and white oak corner to **Wm. Schooley's** other tract, thence with his line S 61° W 152 poles to the first station containing and laid out for 412 acres of land more or less. Now this indenture witnesseth that the said **Catesby Cocke** by his attorney in fact **Aneas Campbell** who by virtue of letters of attorney to him given by the said **Catesby Cocke** bearing date the (blank space) day of December, 1759 recorded in Loudoun County Office, for and in consideration of the sum of 35 pounds current money of Virginia to him in hand paid by the said **Joseph Caldwell,** the receipt whereof the said **Catesby Cocke** by his attorney in fact **Aneas Campbell** doth hereby acknowledge and himself fully paid and satisfied thereof and every part thereof, hath granted bargained sold alienated released and confirmed and by these presents doth bargain and sell alien release and confirm unto the said **Joseph Caldwell** and his heirs all and singular the said 412 acres of land situate bounded and being as is above set forth and described together with all houses barns buildings orchards ways waters watercourses woods meadows swamps rights liberties improvements hereditaments and appurtenances with the rents issues and profits thereof. To have and to hold the said 412 acres of land

more or less and premises hereby granted alienated released and confirmed or mentioned and intended to be granted and released with the appurtenances unto the said **Joseph Caldwell** his heirs and assigns forever, **Catesby Cocke**. Sealed and delivered in the presence of **Nich. Minor, Francis Hague,** and **Jas. Hamilton.** Proven on 6/10/1760. Lease and Release, Loudoun County Deed Book B, pp. 2-6

8.   5/10 and 5/11/1760, **James Hamilton** of the County of Loudoun and Colony of Virginia and **Priscilla** his wife of the one part to **Patrick Holland** of the County and Colony aforesaid of the other part. Whereas there is a certain tract or parcel of land situate lying and being in the County of Loudoun aforesaid on the north side of the **Kittocton Mountain** and bounded as followeth viz. Beginning at a crooked white oak on a hillside corner to **John Ball** thence with **Ball's** line S 4° W 171 poles to two hickories corner to **Francis Hague's** purchase, then with his line N 73° E 154 poles to a black oak on a hill by a **path** corner said **Hague,** then with another of his lines N 16° W 116 poles to a chestnut and two red oaks on a point, thence with another of **Hague's** lines East 108 poles to a black oak in a gully **Hague's** corner, then with **Hague** S 10° E 105 poles to a red oak on a hillside corner **Wm. Schooley's** second purchase, then with his line S 75° E 175 poles to a red oak and white oak corner to said **Schooley, Jos. Caldwell,** and **Aneas Campbell's Reserve,** then with **Caldwell's** line N 51° W 215 poles to a red oak on a hillside **Caldwell's** corner, then with another of his lines S 73° W 243 poles to the first station containing 260 acres of land more or less. The same being of a tract of land granted to **Catesby Cocke Gent**. by patent from the Proprietor's Office of the Northern Neck of Virginia and by the said **Catesby Cocke** transferred to **James Hamilton** by his attorney in fact **Aneas Campbell** by deeds of lease and release which is recorded in Loudoun County Office. Now this indenture witnesseth that the said **James Hamilton** and **Priscilla** his wife for and in consideration of the sum of 20 pounds current money of Virginia to him in hand paid by the said **Patrick Holland** the receipt whereof the said **James Hamilton** and **Priscilla** his wife doth hereby acknowledge thereof and every part thereof, hath granted bargained sold alienated released and confirmed and by these presents doth bargain and sell release and confirm unto the said **Patrick Holland** and his heirs and assigns forever all and singular the said 260 acres of land situate bounded and being as is above set forth and described together with all houses orchards watercourses and all other appurtenances with the rents issues and profits thereof. To have and to hold the said 260 acres of land hereditaments and premises hereby granted and released with the appurtenances unto the said **Patrick Holland** his heirs and assigns forever, **Jas. Hamilton** and **Priscilla Hamilton.** Sealed and delivered in the presence of **Nich. Minor, Lee Massey,** and **Phil Noland**. Proven on 8/10/1762. Lease and Release, Loudoun County Deed Book C, Part 1, pp. 350-355

9.   8/11 and 12/1760, **Catesby Cocke Esq**. of the County of Fairfax by his attorney in fact **Aneas Campbell** of the County of Loudoun of the one part to **James Hamilton Gent**. of the said County of Loudoun aforesaid of the other part. Witnesseth that the said **Catesby Cocke** for and in consideration of the sum of 40 pounds current money of Virginia to the said **Catesby Cocke** in hand paid by the

said **James Hamilton** at or before the sealing and delivery of these presents the receipt whereof the said **Catesby Cocke** by his attorney in fact **Aneas Campbell** doth hereby acknowledge, have granted bargained sold aliened released and confirmed and by these presents do grant bargain sell alien release and confirm unto the said **James Hamilton** (in his actual possession now by virtue of a bargain and sale to him thereof made by the said Catesby Cocke by his attorney in fact Aneas Campbell for one whole year by indenture bearing date the day before the date of these presents and by force of the statute for transferring uses into possessions) and his heirs forever all that tract or parcel of land situate lying and being in the County of Loudoun aforesaid in and about the **Kittocton Mountain**, being part of a tract granted to the said **Catesby Cocke and John Mercer** by a patent from the Proprietor's Office of the Northern Neck of Virginia bearing date the 18th day of December (year not entered), the same being bounded as followeth viz. Beginning at a white oak in a line of **Mahlon Janney's** by his fence marked **WFX - CM** being corner to the original survey of **Cocke and Mercer** and to land of **William Henry Fairfax** extending thence S 88° E 166 poles to a small red oak and hickory corner to **John Ball** on a hillside, thence with **Ball's** line S 5° E 121 poles to two marked hickory bushes, thence with said **Ball** S 1° E 187 poles to the dividing line between said **Cocke and Mercer,** thence with said line S 87° W 115 poles to the line of the said **William Henry Fairfax**, thence with his line N 1° W 232 poles to a hickory and two white oaks in the fork of a branch, then with said **Fairfax** line N 34° W 106 poles to the first station containing 240 acres. Also, one other tract or parcel of land situate lying and being in the same County of Loudoun and part of the same tract taken up by said **Cocke and Mercer** bounded as followeth viz. Beginning at a crooked white oak on hillside corner to **John Ball** extending thence with said **Ball's** line S 4° W 171 poles to two hickories corner to **Francis Hague,** thence with his line N 73° E 154 poles to a black oak on a hill by a **path** corner to said **Hague,** (then) with another of his lines N 16° W 116 poles to a chestnut sapling corner to **Hague,** then East 108 poles to a black oak in a gully corner to **Hague,** then S 10° E 105 poles to a red oak corner to **William Schooley,** then with his line N 75° E 175 poles to a red oak and Wo (white oak) corner to said **Schooley** and **Joseph Caldwell,** thence with **Caldwell's** line N 51° W 215 poles to a red oak on hillside, thence with another of **Caldwell's** lines S 73° W 243 poles to the beginning containing 260 acres be the same more or less according to the above mentioned boundaries, and all houses buildings edifices orchards ways watercourses easements profits commodities hereditaments and appurtenances whatsoever to the above mentioned two tracts of land and premises hereby granted or in any part thereof belonging or in any wise appertaining. To have and to hold the said two tracts of land and all and singular other the premises hereby granted and released and every part and parcel thereof with their and every of their appurtenances unto the said **James Hamilton** his heirs and assigns forever, **Catesby Cocke**. Proven on 8/12/1760. Lease and Release, Loudoun County Deed Book B, pp. 11-16

10.   4/15 and 4/16/1772, **James Hamilton Gent**. Of the County of Loudoun of the one part to **James Kennady (Kennedy)** of the County of Loudoun, weaver, of the other part. Witnesseth that for and in consideration of the sum of 14 pounds

current money of Virginia to the said **James Hamilton** in hand paid by the said **James Kennady** at or before the sealing and delivery of these presents the receipt whereof he doth hereby acknowledge, and thereof doth acquit and discharge the said **James Hamilton** his heirs executors administrators, and by these presents he the said **James Hamilton** pursuant to a decree of the Honorable, the General Court in chancery hath granted bargained sold aliened released and confirmed and by these presents doth grant bargain sell alien release and confirm unto the said **James Kennady** and to his heirs a certain parcel of land situate in the County of Loudoun whereon the said **James Kennady** now lives, being part of a larger tract of land which formerly belonged to **Catesby Cocke** and which was laid off by **John Hough** into several lots of which the parcel of land hereby conveyed is one lot and bounded according to that survey made by the said **Hough** and is supposed to contain 260 acres be the same more or less, and all houses buildings orchards ways waters watercourses profits commodities hereditaments and appurtenances whatsoever to the said premises hereby granted or any part thereof belonging or in any wise appertaining and the reversion and reversions remainder and remainders issues profits thereof and also all the estate right title interest use trust property claim and demand whatsoever of him the said **James Hamilton** of in and to the said premises and all deeds evidences and writings touching or in any wise concerning the same. To have and to hold the lands hereby conveyed and all and singular other the premises hereby granted and released and every part and parcel thereof with their every of their appurtenances unto the said **James Kennady** his heirs and assigns forever, **Jas. Hamilton**. Sealed and delivered in the presence of **W. Ellzey, Joseph Janney**, and **Mahlon Taylor**. Proven on 8/27/1772. Lease and Release, Loudoun County Deed Book I, pp. 54-58.

11. 4/16 and 4/17/1772, **James Kennady (Kennedy)** of the County of Loudoun, weaver, and **Margaret** his wife of the one part to **Joseph Janney and Mahlon Taylor** of the County aforesaid, merchants, of the other part. Witnesseth that for and in consideration of the sum of 180 pounds current money of Virginia to the said **James Kennady** in hand paid by the said **Joseph Janney and Mahlon Taylor** at or before the sealing and delivery of these presents the receipt whereof he doth hereby acknowledge, have granted bargained sold aliened released and confirmed and by these presents do grant bargain sell alien release and confirm unto the said **Joseph Janney and Mahlon Taylor** and their heirs a certain parcel of land situate in the said County of Loudoun whereon the said **James Kennady** now lives being part of a larger tract of land which formerly belonged to **Catesby Cocke** and which was laid off by **John Hough** in several lots of which the parcel of land hereby granted and released is one, and is bounded according to that survey made by **John Hough** supposed to contain 260 acres be the same more or less, (and) joining the tract of land which the said **Joseph Janney** purchased from **John Griffith** as follows viz. Beginning at a white oak in a line of **Mahlon Janney** marked WFX - CM extending thence S 88° E 166 poles to a small red oak and hickory corner to **John Ball's** land on hillside, then with **Ball's** line S 5° E 121 poles to two hickory bushes **Ball's** corner, then with another of his lines S 1° E 177 poles to the dividing line of **Cock** (sic) **and Mercer,** then with said line S 87° W 115 poles to the line of a tract formerly **William Henry Fairfax,** then

with said line N 1° W 222 poles to a hickory and white oak in the fork of a branch marked **WFX - CM**, thence N 34° W 106 poles to the first station containing 140 acres more or less and all houses buildings orchards ways waters watercourses profits commodities hereditaments and appurtenances whatsoever to the said premises hereby granted or any part thereof belonging or in any wise appertaining. To have and to hold the lands hereby conveyed and all and singular other the premises hereby granted and released and every part and parcel thereof with their and every of their appurtenances unto the said **Joseph Janney and Mahlon Taylor** their heirs and assigns forever, **James** his J mark **Kennady**. Sealed and delivered in the presence of **William Ellzey**, **Thomas Lewis**, and **Robert Hamilton**. Proven on 8/27/1772. Lease and Release, Loudoun County Deed Book K, pp. 175-179

12. 5/25 and 5/26/1773, **Joseph Janney** and **Hannah** his wife of the County of Loudoun and **Mahlon Taylor** of the County of Loudoun of the one part to **Jonathan Myers** of the County aforesaid of the other part. Witnesseth that for and in consideration of the sum of 300 pounds current money of Virginia to the said **Joseph Janney and Mahlon Taylor** in hand paid by the said **Jonathan Myers** at or before the sealing and delivery of these presents the receipt whereof he doth hereby acknowledge, doth grant bargain sell alien release and confirm unto the said **Jonathan Myers** and heirs all that tract or parcel of land situate in Loudoun County aforesaid on a small branch of **Kittocton Creek**, 240 acres of which is part of a tract granted to **Cock and Mercer,** the remainder is part of a tract granted to **William Henry Fairfax** and by the several patentees transferred to others and in course and due for to the said **Janney and Taylor,** the whole bounded as followeth viz. Beginning at two white oaks by **Mahlon Janney's** fence marked **CM - FA** corner to land taken up by **Francis Awbrey** and **Cock** (sic) **and Mercer,** extending thence with **Mahlon Janney's** line in part East 168 poles to a small hickory and red oak sapling on a hillside corner to **James Ball**, then with his line S 5° E 124 poles to two small hickories from one root, then S 1° E 168 poles to a small hickory in the dividing line of **Cock and Mercer,** then binding with said line S 87° W 112 poles to a white oak in one of the original lines of said **Cock and Mercer,** then with the same N 3° W 40 poles to a hickory at the head of a great gully, then S 89° W 115 poles to a stake near a marked white oak, then N 21° W 201 poles to a marked black oak on a hillside joining the aforesaid land of **Awbrey,** then with a line of that tract N 50° E 102 poles to the beginning containing 395 acres, and all houses buildings orchards ways waters watercourses profits commodities hereditaments and appurtenances whatsoever to the said premises hereby granted or any part thereof belonging or any wise appertaining. To have and to hold the lands hereby conveyed and all and singular other the premises hereby granted and released and every part and parcel thereof with their and every of their appurtenances unto the said **Jonathan Myers** his heirs and assigns forever, **Joseph Janney**, **Mahlon Taylor**, and **Hannah Janney**. Proven on 6/14/1773. Lease and Release, Loudoun County Deed Book I, pp. 385-391

13. Know all men by these presents that I **Mahlon Taylor** of the County of Hunterdon in West New Jersey have for sundry good causes nominated

constituted and appointed and by these presents do nominate constitute and appoint and in my stead and place put my trusty friend **Thomas Hague** of the County of Loudoun in the Colony of Virginia, my true and lawful attorney to ask demand recover and receive for me and in my name to attach fees & c, or to proceed in any other regular course of law for the recovery of sundry bonds, bills, notes & c., committed to his charge to finish for me all and singular thing and things which shall or may be necessary touching or concerning the same (as) fully and thoroughly as I the said **Mahlon Taylor** in my own person might or could do about the same. In witness whereof I have hereunto set my hand and seal the (blank space) day of April, 1774, **Mahlon Taylor**. Sealed and delivered in the presence of **Strainge Backhouse**. Proven on 12/13/1774. Letter of Attorney, Loudoun County Deed Book K, p. 361

14.   3/10 and 11/1783, **William Schooley** of the County of Westmorland and Sate of Pennsylvania of the one part to **Joseph Janney** of the County of Loudoun and State of Virginia of the other part. Whereas there is a certain tract or parcel of land situate lying and being in the County of Loudoun aforesaid being part of a larger tract of land granted by a patent from the Proprietor's Office to **Catesby Cocke and John Mercer** and relinquished by the said **Mercer** to the said **Cocke** by a division thereof, and by the said **Cocke** conveyed to the said **William Schooley** by deeds of lease and release bearing date 5/1/1760, and bounded as followeth viz. Beginning at a white oak in a valley in a line of **William Hough's** land formerly belonging to **Francis Hague** deceased, the beginning corner of **James Ball's** land, and extending thence with the said **Ball's** line N 75° E 140 poles to two white oaks in a poison field another of **Ball's** corners, thence S 16° E 61 poles to a hickory by a road corner to **Joseph Caldwell,** then with his line N 61° E 152 poles to a line of the heirs of **Joseph McGeach's deceased**, thence with said line N 47° W 190 poles to two red oak sapling in one of the dividing lines of **Cocke and Mercer** original owners of the said land and corner to the heirs of **Joseph McGeach deceased** aforesaid, thence with the said **Cocke and Mercer's** dividing line S 50° W 195 poles to a heap of stones by a marked white oak in a line of **William Hough's** land aforesaid it being also a line of the original survey of the said **Cocke and Mercer**, thence with said line S 16° E 87 poles to the first station containing 201 acres more or less. Now, this indenture witnesseth that the said **William Schooley** for and in consideration of the sum of 400 pounds current money of Virginia to him in hand paid by the said **Joseph Janney** the receipt whereof is hereby acknowledged, hath granted bargained and sold aliened released and confirmed by these presents unto the said **Joseph Janney** all and singular the said tract or parcel of land above mentioned containing 201 acres more or less situate bounded and being as above set forth and described together with all houses barns buildings orchards ways water courses woods meadows swamps rights liberties improvements hereditaments and appurtenances with the rents issues and profits thereof. To have and to hold the said land and premises hereby granted alienated released and confirmed or mentioned and intended to be granted and released unto the said **Joseph Janney** his heirs and assigns forever, **William** his X mark **Schooley**. Sealed and delivered in the presence of **Mahlon**

Janney, **Wm. Hough**, and **Thomas Mathews**. Proven on 8/11/1783. Lease and Release, Loudoun County Deed Book N, Part 2, pp. 472-475.

15. 4/10/1786, **James Ball** of the County of Loudoun and Commonwealth of Virginia and **Mary** his wife of the one part to **Patrick McHolland** of the County aforesaid of the other part. Witnesseth that the said **James Ball** for and in consideration of the sum of 30 pounds current money of Virginia to him in hand paid by the said **Patrick McHolland** the receipt whereof the said **James Ball** and **Mary** his wife doth hereby acknowledge, hath bargained sold aliened released and confirmed and by these presents doth grant bargain sell release and confirm unto the said **Patrick McHolland** his heirs and assigns 80 acres of land more or less with the appurtenances hereafter mentioned, situate lying and being in the County of Loudoun aforesaid on **Kittockton Mountain**, being part of a tract granted to **Cock** (sic) **and Mercer** and also part of 290 acres sold by their attorney in fact **Enes** (sic) **Campbell** to **John Ball** by his deed recorded in Loudoun County Court reference thereunto being had will more fully and at large appear. The said 80 acres bounded as followeth viz. Beginning at a small red oak and hickory corner to **John Pyott Jr.** and extending thence S 80° E 60 poles to a large black oak in the line of said **Ball,** thence S 4° W 78 poles to three hickories corner to **Francis Hague's** land, thence with said **Hague's** line S 12° W 208 poles to the dividing line of **Cock and Mercer,** then with that line S 87° W 12 poles to a corner of **James Kenady** (sic), then with his line N 1 W 198 poles to two hickory bushes on a hillside above said **Kenady's house,** then with **Kenady's** line N 5 W 121 poles to the first station containing 80 acres of land more or less, together with all houses edifices buildings gardens orchards woods ways water watercourses privileges and appurtenances to the same belonging or in any wise appertaining. To have and to hold the said 80 acres more or less of land and all and singular the premises hereby granted or mentioned and intended to be granted with the appurtenances unto the said **Patrick McHolland** his heirs and assigns forever, **James Ball** and **Mary** her X mark **Ball**. Lease and Release, Loudoun County Deed Book N, Part 1, pp. 94-99

16. 9/8/1800, **James Ball** and **Ruth** his wife of Loudoun County in Virginia of the one part to **James Paxon** of the aforesaid County and State of the other part. Witnesseth that the said **James Ball** and **Ruth** his wife for and in consideration of the sum of 30 pounds lawful money to them in hand paid by the said **James Paxon** the receipt whereof they do hereby acknowledge, and by these presents hath granted bargained sold and confirmed and doth hereby fully freely and absolutely grant bargain sell and confirm unto the said **James Paxon** his heirs and assigns one certain messuage or lot of land situate in Loudoun County aforesaid butted and bounded as followeth viz. Beginning at three small hickories corner to **Jonathan Myer's** heirs then with their line N 80° W 52 poles to a heap of stones, then N 22-½° W 52-½ poles to a stone, then S 88° E 52-2/3 poles to a small hickory on a hillside, then S 22° W 52-½ poles to the beginning containing 17 acres be the same more or less, together with the houses thereon and all and singular the appurtenances unto the said messuage or lot of land belonging or any ways appertaining. To have and to hold the hereby granted and described messuage or lot of land and premises with every of their appurtenances unto him

the said **James Paxon** his heirs and assigns forever, **James Ball** and **Ruth Ball**. Proven on 9/8/1800. Deed. Loudoun County Deed Book 2A, pp. 119-121.

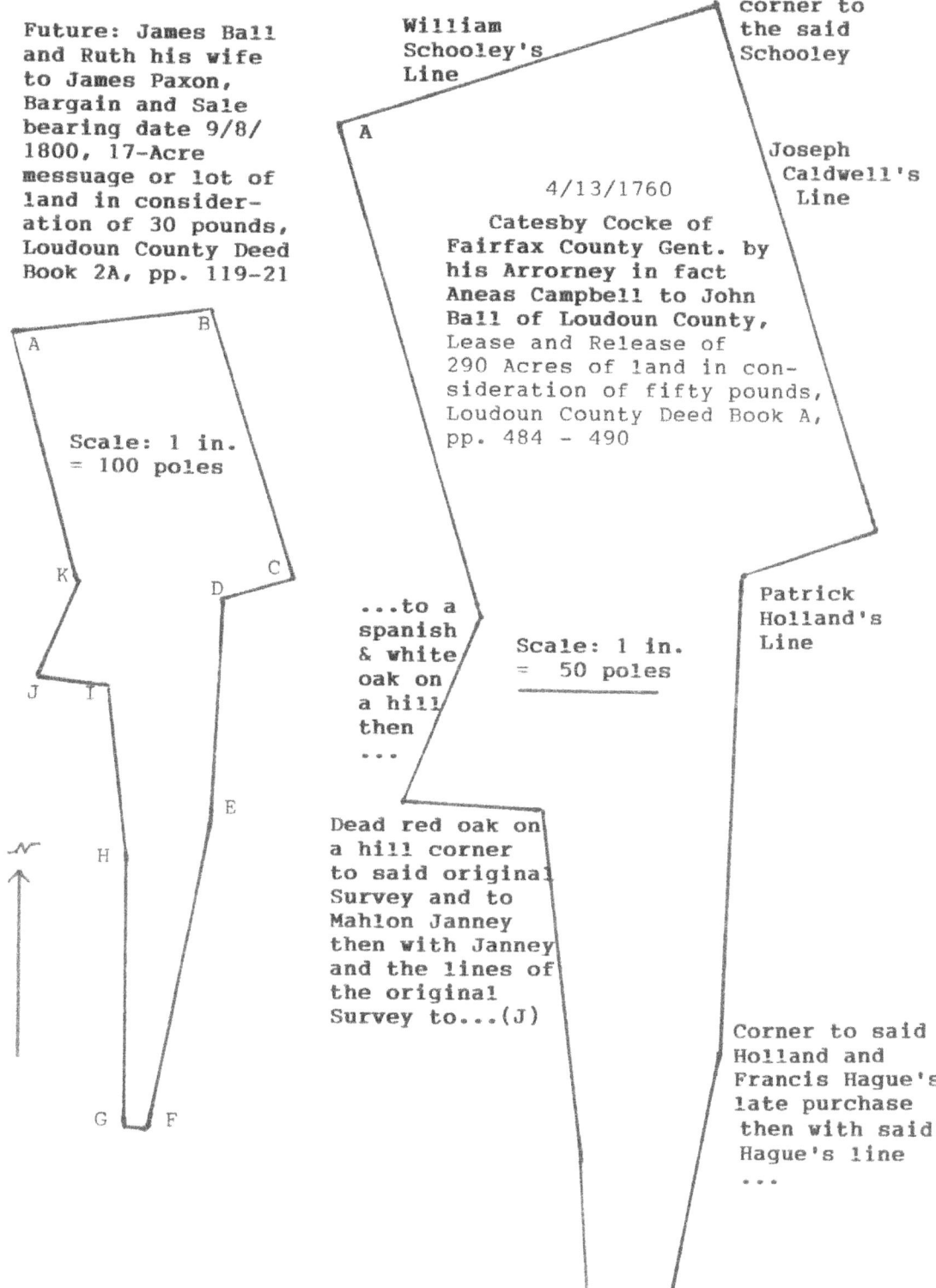

April 13, 1760
Catesby Cocke of Fairfax County Gent. by his Attorney in fact Aneas Campbell Gent. of Loudoun County to Joseph McGeach of Loudoun County, Lease and Release of 600 Acres of Land in consideration of thirty five pounds, Loudoun County Deed Book A, pp. 496 - 502

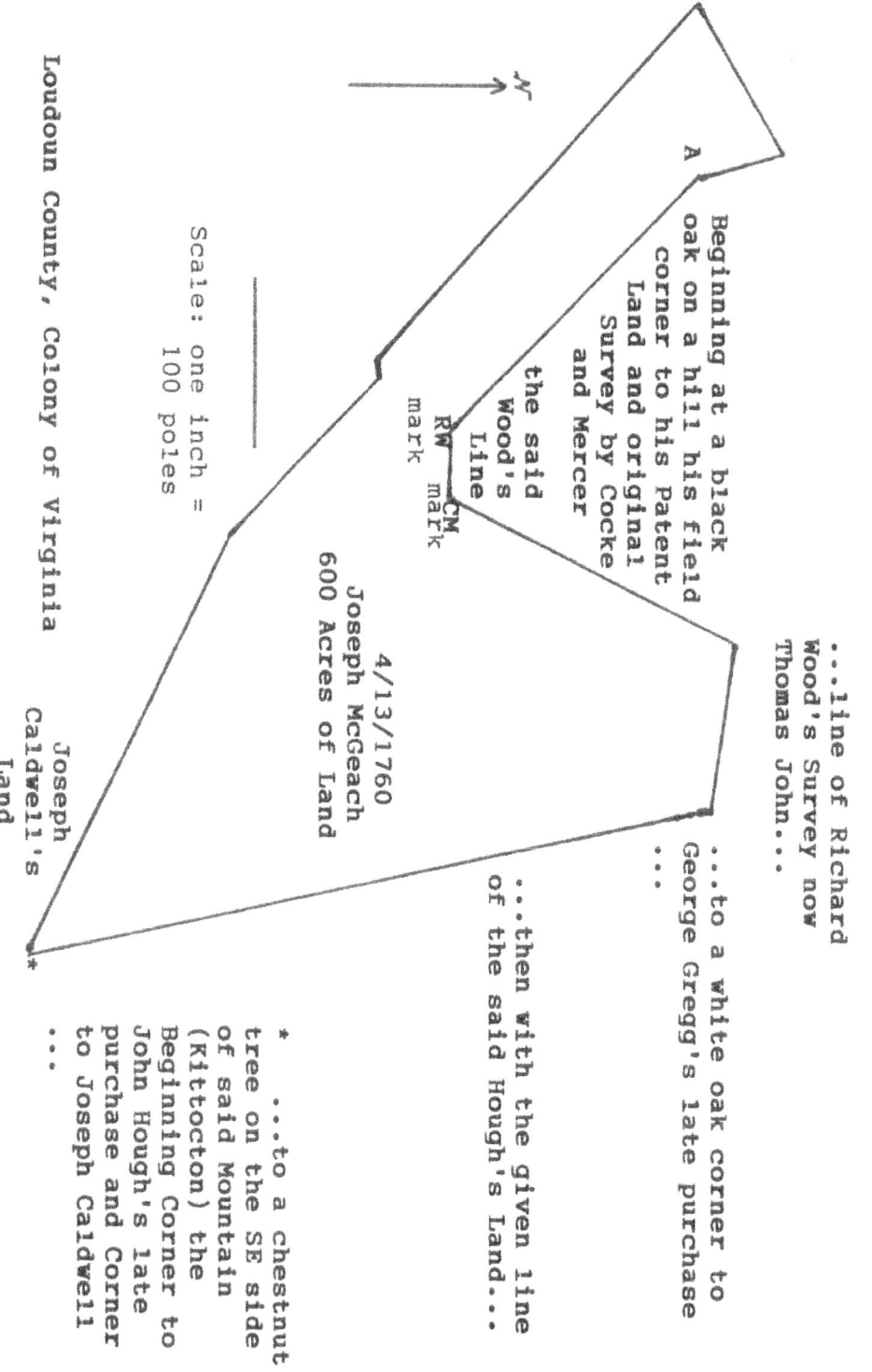

Beginning at a black oak on a hill his field corner to his Patent Land and original Survey by Cocke and Mercer the said Wood's Line

CM mark
RW mark

...line of Richard Wood's Survey now Thomas John...

...to a white oak corner to George Gregg's late purchase...

...then with the given line of the said Hough's Land...

4/13/1760
Joseph McGeach
600 Acres of Land

* ...to a chestnut tree on the SE side of said Mountain (Kittocton) the Beginning Corner to John Hough's late purchase and Corner to Joseph Caldwell...

Joseph Caldwell's Land

Scale: one inch = 100 poles

Loudoun County, Colony of Virginia

...and whereas there is another parcel of land within the Bounds of the above said Original Survey of Cocke and Mercer Bounded as follower viz. ...

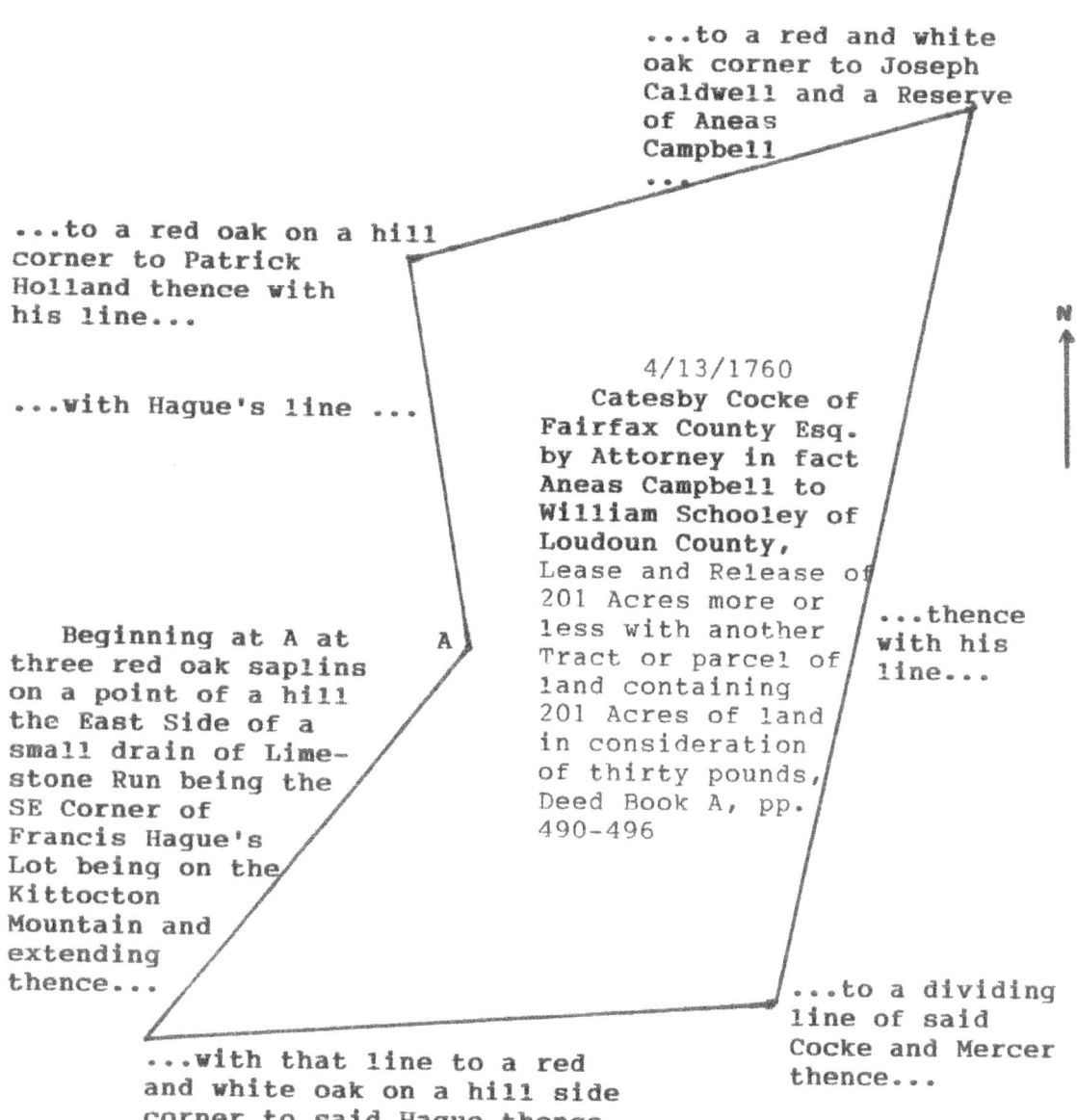

...to a red and white oak corner to Joseph Caldwell and a Reserve of Aneas Campbell...

...to a red oak on a hill corner to Patrick Holland thence with his line...

...with Hague's line ...

4/13/1760
Catesby Cocke of Fairfax County Esq. by Attorney in fact Aneas Campbell to William Schooley of Loudoun County, Lease and Release of 201 Acres more or less with another Tract or parcel of land containing 201 Acres of land in consideration of thirty pounds, Deed Book A, pp. 490-496

...thence with his line...

Beginning at A at three red oak saplins on a point of a hill the East Side of a small drain of Limestone Run being the SE Corner of Francis Hague's Lot being on the Kittocton Mountain and extending thence...

...with that line to a red and white oak on a hill side corner to said Hague thence...

...to a dividing line of said Cocke and Mercer thence...

1 in. = 50 poles

...by his Attorney in fact Aneas Campbell who by virtue of Letters of Attorney given the said Aneas Campbell by the said Catesby Cocke bearing date the eighteenth Day of December Domini one thousand seven hundred and fifty nine & recorded in Loudoun County Office...

one inch = 50 poles

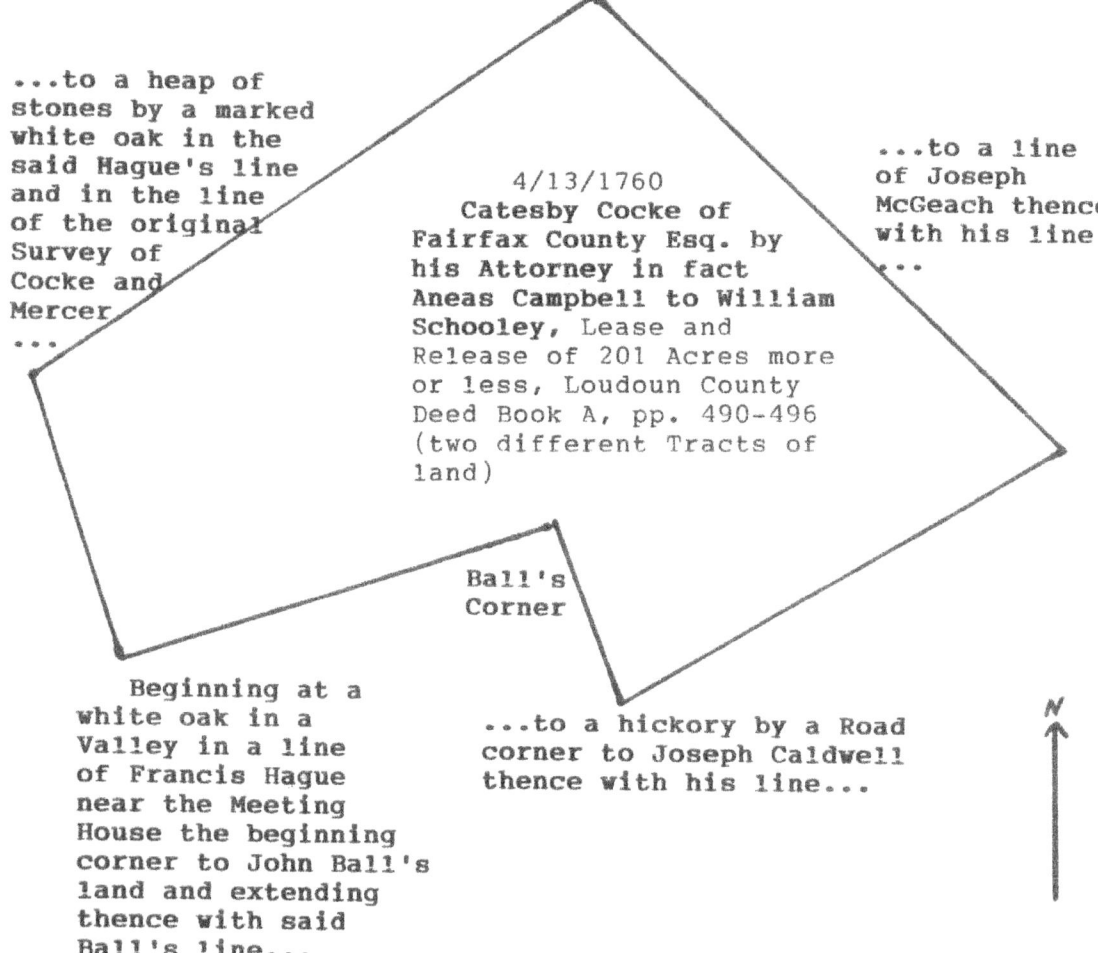

...to two red oak saplins in one of the Dividing lines of said Cocke and Mercer and corner to said McGeach thence with said Dividing line...

...to a heap of stones by a marked white oak in the said Hague's line and in the line of the original Survey of Cocke and Mercer...

4/13/1760
Catesby Cocke of Fairfax County Esq. by his Attorney in fact Aneas Campbell to William Schooley, Lease and Release of 201 Acres more or less, Loudoun County Deed Book A, pp. 490-496 (two different Tracts of land)

...to a line of Joseph McGeach thence with his line...

Ball's Corner

Beginning at a white oak in a Valley in a line of Francis Hague near the Meeting House the beginning corner to John Ball's land and extending thence with said Ball's line...

...to a hickory by a Road corner to Joseph Caldwell thence with his line...

N

180

...and whereas there is another parcel of land within the Bounds of the above said Original Survey of Cocke and Mercer Bounded as follower viz. ...

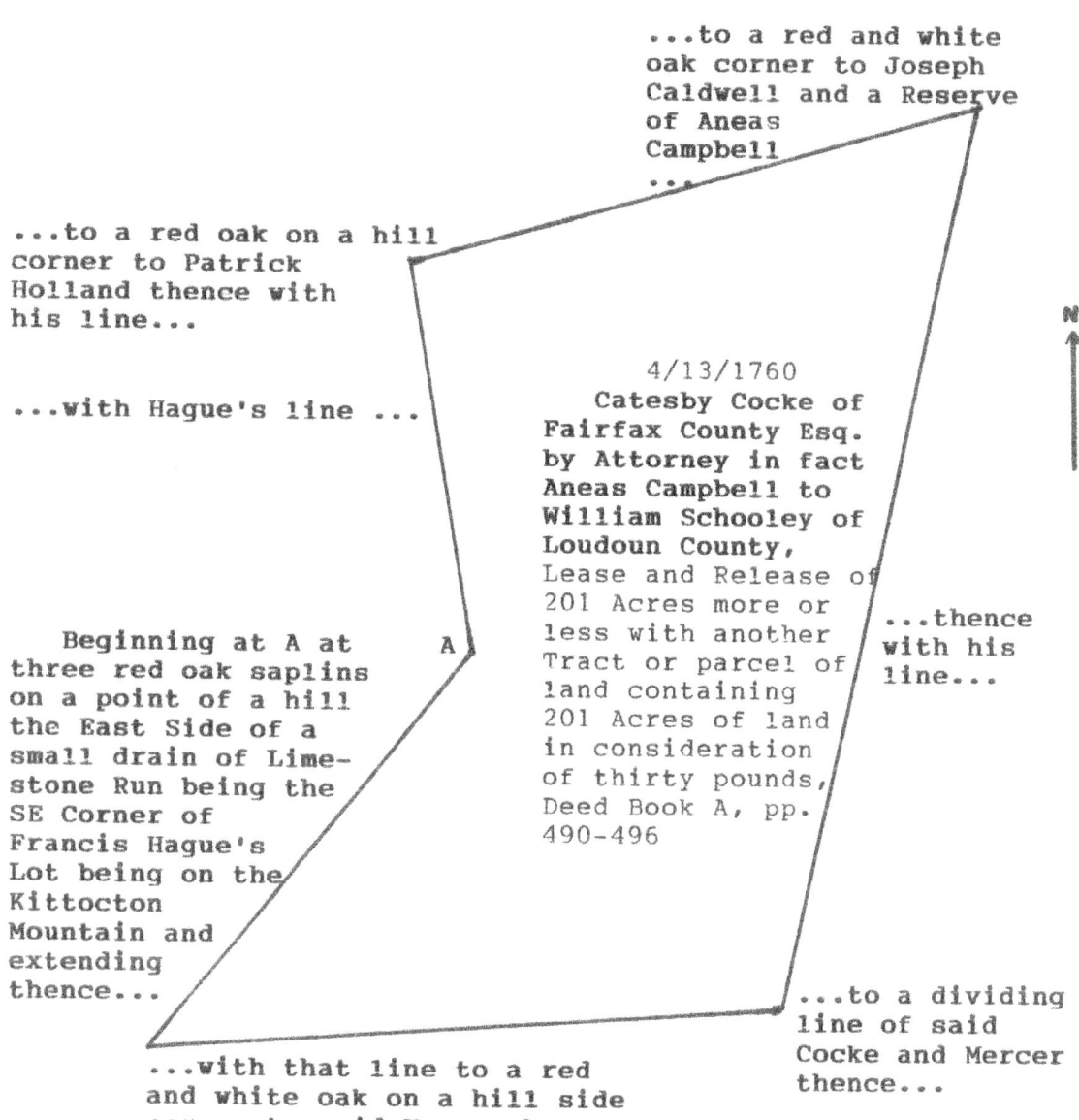

...to a red and white oak corner to Joseph Caldwell and a Reserve of Aneas Campbell...

...to a red oak on a hill corner to Patrick Holland thence with his line...

...with Hague's line ...

4/13/1760
Catesby Cocke of Fairfax County Esq. by Attorney in fact Aneas Campbell to William Schooley of Loudoun County, Lease and Release of 201 Acres more or less with another Tract or parcel of land containing 201 Acres of land in consideration of thirty pounds, Deed Book A, pp. 490-496

...thence with his line...

Beginning at A at three red oak saplins on a point of a hill the East Side of a small drain of Limestone Run being the SE Corner of Francis Hague's Lot being on the Kittocton Mountain and extending thence...

...with that line to a red and white oak on a hill side corner to said Hague thence...

...to a dividing line of said Cocke and Mercer thence...

1 in. = 50 poles

...by his Attorney in fact Aneas Campbell who by virtue of Letters of Attorney given the said Aneas Campbell by the said Catesby Cocke bearing date the eighteenth Day of December Domini one thousand seven hundred and fifty nine & recorded in Loudoun County Office...

one inch = 50 poles

...to two red oak saplins in one of the Dividing lines of said Cocke and Mercer and corner to said McGeach thence with said Dividing line...

...to a heap of stones by a marked white oak in the said Hague's line and in the line of the original Survey of Cocke and Mercer...

4/13/1760
Catesby Cocke of Fairfax County Esq. by his Attorney in fact Aneas Campbell to William Schooley, Lease and Release of 201 Acres more or less, Loudoun County Deed Book A, pp. 490-496 (two different Tracts of land)

...to a line of Joseph McGeach thence with his line...

Ball's Corner

Beginning at a white oak in a Valley in a line of Francis Hague near the Meeting House the beginning corner to John Ball's land and extending thence with said Ball's line...

...to a hickory by a Road corner to Joseph Caldwell thence with his line...

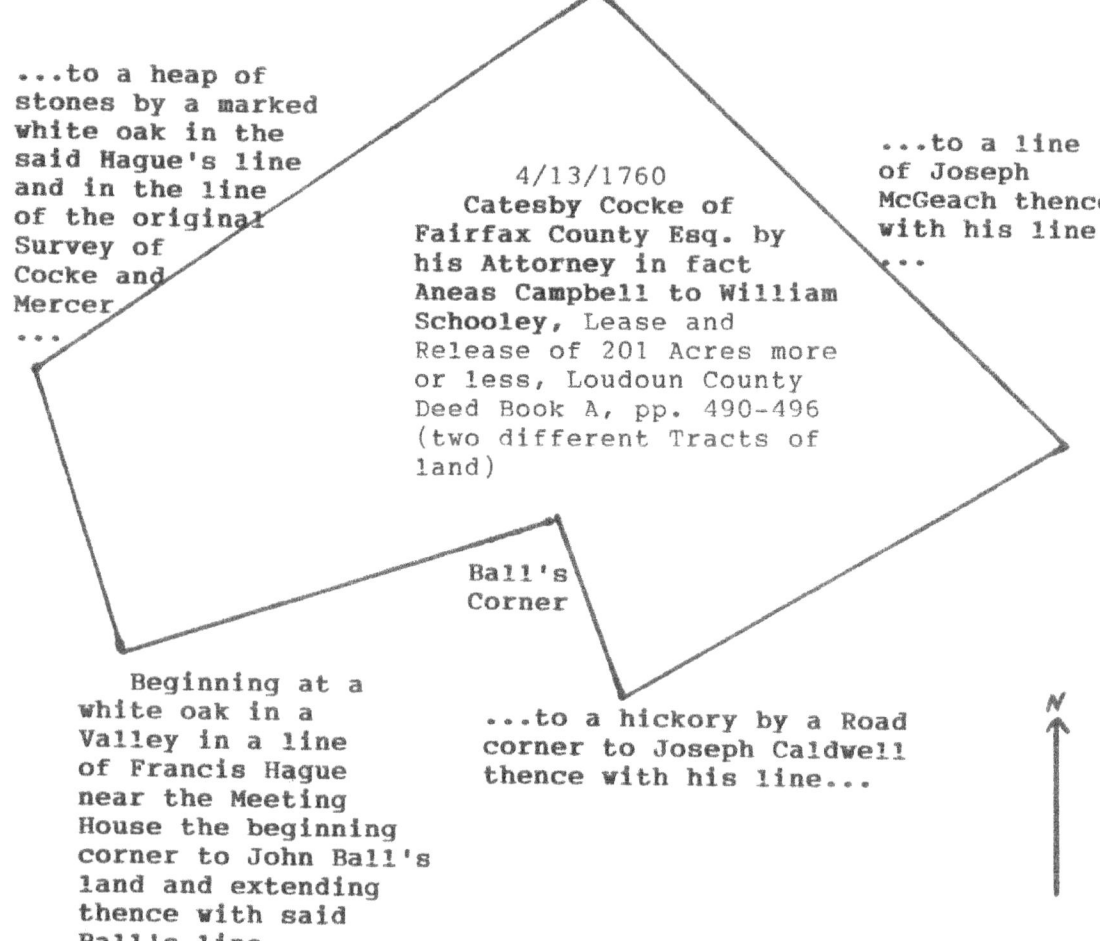

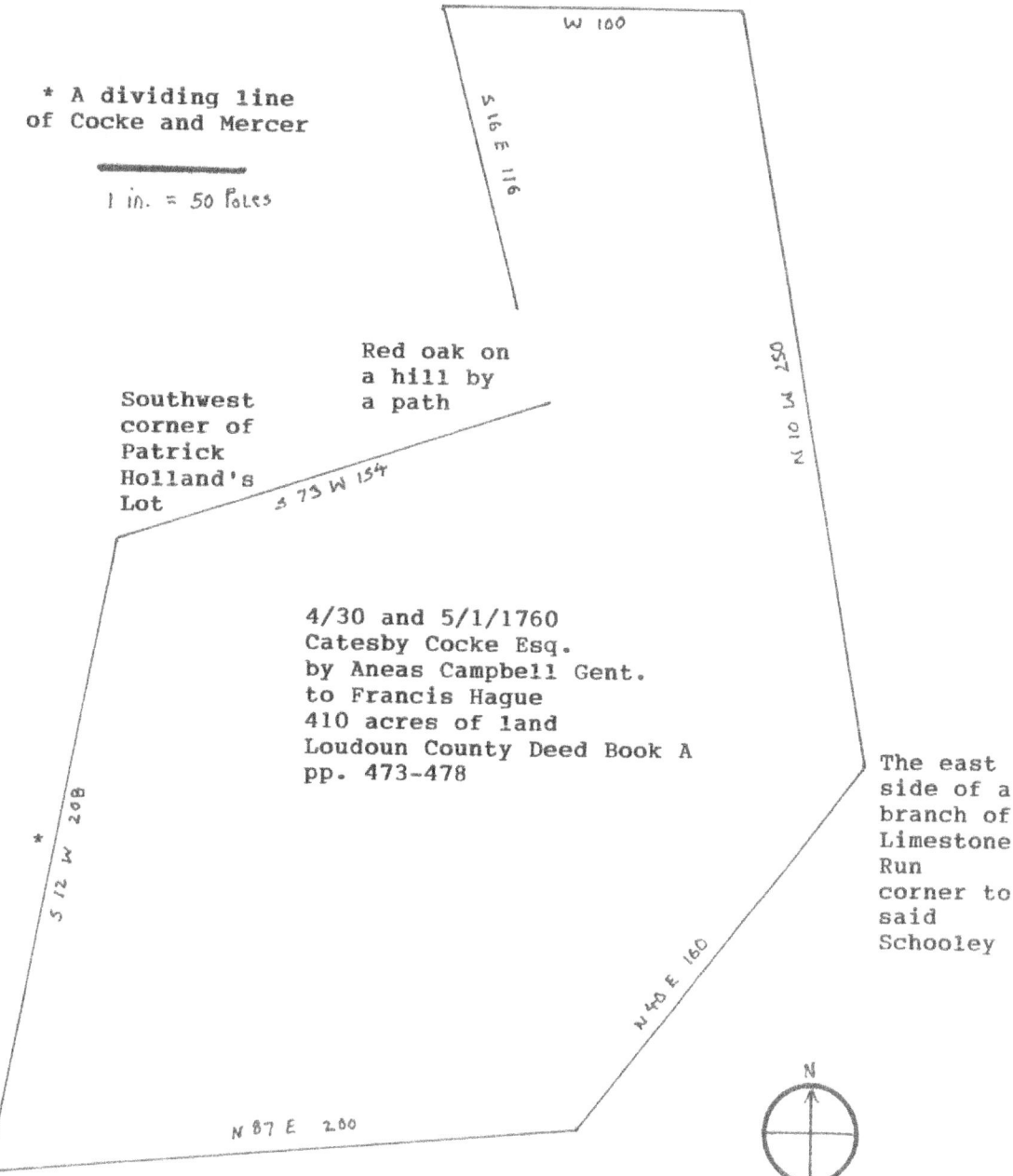

May 1, 1760

Catesby Cocke of Fairfax County Gent. by his Attorney in fact Aneas Campbell Gent. of Loudoun County to Joseph Caldwell of Loudoun County, Lease and Release of four hundred and twelve Acres of Land, Loudoun County Deed Book B, pp. 2 - 6

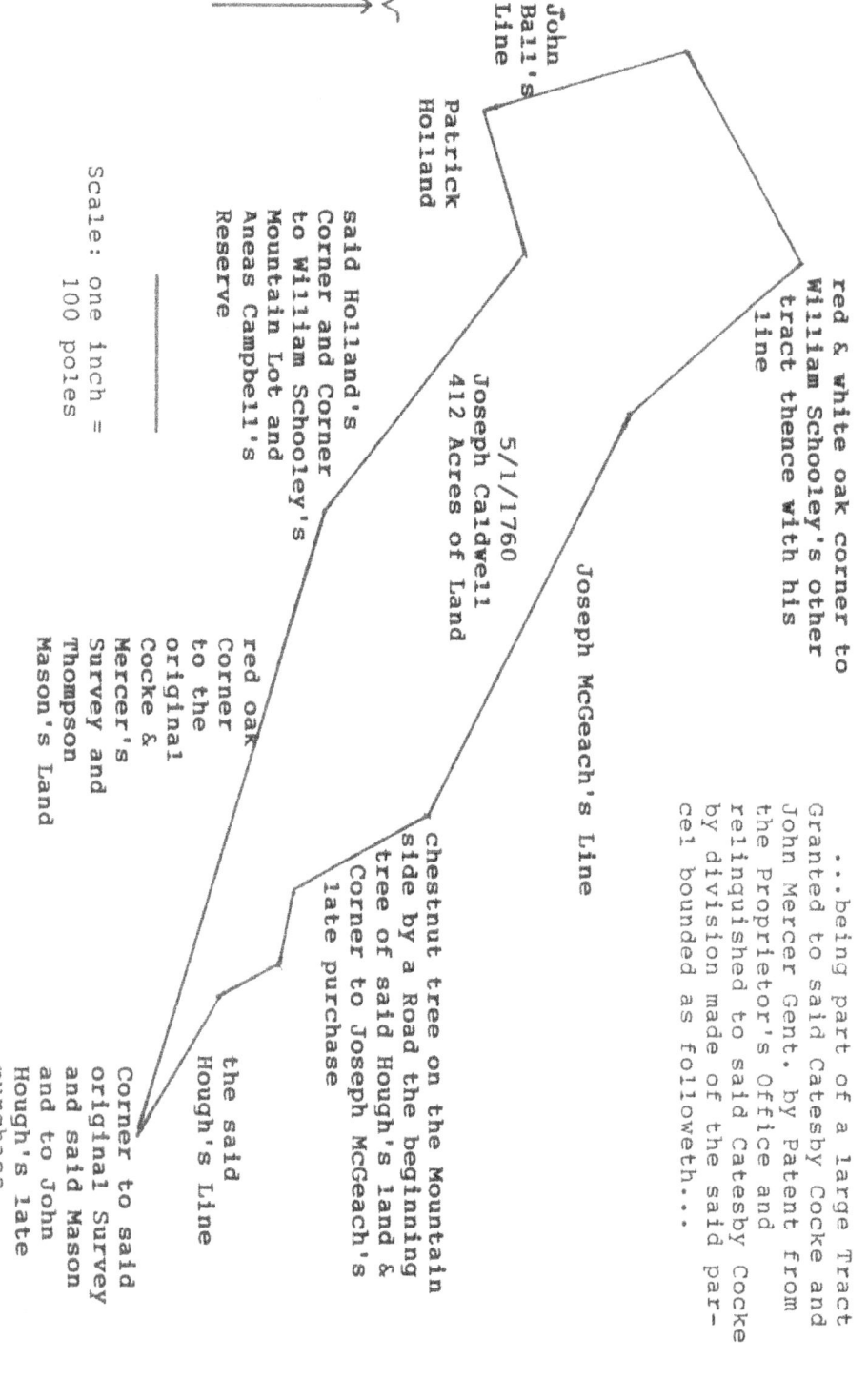

John Ball's Line

Patrick Holland

said Holland's Corner and Corner to William Schooley's Mountain Lot and Aneas Campbell's Reserve

Scale: one inch = 100 poles

5/1/1760
Joseph Caldwell
412 Acres of Land

Joseph McGeach's Line

red & white oak corner to William Schooley's other tract thence with his line

red oak corner to the original Cocke & Mercer's Survey and Thompson Mason's Land

chestnut tree on the Mountain side by a Road the beginning tree of said Hough's land & Corner to Joseph McGeach's late purchase

the said Hough's Line

Corner to said original Survey and said Mason and to John Hough's late purchase

...being part of a large Tract Granted to said Catesby Cocke and John Mercer Gent. by Patent from the Proprietor's Office and relinquished to said Catesby Cocke by division made of the said parcel bounded as followeth...

182

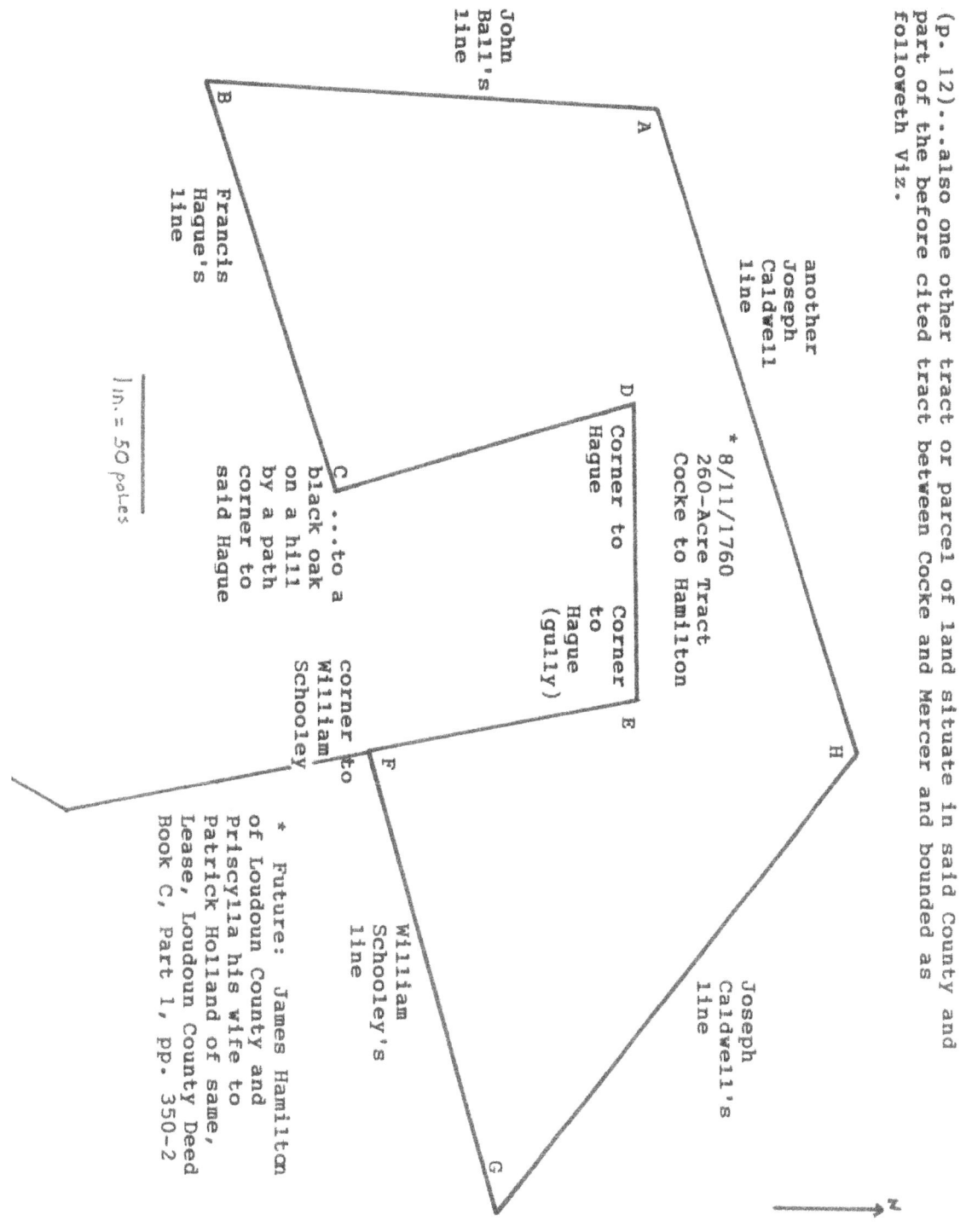

(p. 12)...also one other tract or parcel of land situate in said County and part of the before cited tract between Cocke and Mercer and bounded as followeth viz.

* 8/11/1760 260-Acre Tract Cocke to Hamilton

* Future: James Hamilton of Loudoun County and Priscylla his wife to Patrick Holland of same, Lease, Loudoun County Deed Book C, Part 1, pp. 350-2

Deed: Two tracts or parcels of land

Beginning at a white oak in a line of Mahlon Janney by his fence marked WFX CM being corner to William Henry Fairfax and the original survey of Cocke and Mercer thence...

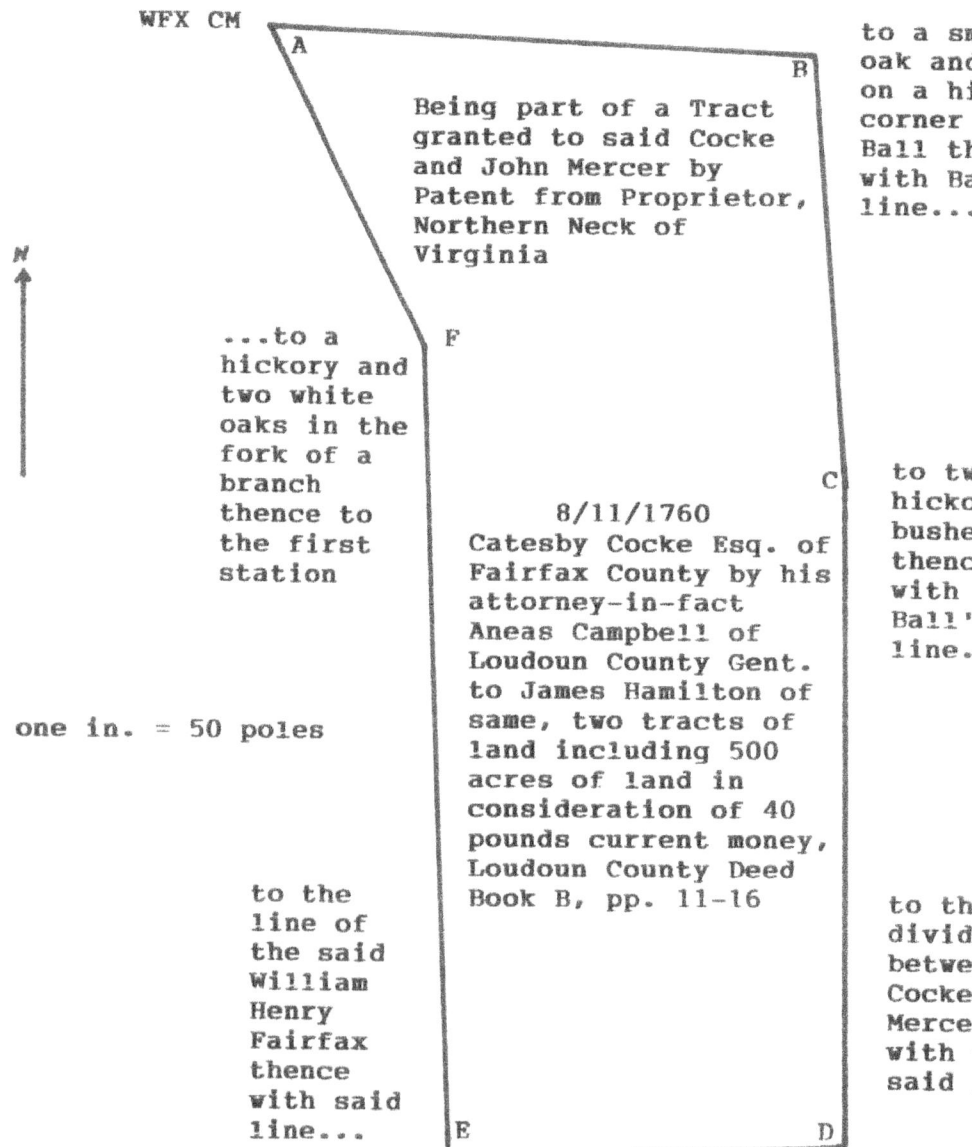

WFX CM

A — B

Being part of a Tract granted to said Cocke and John Mercer by Patent from Proprietor, Northern Neck of Virginia

to a small red oak and hickory on a hill side corner to John Ball thence with Ball's line...

N ↑

...to a hickory and two white oaks in the fork of a branch thence to the first station

F

one in. = 50 poles

8/11/1760
Catesby Cocke Esq. of Fairfax County by his attorney-in-fact Aneas Campbell of Loudoun County Gent. to James Hamilton of same, two tracts of land including 500 acres of land in consideration of 40 pounds current money, Loudoun County Deed Book B, pp. 11-16

C

to two hickory bushes thence with said Ball's line...

to the line of the said William Henry Fairfax thence with said line...

E — D

to the dividing line between said Cocke and Mercer thence with the said line...

Part of a Tract of land formerly of Catesby Cocke's, which was laid-off by John Hough in surveyed lots of which the subject parcel of land was one and supposed to contain two hundred & sixty acres more or less: Joining on a Tract of land which the said Joseph Janney purchased from John Griffith and beginning at a white oak in a line of Mahlon Janney marked WX CM extending thence...

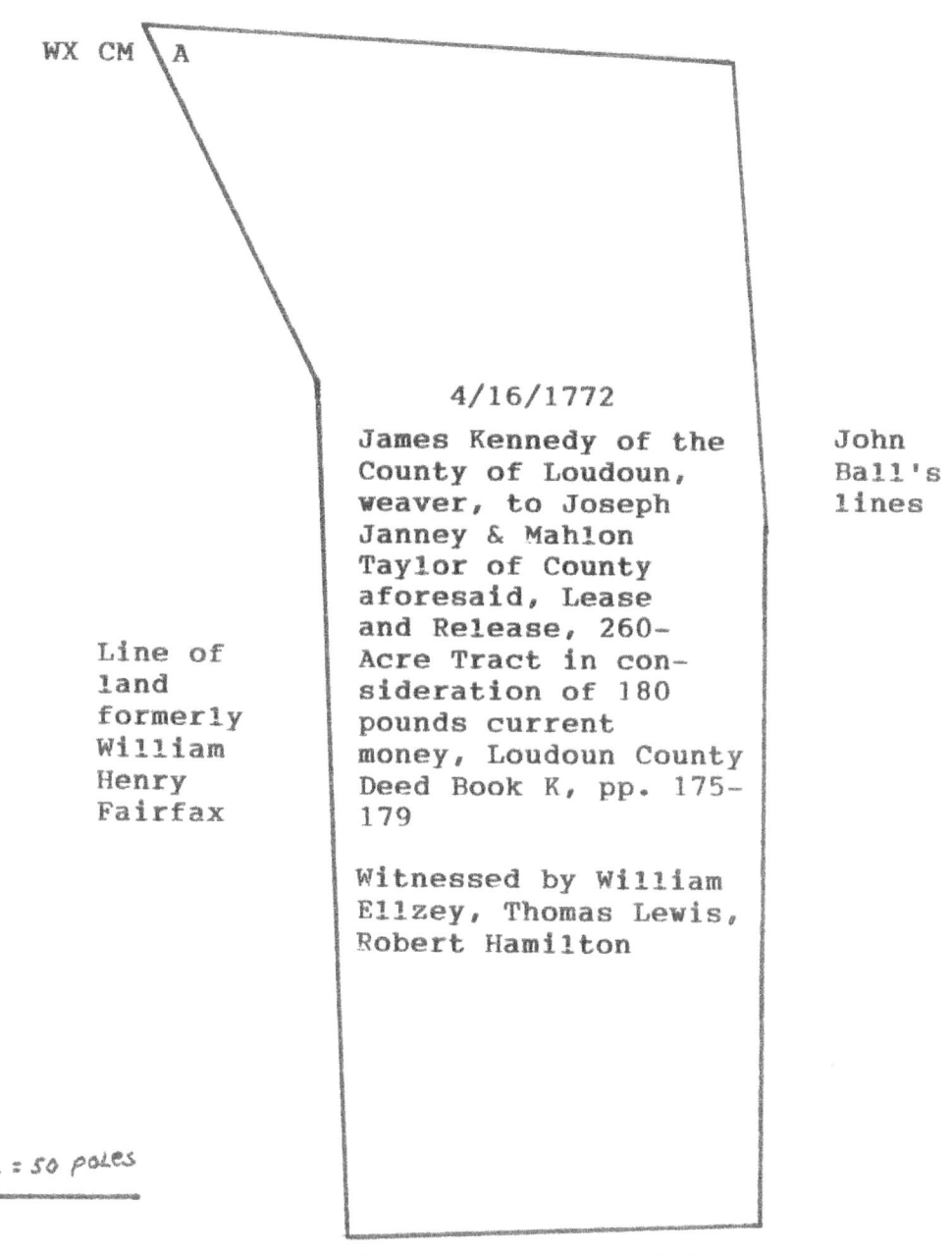

4/16/1772

James Kennedy of the County of Loudoun, weaver, to Joseph Janney & Mahlon Taylor of County aforesaid, Lease and Release, 260-Acre Tract in consideration of 180 pounds current money, Loudoun County Deed Book K, pp. 175-179

Witnessed by William Ellzey, Thomas Lewis, Robert Hamilton

Line of land formerly William Henry Fairfax

John Ball's lines

1 in. = 50 poles

Cocke & Mercer Dividing Line

This Indemnture of Lease and Release made 4/16/1780 between James Ball of Loudoun County and Patrick McHolland of Loudoun County, Bargain and Sale of 80 Acres of Land in consideration of the sum of thirty pounds, Loudoun County Deed Book N, Part 1, pp. 94 - 98

Beginning at a small black oak and hickory corner to John Pyott Junior extending thence...

[Diagram: Parcel labeled A, B, C, F, E, D — "4/16/1780 Patrick McHolland 80 Acres", with north arrow]

...to a large black oak in a line of said Ball thence...

...to two hickories corner to Francis Hague's Land thence with the said Hague line...

...to two hickory bushes on a hillside above Kenady's House and then with the said Kenady's line to the first station

...to a corner of James Kenady's and then with his line ...

...to the dividing line of Cocke and Mercer then with that line...

John Mercer's Partition from Cocke & Mercer's Tract (circa 1742)

The section concerns the parceling of a certain tract land said to contain 5,985 acres that was situated on or about the Catoctin Creek and Catoctin Mountain, which Catesby Cocke and John Mercer had jointly obtained by grant from Thomas, Lord Fairfax and Baron Cameron, the Proprietor of the Northern Neck of Virginia, dated 4/13/1742. Afterwards, John Mercer would relinquish a portion of it to Catesby Cocke in a division thereof made by a Deed of Partition recorded in the County of Fairfax bearing date 12/31/1750. In turn, John Mercer was transformed into John Mercer & Sons who appointed John Hough as their true and lawful attorney in fact over their remaining share of the given acreage by virtue of letter of attorney given him bearing date November 3rd, 1762, and recorded in the General Court of Virginia, Williamsburg.

According to the plan and draft of the said 5,985 acres of land and the division and partition thereof annexed into four lots numbered 1, 2, 3, and 4. The first lot contained 1,361 acres and 1 rood and 6 perches; the second lot contained 1,532 acres and 2 roods and 38 perches; the third lot contained 1,801 acres and 1 rood and 12 perches; the fourth lot contained 1,431 acres and 3 roods and 12 perches. The second and third of which contiguous lots were allotted to the said Catesby Cocke and his heirs and assigns, and the first and fourth separate lots were allotted to John Mercer and his heirs and assigns upon this division or partition between them.

John Mercer & Sons partition from Cocke & Mercer's survey and tract of land was in two parcels on either side of Catesby Cocke's partition. They were on or about the waters of Catoctin Creek and over Catoctin Mountain to Limestone Run. Its outer limits were bounded by George Gregg's land, John Colvill's land (deceased), and Thomas John's land with at least one marker as in as in TJ (Richard Wood).

John Mercer & Sons partition was laid off and bounded by John Hough for ready trade. It seems these lands sold at the prevailing market rates or higher. John Hough earned more money and at a higher rate than had his contemporary Aneas Campbell while he was doing much the same thing in a similar locale for Catesby Cocke. The author counted earnings attributed to Hough of 830 pounds current money against a volume of 2,279 acres of land. The most expensive parcel of land John Hough sold was to Mary McGeach for and in consideration of monies at the rate of 11-½ shillings per acre of land for a total of 200 acres dated in 1764.

Business was not all good. Joseph Hough purchased a parcel of land, which he was unable to pay thus causing John Hough to post a bond for the obligation. Francis Hague purchased a parcel of land, which he was unable to pay thus causing John Hough to post a bond for the obligation. And, Benjamin Williams purchased a parcel of land, which he was unable to pay thus causing John Hough to post a bond for the obligation. Apparently, Williams could not make good on it, which led to the succession of James Hamilton. Finally, Benjamin Hiatt implied he was neither contented nor fully satisfied in his dealings with John Hough per real estate, and in 1771 he empowered and authorized Amos Thompson to claim, demand, or sue for a certain tract of land on Catoctin Mountain, which he had purchased from John Hough for John Mercer & Sons.

John Hough would have earned monies here in a number of different ways. To begin with, as acting attorney for John Mercer & Sons he presumably earned a commission income for arranging real estate transactions. Also, he was a surveyor who in all probability would have earned a fee income for services rendered. Moreover, he was on the face of it a private banker who in all probability would have earned monies for financial services rendered.

1. 12/31/1750, **Catesby Cocke** Gent. of the Parish of Truro in the County of Fairfax of the one part to **John Mercer** Gent. of Marlborough in the County of Stafford of the other part. Whereas the **Rt. Hon. Thomas, Lord Fairfax and Baron Cameron**, in that part of Great Britain called Scotland, Proprietor of the Northern Neck of Virginia by his deed bearing date 4/13/1742 did give grant and confirm unto **Catesby Cocke and John Mercer** one certain tract or parcel of land in the County of Prince William and bounded according to a survey thereof by **John Warner** as followeth. Beginning at A, a white hickory marked **PL** and **JM** on the south side of **Kittockton Run** by the mouth of a drain and is corner of a tract granted unto **John Mead and Richard Averill**, also corner of **Colo. John Colvill's** land, and running thence with the lines of the said **Mead and Averill** S 53° E 202 poles and found B, the corner a spanish oak 4 poles on the left from B, (thence) S 16° E 390 poles to C, a spanish oak on an hill the corner, also another spanish oak marked **CM**, thence S 22° – 30' W 74 poles to D, a large red oak on an hill another corner marked **CM**, thence N 88° W 114 poles to E, a white oak in the line of the said **Mead and Averill** and corner to the land of **Colo. John Colvill,** and also corner to the land surveyed for **Cornelius Eltinge** now belonging to **William Fairfax Esquire,** which tree is marked **WFx** and **CM**, then along the lines of that tract S 34° E 106 poles to F, an hickory and white oak in the fork of a branch of Kittockton called **Amos's Branch** marked **WFx** and **CM**, (thence) S 1° E 578 poles and found G, the corner two white oaks in the line of the land of **Capt. Benjamin Grayson** nine poles on the left and standing on the side of a mountain near one of the head drains of **Limestone Run** and marked CM, from the said two white oaks running along the lines of **Grayson** N 19° E 26 poles to H, four small and one large spanish oak (marked) **CM** on the head of a drain of the said **Limestone**, (thence) East 310 poles to I, three beeches standing on the NW side of the said **Limestone Run** six poles above a fork of the said run and in an island of the same between the broken hills or mountains and is marked **CM**, (thence) S 34° E 114 poles to K, two small white oaks on a drain of the said **Limestone** and on the south side of the top of an hill or mountain and marked **CM**, then with the given line of the said **Grayson's** land S 11° W 424 poles to L, a white oak on the side of the broken hills or mountains and the end of the dividing line of two tracts of the said **Grayson's** (marked) **CM**, then with the given line of the said tract of the said **Grayson's** S 11° W 94 poles to M, a white oak on the north side of the **North Fork of Tuskarora Run** and in the line of the said **Grayson** and in the line of the land of **John Richardson** and marked **CM**, then with **Richardson's** line N 29° E 15 poles to N, a white oak and red oak both dying marked **FA** and corner to the said **Richardson's** land and the land of **Francis Awbrey** now **Mrs. Mason's**, there (are) two large white oaks near

marked **CM** and is near a pond of water, then with the said **Awbrey's** or **Mason's** lines N 17° E 280 poles and found O, the corner three black oaks on an hill marked **CM** on the north side of a branch of **Cool Spring** 18 poles on the left from O, their three black oaks run(ning) N 36° E 82 poles to P, a large white oak and small hickory and poplar (marked) **CM** in a branch of the **Cool Spring**, (thence) N 25° E 150 poles to Q, a black oak on a stony point, thence N 20° E 184 poles to R, a black gum and poplar on the south side of the **South Fork of Limestone** near a point of rocks the end of piney mountain marked **CM**, (thence) N 25° E 186 poles to S, three red oaks at the head of a valley, (thence) N 19° E 148 poles to T, the line of the land of **Joseph Dixon** then with the lines of the said **Dixon's** land N 14° W 53 poles to U, a dead red oak marked, a chestnut oak, a red oak and white oak (marked) **CM**, then with another of **Dixon's** lines N 34° E 102 poles to W, a large white oak, (thence) N 63° E 44 poles to X, a white oak under the hill two poles on the left, (thence) N 30° E 48 poles to Y, a red oak on the side of one of the broken hills or mountains and corner of the said **Dixon** and **Awbrey** now **Mason's**, thence S 72° – 30' E 234 poles to Z, a red oak and three white oaks corner of **Francis Awbrey** or **Mason's** and **Patrick Lynch's** 1,537 acre tract now the said **Cocke's** six poles on the left marked **FA** and **CM**, standing on a branch of **Limestone** then with the lines of the said **Cocke's** tract N 58° – 30' W 102 poles to &, a white oak marked **CM**, (thence) N 29° W 44 poles to a, two spanish oaks growing from one root (marked) **CM**, (thence) S 75° – 30' W 52 poles to b, an hickory (marked) **CM**, (thence) N 49° W 96 poles to c, a chestnut and red oak on the top of one of the broken hills or mountains the beginning tree of the land marked **CM**, thence with the given line of the said tract N 14° W 452 poles to d, the said **Cocke's** 1,488 acre tract, then with that line N 80° W 104 poles to e, the given line of the land formerly **Richard Wood's**, then with that line S 27° W 192 poles to f, a red oak the old corner of **Wood's** marked **CM**, also found a white oak near marked **CM**, from the old corner red oak went along **Wood's** line West 42 poles to g, a white oak the corner of **Wood's** marked **RW**, (thence) N 45° W 199 poles to h, a red oak the old corner on the side of the said hill or mountain N 17° W 188 poles to i, a small hickory and two black oaks on an hill by a broken white oak the old corner near a branch, (thence) N 57° E 134 poles to k, a black oak in the line of the said **Wood** and also in the line of the said tract of the said **Cocke's** 1,488 acre tract then with the line of that tract N 20° W 429 poles to l, a white oak and two black oaks by the north side of **Kittockton Run** near a grove of small pines corner to said **Cocke** and also corner to piece of land of **Colo. Colvill's** then with said **Colvill's** line N 30° W 126 poles to m, two small black oaks in a line of **Colo. Colvill's Kittockton Creek Tract**. Finally, with a line of that tract S 27° W 701 poles to the beginning crossing **Kittockton Creek** at 89 poles, 125 poles, 259 poles, 309 poles, 369 poles and twice more just by the beginning containing 5,985 acres. Together with all rights members and appurtenances thereunto belonging royal mines excepted and a full third part of all lead copper tin coals iron mines and iron ore that should be found thereon. To have and to hold the said 5,985 acres of land together with all rights profits and benefits to the same belonging or in any wise appertaining except before excepted to them the said **Cocke and John Mercer** their heirs and assigns forever. They the said **Catesby Cocke and John Mercer** their heirs and assigns therefore yielding and paying to the said proprietor his heirs and assigns or to his certain attorney or attorneys, agent or agents, or to the certain attorney or attorneys of his heirs and assigns proprietors of the said Northern Neck yearly and every year on the Feast of St. Michael the Archangel the fee rent of one shilling sterling money for every fifty acres of land thereby granted and so proportionably for a greater or lesser quantity as by the said deed relation being thereunto had may fully appear. And, whereas the said **Catesby Cocke and John Mercer** have entered unto the said 5,985 acres of land and premises and now stand seized thereof to them and their heirs forever, and have made and agreed upon a full and complete partition and division of the said land and premises with the appurtenances so that they the said **Catesby Cocke and John Mercer** and their heirs may for the future severally and respectively have hold occupy possess and enjoy their several and respective parts and portions of the said lands and premises with the appurtenances separately and divided from the other. Now this indenture witnesseth that the said **Catesby Coke and John Mercer** have made and by these presents do with one assent and consent for themselves and their heirs make a full and complete division of the said 5,985 acres of land and premises with the appurtenances in manner and form following. That is to say **Catesby Cocke** his heirs and assigns shall and may from hence forth have hold occupy and enjoy to the said **Catesby Cocke** his heirs and assigns forever all that part or parcel of the said 5,985 acres of land and premises with the appurtenances bounded as followeth. Beginning at T in the line of the land of **Joseph Dixon** and thence running the several courses and distances herein before mentioned to the letters U, W, X, Y, Z, &, a, b, c, d, e, f, g, h, then N 17° W 68 poles, then S 59° W 300 poles to the line of **Mead and Averill,** then S 16° E 272 poles to one of their corners at C, and thence running the several courses and distances herein before mentioned to the letters D, E, F, then S 1° E 232 poles, then N 87° E 660 poles to the beginning at T, in the line of **Dixon** aforesaid. And, that the said **John Mercer** his heirs and assigns shall and may from henceforth have hold occupy and enjoy to the said **John Mercer** his heirs and assigns all the rest and residue of the said 5,985 acres of land and premises with the appurtenances lying in two several pieces or parcels on each side of the part or parcel of the said **Catesby Cocke** herein before described. One piece or parcel thereof being bounded as followeth that is to say. Beginning at the said **Catesby Cocke's** corner in the line from the letter h, before mentioned and running thence N 17° W 120 poles to i, a small hickory and two black oaks on a hill by broken white oak the old corner near a branch herein before mentioned and thence running the several courses and distances herein before also mentioned to the letters k, l, m, A, B, a corner spanish oak of **Mead and Averill,** then with their line S 16° E 118 poles to the said **Catesby Cocke's** corner in the said line, then along the line before mentioned dividing this parcel from the said **Catesby Cocke's** land N 59° E 300 poles to the beginning in the line from h, to i, aforesaid. The other part or parcel assigned or allotted to the said **John Mercer** being bounded as followeth that is to say. Beginning at the said **Catesby Cocke's** corner in the line from the letter F, before mentioned and running thence S 1° E 346 poles, nine poles on the right of g, two white oaks in the line of the land of **Benjamin Grayson** herein before mentioned and thence running the several courses and distances herein before mentioned to the letters H, I, K, L, M, N, O, P, Q, R, S, T, and thence S 87° W 660 poles along the line of the line before mentioned dividing this parcel from the said **Catesby Cocke's** land. In witness whereof the parties to these presents have hereunto set their hands and seals the day and year first before written, **Catesby Cocke, J. Mercer**. Sealed and delivered in the presence of us **Chas. Green, Richd. Parker, George Mercer**. Proven on 3/26/1751. Deed of Partition, Fairfax County Deed Book C, pp. 99- 106

2. 11/3/1762, **John Mercer Esq. and George Mercer Esq. and James Mercer Esq.** or **John Mercer and Sons** to **John Hough**, Letter of Attorney, General Court of Virginia

3. 6/13 and 6/14/1763, **John Mercer Esq.** of Marlborough and County of Stafford and Colony and Dominion of Virginia, and **George Mercer Esq.** of the County of Frederick and Colony aforesaid, and **James Mercer Esq.** of the County of Spotsylvania and Colony aforesaid by their attorney in fact **John Hough** of the County of Loudoun, Colony and Dominion aforesaid of the one part to **Joseph Cox** late of the Province of West New Jersey now of said County of Loudoun of the other part. Whereas the said **John Mercer** obtained a grant jointly with **Catesby Cocke Esq.** from **Thomas, Lord Fairfax,** Proprietor of the Northern Neck of Virginia, bearing date the 13th day of April, 1741 for a certain tract of land in the County of Prince William now Loudoun, containing 5,985 acres and about the **Kittocton Creek and Mountain**, which tract of land was divided between them as by a partition deed recorded in the County Court of Fairfax as may appear, part of which division now being laid off and bounded as followeth viz. Beginning at A, a chestnut tree standing in a line of land granted to **Benjamin Grayson** now the property of the said **John Mercer & Co.** and the south side of **Limestone Run** above a fork of the same three poles above a marked beech tree one of the original corners to the aforesaid larger tract extending thence North 214 poles to a small hickory on a ridge of said Mountain to B, then West 150 poles to C a leaning white oak, thence South 14 poles to a spanish oak and red oak corner to lot laid of for (blank space), then the same course continued with his line in all 214 poles to D, the aforesaid line of **Benjamin Grayson**, then with said line East 150 poles to the first station containing 200 acres of land. Now this indenture witnesseth that the said **John Mercer, George Mercer,** and **James Mercer** by their attorney in fact **John Hough** who by virtue of a letter of attorney given to the said **John Hough** by the said **John Mercer, George Mercer,** and **James Mercer** bearing date the 3rd day of November, 1762 duly proven and recorded in the General Court for Virginia, for and in consideration of the sum of 40 pounds current money to them in hand paid by the said **Joseph Cox** the receipt whereof they do and every of them doth hereby acknowledge by their attorney in fact **John Hough,** and for other causes and considerations them thereunto moving, they the said **John Mercer, George Mercer,** and **James Mercer,** by their attorney in fact **John Hough** have and every of them hath granted bargained and sold aliened released and confirmed and by these presents do and every of them doth fully freely and absolutely grant

bargain sell alien release and confirm unto the said **Joseph Cox** and to his heirs and assigns forever. To have and to hold the said land hereditaments all and singular the premises before mentioned with the appurtenances unto the said **Joseph Cox** his heirs and assigns forever, **John Mercer, Geo. Mercer** and **James Mercer**. Proven on 6/14/1763. Lease and Release, Loudoun County Deed Book C, Part 2, pp. 624-630

4.   12/12 and 12/13/1763, **John Mercer Esq.** of Marlborough in the County of Stafford and Colony and Dominion of Virginia, and **George Mercer Esq.** of the County of Frederick and Colony aforesaid, and **James Mercer Esq.** of the County of Spotsylvania and Colony aforesaid by their attorney in fact **John Hough** of the County of Loudoun, Colony and Dominion aforesaid of the one part to **William Hoge** of the County of Loudoun and Colony aforesaid of the other part. Whereas the said **John Mercer** obtained a grant jointly with **Catesby Cocke Esq.** from **Thomas, Lord Fairfax,** Proprietor of the Northern Neck of Virginia, bearing date the 13th day of April, 1742 for a certain tract of land in the County of Prince William now Loudoun County, containing 5,985 acres on and about **Kittocton Creek and Mountain**, which tract of land was divided between them as by a partition deed recorded in the County Court of Fairfax as may appear, part of which division is being laid off and bounded as followeth viz. Beginning at A, a white oak in a stony bottom by a branch corner to the land where **William Gossett** lives extending with that land N 10° E 226 poles to a small red oak in a line of **Mathew Hickson,** then with his line S 62° W 120 poles to a white oak his corner in a line of **Hugh Howell,** then with his line S 28° E 10 poles to a white oak his corner, then with another of his lines S 62° W 64 poles to two small red oaks corner to **Timothy Howell,** then with his lines South 66 poles to a white oak, then with another of his lines S 32° - 30 minutes E 140 poles to a small hickory, then with **Mary McGeach's** line N 40° E 30 poles to a black oak, then N 65° E 36 poles to the firs station containing 150 acres. Now this indenture witnesseth that the said **John Mercer, George Mercer,** and **James Mercer** by their attorney in fact **John Hough** who by virtue of letter of attorney given to the said **John Hough** by the said **John Mercer, George Mercer,** and **James Mercer** bearing date the 3rd day of November, 1762 duly proven and recorded in the General Court of Virginia, for and in consideration of the sum of 70 pounds current money of Virginia to them in hand paid by the said **William Hoge,** the receipt whereof they do every of them doth hereby acknowledge by their attorney in fact **John Hough,** and for other causes and considerations them thereunto moving they the said **John Mercer, George Mercer,** and **James Mercer** by their attorney in fact **John Hough** have and every of them hath granted bargained and sold aliened released and confirmed and by these presents do and every of them doth fully freely and absolutely grant bargain and sell alien release and confirm unto the said **William Hoge** and to his heirs and assigns forever all that the above mentioned tract or parcel of land situate in the County of Loudoun bounded as is above set forth and described and containing 150 acres as aforesaid, and all houses edifices buildings gardens orchards meadows trees woods waters watercourses easements profits and advantages hereditaments rights and appurtenances whatsoever to the same belonging or in any wise appertaining. To have and to hold the said land

hereditaments all and singular the premises before mentioned with the appurtenances unto the said **William Hoge** his heirs and assigns forever. **John Mercer, George Mercer,** and **James Mercer**. Proven on 2/14/1764. Lease and Release, Loudoun County Deed Book D, Part 1, pp. 67-73

5.   2/13 and 2/14/1764, **John Mercer Esq.** of Marlborough and County of Stafford and Colony and Dominion of Virginia, and **George Mercer Esq.** of the County of Frederick and Colony aforesaid, and **James Mercer Esq.** of the County of Spotsylvania and Colony aforesaid by their attorney in fact **John Hough** of the County of Loudoun, Colony and Dominion aforesaid of the one part to **Mary McGeach** of the County of Loudoun and Colony aforesaid of the other part. Whereas **John Mercer and Catesby Cocke** obtained a grant from **Thomas, Lord Fairfax** for a certain tract of land situate in Fairfax County now Loudoun County, which was divided between the said **John Mercer** and **Catesby Cocke** by a partition deed recorded in Fairfax Court, part of which tract now being laid off and bounded as followeth viz. Beginning at a white oak the south side of **Seers Branch** in a line of **George Gregg** running thence with **Gregg's** line S 17° E 94 poles to a hickory bush near a marked b.o. (black oak) the dividing corner between **Cocke** and **Mercer,** then with said dividing line S 59° W 297 poles to three small hickories in **Francis Hague's** line corner also to said division and **William Schooley,** then N14° E 257 poles to a stake near a marked black oak in a line of **William Hoge,** (then) with his line N 40° E 22 poles to a black oak his corner, (then) with another of his lines N 66° E 35 poles to a white oak in a stony bottom corner to said **Hoge** and **Asa Pancoast,** then with his line S 60° E 66 poles to a poplar in a stony bottom, then S 82° E 58 poles to the first station containing 200 acres of land. Now this indenture witnesseth that the said **John Mercer, George Mercer,** and **James Mercer,** by their attorney in fact **John Hough** by virtue of a letter of attorney given to the said **John Hough** by the said **John Mercer, George Mercer,** and **James Mercer,** bearing date the 3rd day of November, 1762 proved and recorded in the General Court for Virginia, for and in consideration of the sum of 115 pounds current money of Virginia to them in hand paid by the said **Mary McGeach** the receipt whereof they do and every of them doth acknowledge by their attorney in fact **John Hough,** and for other causes and considerations them thereunto moving, they the said **John Mercer, George Mercer,** and **James Mercer,** hath granted bargained sold aliened released and confirmed and by these presents do and every of them doth fully freely and absolutely grant bargain and sell alien release and confirm unto the said **Mary McGeach** and to her heirs and assigns forever all the above mentioned tract or parcel of land situate in the County of Loudoun aforesaid bounded as is above set forth and described and containing 200 acres as aforesaid, and all houses edifices buildings gardens orchards meadows trees woods underwoods ways water watercourses easements profits and advantages hereditaments rights and appurtenances whatsoever to the same belonging or in any wise appertaining. To have and to hold the said land hereditaments all and singular the premises before mentioned with the appurtenances unto the said **Mary McGeach** her heirs and assigns forever. In witness whereof the said **John Mercer, George Mercer,** and **James Mercer** by their attorney in fact **John Hough** duly authorized have

hereunto set their hands and affixed their seals the date and year first above written, **John Mercer, George Mercer,** and **James Mercer**. Proven on 2/14/1764. Lease and Release, Loudoun County Deed Book D, Part 2, pp. 74-80

6.   5/17 and 5/18/1764, **John Mercer Esq**. of Marlborough in the County of Stafford and Colony and Dominion of Virginia, and **George Mercer Esq**. of the County of Frederick and Colony aforesaid, and **James Mercer Esq**. of the County of Spotsylvania and Colony aforesaid by their attorney in fact **John Hough** of the County of Loudoun, Colony and Dominion aforesaid of the one part to **Mathew Hickson** of the County of Loudoun, Colony and Dominion aforesaid of the other part. Whereas the said **John Mercer and Catesby Cocke** obtained a grant from the Proprietor of the Northern Neck in Virginia for 5,985 acres, which tract was divided between them by a partition deed recorded in Fairfax County Court reference thereto being had it will fully appear, part of which tract being now laid off and about the **Kittocton Creek** and bounded as followeth viz. Beginning at two hickory saplings by a **road** in a line of **John Hanby's** land bought of **Colo. Cocke,** corner to the lot where **William Gossett** lived, extending thence N 21° W 348 poles to two black oaks the north side of **Kittocton Creek** near a grove of pines corner to **Colo. Colvill's** land, then with one of his lines N 30° W 126 poles to two black oak saplings, (then) from thence S 26° W 320 poles to several saplings corner to **Hugh Howell,** then with his line S 28° E 155 poles to a white oak, then N 62° E 122 poles to a small red oak, then S 10° W 66 poles to a small red oak corner to said **Gossett's** lot, then with that line East 156 poles to the first station containing 464 acres of land more or less. Now this indenture witnesseth that the said **John Mercer, George Mercer,** and **James Mercer** by their attorney in fact **John Hough** who by virtue of a letter of attorney given to the said **John Hough** by the said **John Mercer, George Mercer,** and **James Mercer** bearing date the 3rd day of November, 1762 duly proven and recorded in the General Court of Virginia, for and in consideration of the sum of 185 pounds current money of Virginia to them in hand paid by the said **Mathew Hickson,** the receipt whereof they do and every of them doth acknowledge by their attorney in fact **John Hough,** and for other good causes and considerations them thereunto moving they the said **John Mercer, George Mercer,** and **James Mercer** and every of them hath granted bargained sold aliened released and confirmed and by these presents do and every of them doth fully freely and absolutely grant bargain and sell alien release and confirm unto the said **Mathew Hickson** and to his heirs and assigns forever all the above mentioned tract or parcel of land situate in the County of Loudoun aforesaid bounded as is above set forth and described and containing 464 acres as aforesaid, and all houses edifices buildings gardens orchards meadows trees woods underwoods ways water watercourses easements profits advantages hereditaments rights and appurtenances whatsoever to the same belonging or in any wise appertaining. To have and to hold the said land hereditaments and all and singular the premises with the appurtenances unto the said **Mathew Hickson** his heirs and assigns forever, **John Mercer, Geo. Mercer,** and **James Mercer**. Sealed and delivered in the presence of **Timothy Howell, John Howell,** and **Abner Howell**. Proven on 8/14/1764. Lease and Release, Loudoun County Deed Book D, part 1, 234-241

7. 5/17 and 5/18/1764, **John Mercer Esq**. of Marlborough in the County of Stafford and Colony and Dominion of Virginia, and **George Mercer Esq**. of the County of Frederick and Colony aforesaid, and **James Mercer Esq**. of the County of Spotsylvania of the one part to **Hugh Howell** of the County of Loudoun, Colony and Dominion aforesaid of the other part. Whereas the said **John Mercer** obtained a grant from the Proprietor's Office of the Northern Neck in Virginia for 5,985 acres, which tract was divided between them by a patent deed recorded in Fairfax County Court reference thereto being had it will more fully appear, part of which tract being now laid off near the **Kittocton Creek** and bounded as followeth viz. Beginning at a white oak corner to **William Hoge** extending thence S 60° W 250 poles to a hickory in a line of **John Hough**, then with his line N 27° E 290 poles to a corner of **Mathew Hickson** the north side of **Kittocton Creek**, thence with said **Hickson's** line S 28° E 165 poles to the first station containing 125 acres of land more or less. Now this indenture witnesseth that the said **John Mercer, George Mercer,** and **James Mercer** by their attorney in fact **John Hough** who by virtue of a letter of attorney given to the said **John Hough** by the said **John Mercer, George Mercer,** and **James Mercer** bearing date the 3rd day of November, 1762 duly proven and recorded in the General Court of Virginia, for and in consideration of the sum of 50 pounds current money of Virginia to them in hand paid by the said **Hugh Howell** the receipt whereof they do and each of the doth acknowledge by their attorney in fact **John Hough,** and for other cause and considerations them thereunto moving they the said **John Mercer, George Mercer,** and **James Mercer** have and each of them hath granted bargained sold aliened released and confirmed and by these presents do and every of them doth fully freely and absolutely grant bargain and sell alien release and confirm unto the said **Hugh Howell** his heirs and assigns forever all the above mentioned tract or parcel of land situate in the County of Loudoun bounded as is above set forth and described containing 125 acres as aforesaid, and all houses edifices buildings gardens orchards meadows trees woods underwoods ways water watercourses easements profits and advantages hereditaments and appurtenances whatsoever to the same belonging or in any wise appertaining. To have and to hold the said land hereditaments all and singular the premises before mentioned with the appurtenances unto the said **Hugh Howell** his heirs and assigns forever, **John Mercer, Geo. Mercer,** and **James Mercer**. Sealed and delivered in the presence of **Timothy Howell, John Howell,** and **Abner Howell**. Proven on 8/14/1764. Lease and Release, Loudoun County Deed Book D, Part 1, pp. 241-247.

8. 9/9 and 9/10/1765, **John Mercer Esq**. of Marlborough in the County of Stafford and Colony and Dominion of Virginia, and **George Mercer Esq**. of the County of Frederick and Colony aforesaid, and **James Mercer Esq**. of the County of Spotsylvania and Colony aforesaid by their attorney in fact **John Hough** of the one part to **Joseph Hough** of the County of Loudoun and Colony aforesaid of the other part. Whereas the said **John Mercer and Catesby Cocke** obtained a grant from the Proprietor's Office of the Northern Neck in Virginia for a certain tract of land in the County of Prince William now Loudoun containing 5,985 acres of land about the **Kittocton Creek and Mountain**, and a division

made between by partition deeds part of which tract now being laid off and bounded as followeth viz. Beginning at several small hickories on a knoll one of the original corners and corner to **George Gregg's** land and standing on the north side of a branch commonly called **Sears Branch** and extending thence with **Gregg's** line S 17° E 22 poles to a white oak by a **path** ten poles south side of said branch corner to **Mary McGeach's** late purchase, then with her line N 82° W 58 poles to a poplar in a stony bottom, then N 60° W 66 poles to a white oak in a stony bottom by the south side of said branch corner to **William Hoge's** land and the said **Mary McGeach,** then with **Hoge's** line N 10° E 159 poles to a small black oak, then East 150 poles to two hickory saplings by a **road** (the) beginning corner of **Mathew Hickson's** land in a line of **John Hanby,** then with his line S 21° E 126 poles to a black oak in a line of **George Gregg,** then with his line S 57° W 134 poles to the beginning containing 150 acres of land. Now this indenture witnesseth that the said **John Mercer, George Mercer,** and **James Mercer** by their attorney in fact **John Hough** who by a letter of attorney given to the said **John Hough** by the said **John Mercer, George Mercer,** and **James Mercer** bearing date the 3rd day of November, 1762 duly proven and recorded in the General Court for Virginia, for and in consideration of the sum of 75 pounds current money of Virginia to them in hand paid by the said **Joseph Hough** the receipt whereof they do and every of them doth hereby acknowledge by their attorney in fact **John Hough,** and for other causes and considerations them thereunto moving, they the said **John Mercer, George Mercer,** and **James Mercer** by their attorney in fact **John Hough** have and every of them hath granted bargained and sold aliened released and confirmed and by these presents do and every of them doth fully freely and absolutely grant bargain and sell alien release and confirm unto the said **Joseph Hough** his heirs and assigns forever all that the above mentioned tract or parcel of land situate in the County of Loudoun bounded as is above set forth and described and containing 150 acres of land as aforesaid, and all houses edifices buildings gardens orchards meadows trees woods ways water watercourses easements profits and advantages hereditaments rights and appurtenances whatsoever to the same belonging or in any wise appertaining. To have and to hold the said land hereditaments and all and singular the premises before mentioned with the appurtenances unto the said **Joseph Hough** his heirs and assigns forever, **John Hough** for **John Mercer, Geo. Mercer,** and **James Mercer**. Proven on 9/10/1765. Lease and Release, Loudoun County Deed Book D, Part 2, pp. 600-607

9. 10/11 and 10/13/1765, **John Mercer Esq.** of Marlborough in the County of Stafford and Colony of Virginia, and **George Mercer Esq.** of the County of Frederick and Colony aforesaid, and **James Mercer Esq.** of the County of Spotsylvania and Colony aforesaid by their attorney in fact **John Hough** of the County of Loudoun and Dominion aforesaid of the one part to **Colo. James Hamilton** of the County of Loudoun of the other part. Whereas the said **John Mercer and Catesby Cocke** obtained a patent from the Proprietor of the Northern Neck for (blank space) acres of land about the **Kittocton Creek and Mountain,** which was divided between them by a partition recorded in Fairfax Court part of which tract now being laid off and bounded as followeth viz.

Beginning at a marked chestnut tree standing by the side of the **Limestone Branch** on the breaks of **Kittocton Mountain** and the beginning corner of **Joseph Cocks** (Cox) land near a marked beach in an island of said run corner to **Benjamin Haite's** (Hiatt) lot, extending thence East 3 poles to said beach, then with the line of said **Haite** (Hiatt) S 34° E 60 poles to two small white oaks, then East 91 poles to a white oak and black oak on a high hill, then North 247 poles to a stake on a hillside near a valley, then West 130 poles to a line of **Joseph Cox,** then with his line South 200 poles to the first station containing 200 acres of land. Now this indenture witnesseth that the said **John Mercer, George Mercer**, and **James Mercer** by their attorney in fact **John Hough** who by a letter of attorney and for and in consideration of the sum of 40 pounds current money of Virginia to them in hand paid by the said **James Hamilton** the receipt where of is hereby acknowledged, and for other good causes and considerations them thereunto moving, hath granted bargained sold aliened released and confirmed and by these presents do and every of them doth fully freely and absolutely grant bargain and sell alien release and confirm unto the said **James Hamilton** and to his heirs and assigns forever all the above mentioned tract or parcel of land situate in the County of Loudoun aforesaid bounded as is above set forth and described and containing 200 acres as aforesaid, and all houses edifices gardens orchards meadows trees woods underwoods ways water watercourses easements profits and advantages hereditaments rights and appurtenances whatsoever to the same belonging or in any wise appertaining. To have and to hold the said land hereditaments all and singular the premises before mentioned with the appurtenances unto the said **James Hamilton** his heirs and assign forever, **John Mercer, George Mercer and James Mercer**. Proven on 10/11/1765. Lease and Release, Loudoun County Deed Book D, Part 2, pp. 650-655

10. 5/8 and 5/9/1766, **John Mercer Esq**. of Marlborough in the County of Stafford and Colony and Dominion of Virginia, and **George Mercer** of the County of Frederick and Colony aforesaid, and **James Mercer Esq**. of the County of Spotsylvania and Colony aforesaid of the one part to **James Ratikin** of the County of Loudoun and Colony aforesaid of the other part. Whereas the said **John Mercer** obtained a grant jointly with **Catesby Cocke Esq**. from **Thomas, Lord Fairfax,** Proprietor of the Northern Neck of Virginia, bearing date the 13th day of April, 1742 for a certain tract of waste land in the County of Prince William now of the County of Loudoun, containing 5,985 acres of land on and about the **Kittocton Creek and Mountain**, which tract of land was divided between them as by a partition deed recorded in the County Court of Fairfax may appear, part of which division being now laid off and bounded as followeth viz. Beginning at a large white oak corner to **Benjamin Williams** late purchase and in a line of **John Cavins** extending thence with said **Williams** line N 88° E 160 poles to a spanish oak in a line of **Joseph Cox,** then with his line South 120 poles, then S 88° W 160 poles to a hickory in the aforesaid line of **Cavins,** then with said line N 2° W 120 poles to the first station containing 115 acres of land. Now this indenture witnesseth that the said **John Mercer, James Mercer,** and **George Mercer** by their attorney in fact **John Hough** who by virtue of a letter of attorney given the said **John Hough** by the said **John Mercer, George Mercer,** and

James Mercer, bearing date the 3rd day of November, 1762 duly proven and recorded in the General Court, for and in consideration of the sum of 40 pounds current money of Virginia to them in hand paid by the said **James Ratikin** the receipt they do and every of them doth hereby acknowledge, hath granted bargained and sold aliened released and confirmed and by these presents and every of them doth fully freely and absolutely grant bargain and sell aliened release and confirmed unto the said **James Ratikin** and to his heirs and assigns forever all the above mentioned tract or parcel of land situate in the County of Loudoun and bounded as is above set forth described and containing 115 acres of land as aforesaid, and all houses edifices buildings gardens orchards meadows trees woods underwoods way(s) waters watercourses easements profits and advantages hereditaments rights and appurtenances whatsoever to the same belonging or in any wise appertaining. To have and to hold the said land hereditaments all and singular the premises before mentioned with the appurtenances unto the said **James Ratikin** heirs and assigns forever, **John Mercer, George Mercer and James Mercer.** Proven on 5/12/1766, Lease and Release, Loudoun County Deed Book E, pp. 26-31

11. 6/9 and 6/10/1766, **Joseph Hough** of the County of Loudoun of the one part to **John Hough** of the County aforesaid of the other part. Whereas there is a certain tract or parcel of land situate in the County of Loudoun aforesaid bounded as followeth viz. Beginning at several hickories on a knoll an original corner to **Cock** (sic) **and Mercer's** survey and standing on the north side of a branch that issues from **George Gregg's Sawmill** and being a corner to the said **George Gregg,** and extending thence with his line S 17° E 20 poles to a white oak by a **path** ten poles the south side of the said branch corner to **Mary McGeach's** land purchased of **Mercer,** then with her line N 82° W 58 poles to a poplar in a stony bottom, then N 60° W 66 poles to a white oak in a stony bottom by the south side of said branch corner to said **Mary McGeach** and to **William Hoge,** then crossing said branch with **Hoge's** line N 10° E 159 poles to a small black oak, then East 159 poles to a small black oak, then East 150 poles to two hickory saplings by a **road** corner to **Mathew Hickson** and in a line of **John Hanby,** then with **Hanby's** line S 24° E 120 poles to a black oak in a line of **George Gregg,** then with said line S 57° E 134 poles to the beginning, containing 150 acres of land. It being part of a tract patented to **Cock and Mercer** and by said **Mercer** transferred to the said **Joseph Hough** by deeds bearing date the 9th and 10th days of September, 1765. Now this indenture witnesseth that the said **Joseph Hough** for and in consideration of the sum of 80 pounds current money of Virginia in hand paid by the said **Joseph Hough,** the receipt whereof the said **John Hough** doth hereby acknowledge and himself fully satisfied thereof and every part thereof, hath granted bargained sold alienated released and confirmed and by these presents doth bargain and sell alien release and confirm unto the said **John Hough** and his heirs and assigns all and singular the said 150 acres of land bounded and being as is above set forth and described, together with all houses barns buildings ways waters woods meadows rights liberties improvements hereditaments and appurtenances with the rents issues and profits of the same. To have and to hold the said land and premises hereby granted released and

confirmed or mentioned and intended to be granted and released with the appurtenances unto the said **John Hough** his heirs and assigns forever, **Jos. Hough**. Proven on 6/10/1766. Lease and Release, Loudoun County Deed Book E, pp. 77-81

12. 3/9 and 3/10/1767, **John Mercer Esq**. of Marlborough in the County of Stafford and Colony of Virginia, and **George Mercer Esq**. of the County of Frederick and Colony aforesaid, and **James Mercer Esq**. of the County of Spotsylvania and Colony aforesaid by their attorney in fact **John Hough** of the County of Loudoun, Colony and Dominion aforesaid of the one part to **Timothy Howell** of the County of Loudoun and Colony aforesaid of the other part. Whereas the said **John Mercer and Catesby Cocke** obtained a grant from the Proprietor's Office of the Northern Neck of Virginia for a certain tract of land in the County of Prince William now Loudoun containing 5,985 acres of land and a division made between by partition deed recorded in Fairfax County Court, part of which tract now being laid off and bounded as followeth viz. Beginning at several white oak saplings on a stony point the east side of the **South Fork of Kittocton** in a line **John Hough's** land extending thence S 55° E 260 poles to a heap of stones in a line of **Mary McGeach's** late purchase, then with said line N 14° E 107 poles to a stake, then S 40° W 8 poles to a small hickory corner to **William Hogue**, (then) with his line N 32-½° W 140 poles to a white oak his corner, (then) with another of his lines North 66 poles to his corner and corner to **Hugh Howell,** then with said **Howell's** line S 60° W 128 poles to a hickory in the aforesaid line of **John Hough,** then with said line S 26° W 75 poles to the beginning containing 190 acres of land be the same more or less. Now this indenture witnesseth that the said **John Mercer, George Mercer,** and **James Mercer,** by their attorney in fact **John Hough** who by a letter of attorney given to the said **John Hough** by the said **John Mercer, George Mercer,** and **James Mercer,** bearing date the 3rd day of November, 1762 duly proved and recorded in the General Court for Virginia, for and in consideration of the sum 95 pounds current money of Virginia to them in hand paid by the said **Timothy Howell** the receipt whereof they do and every of them doth hereby acknowledge, and for other causes and considerations them thereunto moving, they the said **John Mercer, George Mercer,** and **James Mercer** by their attorney in fact **John Hough** have and every of them hath granted bargained and sold aliened released and confirmed and by these presents do and every of them do, fully freely and absolutely grant bargain and sell alien release and confirm unto the said **Timothy Howell** and to his heirs and assigns forever all that the above mentioned tract or parcel of land situate in the County of Loudoun and bounded as is above set forth and described and containing 190 acres of land as aforesaid, and all houses edifices buildings gardens orchards meadows trees woods ways water watercourses easements profits and advantages hereditaments rights and appurtenances whatsoever to the same belonging or in any wise appertaining. To have and to hold the said land hereditaments all and singular the premises above mentioned with the appurtenances unto the said **Timothy Howell** his heirs and assigns forever, **John Hough** for **John Mercer, George Mercer,** and **James**

Mercer. Proven on 3/10/1767. Lease and Release, Loudoun County Deed Book E, pp. 287-293

13.   3/7 and 3/8/1770, **William Hoge** of the County of Loudoun and Dominion of Virginia and **Mary** his wife of the one part to **John Hough** of the said County of Loudoun of the other part. Witnesseth that for and in consideration of the sum of 400 pounds current money of Virginia to the said **William Hoge** and **Mary** his wife in hand paid by the said **John Hough** at or before the sealing and delivery of these presents the receipt whereof they do hereby acknowledge, hath granted bargained sold aliened released and confirmed and by these presents doth grant bargain sell alien release and confirm unto the said **John Hough** and his heirs all that tract or parcel of land situate in the County of Loudoun aforesaid on a branch of **Kittocton Creek** called **Seers Branch** (sic) and further bounded as followeth viz. Beginning at A, a white oak in a stony bottom by a branch corner to land the said **John Hough** purchased of **John Mercer Esq. and Sons** also corner to land **Mary McGeach** purchased of said **Mercer** and extending thence with said **John Hough's** line N 10° E 226 poles to a small red oak in a line of **Mathew Hickson**, then with said line S 62° W 120 poles to a white oak his corner in a line of **Hugh Howell**, then with his line S 28° E 10 poles to a white oak his corner, then with his line S 62° W 64 poles to two small red oaks corner to **Timothy Howell**, then with his line South 66 poles to a white oak, (then) still with his line S 32° 30 minutes E 140 poles to a small hickory, then with said **Mary McGeach's** lines N 40° E 30 poles to a black oak, then N 65° E 36 poles to the first station containing 150 acres more or less, being a parcel of land sold and conveyed by **John Mercer and Sons** to the said **William Hoge** by deeds bearing date the 12th and 13th days of December, 1763 and recorded in Loudoun County Court, the same part of a larger tract granted to **Cocke and Mercer** and divided between them, and all houses buildings orchards ways waters watercourses profits commodities hereditaments and appurtenances whatsoever to the said premises hereby granted or any part thereof belonging or in any wise appertaining. To have and to hold the land hereby conveyed and all and singular other the premises hereby granted and released and every part and parcel thereof with their and every of their appurtenances unto the said **John Hough** his heirs and assigns forever, **Willm. Hoge** and **Mary Hoge**. Proven on 3/18/1770. Lease and Release, Loudoun County Deed Book G, pp. 236-239 (Note: Also, see John Hough to William Hoge, Loudoun County Deed Book G, pp. 239-240)

14.   10/15/1771, Know all men by these presents that I **Benjamin Hiatt** of Connecticut Farms in the Colony of Elizabeth Town, Essex County, New Jersey, Minister of the Gospel, have and do hereby constitute and appoint my trusty friend **Amos Thompson**, Minister of the Gospel in Loudoun County, Virginia, my true and lawful attorney to claim demand or sue for, for me and in my name, a certain tract of land that I purchased of **John Hough** attorney for **John, George and James Mercer's** lying on **Kittocton Mountain** in Loudoun County, Virginia, at his discretion and fully confirming in his knowledge and integrity. I hereby give and grant unto any said attorney clear and absolute power to settle and adjust all difference that have or may arise between me and **Hamilton Rogers** or any other person or persons whatsoever about the aforesaid tract of land or anything

thereto relating either by proposition, arbitration, or a course of law at his discretion fully, clearly, and absolutely as I myself could do were I present, and further I give and grant unto my said attorney full power and authority to rent or lease or other ways at his discretion or to convey by lawful deeds a fee simple of in and to the said tract of land fully and clearly as I could myself were I personally present. In witness whereof I have hereunto set my hand & seal this15th day of October, 1771, **Benjamin Haitt** (sic). At a Court held for Loudoun County May the 26th, 1772, this Power of Attorney was proved by oaths of **Josias Clapham Gent.**, **Josias Clapham**, and **Neal McGinnis**, witnesses thereto and ordered to be recorded. **Chas. Binns**, Clerk of Court. Loudoun County Deed Book H, pp. 427-428

15. 8/6 and 8/7/1773, **John Hough** of the County of Loudoun of the one part to **Joseph Janney** of the same County of the other part. Witnesseth that for and in consideration of the sum of 60 pounds current money of Virginia to the said **John Hough** in hand paid by the said **Joseph Janney** at or before the sealing and delivery of these presents the receipt whereof he doth acknowledge, hath granted bargained sold aliened released and confirmed unto the said **Joseph Janney** and his heirs a certain parcel of land situate in Loudoun County aforesaid and bounded as followeth viz. Beginning at a black oak marked **TJ** standing by the **road** crossing the mountain and the northeast corner of **George Gregg's** land and corner to the land the said **Joseph Janney** purchased of **John Hanby** or near the same, and extending thence with a line of **John Hanby's** N 23° W 100 poles to a hickory sapling by the **road leading to Kirk's Mill** and corner to **William Hickson's** land, then along the **road** S 11° W 34 poles to a white oak, then S 15° W 18 poles to a hickory, then S 10° W 34 poles to a black oak, then S 18° W 44 poles to a spanish oak by the **road**, then S 35° W 14 poles to a black oak, then S 17° W 20 poles to a black oak by the south side of the first mentioned **mountain road** near the line of **George Gregg**, then binding with that **road** N 55° E 116 poles to the beginning containing 32 acres, being a detached parcel of land lying **between the two roads** and part of a tract the said **John Hough** purchased of **John Mercer and Sons**, and all houses buildings orchards ways waters watercourses profits commodities hereditaments and appurtenances whatsoever to the said premises hereby granted or any part thereof belonging or in any wise appertaining. To have and to hold the lands hereby conveyed and all and singular other the premises hereby granted and released and every part and parcel thereof with their and every of their appurtenances unto the said **Joseph Janney** and assigns forever, **John Hough**. Proven on 8/9/1773. Lease and Release, Loudoun County Deed Book I, pp. 329-333

16. 4/8 and 4/9/1774, **Mathew Hixon** of the County of Loudoun County and Colony of Virginia of the one part to **William Hixon** of the same County and Colony aforesaid of the other part. Whereas the said **Mathew Hixon** obtained a deed for a tract of land of **John, James**, and **George Mercer, Esquires**, which deed is recorded in Loudoun County Court reference thereto being had will more fully and at large appear, part of which tract being now laid off and bounded as followeth viz. Beginning at two hickory saplings on a line of **John Hanby's** and extending thence N 21° W 158 poles and 35 links to a black oak near a **grave**,

then S 73° W 114 poles to two white oaks upon a hillside, thence N 19° W 90 poles to a poplar upon the bank of **Kittocton**, then up the said Creek with the meanders of the same 162 poles to a poplar among a bunch of rocks in a line of **John Hough's**, then S 26° W 54 poles to a hickory, (then) S 28° E 155 poles to a white oak, (then) N 62° E 120 poles to a small red oak, (then) S 10° W 66 poles to a small red oak corner to **Gossett's** lot, then East 156 poles to the first station containing 217 acres. Now this indenture witnesseth that the said **Mathew Hixon** for and in consideration of the sum of 50 pounds Virginia currency to him in hand paid by the said **William Hixon** the receipt whereof he doth hereby acknowledge and for other causes and considerations him thereunto moving, he the said **Mathew Hixon** hath granted bargained sold aliened released and confirmed and by these presents doth fully freely and absolutely grant bargain and sell alien release and confirm unto the said **William Hixon** and to his heirs and assigns forever all the above mentioned tract or parcel of land situate in the County of Loudoun aforesaid bounded as is above set forth and described and containing 217 acres as aforesaid, and all houses edifices buildings gardens orchards meadows trees woods underwoods ways waters watercourses easements profits advantages hereditaments rights and appurtenances whatsoever to the same belonging or in any wise appertaining. To have and to hold the said land hereditaments and all and singular the premises with the appurtenances unto the said **Wm. Hixon** his heirs and assigns forever, **Mathew** his M mark **Hixon**. Sealed and delivered in the presence of **Hugh** his H mark **Howell, Joseph Bonham**, and **Charles Howell**. Proven on 4/11/1774. Lease and Release, Loudoun County Deed Book K, pp. 144-149

17. 4/8 and 4/9/1774, **Mathew Hixon** of the County of Loudoun of the one part to **Timothy Hixon** of the same place of the other part. Whereas the said **Mathew Hixon** obtained a deed for a tract of land of **John, James**, and **George Mercer, Esquires** which deed is recorded in Loudoun County Court reference thereto being had it will more fully and at large appear part of which tract being now laid off and bounded as followeth viz. Beginning at a black oak near a **grave** and extending N 21°W 189 poles to two black oaks corner to **Colo. Colvill's** land, then N 30° W 126 poles to two black oak saplings, from thence S 26° W 266 poles to a poplar among a bunch of rocks, then down **Kittocton Creek** with the meanders of the same 162 poles to a poplar, then S 19° E 90 poles to two white oak saplings in a hillside, from thence 114 poles to the beginning containing 247 acres. Now this indenture witnesseth that the said **Mathew Hixon** for and in consideration of the sum of 50 pounds Virginia currency to him in hand paid by the said **Timothy Hixon** the receipt whereof he doth hereby acknowledge and for other causes and considerations him thereunto moving, him the said **Mathew Hixon** hath granted bargained sold aliened released and confirmed and by these presents doth fully freely and absolutely grant bargain and sell alien release and confirm unto the said **Timothy Hixon** and to his heirs and assigns forever all the above mentioned tract or parcel of land situate in the County of Loudoun aforesaid and bounded as is above set forth and described and containing 247 acres as aforesaid, and all houses edifices buildings gardens orchards meadows trees woods underwoods ways water watercourses easements profits advantages

hereditaments rights and appurtenances whatsoever to the same belonging or in any wise appertaining. To have and to hold the said land hereditaments and all and singular the said premises with the appurtenances unto the said **Timothy Hixon** his heirs and assigns forever, **Mathew** his M mark **Hixon**. Sealed and delivered in the presence of **Hugh** his H mark **Howell, Joseph Bonham**, and **Charles Howell**. Proven 4/11/1774. Lease and Release, Loudoun County Deed Book K, pp. 149-155

18.   2/17/1775, **George Mercer Esquire** formerly of the Colony of Virginia at present of the City of London of the first part, and **James Mercer** of the County of Spotsylvania attorney at law of the second part, and the said **James Mercer** acting executor of the last will and testament of **Mrs. Anne Mercer deceased** late of Marlborough in the County of Stafford who was sole devisee and executrix of **John Mercer Esquire deceased** late of the same place of the third part, to **James Hamilton** of the County of Loudoun of the fourth part. Whereas the aforementioned **John Mercer** in his lifetime (blank space) and the said **George Mercer** and **James Mercer** were seized in fee of certain land in the County of Loudoun as tenants in common, the said **John Mercer** in moiety, and the said **George** and **James** each as quarter part, and in tending to dispose the same without division and to divide the purchase money in proportions aforementioned by their joint and several letter of attorney bearing date the 3rd day of November, 1762 now of record in the General Court did constitute and appoint **John Hough** of the said County of Loudoun their joint and several attorney thereby empowering the said **John Hough** to sell and dispose of the said lands in such manner as he should think proper and to convey the same to the purchaser. And, whereas the said **John Hough** by virtue of the said letter of attorney on the 27th day of September, 1765 in the lifetime of the said **John Mercer** did sell to **Benjamin Williams** 200 acres part of the said lands for the consideration of 40 pounds, which the said **Benjamin Williams** being then unable to pay the said **Hough** passed his bond bearing date the day and year last mentioned for making proper deeds to the said **Benjamin Williams** upon payment of the said consideration money, and put the said **Benjamin Williams** in possession thereof under the purchase aforesaid until the 10th day of (blank space) when he sold the same to the above said **James Hamilton** for valuable consideration and assigned the said **John Hough's** bond to the said **James Hamilton** who entered into the said lands and has continued in possession of the same ever since as may appear by the said bond and assignment thereof now delivered up to be cancelled. And, whereas the said **John Mercer Esquire** departed this life in the month of October, 1768 before the said **Hough** had made deeds to the said **Anne Mercer** and by her last will and testament of record in the County of Stafford devised his whole estate to the aforementioned **Anne Mercer** his wife in fee and thereof appointed her sole executrix. And, also whereas the said **Anne Mercer** departed this life in the month of September, 1770 before the deeds were made to the said **Williams** or **Hamilton** and by her last will and testament also of record in the said County of Stafford devised her estate to and among her children subject nevertheless to the payment of debts as well of the said **John Mercer** as her own, and of her said will appointed **Alexander Rose Esquire** and the said **James**

Mercer and her son **Mungo Roy Mercer** executors authorizing them or any of them who should undertake the said executorship to sell any part of her estate either real or personal as they or such acting executor should judge most proper for the purpose aforesaid. And, whereas the said **Mungo Roy Mercer** being under age departed this life before probate of the said will and the said (losses to the margin) the executorship upon record, the aforementioned **James Mercer** alone took upon himself the said executorship by probate thereof now remaining of record among the proceedings of the said Court of Stafford. And, whereas the said **James Hamilton** hath long since paid the aforementioned purchase money to the said **John Hough** but it is doubted whether the said **Hough's** power was not revoked as to the said **John Mercer** by his death, and the said **James Mercer** is advised that he may well convey the said **John Mercer** in the said lands so sold to the said **James Hamilton** as aforesaid under power given him by the will of the said **Anne Mercer** as afore recited. Now to the end that the said **James Hamilton** may have a good and sufficient conveyance of the said 200 acres of land so sold by the said **Hough** as aforesaid, this indenture witnesseth that the aforenamed **George Mercer Esquire** and the said **James Mercer** as well in his own right as executor of the said **Anne Mercer** deceased for and in consideration of the premises and for and in consideration of the said sum of 40 pounds to the said **John Hough** for their use paid by the said **James Hamilton** as aforesaid and for the further consideration of the sum of 5 shillings sterling money of Great Britain to them the said **George Mercer** and **James Mercer** as well in his own right as executor for **Anne Mercer** deceased in hand paid by the aforementioned **James Hamilton** the receipt whereof they do hereby severally acknowledge, have given granted bargained and sold aliened released and confirmed and by these presents do give grant bargain and sell alien release and confirm unto the said **James Hamilton** his heirs and assigns all that tract or parcel of land aforementioned situate lying and being in the County of Loudoun and bounded as follows viz. Beginning at a large white oak on the **Kittocton Mountain** corner to **James Ratikin** and in a line of **John Cavins** extending thence with **Cavins** line N 3° W 142 poles to a white oak on a hill the dividing corner between **Cock and Mercer,** then with the said dividing line N 86° E 226 poles to a small hickory in a valley by a **path**, then South 115 poles to two red oaks in **Joseph Cox's** line then with said line West 40 poles to a white oak **Cox's** corner, then with **Cox's** line South 13 poles to a spanish oak corner to said **James Ratikin,** then with **Ratikin's** line S 88° W 160 poles to the beginning containing 200 acres of land, excepting out of the same 10 acres of the said land laid off to **Patrick McVey** and sold to him by the said **Benjamin Williams,** and which said **James Hamilton** is to convey to the said **Patrick McVey** or can set to be done according to a survey thereof made by the said **Hough** on the sale thereof, and also all the estate right title claim and demand property and use either in law or equity of them the said **George Mercer** and **James Mercer** as well in his own right as executor of the said **Anne Mercer** deceased or either of them of in and to the said tract or parcel of land with the appurtenances to the same belonging or in any wise appertaining. To have and to hold the said tract or parcel of land aforementioned and premises with their every of their appurtenances unto the said **James Hamilton** his heirs and assigns forever, **John Hough** for **George Mercer, James Mercer, James Mercer** executor of **Anne Mercer**. Sealed and delivered in the presence of **Morgan Alexander, William Robinson, Francis Peyton, Valentine Harrison**, and **Henry Peyton**. Proven on 9/11/1775. Deed, Loudoun County Deed Book L, pp. 392- 396

19.   2/17/1775, This indenture quadripartite between **George Mercer Esquire** formerly of the Colony of Virginia at present of the City of London of the first part, and **James Mercer** of the County of Spotsylvania attorney in fact of the second part, and the said **James Mercer** acting executor of the last will and testament of **Mrs. Anne Mercer** late of Marlborough in the County of Stafford deceased who was sole devisee and executrix of **John Mercer deceased** late of the same place of the third part, and **Joseph Hough** of the County of Loudoun of the fourth part. Whereas the aforementioned **John Mercer** in his lifetime and the said **George Mercer** and **James Mercer** were seized in fee of certain land in the County of Loudoun as tenants in common, the said **John Mercer** in moiety, and the said **George** and **James** each a quarter part, and intending to dispose the same without a division and to divide the purchase money in proportion aforementioned by their joint and several letter of attorney bearing date the 3rd day of November, 1762 now of record in the General Court did constitute and appoint **John Hough** of the said County of Loudoun their joint and several attorney thereby empowering the said **John Hough** to sell and dispose of the said land in such manner as he should think most proper and to convey the same to the purchasers. And, whereas the said **John Hough** by virtue of the said letter of attorney on the 2nd day of September, 1767 in the lifetime of the said **John Mercer** did sell to **Joseph Hough** 200 acres part of the said lands for the consideration of 40 pounds current money of Virginia, which the said **Joseph Hough** being then unable to pay the said **Hough** passed his bond bearing date the day and year last mentioned for making proper deeds to the said **Joseph Hough** upon payment of the said consideration money, and put the said **Joseph Hough** in possession of the said 200 acres who continued possession thereof under the purchase aforesaid ever since as may appear by the said bond now delivered up to be cancelled. And, whereas the said **John Mercer Esq**. departed this life in the month of October, 1768 before the said **Hough** had made deeds to the said **Joseph** and by his last will and testament now of record in the County Court of Stafford devised his whole estate to the above named **Anne Mercer** (losses to margin) and thereof appointed her sole executrix. And, also whereas the said **Anne Mercer** departed this life in the month of September, 1770 before deed were made to the said and by her last will and testament also of record in the said County of Stafford devised her estate to and among her children subject nevertheless to the payment of debts as well of the said **John Mercer** as her own, and of her said will appointed **Alexander Rose Esquire** the said **James Mercer** and her son **Mungo Roy Mercer** executors authorizing them or any of them who should undertake the said executorship to sell any part of her estate either real or personal as they or such acting executor should judge most proper for the purposes aforesaid. And, whereas the said **Mungo Roy Mercer** being under aged departed this life before probate of the said will and the said **Alexander Rose** having renounced the

executorship upon record, the aforementioned **James Mercer** alone took upon himself the said executorship by probate thereof now remaining of record among the proceedings of the said Court of Stafford. And, whereas the said **Joseph Hough** hath since paid the aforementioned purchase money to the said **John Hough** but it is doubted whether the said **Hough's** power was not revoked as to the said **Mercer** by his death and the said **James Mercer** is advised that he may well convey the said **John Mercer** interest in the said lands so sold to the said **Joseph Hough** as aforesaid under the powers given him by the said will of the said **Anne Mercer** as aforerecited. Now to the end that the said **Joseph Hough** may have a good and sufficient conveyance of the said 200 acres of land so sold by the said **Hough** as aforesaid, this indenture witnesseth that the aforementioned **George Mercer Esquire** and the said **James Mercer** as well in his own right as executor of the said **Anne Mercer** deceased for and in consideration of the sum of 5 shillings sterling money of Great Britain to them the said **George Mercer** and **James Mercer** as well in his own right as executor of the said **Anne Mercer** deceased in hand paid by the aforenamed **Joseph Hough** the receipt whereof they do hereby severally acknowledge, have given granted bargained and sold aliened released and confirmed and by these presents do severally give grant bargain and sell alien release and confirm unto the **Joseph** his heirs and assigns all that tract or parcel of land aforementioned situate lying and being in the County of Loudoun and bounded as follows viz. Beginning at two small hickories in a valley in the dividing line between **Cock** (sic) **and Mercer** and to a parcel of land sold **Benjamin Williams** now **James Hamilton** extending thence South 115 poles to two red oaks in **Joseph Cox's** line corner to said **Benjamin Williams** survey, then with said **Cox's** line East 103 poles to a white oak and a small hickory corner to said **Cox,** then with another of his lines South 37 poles to 3 spanish oaks corner to **James Hamilton's** other tract, then binding with his line east 125 poles to his corner two oak saplings on a hillside, thence still East 25 poles to a black and white oak, then North 87 poles to a white oak on a hill, then N 28° W 85 poles to the aforesaid dividing line of **Cock and Mercer,** then with said line S 87° W 210 poles to the beginning containing 200 acres and all the estate right title interest claim and demand property and use either in law or equity of them the said **George Mercer** and **James Mercer** as well of his own right as executor of the said **Anne Mercer deceased** or either of them of in and to the said tract or parcel of land with the appurtenances to the same belonging or in any wise appertaining. To have and to hold the said tract or parcel of land aforementioned and premises with their and every of their appurtenances unto the said **Joseph Hough** and his heirs and assigns forever, **John Hough** for **Geo. Mercer, James Mercer,** and **(James) Mercer** executor of **Anne Mercer**. Sealed and delivered in the presence of **Morgan Alexander, William Robinson, Francis Peyton, Valentine Harrison,** and **Henry Peyton**. Proven on 9/8/1775. Deed, Loudoun County Deed Book L, pp. 396-401

20.   2/17/1775, This indenture quadripartite between **George Mercer** formerly of the Colony of Virginia Esquire at present of the City of London of the first part, and **James Mercer** of the County of Spotsylvania attorney at law of the second part, and the said **James Mercer** acting executor of the last will and

testament of **Mrs. Anne Mercer** late of Marlborough in the County of Stafford deceased who was sole devisee and executrix of **John Mercer Esquire** late of the same place deceased of the third part, to **Francis Hague** of the County of Loudoun of the fourth part. Whereas the aforenamed **John Mercer Esquire** in his lifetime and the said **George Mercer** and **James Mercer** were seized in of certain lands in the County of Loudoun as tenants in common the said **John Mercer** in a moiety and the said **George** and **James** each a quarter part and intending to dispose of the same without divisions and dividends (losses to margin) proportions aforenamed by their joint and several letter of attorney bearing date 11/3/1762, now of record in the General Court did constitute and appoint **John Hough** of the said County of Loudoun their joint and several attorney thereby empowering the said **John Hough** to sell and dispose of the said lands in such manner as he should think proper and to convey the same to the purchasers. And, whereas the said **John Hough** by virtue of the said letter of attorney on 9/2/1767 in lifetime of the said **John Mercer** did sell to the aforenamed **Francis Hague** 85 acres part of the said lands for the consideration of 42 pounds Virginia currency, which the said **Francis Hague** being then unable to pay the said **John Hough** passed his bonds bearing date the day and year last mentioned for making proper deeds to the said **Francis Hague** upon payment of the said consideration money and put the said **Francis Hague** in possession of the said 85 acres who has continued in possession thereof under the purchase aforesaid as may appear by the said **John Hough's** bond now divided up to be cancelled. And, whereas the said **John Mercer Esquire** departed this life in the month of October, 1768 before the said **Hough** had made deeds to the said **Francis Hague** and by his last will and testament now of record in the County Court of Stafford devised his whole estate to the aforenamed **Anne Mercer** his wife in fee and thereof appointed his sole executor. And, also whereas the said **Anne Mercer** departed this life in the month of September, 1770 and before deeds were made to the said **Francis Hague** and by her last will and testament also of record in the said County of Stafford devised her (losses to margin) among her children subject nevertheless to the payment of debts as well of the said **John Mercer** deceased as her own, and of her said will appointed **Alexander Rose Esquire** the said **James Mercer** and her son **Mungo (Roy) Mercer** executors authorizing them or any of them who should undertake the said executorship to sell any part of her estate either real or personal as they or such acting executor should judge most proper to the purposes aforesaid. And, whereas the said **Mungo Roy Mercer** being underage departed this life before probate of the said will and the said **Alexander Rose** having renounced the executorship up on record, the aforenamed **James Mercer** alone took upon himself the said executorship as may appear by probate thereof remaining of record among the proceedings of the said County of Stafford. And, whereas the said **Francis Hague** hath long since paid the aforementioned purchase money to the said **John Hough** but it is doubted whether the said **Hough's** power was not revoked as to the said **Mercer** by his death and the said **James Mercer** is advised that he may well convey the said **John Mercer's** interest in the said lands so sold to the said **Francis Hague** as aforesaid under the powers given him by the will of the said **Anne Mercer** as aforerecited. Now to the end that the said **Francis**

Hague may have good and sufficient conveyance of the said 80 (sic) acres of land so sold by the said **Hough** as aforesaid, this indenture witnesseth that the aforementioned **George Mercer Esquire** and the said **James Mercer** in his own right as well as executor of the said **Anne Mercer deceased** for and in consideration of the premises and for and in consideration of the sum of 45 pounds to the said **John Hough** for their use paid by the said **Francis Hague** as aforesaid and for the further consideration of the sum of 5 shillings sterling money of Great Britain to them the said **George Mercer** and **James Mercer** as well in his own right as executor of the said **Anne Mercer** and in hand paid by the aforenamed **Francis Hague** the receipt whereof they do hereby severally acknowledge, have given granted bargained and sold aliened released and confirmed and by these presents do severally give grant bargain an sell alien release and confirm unto the said **Francis Hague** his heirs and assigns all that certain tract or parcel of land aforementioned situate lying and being in the County of Loudoun and bounded as follows viz. Beginning at a white hickory in a bottom corner to **Hague** and to **John Hough** extending thence with **Hough's** line N 27° E 55 (56?) poles to a small white oak corner to **Andrew Brown,** then with **Brown's** line S 53° E 260 poles to a heap of stones in **Mary McGeach's** line, then with said line S 14° W 125 poles to three small hickories in a line of said **Hague's** land, then with said line N 15° W 125 poles to a black oak and white oak, then with another of said **Hague's** lines N 53° W 190 poles to the beginning containing according to a survey thereof made by the said **John Hough** on the sale thereof 85 acres and all the estate right title claim demand property and use either in law or equity of them the said **George Mercer** and **James Mercer** as well in his own right as executor of the said **Anne Mercer** deceased or either of them of in and to the said tract or parcel of land with the appurtenances to the same belonging or in any wise appertaining. To have and to hold the said tract or parcel of land aforementioned and premises with their and every of their appurtenances unto the said **Francis Hague** and his heirs and assigns forever, **John Hough** for **George Mercer, James Mercer** and **James Mercer** executor of **Anne Mercer**. Sealed and delivered in the presence of **Morgan Alexander, William Robinson, Francis Peyton, Valentine Harrison,** and **Henry Peyton**. Proven on 9/11/1775. Deed, Loudoun County Deed Book L, pp. 401-406

21. 3/18/1782, **William Cavins** of the County of Loudoun and Commonwealth of Virginia and **Mary** his wife of the one part to **John McGeach** of the County of Loudoun and Commonwealth aforesaid of the other part. Whereas **John Mercer and Catesby Cox** (sic) obtained a grant from **Thomas, Lord Fairfax** for a certain tract of land situate in Fairfax County now Loudoun, which was divided between (the) said **John Mercer and Catesby Cock** (sic) by a partition deed and recorded in Fairfax County Court, part of which tract was sold and laid off to **Mary McGeach** now **Mary Cavins** containing 200 acres and conveyed to her by indentures of lease and release and recorded in Loudoun County Court, part of which tract is now laid off and bounded as followeth viz. Beginning at three small hickories in a line of **Francis Hague** and corner to the division of **Cocke and Mercer** and **William Schooley**, thence with said division line of **Cocke and Mercer** N 59° E to the corner between said **John McGeach**

and his brother **Joseph McGeach,** thence with that line and its run and marked to the original line of said two hundred acre tract, and then with the lines of that tract to the beginning containing 100 acres of land. Now this indenture witnesseth that the said **William Cavins** and **Mary** his wife for and in consideration of the sum of 20 pounds current money of Virginia to them in hand paid by the said **John McGeach** the receipt whereof is hereby acknowledged and for other causes and considerations them thereunto moving, the said **William Cavins** hath granted bargained and sold aliened released and confirmed and by these presents do fully freely and absolutely grant bargain and sell alien release and confirm unto the said **John McGeach** and to his heirs and assigns forever. To have and to hold the said land hereditaments all and singular the premises before mentioned with the appurtenances unto the said **John McGeach** his heirs and assigns forever, **William Cavins, Mary** her M mark **Cavins.** Sealed and delivered in the presence of **Josh Danniel, Isaac Vandevanter,** and **John Henry.** Proven on 11/11/1782. Lease and Release, Loudoun County Deed Book N, Part 2, pp. 380-385.

22.   3/1/1803, **Timothy Hixson** of the County of Loudoun of the one part to **Ruben Hixson** of the same County of the other part. Witnesseth that for and in consideration of the sum of $ 2,000 to him in hand paid by the said **Ruben Hixson** the receipt whereof is hereby acknowledged by the said **Timothy Hixson** and himself content and fully satisfied, having granted bargained and sold aliened released and confirmed and by these presents doth grant bargain alien sell and release and confirm unto the said **Ruben Hixson** his heirs and assigns forever all that tract or parcel of land situate lying and being in the County of Loudoun aforesaid and joining to the lands of the heirs of **William Hixson deceased** being part of a larger tract of land belonging to the said **Timothy Hixson** and is bounded as followeth viz. Beginning at two hickories on the west side of **Kittocton Creek** and supposed to be in the line of **Colvin's (Colvill's)** extending thence with that line S 28° W 128 poles to a poplar corner to said **Timothy Hixson** and other lands of said **Ruben Hixson,** from thence with said **Kittocton Creek** and binding therewith the several meanders thereof to the beginning containing and laid out for 63 acres of land be the same more or less. Also, one half an acre of land upon the south side of **Kittocton** for the purpose of an **abutment for a mill-dam** with liberty to pass and re-pass thereunto for the purpose of building and repairing said abutment, and also the reversion and reversions remainder and remainders of said tract the rents and services thereof with all the estate right title interest property claim and demand of him the said **Timothy Hixon** of in and to the said tract of land aforesaid and every part and parcel thereof to him the said **Ruben Hixon.** To have and to hold the said tract of land and premises and every part and parcel thereof to him the said **Ruben Hixon** his heirs and assigns forever with the appurtenances thereto belonging or in any wise appertaining, **Timothy Hixson.** Sealed and delivered in the presence of **Henry Huff Jr., John Martin Jr., John Kleinhoff,** and **Geo. Mull.** Proven on 5/9/1803. Bargain and Sale, Loudoun County Deed Book 2C, pp. 299-301

The dividing corner
between Cocke and
Mercer then with
the dividing line...

to a small
hickory in a
valley by
a path

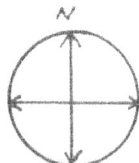

on the K. Hacton Mountain

Formerly Benjamin Williams purchase

2/17/1775

George Mercer of the City of
London of the first part and James
Mercer of Spotsylvania County of the
second part and the said James
Mercer as acting executor of the
third part by their joint and
several attorney John Hough of Loudoun County to James Hamilton of
Loudoun County of the fourth part,
Deed, 200 acres, Deed Book L,
pp. 392-396

See ** Line of John
Mercer and Sons by
John Hough to James
Hamilton, Lease and
Release 200 acres,
Deed Book D, Part 2,
pp. 650-654 dated
10/11 and 10/13/1765

C   B

6/13/1763 and 6/14/1763

5/8 and 5/9/1766
John Mercer and Sons by
their attorney in fact
John Hough of Loudoun
County to James Ratikin
of Loudoun County, Lease
and Release 115 acres of
land, Loudoun County Deed
Book E, pp. 26-31

John Mercer Esq. of
Stafford County and George
Mercer of Frederick County
Esq. and James Mercer of
Spotsylvania Esq. by their
attorney in fact John
Hough of Loudoun County to
Joseph Cox late of the
Province of New Jersey now
of Loudoun County, Lease
and Release 200 acres of
land, Loudoun County Deed
Book C, Part 2, pp. 624 -
631

**

D   A

See * Line of John Cavin's

the south side
of Limestone
Run above a fork
of the same

1 in. = 50 poles

Beginning at A a white oak on the South Side of Seirs Branch in a line of George Gregg running then with the said Gregg's Line S17E 94 poles to a hickory bush near a marked black oak in the dividing line between Cocke and Mercer...

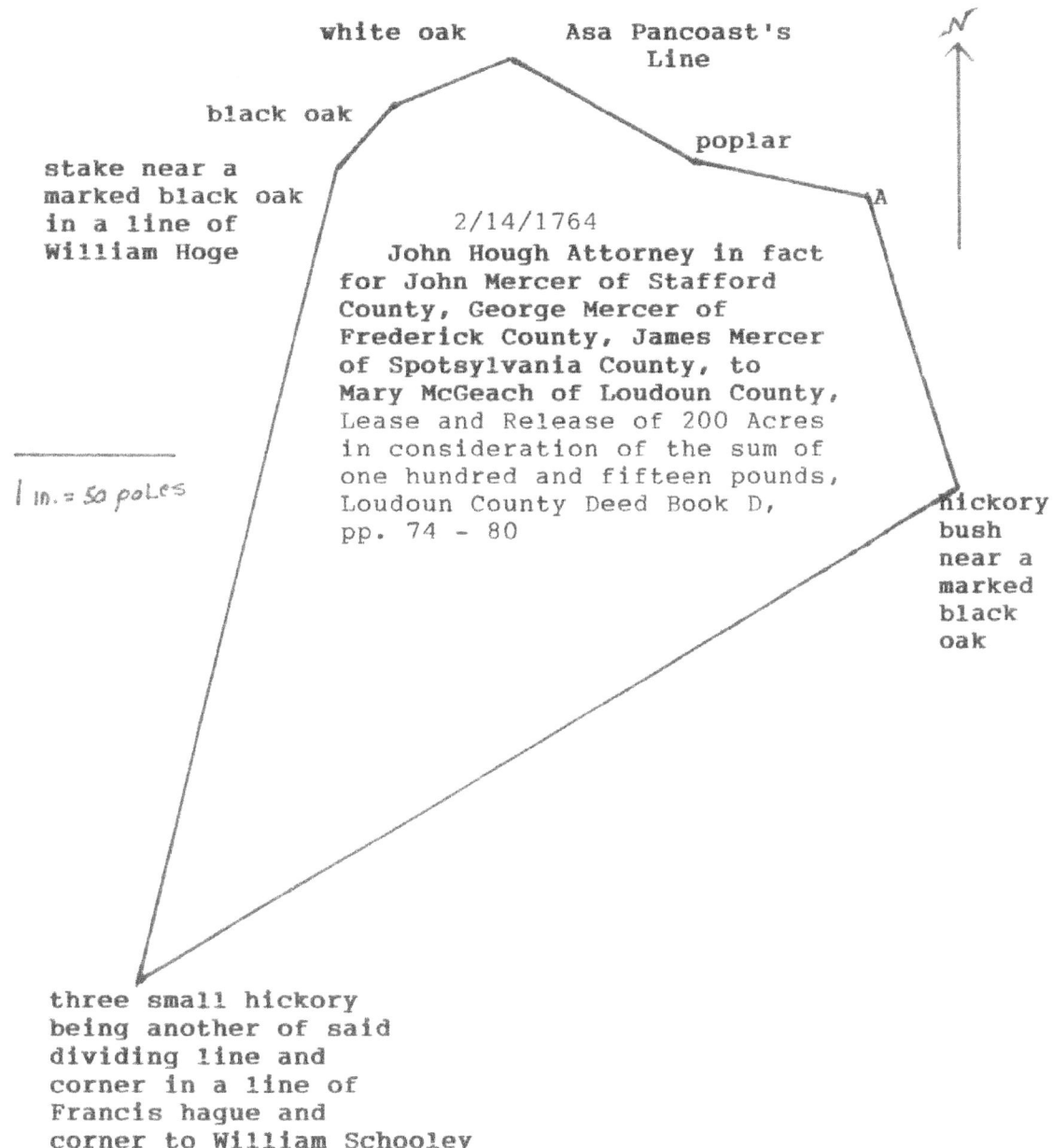

2/14/1764
John Hough Attorney in fact for John Mercer of Stafford County, George Mercer of Frederick County, James Mercer of Spotsylvania County, to Mary McGeach of Loudoun County, Lease and Release of 200 Acres in consideration of the sum of one hundred and fifteen pounds, Loudoun County Deed Book D, pp. 74 - 80

Loudoun County, Virginia

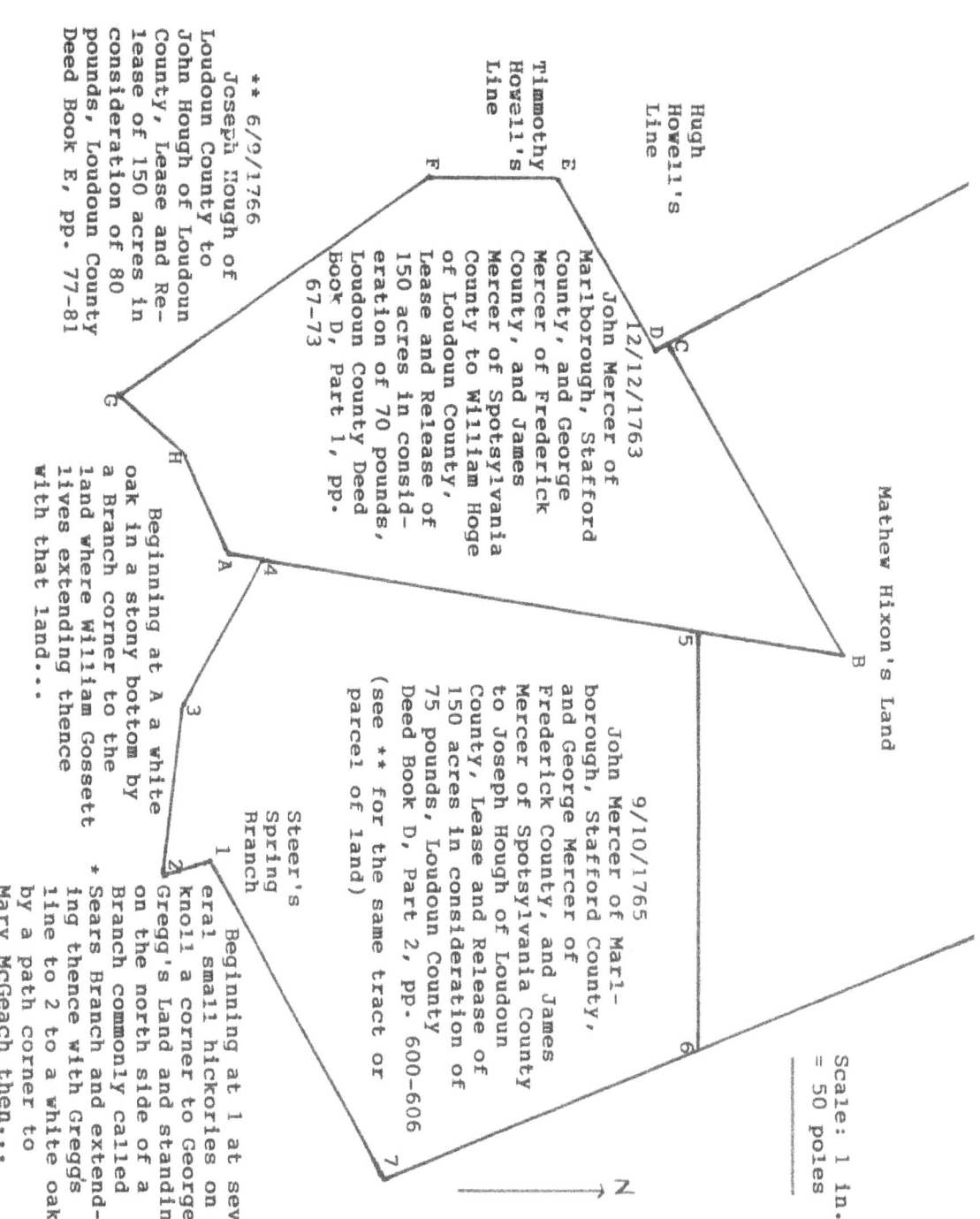

212

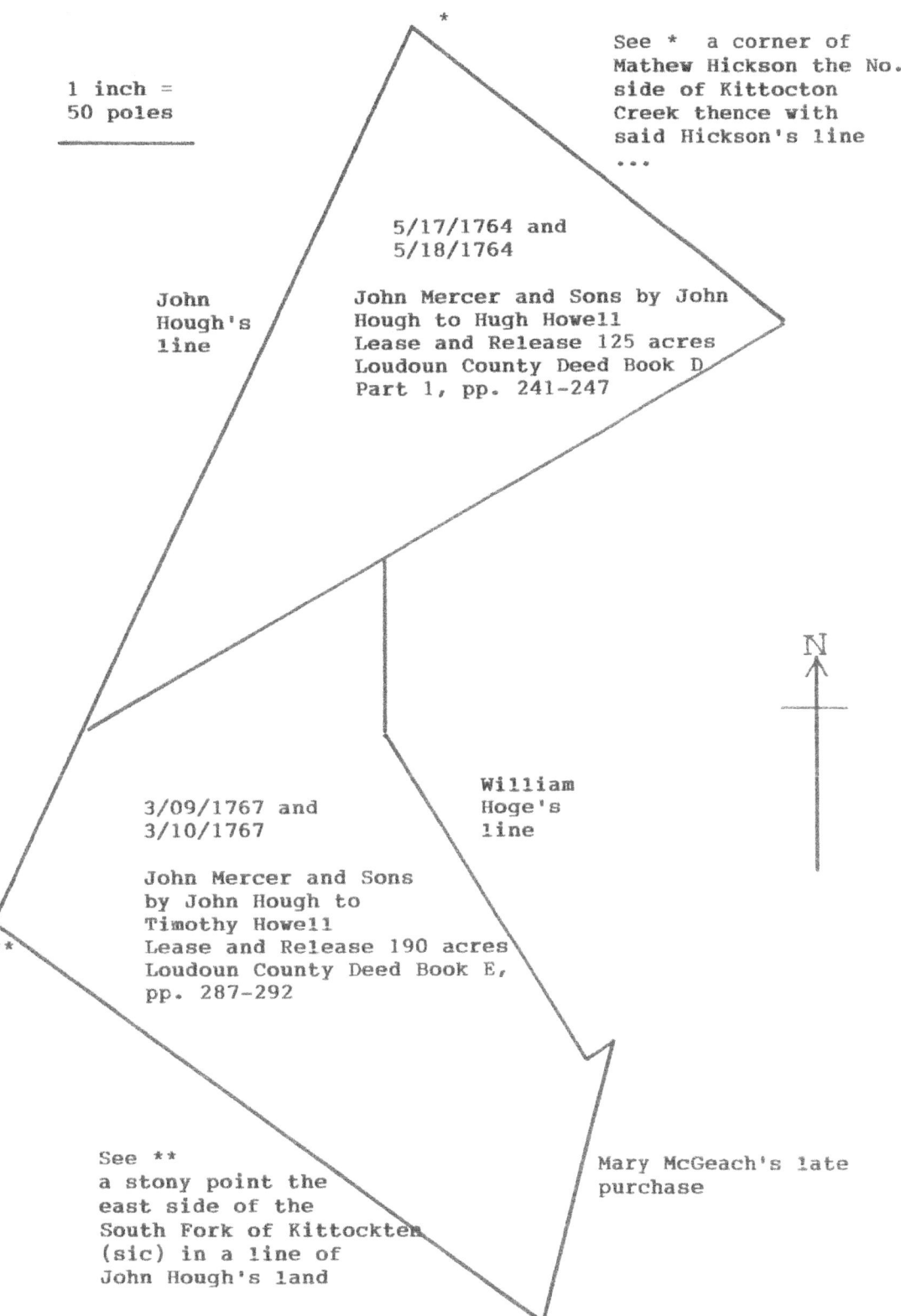

8/11/1773 John Hough of Loudoun County to Joseph Janney of Loudoun County, Lease and Release of 32 acres of land in consideration of sixty pounds, ...Beginning at A at a black oak marked standing by the Road crossing the Mountain and the NE corner of George Gregg's Land and a corner to the land the said Joseph Janney purchased of John Hanby, or near the same, and extending thence with a line of John Hanby's to B to a hickory sapling by the Road leading to Kirk's Mill and corner to William Hickson's (Hixon) Land, then along the Road to C to a white oak then to D to a hickory, then to E to a black oak, then to F to a spanish oak by the Road, then to G to a black oak, then to H to a black oak by the south side of the first mentioned Road near the line of George Gregg, then binding with that Road to the beginning containing 32 acres being a detached parcel of land lying between the two Roads, and part of a Tract the said John Hough purchased of John Mercer and Sons through Joseph Hough, Loudoun County Deed Book I, pp. 329-333

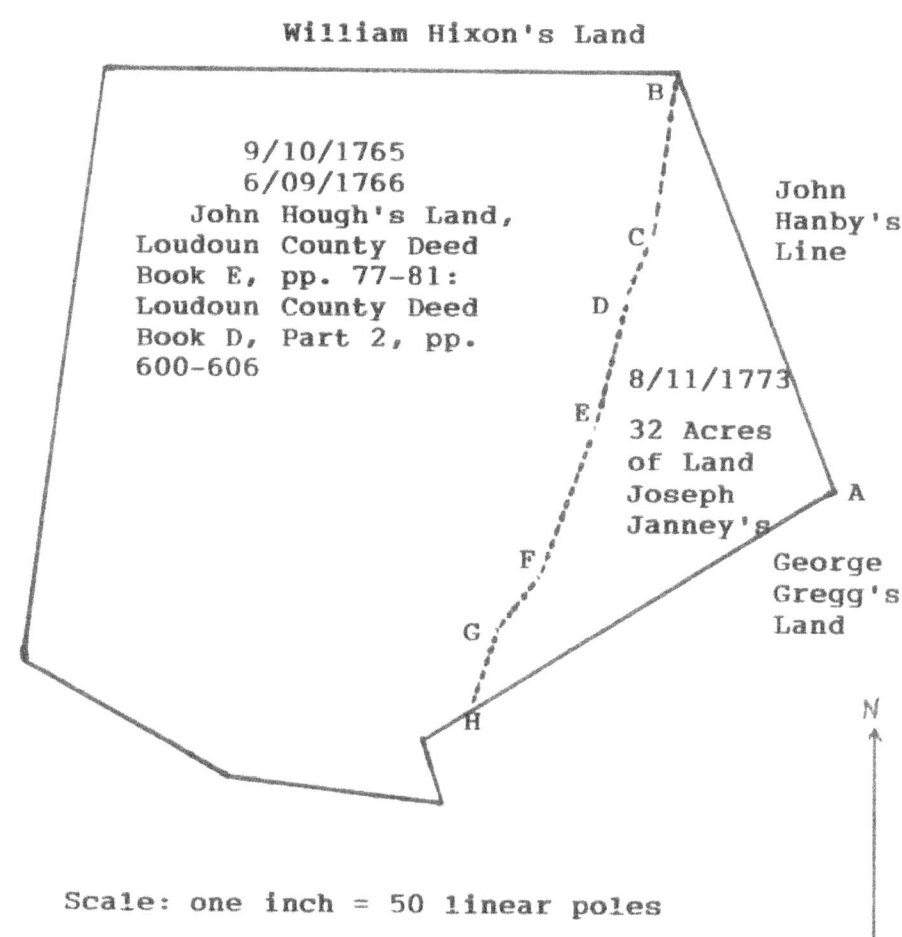

Scale: one inch = 50 linear poles

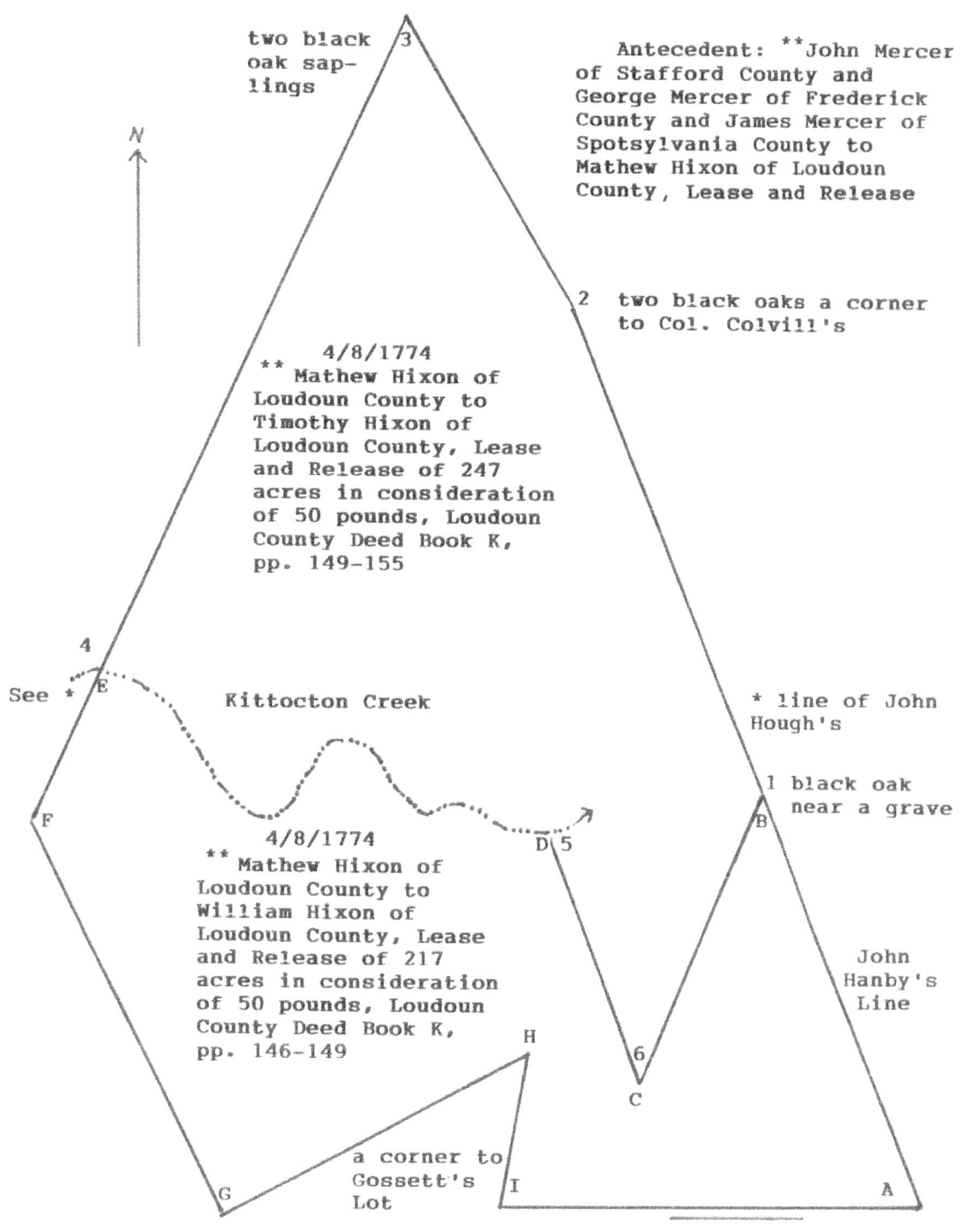

George Mercer Esq. of the City of London of the first part, and James Mercer of the County of Spotsylvania attorney at law of the second part, and the said James Mercer acting executor of the last will and testament of Anne Mercer late of Marlborough in the County of Stafford of the third part, to Francis Hague of Loudoun Count of the fourth part

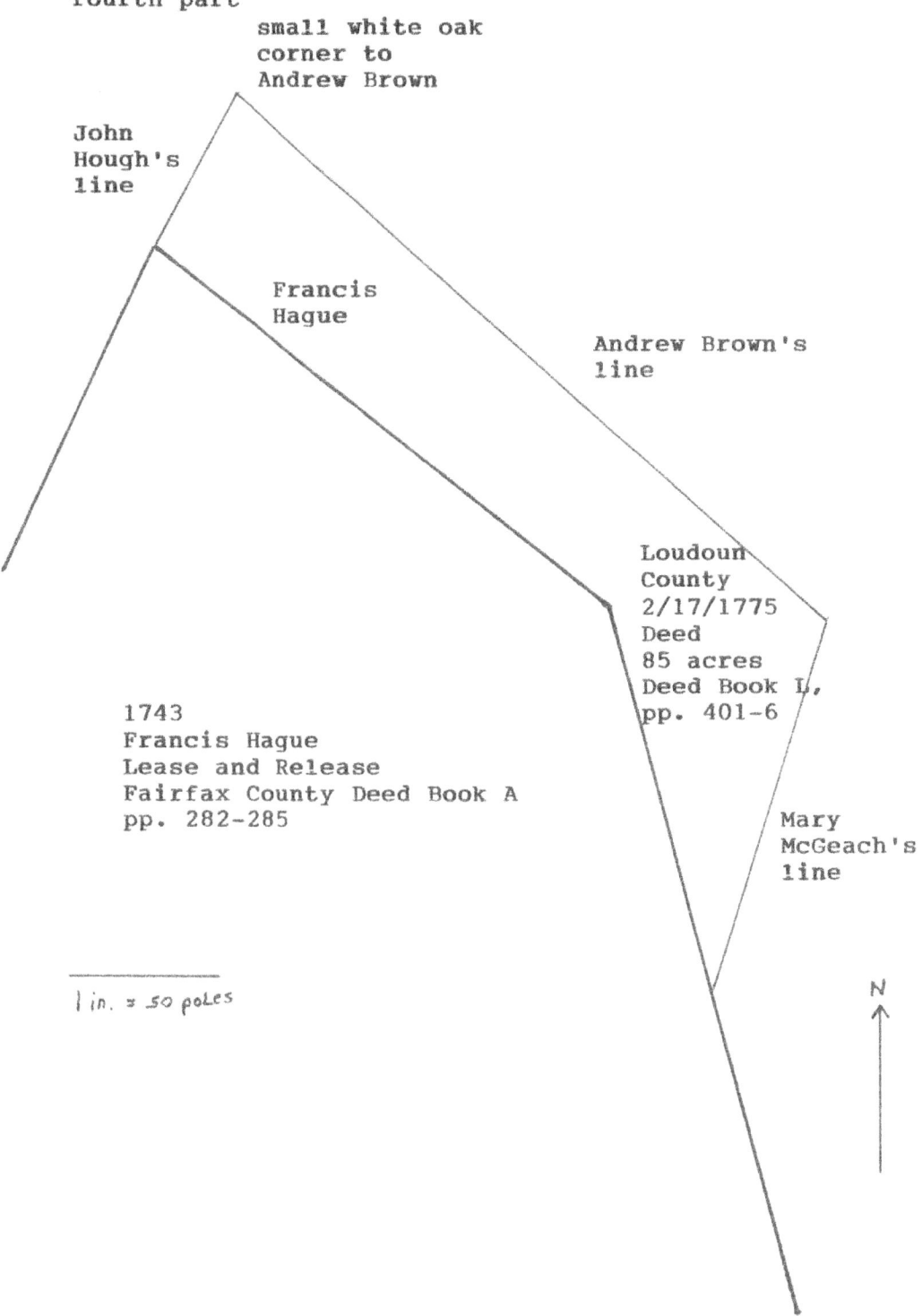

George Mercer Esq. of the City of London of the one part and James Mercer of Spotsylvania County of the second part and the said James Mercer as acting executor of Mrs. Anne Mercer deceased by their joint and several attorney John Hough of Loudoun County to Joseph Hough of the County of Loudoun, Deed, 200 acres of land, Loudoun County Deed Book L, pp. 396-401, bearing date the 17th day of February, 1775

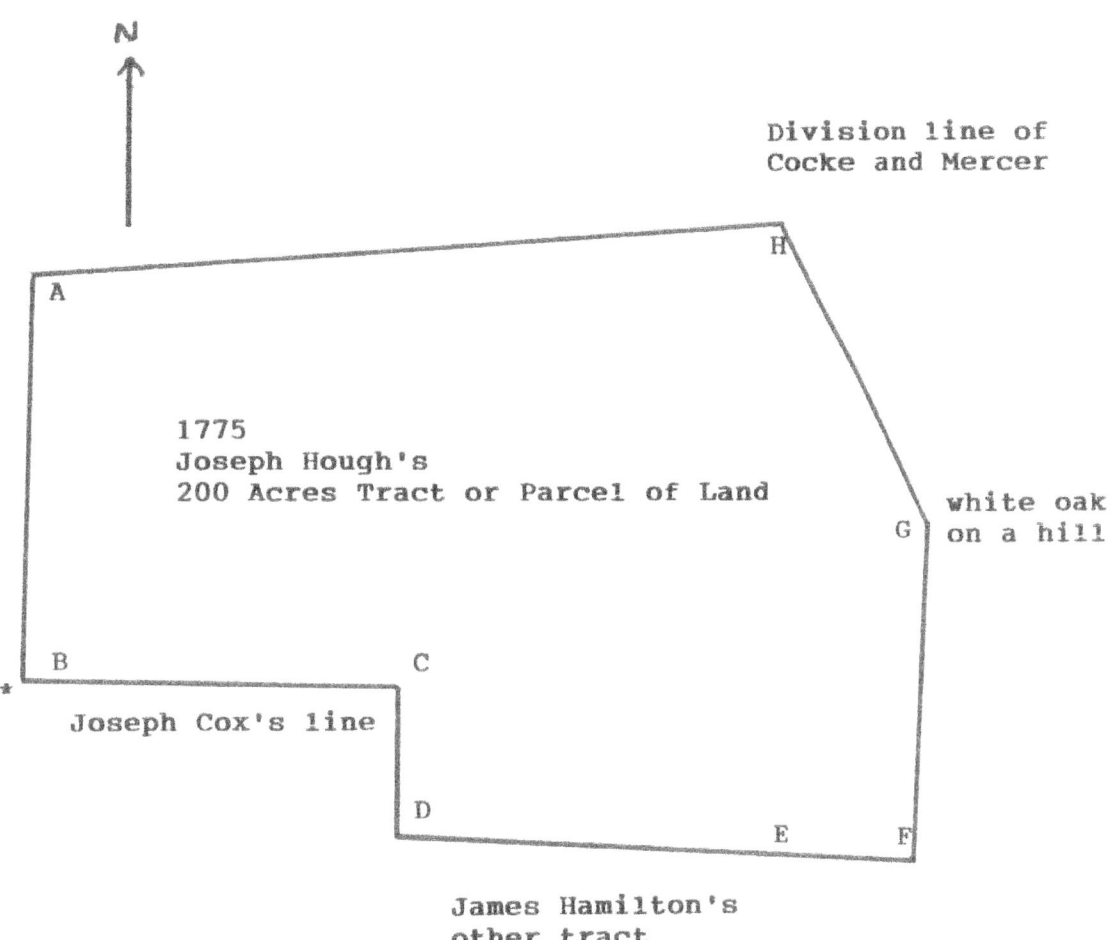

Waterford (circa 1781)

About the year 1733 John Mead acquired release of 703 acres from Catesby Cocke, which land had originated in the Northern Neck Proprietary. Within a period of nearly ten years time he had parceled the same tract unto presumably Amos Janney, David Griffith, and Francis Hague. The southern boundary line of Francis Hague's parcel of land appears to have been formulated around the site of a piece of land on the South Fork of Catoctin Creek, which belonged to Amos Janney. This landscape site evolved into the village or town of Waterford.

The people who settled in this locality largely shared a common church, culture, and language. After the time of Amos Janney's death in circa 1747, Francis and Jane Hague would become without doubt leaders of their Quaker community; many were Irish Quakers. He was essential to the ultimate improvement of the ground on or about Waterford. It is noted that Francis Hague was aided in his endeavors by slaves who labored on his account. It was not uncommon at that time for the folk here to be slave owners or to employ slave laborers, or deal in slaves.

Amos Janney's heir at law, Mahlon Janney, traded ten acres of land dated in 1755 to trustees, "to suffer and permit such of the people called Quakers inhabiting within the said County of Fairfax (Loudoun County established 1757) to erect and build such and so many meetinghouses, schoolhouses and yards or places of burial," which acreage came from landed property apparently descended from Amos Janney. By 1762 Mahlon Janney was the master of a mill in this neighborhood, which likewise was around the time he formally traded lots of land with Francis Hague. At which point Francis Hague was in possession of the aforesaid piece of land containing 12 acres lying at that time adjacent to Mahlon Janney's Mill. Subsequently, Francis Hague released the same lot of land unto his son Thomas Hague dated in 1773.

Around the time of the end of the American Revolutionary War bearing date in 1781, Thomas Hague sold the given lot of land unto Joseph Janney. In turn, Joseph Janney marked off the real estate into fifteen pieces of land for ready trade. One of Janney's early patrons was Thomas Moore (Sr.), lately from Pennsylvania. He built a residence here and called his place "Waterford" after his native home in Ireland.[1] The earliest published reference the author has ever seen for Waterford was dated January 1, 1787, which was an advertisement for two

---

[1] "Thomas Moore was a remarkable man. His father, Thomas Moore, an Irish Quaker, came to this country early in the last century, settled first in Pennsylvania, where he married, and afterwards moved to Loudoun County, Virginia, where he built a residence and called the place Waterford, after his native home. Here the son Thomas carried on the business of cabinet-maker which he had learned. About the year 1794 he moved to Maryland, having married Mary Brooke, daughter of Roger Brooke of Brooke Grove, Montgomery County. Here he commenced farming on the estate of his wife and soon distinguished himself as a practical farmer", T.H.S. Boyd, The History of Montgomery County, Maryland: From its Earliest Settlement in 1650 to 1879, as was published in 1879. A facsimile reprint with a new index published in 2001 by Heritage Books, Bowie, Maryland, 2001, pp. 89-91

runaway servants in the Virginia Journal and Alexandria Advertiser for James Moore and John Coffee of "Waterford".[1]

An early force for industrial progress in Waterford was William Paxson. By 1789 he was the principal of a wire weaving business, which made and sold rolling screens, and all kinds of fan riddles, shaking screens and the like.[2] A short list of some other early persons and entities of importance here should include in no particular order Amos Janney and son Mahlon Janney as above; Francis Hague and son Thomas Hague as above; Joseph Janney as above; brothers Thomas Moore (Jr.), James Moore as above and Asa Moore; brothers Abner Williams and John Williams; James Griffith; William Hough; Thomas Phillips; Robert Braden; Fleming Patterson; Moore & Phillips; and the tanyard on "tanyard run" (Waterford).

1. 5/1 and 5/2/1781, **Thomas Hague** of Loudoun County in Virginia and **Sarah** his wife of the one part to **Joseph Janney** of the same County of the other part. Witnesseth that for and in consideration of the sum of 200 pounds in gold and silver current money of Virginia to the said **Thomas Hague** and **Sarah** his wife in hand paid by the said **Joseph Janney** at or before the sealing and delivery of these presents, the receipt whereof they do hereby acknowledge, have granted bargained sold aliened released and confirmed and by these presents doth grant bargain sell alien release and confirm unto the said **Joseph Janney** and his heirs all that tract or parcel of land situate in Loudoun County aforesaid joining **Mahlon Janney's Mill Lot** and further bounded as followeth viz. Beginning at a white oak standing near the **road** corner to **Mahlon Janney's Mill Lot** and extending thence N 2-½° E 30 poles to a hickory on a hill, then S 81° E 26 poles to a white oak bush, then S 1-½° W 64 poles to a white oak bush by **Mahlon Janney's** fence, then with said **Mahlon Janney's** line N 65° W 29 poles to a small hickory by the **millrace**, then down the **race** N 5° W 20 poles to a large white oak, then N 27° E 4 poles to the beginning containing 12 acres be the same more or less. Also, another tract or parcel of land joining the above bounded as followeth viz. Beginning at a white oak standing by **Mahlon Janney's Sawmill** corner to said **Janney's Mill Lot** extending thence up the west side of the said **race** S 20° E 14 poles to a white oak on the **race** bank, then continuing up the **race** S 2° E 9 poles, then with another of his lines N 66° W 12 poles to a black oak sapling the west side of **Kittockton Creek**, then N 18° E 26 poles to a gum tree standing near the **ford** then crossing the said Creek and up the **Mill tailrace** S 58° E 39 poles to the beginning containing 5-¾ acres, which two parcels of land above described by buts and bounds are part of a larger tract containing 303 acres, which **Francis Hague** purchased of **John Mead** (and) the said **Francis Hague** conveyed the two small parcels above mentioned to the above named **Thomas Hague** his son by deeds bearing date the 19th and 20th days of March, 1773 and all

---

[1] Wesley E. Pippenger and James D. Munson, The Virginia Journal and Alexandria Advertiser, Volume III, p. 254: The Virginia Journal and Alexandria Advertiser, Volume IV, Willow Bend Books, Westminster, Maryland, p. 7

[2] Wesley E. Pippenger and James D. Munson, The Virginia Journal and Alexandria Advertiser, Volume IV, Willow Bend Books, Westminster, Maryland 2001, p. 218

houses buildings orchards ways water watercourses profits commodities hereditaments and appurtenances whatsoever to the said premises hereby granted or any part thereof belonging or in any wise appertaining. To have and to hold the lands hereby conveyed and all and singular other the premises hereby granted and released and every part and parcel thereof with their and every of their appurtenances unto the said **Joseph Janney** his heirs and assigns forever, **Thomas Hague** and **Sarah Hague**. Sealed and delivered in the presence of **Samuel Murrey, Patk. Cavan, William Taylor,** and **John Dodd**. Proven on 4/13/1784. (Note: This entry is repeated for purposes of clarity in the section concerning John Mead's Tract from Catesby Cocke.)

2. 8/17/1784, **Joseph Janney** of the County of Fairfax and State of Virginia, merchant, of the one part to **Thomas Moore Jr.** of the County of Loudoun and State aforesaid of the other part. Witnesseth that the said **Joseph Janney** for and in consideration of the sum of 6 pounds lawful money of Virginia to him in hand paid by the said **Thomas Moore** the receipt whereof he doth hereby own and acknowledge, hath granted bargained sold aliened and confirmed and doth hereby fully freely and absolutely grant bargain sell alien and confirm unto him the said **Thomas Moore** his heirs and assigns one certain messuage or lot of land situate in Loudoun County aforesaid being part of a larger lot belonging to the said **Joseph Janney** butted and bounded as followeth viz. Beginning at a hickory tree in **William Hough's** line and extending thence with said line S 1° - 30 minutes W 110 feet to a large black oak corner to **Mahlon Janney** and **William Hough**, thence with **Mahlon Janney's** line the same course 53 feet, thence S 73° E 51 feet, thence N 15° E 162 feet to the upper corner of **Joseph Janney's stable**, thence S 82° W 74 feet to the hickory the place of beginning, together with the dwelling houses thereon and all and singular the appurtenances unto the said messuage or lot of land belonging or in any ways appertaining unto him the said **Thomas Moore** his heirs and assigns forever. To have and to hold the hereby granted bargained and described messuage or tenement lot of land and premises with every of their appurtenances unto him the said **Thomas Moore** his heirs and assigns forever, **Joseph Janney** and **Hannah Janney**. Signed, sealed and delivered in the presence of **Jonah Thompson, Joseph Mandeville,** and **Andrew Copeland**. Proven on 9/13/1784. Bargain and Sale, Loudoun County Deed Book O, pp. 158-160

3. 6/17/1785, **Thomas Moore Jr.** of the County of Loudoun and State of Virginia of the one part to **John Sutton** of Alexandria in the County of Fairfax and State aforesaid of the other part. Witnesseth that the said **Thomas Moore** for and in consideration of the sum of 100 pound to him in hand paid by the said **John Sutton** the receipt whereof he doth hereby acknowledge, hath granted bargained sold aliened and confirmed and doth hereby fully freely and absolutely grant bargain sell and confirm unto him the said **John Sutton** his heirs and assigns one certain messuage or tenement and lot of land situate in Loudoun County aforesaid butted and bounded as followeth viz. Beginning at a hickory tree in **William Hough's** line and extending thence S 1° – 30 minutes W 110 feet to a large black oak corner to **Mahlon Janney** and **William Hough,** thence with **Mahlon Janney's** line the same courses 53 feet, thence S 73° E 51 feet along

Joseph Janney's line, thence along the same line N 15° E 162 feet to the upper corner of **Joseph Janney's stable**, thence with **William Hough's** line S 82° W 74 feet to the hickory the place of beginning, together with the dwelling house thereon and all and singular the appurtenances thereunto belonging or in any wise appertaining. To have and to hold the hereby granted, bargained and described messuage or tenement lot of land and premises with every of their appurtenances unto him the said **John Sutton** his heirs and assigns forever. Provided, and it is nevertheless the true intent and meaning of this indenture that if the above named **Thomas Moore** his heirs executors, administrators or any of them, shall well and truly pay or cause to be paid unto the said **John Sutton** or his certain attorney, heirs, executors or administrators or any of them the just and full sum of 100 pounds current money of Virginia with the lawful interest for the same on or before the seventeenth day of the sixth month in the year of our Lord 1786 without fraud or further delay, then the said **John Sutton** his heirs, executors, administrators or assigns shall release or cause to be released unto the said **Thomas Moore** his heirs executors administrators all and singular the above mentioned and granted messuage and premises with their appurtenances. But, in failure of the above payment of the sum of 100 pounds current money of Virginia with interest for the same then the said **John Sutton**, his certain attorney, his heirs, executors or assigns shall and may at any time enter into and take possession of the aforesaid granted lot, messuage and premises and hold the same free and clear and freed and cleared from all hindrance or molestation of or from the said **Thomas Moore** or any acting or claiming under him or from the right claim or demand of him the said **Thomas Moore** or any person whatsoever, **Thomas Moore Jr., John Sutton**. Signed, sealed and delivered in the presence of **Asa Moore, Thos.** his X mark **Brown**, and **Elizabeth Richardson**. Proven on 9/12/1785. Mortgage, Loudoun County Deed Book O, pp. 423-426.

4. 6/12/1785, **Joseph Janney** of the County of Loudoun and State of Virginia of the one part to **Richard Richardson** of the County of Frederick and State of Maryland of the other part. Witnesseth that the said **Joseph Janney** for and in consideration of the sum of 10 pounds lawful money of Virginia to him in hand paid by the said **Richard Richardson** the receipt whereof he doth hereby own and acknowledge, hath granted bargained sold aliened and confirmed and doth hereby fully freely and absolutely grant bargain sell and confirm unto him the said **Richard Richardson** his heirs and assigns one certain messuage or lot of land situate in Loudoun County aforesaid being part of a larger tract belonging to the said **Joseph Janney** butted and bounded as followeth viz. Beginning at a stone on the south side of the **tanyard run near the road** thence N 50° – 60 minutes E 10 perches, thence S 39° - 30 minutes E 8 perches, thence S 39° - 30 minutes W 10 perches, thence N 50° - 60 minutes W 8 perches to the place of beginning, together with all and singular the appurtenances thereunto belonging or in any wise appertaining unto the said messuage or lot of land, and the reversion and reversions, rents issues and profits thereof. To have and to hold the hereby granted bargained and described premises with every of their appurtenances unto him the said **Richard Richardson** his heirs and assigns

forever, **Joseph Janney** and **Hannah Janney**. Proven on 6/12/1786. Bargain and Sale, Loudoun County D, Part 2, pp. 338-339

5.   6/12/1785, **Joseph Janney** of the County of Loudoun and State of Virginia of the one part to **Joseph Pierpoint** of the County of Frederick and State of Maryland of the other part. Witnesseth that the said **Joseph Janney** for and in consideration of the sum of 10 pounds lawful money of Virginia to him in hand paid by the said **Joseph Pierpoint,** the receipt whereof he doth hereby own and acknowledge, hath granted bargained sold aliened and confirmed, and doth hereby fully freely and absolutely bargain sell and confirm unto him the said **Joseph Pierpoint** his heirs and assigns one certain messuage or lot of land situate in Loudoun County aforesaid, being part of a larger tract belonging to **Joseph Janney** culled and bounded as followeth viz. Beginning at a corner of **Richard Richardson's** lot this day purchased of **Joseph Janney** thence N 50° - 60 minutes E 10 perches, thence S 39° - 30 minutes E 8 perches, thence S 39° - 30 minutes W 10 perches, thence N 50° - 60 minutes W 8 perches to the place of beginning, together with all and singular the appurtenances thereunto belonging or in any wise appertaining unto the said messuage or lot of land, and the reversion and reversions, rents issues and profits. To have and to hold the hereby granted bargained and described premises with every of their appurtenances unto him the said **Joseph Pierpoint** his heirs and assigns forever, **Joseph Janney** and **Hannah Janney**. Proven on 6/12/1786Bargain and Sale, Loudoun County Deed Book P, Part 2, pp. 340-341

6.   2/10/1791, **Joseph Janney** of Loudoun County in the State of Virginia and **Hannah** his wife of the one part to **Stephen Wilson** of the said County of the other part. Witnesseth that the said **Joseph Janney** for and in consideration of the sum of 5 pounds current money of Virginia to him in hand paid by the said **Stephen Wilson** the receipt whereof the said **Joseph Janney** doth hereby acknowledge and himself therewith to be fully satisfied and paid, have granted bargained and sold aliened released and confirmed and by these presents doth grant bargain sell alien released and confirm unto him the said **Stephen Wilson** his heirs and assigns forever all that lot or parcel of land situate in Loudoun County in the little town called **Waterford** and whereon **William Paxton** now dwells and who has built on and improved. Bounded as followeth viz. Beginning at a planted stone corner to **Joseph Pairpoints** lot extending thence S 40° E 4 poles to another stone corner to **Benjamin Richmire** lot, then N 50° E 10 poles to **William Hough's** line, then N 40° W 4 poles corner to said **Joseph Pairpoint,** then with his line S 50° W 10 poles to the beginning containing one quarter of an acre be the same more or less, being part of the 17 acres of land the said **Joseph Janney** purchased of **Thomas Hague**, and the reversion and reversions, remainder and remainders, rents issues and profits of all and singular the said lot or quarter of an acre of land and premises above mentioned with the appurtenances thereto belonging and every part and parcel thereof. To have and to hold the said lot of land and premises above mentioned to him the said **Stephen Wilson** his heirs and assigns forever, **Joseph Janney** and **Hannah Janney**. Proven on 4/12/1791. Bargain and Sale, Loudoun County Deed Book S, pp. 325-328

7. 2/14/1791, **Joseph Janney** of the County of Loudoun and State of Virginia of the one part to **Mahlon Janney** of the same place of the other part. Witnesseth that the said **Joseph Janney** for and in consideration of the sum of 24 pounds to him in hand paid by the said **Mahlon Janney** the receipt whereof he the said **Joseph Janney** doth hereby acknowledge, hath granted bargained and sold aliened released and confirmed and by these presents doth grant bargain sell alien release and confirm unto the said **Mahlon Janney** and his heirs and assigns forever all that lot of 5 acres (and) 1 rood and premises laying in the County of Loudoun aforesaid and bounded as follows. Beginning at a white oak near **Mahlon Janney's Sawmill** thence N 63° - 30 minutes W 39-½ perches to a gum on west side of Catoctin Creek near the **road**, then S 19° - 30 minutes E 26 perches to a marked white oak bush near a black oak stump corner to **Mahlon Janney** and **William Hough**, then S 68° - 30 minutes E 12 perches to a stake, then S 4° W 9 perches to a stake, then S 67° E 25 perches to two small gums on the **race** bank, then S 6° - 30 minutes W 18-¼ perches to a plumb tree, then N 25° W 13 perches to the beginning containing 5 acres and 1 rood of land more or less, with the appurtenances thereunto belonging or in any wise appertaining, and the reversion and reversions, reminder and reminders, rents issues and profits of all the said lot and premises above mentioned and intended to be hereby granted and conveyed, and all the estate right title and interest property claim and demand whatsoever of him the said **Joseph Janney** and **Hannah** his wife in and to the said 5 acres and 1 rood of land and premises above mentioned and in and to every part and parcel thereof. To have and to hold the said tract of land and premises above mentioned and intended to be hereby granted and every part and parcel to him the said **Mahlon Janney** his heirs and assigns forever, **Joseph Janney**. Proven on 2/14/1791. Bargain and sale, Loudoun County Deed Book S, pp. 250-252

8. 2/14/1791, **Mahlon Janney** of the County of Loudoun in Virginia of the one part to **Joseph Janney** of the same place of the other part. Witnesseth that the said **Mahlon Janney** for and in consideration of the sum of 10 pounds to him in hand paid by the said **Joseph Janney** the receipt whereof he the said **Mahlon Janney** doth hereby confess and acknowledge and himself therewith to be fully satisfied and paid, have granted bargained and sold aliened released and confirmed unto him the said **Joseph Janney** and to his heirs and assigns forever all that lot of 2 acres of land and premises laying in County of Loudoun aforesaid and bounded as follows. Beginning at a planted stone or stake on the east side of the said **Mahlon Janney's mill-race** in a former line of the said **Mahlon and Joseph Janney's,** extending thence with said line and a line of **William Hough's** S 65-¼° E 32 poles to another planted stone by the **road leading from Leesburg to said Janney's mill**, thence nearly with the said **road** S 7° W 10 poles to two white oak saplings, then N 65° W 32 poles to a persimmon tree on the east side of said **race**, then down the **race** N 7° E 11 poles to the first station containing 2 acres of land more or less, with the premises and appurtenances thereunto belonging or in any wise appertaining, and the reversion and reversions, reminder and reminders, rent issues and profits of all the said lot of two acres of land and premises above mentioned and intended to be hereby granted, and all the estate

right title interest property claim and demand whatsoever of him the said **Mahlon Janney** and **Sarah** his wife of in and to the said 2 acres of land and premises above mentioned and in and to every part and parcel thereof. To have and to hold the said 2 acres of land and premises above mentioned and intended to be hereby granted and every part and parcel to him the said **Joseph Janney** his heirs and assigns forever, **Mahlon Janney**. Proven on 2/14/1791. Loudoun County Deed Book S, pp. 252-255

9. 4/17/1791, **Joseph Janney** of the County of Loudoun and State of Virginia and **Hannah** his wife of the one part to **Asa Moore** of Loudoun County in aforesaid State of the other part. Witnesseth that for and in consideration of the sum of 30 pounds current money of Virginia to the said **Joseph Janney** in hand paid by the said **Asa Moore** at or before the sealing and delivery of these presents the receipt whereof he doth hereby acknowledge, have granted bargained sold aliened released and confirmed and by these presents do grant bargain and sell alien release and confirm unto the said **Asa Moore** and his heirs one certain lot of ground containing one acre be the same more or less bounded as followeth viz. Beginning at a locust stake or post at the place where a small marked white oak stood being the northeast corner of said **Joseph Janney's** land purchased of **Thomas Hague** and standing on a hill and extending thence N 81° W 13 poles to a stake, then South 14 poles to a stake, then S 89° E 13 poles to a stake by the **springhead**, then North 12 poles to the first station containing one acre of land. The said one acre being part of 17 acres the said **Joseph Janney** purchased of **Thomas Hague** and situate in Loudoun County joining **Mahlon Janney's mill land**, and all houses buildings orchards ways waters watercourses profits commodities hereditaments and appurtenances whatsoever to the said premises hereby granted or any part thereof belonging or in any wise appertaining. To have and to hold the lands hereby conveyed and all and singular other the premises hereby granted and released and every part and parcel thereof with their and every of their appurtenances unto the said **Asa Moore** his heirs and assigns forever, **Joseph Janney,** and **Hannah Janney**. Received of **Asa Moore** the sum of 30 pounds current money of Virginia being the consideration mentioned to be paid us on the perfection of this deed. Witness (blank space) hand this 2nd day of December, 1785. Proven on 4/12/1791. Lease and Release, Loudoun County Deed Book S, pp. 323-325

10. 4/14/1794, **John Janney** and **John Janney Jr**. executors of **Joseph Janney deceased** of Loudoun County and State of Virginia of the one part to **John Williams** of the County and State aforesaid of the other part. Witnesseth that the said **John Janney** and **John Janney Jr**. for and in consideration of the sum of 5 pounds lawful money of Virginia to them in hand the receipt whereof they do hereby acknowledge, hath granted bargained and sold aliened unto the said **John Williams** his heirs and assigns one certain messuage or lot of ground in the village of in the County aforesaid butted and bounded as follows viz. Beginning at a planted stone on the east side of the **road leading from Mahlon Janney's Mill to Leesburg** corner to a lot laid of for **Ann Myars** (sic) thence S 40° E 116 feet along said **road** to a stone planted in **William Hough's** line, thence along said line S 1° W 157 feet to the corner post of **Ann Myars's** (sic) lot

224

aforesaid, thence with her line S 47° W 100 feet to the beginning containing 21 perches more or less, together with the houses thereon ad all and singular the appurtenances unto the said messuage or lot of land belonging or any wise appertaining, and the reversion and reversions, reminder and remainders, rents issues and profits thereof. To have and to hold the hereby granted bargained and sold tenement of land and premises with every of their appurtenances unto the said **John Williams** his heirs and assigns, to his or their only proper use benefit thereof forever, **John Janney, John Janney Jr.** Signed, sealed and delivered in the presence of **Benjamin Mead, Wm. Hough, R. Braden,** and **Stephen Wilson**. Proven on 12/10/1794. Bargain and Sale, Loudoun County Deed Book 2C, pp. 21-23

11. 10/4/1796, **John Janney** and **John Janney Jr.** executors of **Joseph Janney deceased** of the County of Loudoun and Commonwealth of Virginia of the one part to **Flemin Patterson** of the County and State aforesaid of the other part. Witnesseth that the said **John Janney** and **John Janney Jr.** for and in consideration of the sum of 50 pounds lawful money of Virginia to them in hand paid by the said **Flemin Patterson** (sic) the receipt whereof they do hereby acknowledge, hath granted bargained and sold aliened unto the said **Flemin Patterson** his heirs and assigns one certain messuage or lot of land in the village of **Waterford** in County aforesaid bounded as follows viz. Beginning at a corner of **Robert Braden's** lot thence N 49° E 124 feet, thence S 1° E 37 feet, thence S 49° W 99 feet, thence N 39° W 27 feet to the beginning containing 3,553 feet more or less, together with the houses improvements and appurtenances thereunto belonging or in any wise appertaining to the said lot or messuage or lot of land and the reversion and reversions, reminder and reminders, rents issues and profits thereunto belonging. To have and to hold the hereby bargained and sold tenement of land with all and every of the appurtenances thereunto belonging unto the said **Flemin Patterson** (sic) his heirs or assigns, to his or their only proper use and behoove forever, **John Janney,** and **John Janney Jr.** Signed, sealed and delivered in the presence of **Asa Moore, R. Braden, Stephen Wilson, James Moore, Richard Griffith,** and **Anthony Wright**. Proven on 12/10/1796. Bargain and Sale, Loudoun County Deed Book X, pp. 277-278

12. 10/4/1796, **John Janney** and **John Janney Jr.** executors of **Joseph Janney deceased** of the County of Loudoun and Commonwealth of Virginia of the one part to **Andrew Brown** of the County and Commonwealth aforesaid of the other part. Witnesseth that the said **John Janney** and **John Janney Jr.** for and in consideration of the sum of 100 pounds lawful money of Virginia to them in hand paid by the said **Andrew Brown** the receipt whereof they do hereby acknowledge, hath granted bargained and sold aliened unto the said **Andrew Brown** his heirs and assigns one certain messuage of lot of land in the village of **Waterford** in the County of Loudoun aforesaid bounded as follows. Beginning at the corner of a lot now in possession of the **Widow Thompson** extending thence N 49° E 165 feet, thence S 1° E 66 feet, thence S 49° W 124 feet, thence to the beginning containing 8,814 feet more or less, together with all houses improvements and appurtenances thereunto belonging or in any wise appertaining to the said lot or messuage of land, and the reversion and reversions, reminder and

reminders, rents issues and profits thereunto belonging. To have and to hold the hereby bargained and sold tenement of land with all and every of the appurtenances thereunto belonging unto the said **Andrew Brown** his heirs and assigns, to his or their only proper use and behoove forever, **John Janney**, and **John Janney Jr**. Signed, sealed and delivered in presence of **Asa Moore, James Moore, R. Braden, Stephen Wilson, Richard Griffith**, and **Anthony Wright**. Proven on 12/12/1796. Bargain and Sale, Loudoun County Deed Book X, pp. 278-280

13. 3/15/1797, **Thomas Janney** of the town of **Leesburg** in the County of Loudoun and State of Virginia to **Flemin Patterson** of the village of **Waterford** in the County and State aforesaid. Witnesseth that in consideration of the sum of $ 120.00 in hand paid by said **Flemon Patterson** the receipt whereof he the said **Thomas Janney** doth hereby acknowledge, hath granted bargained sold alienated unto the said **Flemon Patterson** his heirs and assigns two lots in the village of **Waterford** aforesaid No. (blank space) and No. (blank space) being surveyed in one and butted and bounded as follows. Beginning at a planted stone in the **road or street** corner to **Sarah Thompson's lot** formerly **Stephen Wilson's** then with line of said lot S 49° W 72 perches to a planted stone in **Mahlon Janney's** line, then with said line S 68° E 74 feet to another planted stone in said line, thence N 49° E 20 perches to a planted stone on the **road or street** corner to **Joseph Talbot Jr.**, thence along said **road or street** S 41° W 62 feet to the beginning containing one-half an acre more or less, together with all the buildings thereon and all and singular of the appurtenances unto the said lot or messuage of land belonging or in any wise appertaining, and the reversion and reversions, remainder and reminders, rents issues and profits thereof. To have and to hold the hereby granted and sold tenement of land and premises, with every of their appurtenances unto the said **Flemin Patterson** his heirs or assigns, to his or their only proper use and behoove forever, **Thomas Janney**, and **Sarah E. Janney**. Signed, sealed and delivered in the presence of **Isaac Steere, Evin Griffith, Adam Carnahan**, and **William Smith**. Proven 3/15/1797. Loudoun County Deed Book X, pp. 359-362

14. 4/1797, **William Paxton** of the County of Loudoun and State of Virginia of the one part to **Joseph Talbott** of the village of **Waterford** in the County and State aforesaid of the other part. Witnesseth that in consideration of the sum of 15 pounds in hand paid by said **Joseph Talbott** the receipt whereof he the said **William Paxton** doth hereby acknowledge, hath granted bargained sold aliened unto the said **Joseph Talbott** his heirs or assigns a lot of ground in the village of **Waterford** aforesaid butted and bounded as follows. Beginning at a planted stone in the main road or street corner to **Fleming Patterson** therewith his line reversed S 49° W 20 perches to a planted stone corner to said **Patterson** in **Mahlon Janney's** line, thence with said line S 68° E 74 feet to another planted stone in said line, thence N 49° E 18 perches to a planted stone in the **main road or street**, thence with said street N 41 W 60 feet to the beginning containing 70 square perches more or less, together with the buildings thereon and all and singular the appurtenances unto the said lots or messuage of and belonging or in any wise appertaining, and the reversion and reversions, reminder and reminders,

rents issues and profits thereupon. To have and to hold the hereby granted and sold tenements of land and premises with every of their appurtenances unto the said **Joseph Talbott Jr.** his heirs or assigns, to his or their only proper use benefit or behoove forever, **William Paxson**. Proven on 4/11/1797. Bargain and Sale, Loudoun County Deed Book X, pp. 363-364

15. 1799, **Stephen Wilson** and **Martha** his wife of the County of Loudoun and State of Virginia of the one part to **Sarah Thompson** of the village of **Waterford** in the County aforesaid of the other part. Witnesseth that the said **Stephen Wilson** hath in consideration of 110 pounds current money of Virginia to him in hand paid the receipt whereof the said **Stephen Wilson** hereby acknowledges being fully satisfied therewith, hath granted bargained sold released and confirmed and doth and by these presents sell and confirm unto the said **Sarah Thompson** her heirs and assigns forever all that lot or messuage of land in the village of **Waterford** whereon she now lives. Beginning at a planted stone on **the main road or street** corner to **Evan Griffith's** lot formerly **Joseph Peirpoint's** thence along said **street** S 40° E 4 perches to another planted stone corner to **Flemin** (sic) **Patterson's** lot, thence along said **Patterson's** line N 50° E 10 perches to a planted stone in **William Hough's** line, thence N 40° W 4 perches to a planted stone corner to **Evan Griffith**, thence with said **Griffith's** line S 50° W 10 poles to the beginning containing one-quarter of an acre more or less, together with the rents issues and profits and all and singular of said lot and premises above mentioned with the appurtenances thereunto belonging and every part and parcel thereof, and all the right title property or demand whatsoever of him the said **Stephen Wilson** and **Martha** his wife in said lot and premises and all their appurtenances. To have and to hold the said lot of land premises above mentioned to the said **Sarah Thompson** her heirs and assigns forever with all its appurtenances to the only use and behoove of her the said **Sarah Thompson** her heirs and assigns forever, **Stephen Wilson** and **Martha Wilson**. Signed, sealed and delivered in the presence of **Richard Griffith, Mahlon Janney**, and **Samuel Gover**. Proven on 4/8/1799.

16. 4/9/1799, **John Sutton** of Alexandria of the one part to **Thomas Moore** late of Loudoun County now of Montgomery County, Maryland of the other part. Witnesseth that for diverse good causes and considerations and for the sum of shillings current money of Virginia paid by the said **Thomas Moore** to the said **John Sutton** the receipt whereof is hereby acknowledged, he the said **John Sutton** hath sold aliened released and conveyed and by these presents doth sell alien release and convey unto the said **Thomas Moore** his heirs and assigns all the right title and interest which he the said **John Sutton** has in and to a house messuage or tenement and a lot of land thereunto belonging lying and being in the town of **Waterford** and County of Loudoun in Virginia, formerly the property of the said **Thomas Moore**. To have and to hold unto him the said **Thomas Moore** his heirs and assigns forever, **John Sutton**. Witnessed by **George McCabe, Wm. Byrd Page**, and **Wilson Carey Selden**. Proven on 4/9/1799. Deed, Loudoun County Deed Book Z, pp. 212-213

17. 4/10/1799, **Thomas Moore Jr.** of the County of Montgomery and State of Maryland of the one part to **Asa Moore** of the Village of Waterford and State of

Virginia of the other part. Witnesseth that the said **Thomas Moore Jr.** for and in consideration of the sum of 400 pounds lawful money of Virginia to him in hand paid by the said **Asa Moore** the receipt whereof he doth hereby own and acknowledge, hath granted sold and confirmed and doth hereby full and absolutely grant sell and confirm unto him the said **Asa Moore** his heirs and assigns one certain lot of land situate in **Waterford** aforesaid butted and bounded as followeth viz. Beginning at a hickory tree in **William Hough's** line and extending thence with said line S 1° - 30 minutes W 163 feet, thence S 73° E 51 feet, thence N 15° E 162 feet, thence S 82° W 74 feet to the beginning, together with the dwelling house thereon and all and singular the appurtenances unto the said lot of land belonging or in any ways appertaining and the rents and issues and profits thereof. To have and to hold the hereby granted and described lot of land and premises with every of their appurtenances unto him the said **Asa Moore** his heirs and assigns forever, **Thomas Moore**. Signed, sealed and delivered in the presence of **James Moore, Richard Griffith, J. Willett,** and **Thomas Phillips**. Proven on 9/10/1799. Deed, Loudoun County Deed Book Z, pp. 307-309

18. 2/22/1806, **William Hough** and **Elenor** his wife of Loudoun County and State of Virginia of the one part to **John Williams** of the aforesaid County and State of the other part. Witnesseth that the said **William Hough** for and in consideration of the sum of $ 20.00 unto him the said **William Hough** in hand well and truly paid by the said **John Williams** at or before the sealing and delivery hereof the receipt whereof he doth hereby acknowledge, hath granted bargained sold aliened released and confirmed and by these presents doth grant bargain sell alien release and confirm unto the said **John Williams** his heirs and assigns forever one certain lot or messuage in the town of **Waterford** in the County and State aforesaid and being butted and bounded as follows viz. Beginning at a planted post (in the line of said **Hough** it being a division line between the land formerly given by **Francis Hague** to his son **Thos.** and the land now the property of **Wm. Hough** purchased of said **Francis Hague's** executors) the said post being a corner to **Flemon** (sic) **Patterson** and also a corner for a lot purchased of **Joseph Janney** and conveyed by his executors to the said **John Williams** thence S 40° E 114 feet to a planted stone, thence S 49° W 97-½ feet to a planted stone corner to the said **Williams's** lot conveyed to him by **Joseph Janney's** executors, thence with the line of that lot (it being the said **Hough's** line of division between his land and the part conveyed by **Francis Hague** to his son **Thomas**) N 1° W 153 feet to the beginning containing 20 perches more or less, together with all and singular the rights members liberties improvements hereditaments and appurtenances whatsoever thereunto belonging or in any wise appertaining, and the reversion and reversions, reminder and reminders, rents issues and profits thereof. To have and to hold the all and singular the premises hereby granted with the appurtenances unto the said **John Williams** his heirs and assigns, to the only proper use benefit and behoove of the said **John Williams** his heirs and assigns forever, **William Hough** and **Elenor Hough**. Signed, sealed and delivered in the presence of **Daniel Stone, Thomas Phillips, Joseph Bond,** and **William H. Hough**. Proven on 5/12/1806. Bargain and Sale, Loudoun County Deed Book 2G, pp. 260-261

19.   9/17/1808, **Mahlon Janney** of the County of Loudoun and **Sarah** his wife of the one part to **Jonas Potts** of the same County of the other part. All that messuage tenement plantation **gristmill** and tract of land situate in Loudoun County containing 67 acres and 3 roods and 21 poles of land. Bargain and Sale for and in consideration of the sum of $ 3,000.00, Loudoun County Deed Book 2K, pp. 364-365

20.   4/18/1809, **Mahlon Janney** of the County of Loudoun of the one part to **Samuel Gover** of the County of Loudoun of the other part. Bargain and Sale of a certain lot of land containing 7,766 square feet adjoining the town of **Waterford**. Bargain and Sale for and in consideration of the sum of $ 20.00, Loudoun County Deed Book 2K, pp. 365-366

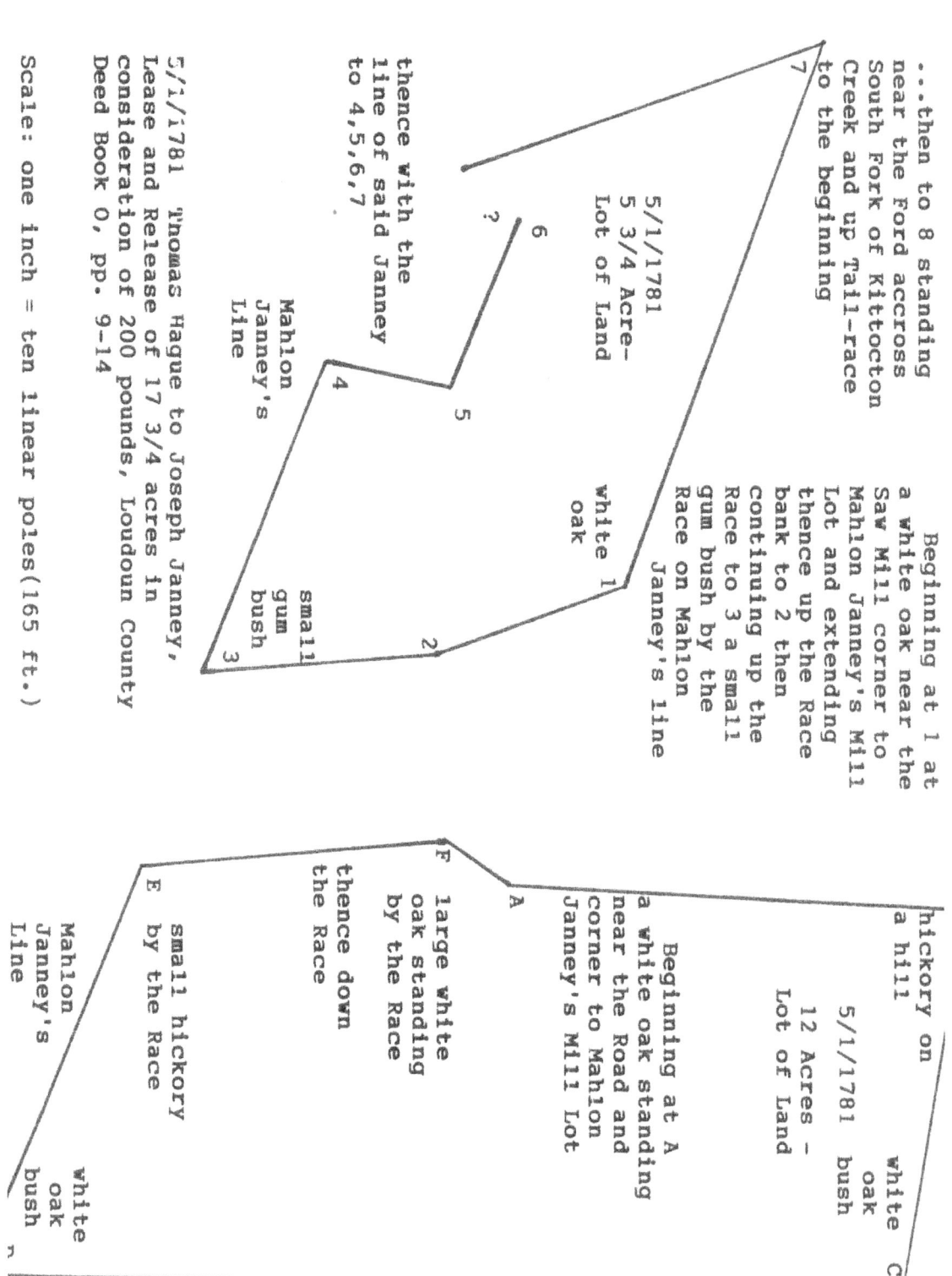

6/17/1785, Thomas Moore Junior of Loudoun County and John Sutton of Alexandria in the County of Fairfax, Mortgage, one hundred pounds, one certain messuage or tenement and land situate in Loudoun County aforesaid butted and bounded as followeth Viz., Loudoun County Deed Book O, pp. 423-426

4/9/1799, John Sutton of Alexandria and Thomas Moore late of Loudoun County now of Montgomery County, Maryland, five hundred pounds current money of Virginia in consideration of Deed, Loudoun County Deed Book Z, pp. 212-213

Note: The 1785 Deed made no mention of a place name whereas the other 1799 Deed refers to the house messuage or tenement and lot of land thereundto belonging & being in the Town of Waterford. The 1785 Deed was witnessed by Thos his X mark Brown and Elizabeth Richardson. The 1799 Deed was witnessed by George McCabe, Wm. Byrd Page, Wilson Carey Selden

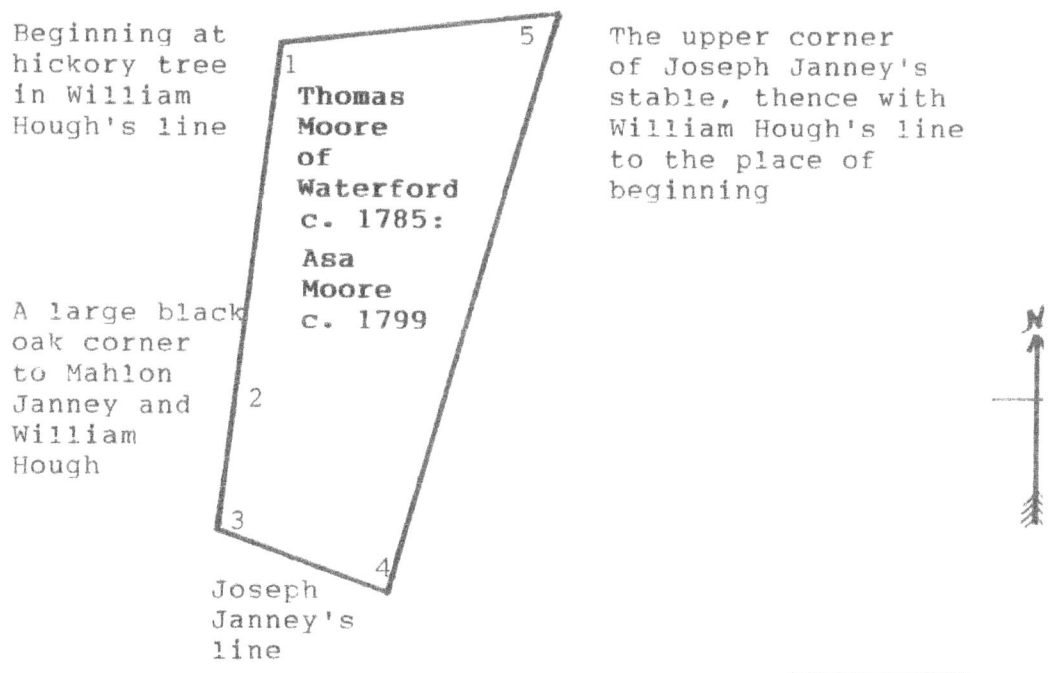

4/10/1799, Thomas Moore Junior of the County of Montgomery, Maryland, to Asa Moore of the village of Waterford, Deed, Loudoun County Deed Book Z, pp. 307-309

1 in. = 50 feet

*   2/16/1791 Joseph Janney of Loudoun County and Hannah his Wife to Stephen Wilson of Loudoun County, Baragain and Sale, ...all that Lot or Parcel of Land situate(d) in Loudoun County in the little Town called Waterford and whereon William Paxton now dwells and who has beuilt on and improved (it) bounded as followeth...Loudoun County Deed Book S, pp. 325-8

*   ...being part of the 17 acres of land the said Joseph Janney purchased of Thomas Hague...

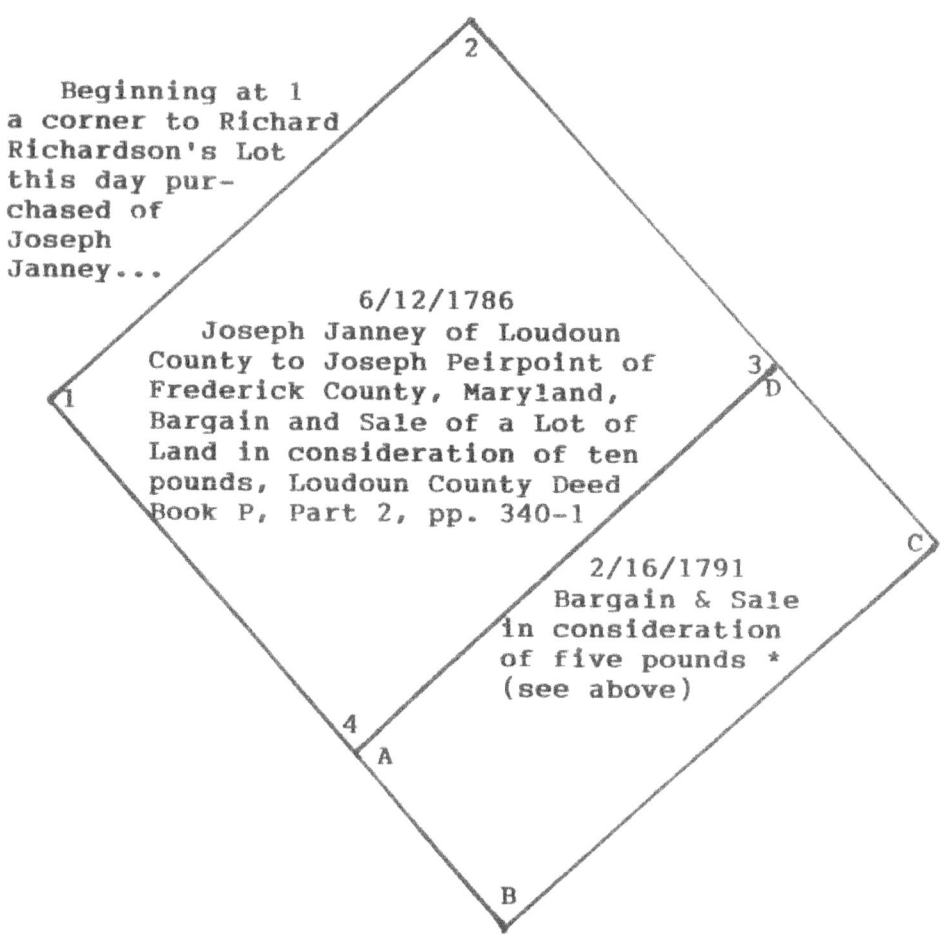

Beginning at 1 a corner to Richard Richardson's Lot this day purchased of Joseph Janney...

6/12/1786
Joseph Janney of Loudoun County to Joseph Peirpoint of Frederick County, Maryland, Bargain and Sale of a Lot of Land in consideration of ten pounds, Loudoun County Deed Book P, Part 2, pp. 340-1

2/16/1791
Bargain & Sale in consideration of five pounds * (see above)

Scale: one inch equals fifty linear feet

February 14, 1791, Mahlon Janney to Joseph Janney, Bargain and Sale, all that lot or two acres of land and premises in consideration of ten pounds, Loudoun County Deed Book S, pp. 252-255

one inch = 100 linear feet

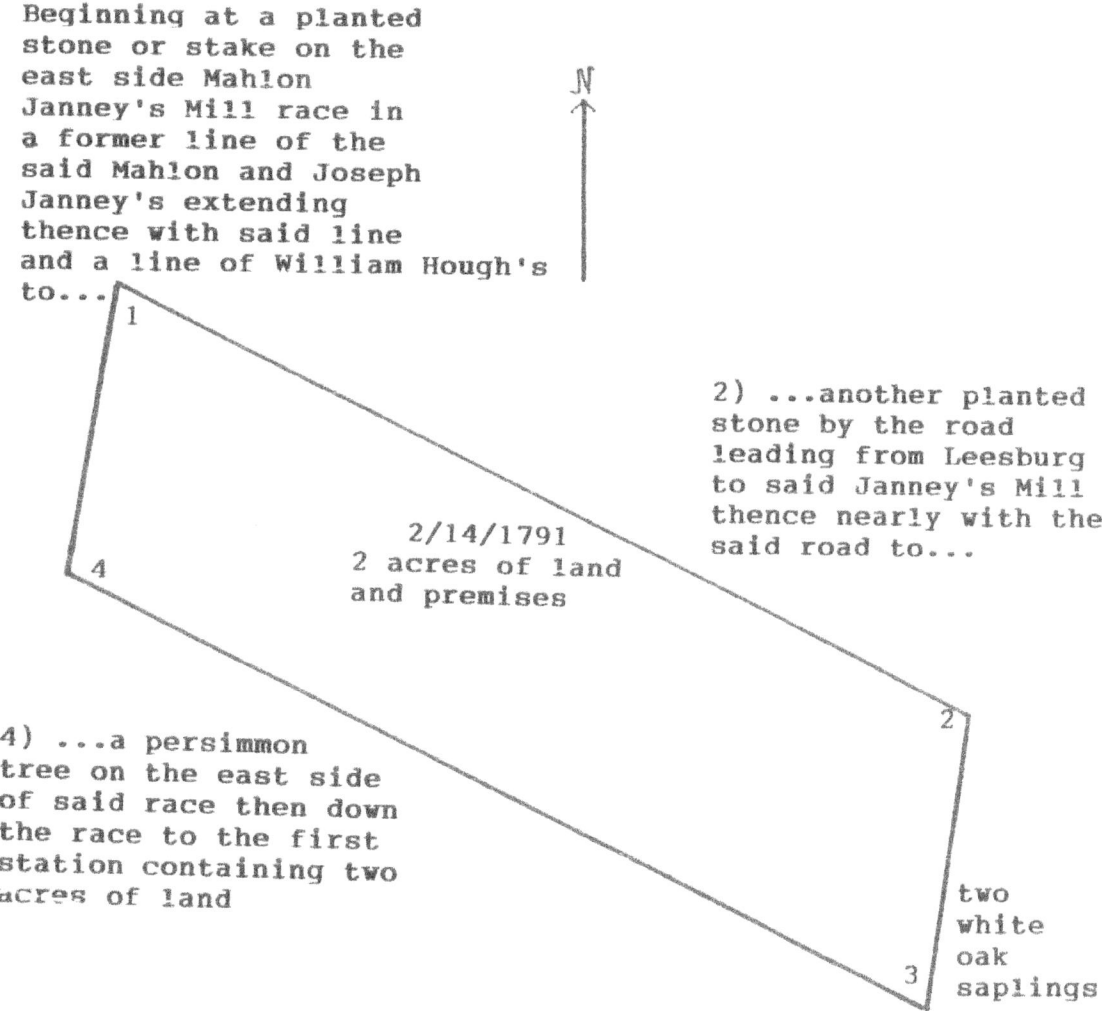

Beginning at a planted stone or stake on the east side Mahlon Janney's Mill race in a former line of the said Mahlon and Joseph Janney's extending thence with said line and a line of William Hough's to...

2) ...another planted stone by the road leading from Leesburg to said Janney's Mill thence nearly with the said road to...

2/14/1791
2 acres of land and premises

4) ...a persimmon tree on the east side of said race then down the race to the first station containing two acres of land

two white oak saplings

2/14/1791 Joseph Janney of the County of Loudoun and Hannah his Wife to Mahlon Janney of the same place, Bargain and sale of five acres, one Road, and Premises, in consideration of the sum of twenty four pounds, Loudoun County Deed Book S, pp. 250-252

Antecedents: Thomas Hague to Joseph Janney dated 5/1/1781, Lease and Release, Loudoun County Deed Book O, pp. 9-14 : Francis Hague to Thomas Hague dated 3/12/1773, Lease and Release, Loudoun County Deed Book I, pp. 168-173

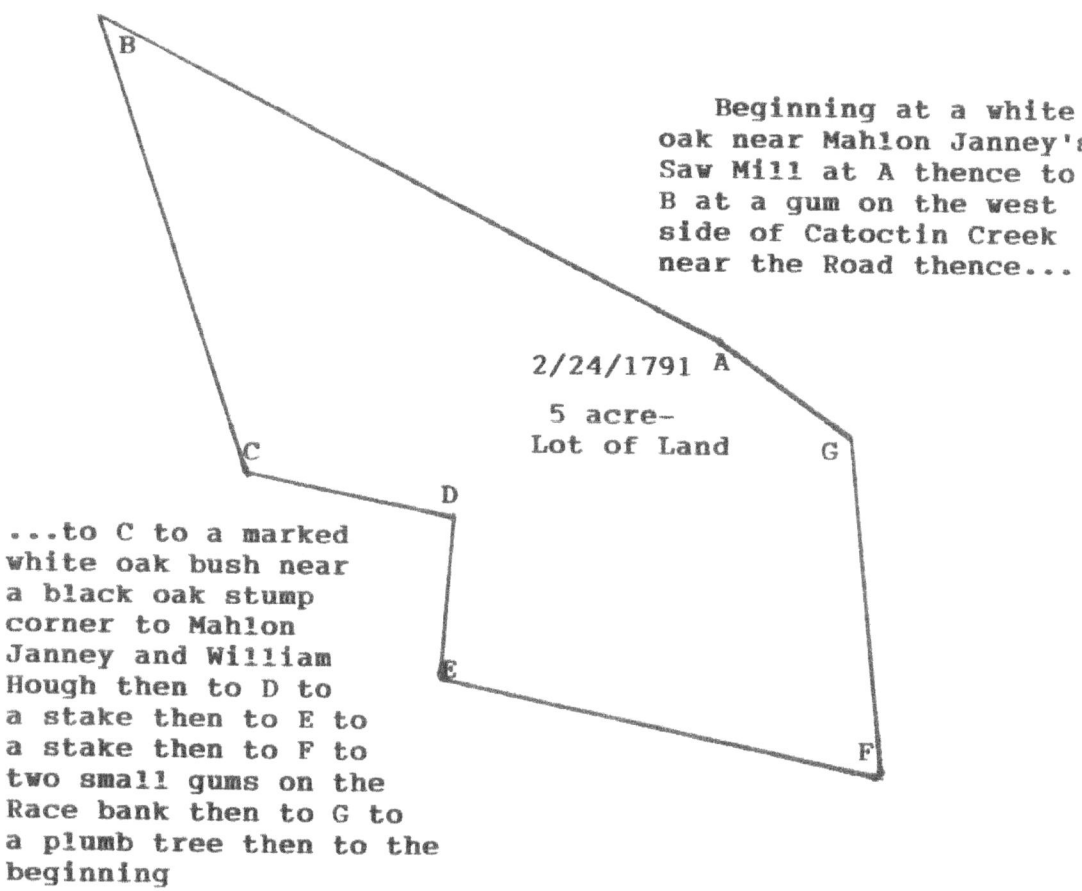

Beginning at a white oak near Mahlon Janney's Saw Mill at A thence to B at a gum on the west side of Catoctin Creek near the Road thence...

2/24/1791
5 acre-
Lot of Land

...to C to a marked white oak bush near a black oak stump corner to Mahlon Janney and William Hough then to D to a stake then to E to a stake then to F to two small gums on the Race bank then to G to a plumb tree then to the beginning

Scale: one inch = ten linear poles or 165 linear feet

* 4/11/1791 Joseph Janney of the County of Loudoun to Asa Moore of the same place, Lease and release of a one acre Lot of land in consideration of the sum of thirty pounds, Loudoun County Deed Book S, pp. 320-325

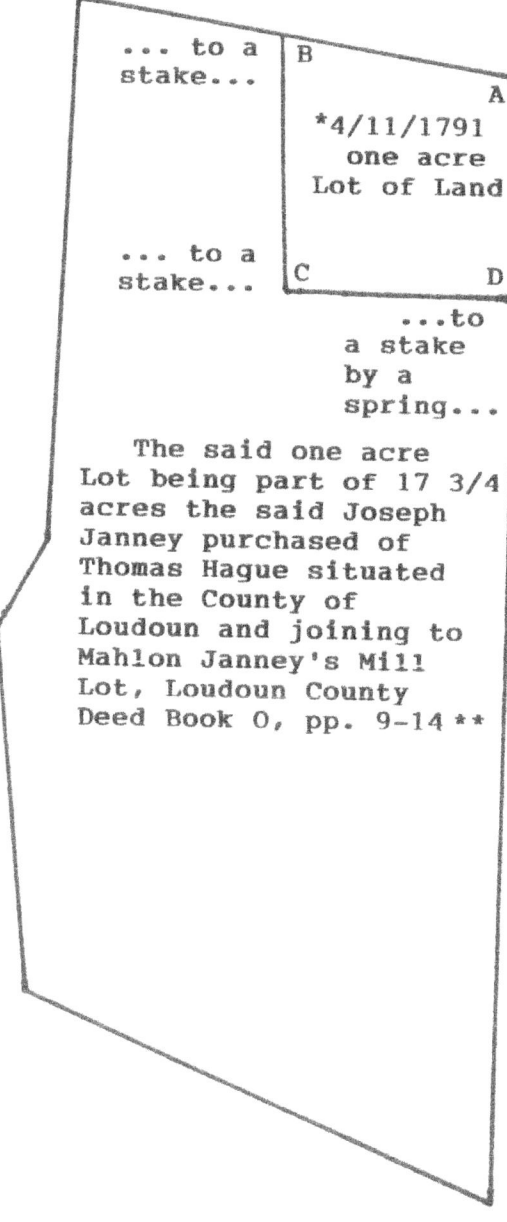

... to a stake...

B   A
*4/11/1791
one acre
Lot of Land

... to a stake...

C   D

...to a stake by a spring...

The said one acre Lot being part of 17 3/4 acres the said Joseph Janney purchased of Thomas Hague situated in the County of Loudoun and joining to Mahlon Janney's Mill Lot, Loudoun County Deed Book O, pp. 9-14 **

Beginning at A at a locust post at the place where a small marked white oak stood it being the NE Corner to the said Joseph Janney's Land which he purchased of Thomas Hague and standing on a hill and extending thence...

** Antecedent: Francis Hague of Loudoun County, Yeoman, to Thomas Hague, Lease and Release of 17 3/4 Acres of Land, Loudoun County Deed Book I, pp. 168-173

Scale: one inch = ten poles

one inch = 50 linear feet

(1) Beginning at a locust stake or post at the place where a small marked white oak stood being the northeast corner to said Joseph Janney's land purchased of Thomas Hague and standing on a hill and extending thence...

4/17/1791
Lease and Release
Joseph Janney of County of Loudoun and Hannah his wife to Asa Moore of County aforesaid, one acre, being part of seventeen acres the said Joseph Janney purchased of Thomas Hague, and situate in Loudoun County joining Mahlon Janney Mill-land and all houses, buildings, ways, orchards...,
Loudoun County Deed Book
pp. 321-325

stake

stake

a stake by the springhead

William Hough and Elenor his Wife of the County of Loudoun to John Williams of Loudoun County...one certain Messuage or Lot of Land in the Town of Waterford...Loudoun County Deed Book 2G, p. 260, Bargain and Sale of twenty eight perches

John Janney and John Janney Junior Executors of Joseph Janney dec. of the County of Loudoun to John Williams of Loudoun County...one certain Messuage or Lot of Land in the Village of Waterford...Loudoun County Deed Book 2C, p. 21, Bargain and Sale of twenty seven perches

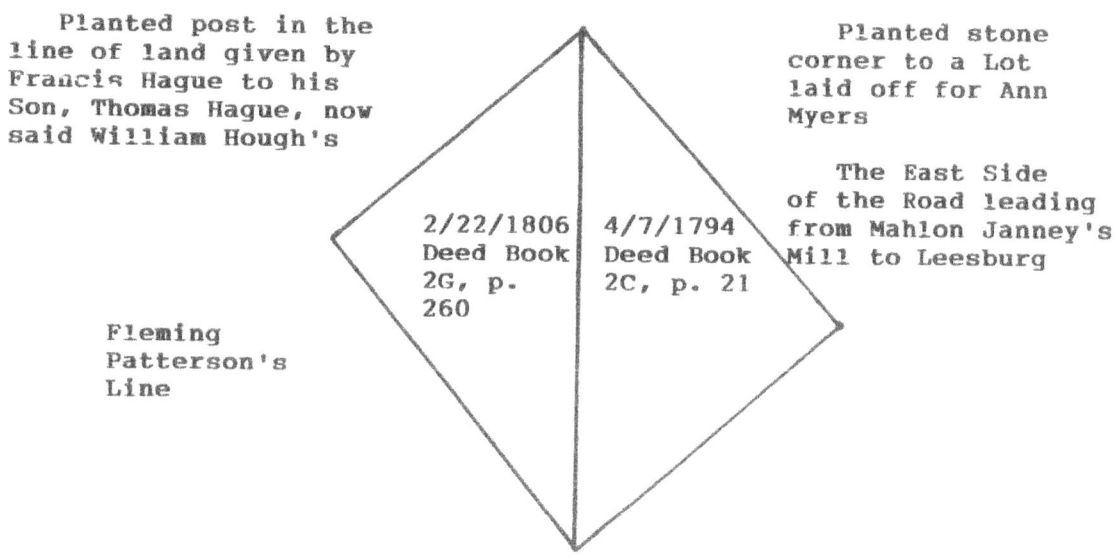

Planted post in the line of land given by Francis Hague to his Son, Thomas Hague, now said William Hough's

Planted stone corner to a Lot laid off for Ann Myers

The East Side of the Road leading from Mahlon Janney's Mill to Leesburg

2/22/1806 Deed Book 2G, p. 260

4/7/1794 Deed Book 2C, p. 21

Fleming Patterson's Line

Scale: one inch = 50 feet
one perch = 16.5 feet

Waterford, Loudoun County, Virginia

October 4, 1796

Janney's Executors to
Flemin(g) Patterson

John Janney and John Janney Junior Executors of Joseph Janney dec. of the County of Loudoun to Flemin(g) Patterson of Loudoun County...witnesseth that for and in consideration of the sum of fifty pounds lawful money of Virginia hath bargained and sold one certain Messuage or Lot of Land containing 3,553 feet more or less in the Village of Waterford...Loudoun County Deed Book X, pp. 277-278

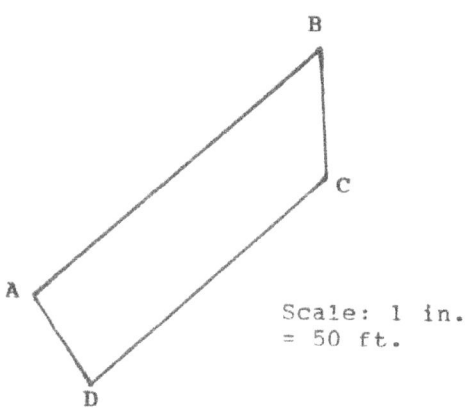

Scale: 1 in. = 50 ft.

Beginning at a corner of Robert Braden's Lot thence N49E 124 feet thence S1E 37 feet thence S49W 99 feet thence N39W 27 feet to the beginning containing 3,553 feet more or less

October 4, 1796

Janney's Executors to
Andrew Brown

John Janney and John Janney Junior Executors of Joseph Janney dec. of the County of Loudoun to Andrew Brown of Loudoun County... witnesseth that for and in consideration of the sum of one hundred pounds lawful money of Virginia hath bargained and sold one certain Messuage or Lot of Land containing 8,814 feet more or less in the Village of Waterford...Loudoun County Deed Book X, pp. 278-280

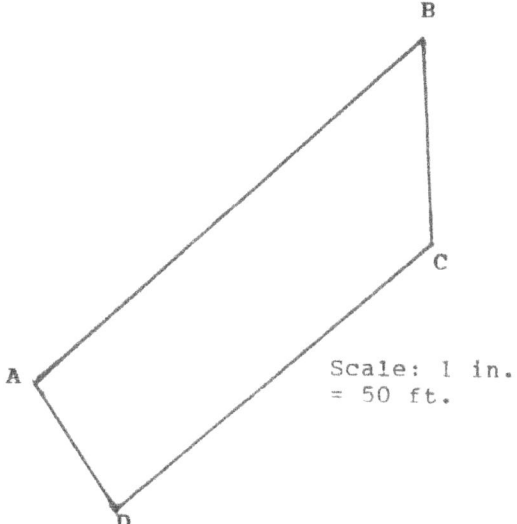

Scale: 1 in. = 50 ft.

Beginning at the corner of the Lot now in possession of the Widow Thompson extending thence N49E 165 feet thence S1E 66 feet thence S49W 124 feet thence to the beginning containing 8,814 feet more or less

Beginning at A a planted stone in the Road or Street corner to Sarah Thompson's Lot formerly Stephen Wilson's then with line of said Lot S49W 22 perches to a planted stone in Mahlon Janney's line then with said S68E seventy four feet to another planted stone in said line then N49E 20 perches to a planted stone of the Street or Road corner to Joseph Talbott Junior then along said Road or Street N41W sixty two feet to the beginning containing one half acre more or less together with the buildings thereon & all and singular of the appurtenances unto said Lot or Messuage of Land belonging...

3/15/1797 Thomas Janney to Fleming Patterson (two Lots) Bargain and Sale Loudoun County Deed Book X, pp. 359-363

April, 1797 William Paxson to Joseph Talbott Jr. Bargain and Sale Loudoun County Deed Book X, p. 363 in consideration of one hundred twenty Seventy square perches of Land Dollars, Loudoun County Deed Book X,

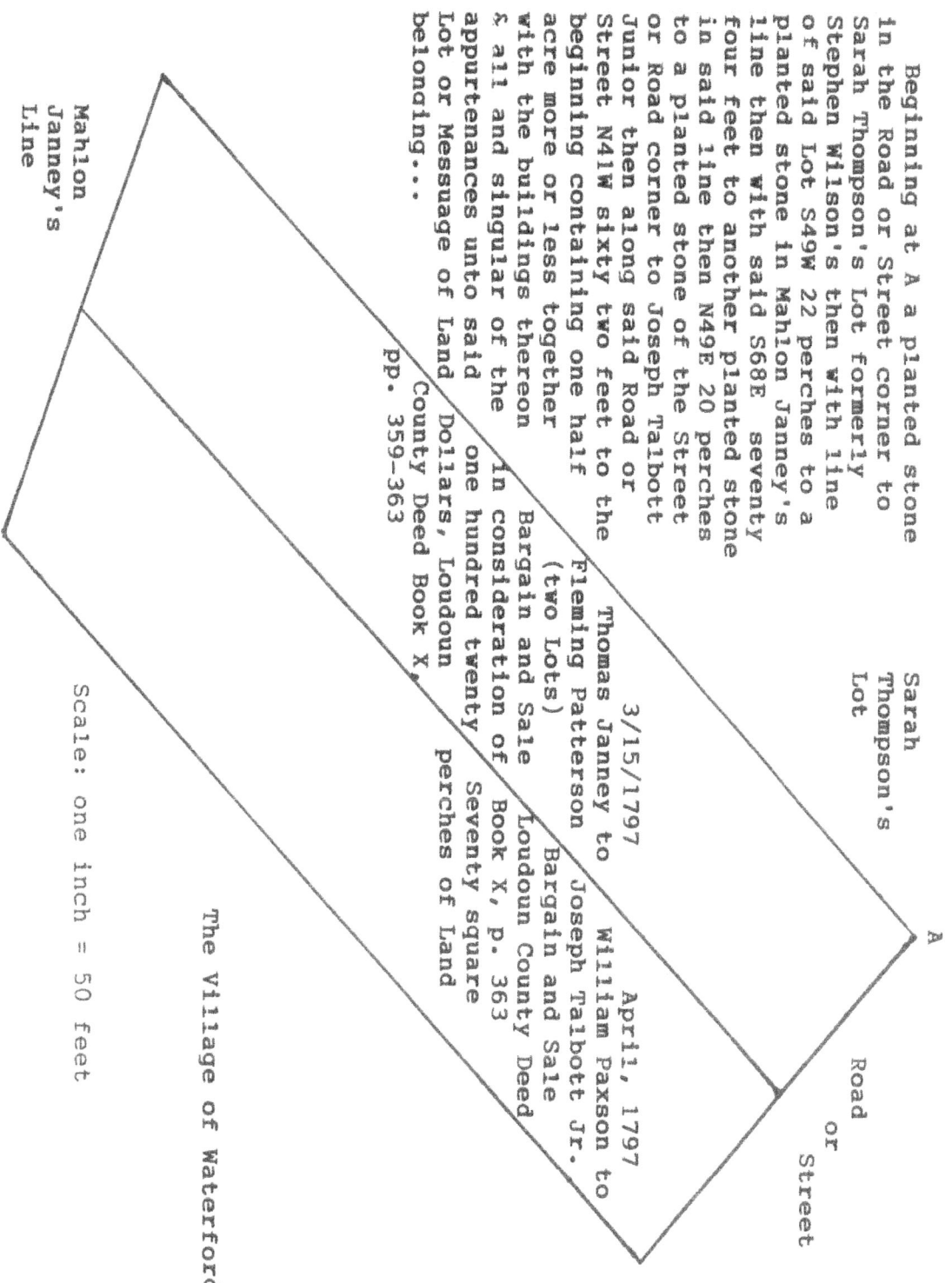

A

Sarah Thompson's Lot

Road or Street

Mahlon Janney's Line

Scale: one inch = 50 feet

The Village of Waterford

239

This Indenture made this tenth day of January in the year 1807, Mahlon Janney of the Town of Waterford in the County of Loudoun to Asa Moore of the Town and County aforesaid, Bargain and Sale, a certain lot of land containing 10,500 square feet in consideration of thirty pounds, Loudoun County Deed Book 2H, pp. 112-113

Witnessed by James Moore, Jas. Talbott, Samuel Gover, Thomas Phillips

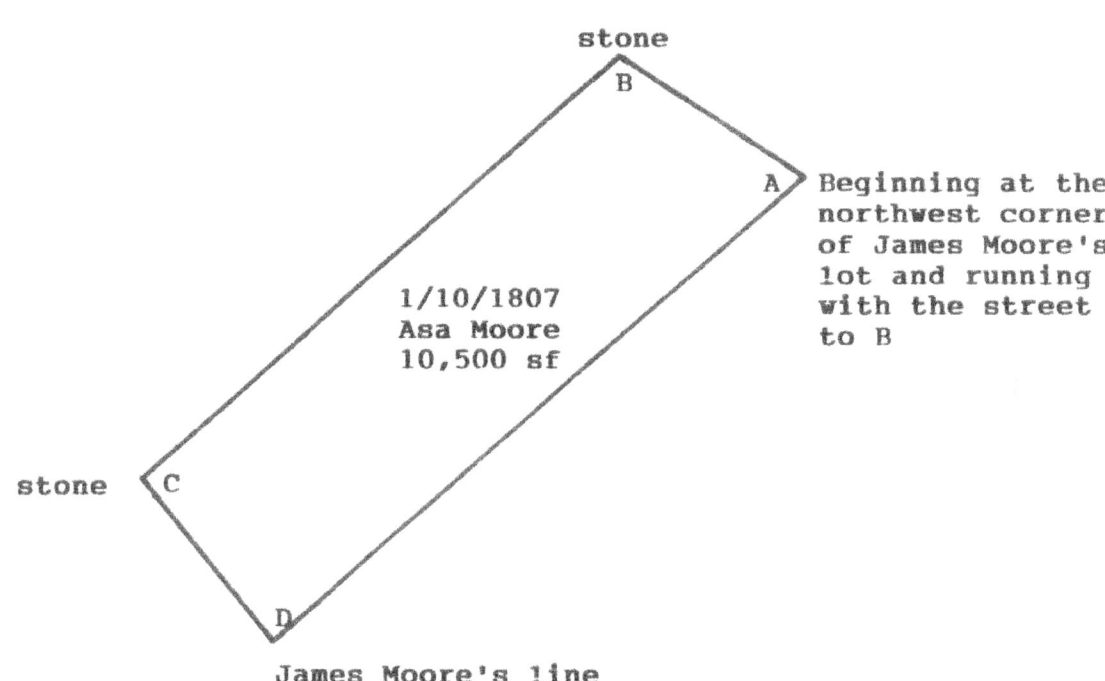

one inch = 50 linear feet

Mahlon Janney of the County of Loudoun and Sarah his wife to Jonas Potts of the same County, Bargain and Sale, all that messuage tenement plantation grist mill and tract of land containing 67 acres situated in Loudoun County aforesaid and bounded as followeth, witnessed by James Moore, W.S. Neale, Thomas Phillips, Loudoun County Deed Book 2K, pp. 364-365, the above document bearing date September 17th 1808

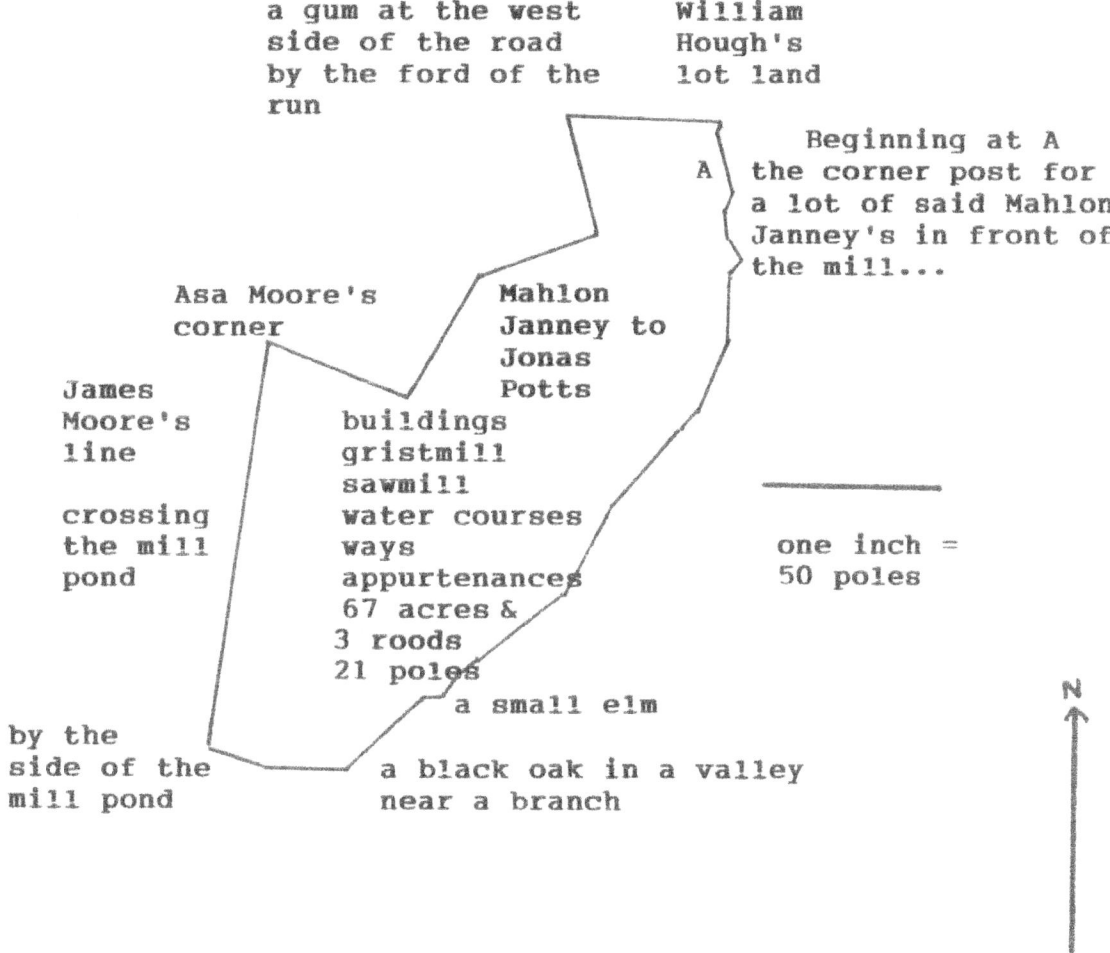

Mahlon Janney of the County of Loudoun to Samuel Gover of County of Loudoun, Bargain and Sale of a certain lot of land adjoining the Town of Waterford, in consideration of twenty dollars, this indenture made bearing date 4/13/1809, Loudoun County Deed Book 2K, pp. 365-366

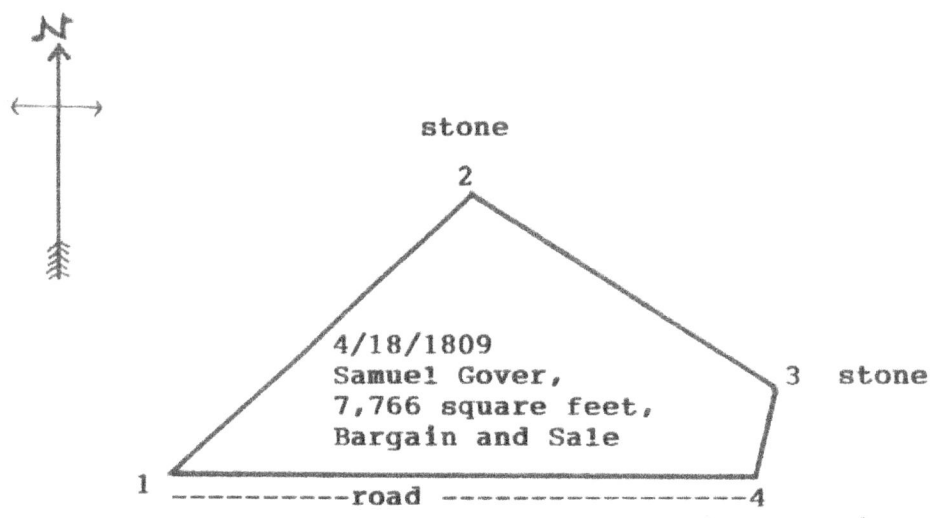

4/18/1809
Samuel Gover,
7,766 square feet,
Bargain and Sale

Beginning at a stone in the edge of the road and corner to Mahlon Myers lot thence with the line of said Myers lot N 49 E 118 feet to a stone, another of said Myers corners, thence

a stone on the side of the road thence with the road to the beginning

one inch = 50 linear feet

A

Abril, Richard, 17
Adam, Andrew, 124, 125, 152
Adams, Andrew, 33, 123
Albertson, Garret, 126
Alexander, Morgan, 205, 206, 208
Amos's Branch, 45, 162
Analostan Island, 12
Anderson, William, 37
Ann, 37
Armstrong, M., 128, 129, 131
Arnold, 103
Aubrey, Francis, 15, 16
Aubrey, Thomas, 10, 15
Averill, 149
Averill, Richard, 10, 13, 45, 46, 162, 188
Awbrey, 5, 9
Awbrey, Elizabeth, 11
Awbrey, Francis, 5, 9, 10, 11, 12, 13, 14, 15, 17, 29, 31, 38, 39, 40, 41, 90, 91, 122, 149, 161, 163, 173, 188
Awbrey, Francis and Frances Tanner, 9
Awbrey, Francis, his Reserve, 90
Awbrey, Francis, his Reserve made with John Colvill, 38
Awbrey, Francis, son of Francis and Frances Awbrey, 12
Awbrey, George, 10, 12, 14, 15
Awbrey, Henry, 12
Awbrey, John, 12, 14
Awbrey, John and Mary, 10
Awbrey, Mary, 14
Awbrey, Richard, 11, 12, 14
Awbrey, Samuel, 10, 11, 14, 18, 19
Awbrey, Sarah, 10, 11, 12
Awbrey, Thomas, 10, 11, 12, 13, 14, 19, 40
Awbrey, Thos., 15
Awbrey's Ferry, 12
Awbrey's ferry road to his ferry landing, 11
Awbrey's ordinary and ferry, 12
Axline, Adam, 133

B

Backhouse, Strainge, 174
Bald Hill, 155
Ball, Farlen (Farling), 154
Ball, Farlin (Farling), 151, 152, 153, 154
Ball, Farling, 97, 153, 154
Ball, Farling and Mary, 155
Ball, James, 52, 173, 174
Ball, James and Mary, 175
Ball, James and Ruth, 175
Ball, John, 166, 168, 170, 171, 172, 175
Ball, Nathan, 97, 104
Ball's Mill, 103
Ball's Mill, Farling, 97
Ball's Road, 96

Beatty, Charles, 35
Beeson, Rachel, 60
Ben, 37
Bennett Esq., Honble., 70
Bennett, Charles, Earl of Tankerville, 27, 35, 41, 122, 123
Bennett, Henry A., 97
Bennett, Henry Astley, 35, 38, 97, 122, 123
Big Road, the, 62
Binns, Chas., 201
Black, Hugh, 153
Blincoe, G.W., 103
Blincoe, Saml., 103
Bond, Joseph, 227
Bonham, Ephraim, 154
Bonham, Joseph, 202, 203
Border, Nicholas, 133
Braddock, Mary, 125
Braddock, Prudence, 125
Braddock, Ralph, 125
Braddock, William, 34, 122, 124, 125
Braden R., 224
Braden, Joseph, 133
Braden, R., 74, 75, 223, 224
Braden, Robert, 224
Brown, Andrew, 52, 208, 224
Brown, Henry, 19, 60, 61, 62, 63, 64, 65, 68, 70, 145
Brown, Henry and Easter, 69
Brown, Henry and Esther, 61, 64, 65
Brown, Henry and Hester, 68
Brown, Henry and Hester (sic), 62
Brown, Henry, deceased, 62, 73
Brown, Henry, deceased, and Esther, widow, 73
Brown, James, son of William Brown of England, 60
Brown, John, 63, 73
Brown, Joseph, 63
Brown, Mary, 61, 63, 64
Brown, Mary, the daughter of Edward Norton, 60
Brown, Mary, widow, later Mary Kirk, 62
Brown, Mercer, 48, 62, 63, 64, 69, 71, 72
Brown, Mercer and Sarah, 62, 69
Brown, Richard, 60, 61, 62, 63, 64, 65, 66, 71
Brown, Richard and Mary, 60
Brown, Richard, deceased, 64, 70
Brown, Richard, his house, malthouse, mill, millhouse, saw, sawmill, brewhouse, outhouses, and sundry accessories, 61
Brown, Richard, son of William Brown and Ann Mercer Brown, 60
Brown, Sarah, 69
Brown, Thos., 220
Brown, William, 19, 62, 63, 64, 73
Brown, William and Hannah, 62, 73
Brown, William, of England, 60
Brown, William, son of William Brown of England, 60
Brown's Mill, Mercer, 62
Butcher, John, 52

C

Cadwallader, Hannah, 96
Cadwallader, Moses, 49
Caldwell, Jos., 170
Caldwell, Joseph, 166, 167, 168, 169, 170, 171, 174
Calrick, Peter, 99
Calrik, Peter, 99
Campbell Jr., Aneas, 130
Campbell, Aneas, 18, 68, 143, 144, 145, 149, 150, 152, 155, 161, 165, 166, 167, 168, 169, 170, 187
Campbell, Aneas, his Reserve, 168, 169, 170
Campbell, Enes, 175
Canady, James, 166
Canady's house, 166
Canady's house (Kennedy), 162
Canby, Benja., 73
Canby, Benjamin, 72
Canby, Saml., 50
Canoy Island, 5, 9
Carnahan, Adam, 6, 225
Carnes, Jacob, 75, 76
Carney, Mary, 28
Carolina Road and Vestal's Gap Road, intersection of, 5, 9
Catharine, daughter of John West Jr., 37
Catharine, John Colvill and Mary Foster's daughter, 28
Catharine, John Colvill's daughter by Mary Foster, 41
Catharine, the wife John West Jr., 93
Catharine, wife of John West Jr., 43
Catoctin Manor, the Backline, 123, 124, 133
Cavan, Patk., 51, 218
Cavan, Patrick, 97
Cavins, John, 197, 204
Cavins, William, 187
Cavins, William and Mary, 208
Charity School, 31
Charles, Earl of Tankerville, 30, 33, 35, 38, 42, 44, 122, 123, 124, 125, 126, 127, 128, 129, 130, 131, 132
Clapham, 12
Clapham, Josias, 19, 150, 201
Clymore, Christian, 100
Cock and Mercer, 172, 173, 175, 198, 204, 206
Cocke, 68
Cocke & Mercer, 5, 46, 149, 161, 187
Cocke and Mercer, 45, 52, 149, 163, 165, 166, 167, 168, 171, 174, 189, 200, 208
Cocke, Catesby, 5, 18, 45, 46, 47, 50, 60, 61, 64, 65, 66, 67, 68, 71, 143, 144, 145, 149, 150, 152, 153, 155, 161, 162, 164, 165, 166, 167, 168, 169, 170, 172, 187, 188, 190, 191, 192, 193, 194, 195, 197, 199
Cocke, Catesby and Mercer, John, 161, 162, 164, 165, 166, 167, 168, 169, 171, 174, 188, 190, 191
Cocke, Catesby by Aneas Campbell, 5
Cocke, Catesby,, 145
Cocks, Joseph, 197
Collins, Abraham H., 74
Collins, Levi, 75
Collins, Levi, the log house occupied by, 76
Colvell, 27
Colvil, 27
Colvil, John, 15
Colvil, John v. Aubrey, Thomas, 10
Colvill, 97
Colvill (?), Joseph, 130
Colvill (Colvil), Capt. John, 25
Colvill (Colville) as Colvin, 30
Colvill (Colville), John, 41
Colvill deceased, Colo. John, 32
Colvill, Capt. John, 25
Colvill, Catharine, 27
Colvill, Colo., 194, 202
Colvill, Colo. John, 26
Colvill, Colo. Thomas, 28
Colvill, Francina (Frances), 37
Colvill, George, 27, 28, 31
Colvill, John, 10, 13, 25, 26, 27, 28, 29, 30, 31, 32, 33, 35, 36, 37, 38, 39, 40, 41, 42, 43, 60, 90, 91, 92, 93, 95, 122, 123, 162, 163, 187, 188, 189
Colvill, John, deceased, 123
Colvill, John, his daughter Catharine by Mary Foster, 30
Colvill, Thomas, 26, 27, 28, 29, 31, 33, 35, 36, 37, 43, 44, 93, 122, 132, 133
Colvill, Thos., 94, 132
Colville (Colvill), clans, 27
Colville of Cleish, 27
Colville, John, 30
Colvin, 27
Colvin (Colvill), 209
Colvin as Colvill (Colville), 30
Colvin, Capt. John, 25
Colvin, clans, 27
Colwell, 27
Combs, Saml., 133
Combs, Samuel, 130, 133
Compton, John, 19
Compton, Mary, 19
Conard and Isaac Steer, a gate corner, 104
Connard, Anthony, 97, 98, 99
Conoy Island, 11
Conoy Island (Heaters Island), 11
Cool Spring, 163, 189
Coombs (Combs), Samuel, 124
Coombs, Mary, 124
Coombs, Saml., 126
Coombs, Samuel, 34, 122, 124, 126, 127
Copeland, Andrew, 219
Cordell, 75
Counce, Adam, 133
Count (Counts), Adam, 130
Count (Counts), Henry, 131
Count, Adam, 34, 122, 131
Count, David, 131
Count, Henry, 34, 122, 131
Count, Kathrine, 131
Count, Mary, 131
Count, Salamy, 131
Counts, Adam, 127, 128
Cox, 204
Cox, Joseph, 191, 192, 197, 204, 206

Crawford, Archd., 128, 129, 131
Crawford, William, 44, 133
Cummings, John, 19
Cunard, Anthony, 102, 104
Cunnard Sr., Edward, 103
Cunnard, Anthony, 97

D

Dade, Francis, 43, 93
Daniel, Josh, 209
Daniel, Joshua, 101
Daphne, 37
Davis, John, 97
Dawson, Abraham, 69, 129, 154, 155
Dawson, Abraham and Ann, 155, 156
Dehaven, Jacob, 72
Dixon, Joseph, 149, 163, 164, 189, 190
Dodd, John, 51, 218
Dodd, Thomas, 49
Dodd, Thos., 31, 44, 94
Dodd, William, 60
Donaldson, James, 43, 93
Donaldson, Stephen, 43, 93
Dorsey, Edwd., 104
Douglass, William, 13
Drean, John, 73
dwelling house and barn, 75

E

Earl of Tankerville, 28, 29, 30, 31, 32, 33, 34, 35, 36, 37, 122
Earl of Tankerville and his brother, Henry Astley Bennett, 62
Earl of Tankerville, Charles Bennett, 27
Ellzey, F., 129, 130
Ellzey, W., 43, 93, 172
Ellzey, William, 173
Eltinge, Cornelius, 162, 188
Emms, Edward, 29
Esther, John and Thomas Colvill's sister, 28
Everheart's Mill, 61

F

Fadeley, Jacob, 73
Fairfax Meetinghouse, 61, 70
Fairfax Meetinghouse, small slice of land adjoining it from Francis Hague deceased, 52
Fairfax Meetinghouse, Trustees of, 52
Fairfax, George William, his Manor, 99
Fairfax, William, 26, 29, 30, 122, 162, 188
Fairfax, William Henry, 122, 161, 171, 172, 173
Fairfax, William Henry, deceased, 161
Farehurst, Jeremiah, 47
Ferguson, Auzabah, 126
Ferguson, James, 34, 122, 124, 125, 126, 127
Ferguson, Margaret, 126
ferry landing, 11

ferry road, 11
ford, 98, 218
ford, the, 51
Foster, Mary, 28, 30
Foxal, Catharine, 127
Foxal, David, 34, 122, 127
Foxal, Elizabeth, 127
France, Nicholas, 96

G

George Mercer, James Mercer and James Mercer as executor for Anne Mercer, 207
George the Second, 123, 124
George the Third, 42, 92, 125, 126, 127, 128, 129, 130, 131, 132
German Settlement, 102
Giles (Colvill), Esther, 27
Giles, Capt. Mathias, 27
Gillingham, Thomas, 98
Goodwin, David, 104
Gossett, 194, 202
Gossett, John, 19
Gossett, Mathias, 19
Gossett, William, 192, 194
Gover, Jesse, 74
Gover, Samuel, 226, 227
Graham, Henry, 128, 129, 130, 131
Grant, John, 124
Grant, William, 34, 122, 123
grave, 201, 202
grave sites, Indian, 10
grave, Indian, 15, 16
Grayson, Benjamin, 162, 165, 188, 191
Great Road, the, 17
Green, Chas., 165, 191
Green, James, 47
Greenhorn, Andrew, 12
Gregg, 167
Gregg, Elizabeth, 92
Gregg, George, 5, 6, 10, 14, 31, 66, 92, 149, 150, 152, 153, 154, 155, 187, 193, 196, 198, 201
Gregg, George and Elizabeth, 42, 151, 152
Gregg, George, yeoman, 39, 90, 91
Gregg, John and Elizabeth, 31
Gregg, William, 155
Gregg's Sawmill, George, 149, 187, 198
Gregory, John, 29
Griffeth (Griffith), David, 45, 46
Griffeth, David, 46, 47
Griffin, William, 19
Griffith (Griffeth) David, 46
Griffith, David, 45, 46, 47
Griffith, Evan, 225
Griffith, Evin, 225
Griffith, John, 162, 172
Griffith, Richard, 224, 226
Griffith, William, 18
gristmill, Mahlon Janney to Jonas Potts, 227
Grubb, Ebenezer, 101, 102
Gunnell, John, 155

H

Hague Thos., son of Francis Hague, 227
Hague, Ann, 46
Hague, Francis, 39, 40, 45, 46, 47, 48, 49, 50, 51, 52, 65, 91, 94, 144, 151, 161, 165, 166, 168, 170, 171, 174, 175, 187, 193, 207, 208, 218, 227
Hague, Francis and Jane, 49
Hague, Francis and Jane Janney, 46
Hague, Francis, deceased, 51
Hague, John, 46
Hague, Samuel, 51, 52
Hague, Thomas, 49, 50, 51, 52, 174, 218, 221, 223
Hague, Thomas and Sarah, 50, 218
Haite, Benjamin, 197
Hall, Sarah, 14, 15
Hall, William, 14, 15
Halling, Margaret, 13, 18
Hamilton, 76
Hamilton Mills, 61, 63
Hamilton, James, 34, 62, 73, 122, 130, 152, 161, 170, 171, 187, 196, 197, 203, 204, 206
Hamilton, James and Priscilla, 170
Hamilton, Jas., 144, 151, 166, 167, 169, 170
Hamilton, John, 73, 74, 75
Hamilton, Priscilla, 130
Hamilton, Robert, 173
Hanbey, John, 40, 91
Hanby, John, 5, 6, 17, 18, 152, 153, 155, 194, 196, 198, 201
Harden, Edward, 154
Harris, Martha, 40, 91
Harris, Samuel and Mary, 5, 6
Harrison, Valentine, 205, 206, 208
Harriss Jr., Samuel, 154
Harriss, Asa, 100
Harriss, Jacob, 71
Hawling, Margaret, 10, 13, 14
Hawling's Bottom, 13
Heaters Island, 11
Henderson, Kathrine, 132
Henderson, Mathew, 132
Henderson, William, 34, 122, 130, 132
Henry, George W., 75
Henry, John, 209
Heryford, John, 43, 93
Hiatt, Benjamin, 187, 200, 201
Hickson, Mathew, 155, 192, 194, 195, 196, 198, 200
Hickson, William, 201
Himming, William, 153
Hirst, John, 52
Hixon, Mathew, 201, 202
Hixon, Ruben, 209
Hixon, Timothy, 74, 104, 202
Hixon, William, 201
Hixon, Wm., 202
Hixson, Timothy, 209
Hixson, William, deceased, 209
Hoge, William, 192, 193, 195, 196, 198, 200
Hoge, William and Mary, 200
Hoge, Willm. and Mary, 200
Hogue, William, 199
Holland, Patrick, 165, 166, 168, 169, 170
Hollingsbury, Isabella, 37
Hollingsworth, Isaac, 17
Hooe and Little, 101, 103
Hooe, Robert Townsend, 38, 123
Hooe, Robert Townshend, 123
Hough 3rd (III), John, 52
Hough Jr., John, 50
Hough Jr., John, deceased, 96
Hough Jr., Wm., 103
Hough, Amos, 50
Hough, Jno., 66
Hough, John, 6, 13, 17, 29, 31, 42, 43, 44, 48, 49, 52, 65, 66, 72, 90, 92, 93, 94, 95, 96, 97, 98, 99, 100, 101, 102, 124, 125, 144, 149, 151, 152, 161, 166, 167, 169, 172, 187, 191, 192, 193, 194, 195, 196, 197, 199, 200, 201, 202, 203, 205, 207, 208
Hough, John (blacksmith), 41
Hough, John (surveyor), 31
Hough, John, blacksmith, 30, 38, 39, 90, 91
Hough, John, blacksmith, and Sarah his wife, 39
Hough, John, deceased, 101, 102, 103
Hough, John, his son, 36
Hough, John, surveyor, 90
Hough, John, where he lived, 101
Hough, Jonah, 101, 102
Hough, Jos., 199
Hough, Joseph, 149, 187, 195, 196, 198, 205, 206
Hough, Mahlon, 101, 102, 103, 156
Hough, Mr., 94
Hough, Samuel, 101, 102, 103
Hough, Sarah, 91, 94
Hough, Thomas, 103
Hough, Thos., 103
Hough, William, 51, 96, 98, 101, 102, 103, 104, 174, 219, 221, 222, 223, 226
Hough, William and Elenor, 227
Hough, William H., 227
Hough, Wm., 101, 102, 103, 104, 156, 175, 223, 227
Hough's Mill, J., 103
Hough's Mill, John, 97
Hough's, John, mill dam, 95
house, miller's, 76
Householder Jr., Adam, 63, 73
Howell, 103, 199
Howell, Abner, 194, 195
Howell, Charles, 202, 203
Howell, Hugh, 192, 194, 195, 199, 200, 202, 203
Howell, John, 194, 195
Howell, Timothy, 192, 194, 195, 199, 200
Huff Jr., Henry, 209
Hull, Samuel, 11

I

Indian grave, 15, 16, 40
Indian grave sites, 10

J

James, Danl., 64
Janney, 94
Janney and Taylor, 173
Janney Jr., John, 223, 224
Janney Jr., Joseph, 223
Janney, Abel, 6, 52
Janney, Amos, 29, 31, 41, 42, 43, 45, 46, 47, 52, 90, 91, 92, 93
Janney, Amos and Mary, 46
Janney, Amos, the late, 39
Janney, Hannah, 173
Janney, Israel, 52, 100
Janney, Jacob, 47, 63, 64, 65
Janney, John, 99, 100, 223, 224
Janney, Joseph, 5, 6, 49, 50, 162, 172, 173, 174, 201, 218, 219, 220, 221, 222, 223, 227
Janney, Joseph and Hannah, 173, 219, 220, 221, 222, 223
Janney, Joseph and Taylor, Mahlon, 162, 172, 173
Janney, Joseph, deceased, 223, 224
Janney, Joseph, his stable, 219
Janney, Mahlon, 45, 48, 49, 50, 52, 94, 95, 99, 100, 161, 166, 171, 172, 173, 175, 219, 221, 222, 225, 226, 227
Janney, Mahlon and Sarah, 222
Janney, Mary, 45
Janney, Sarah, 95, 101
Janney, Thomas, 224
Janney, Thomas and Sarah E., 225
Janney's mill land, Mahlon, 223
Janney's Mill Lot, 49
Janney's Mill Lot, Mahlon, 51, 52, 218
Janney's Mill Lot, Mahlon, the sawmill a corner to, 50
Janney's Mill Lot, the mouth of his mill tailrace, 52
Janney's Mill, Mahlon, 49, 100, 149, 154
Janney's Mill, Mahlon, the millrace, 51, 218
Janney's Mill, the head race of, 49
Janney's Mill, the tailrace, 50
Janney's mill-race, Mahlon, 222
Janney's Sawmill, Mahlon, 51, 218, 221
Janney's, Mahlon, mill dam, 94
Jenners, Abriel, 75
John, Thomas, 5, 67, 152, 153, 167
John, Thos., 5
Johnston, Capt. William, 37
Johnston, Sarah, 37
Johnston, Wm., 155
Jones, James, 68, 69, 146
Jones, William, 17, 18, 68, 69, 144, 146

K

Kavanaugh, John, 7
Kelly, Joseph, 17, 41
Kenady, James, 175
Kenady's house, 175
Kenady's house (Kennedy), 162
Kennady, James, 171, 172
Kennady, James and Margaret, 172
Kennedy, James, 162
Kennedy, James, his house, 161
Kennedy, James, weaver, 161
Kirk, 68
Kirk, William, 33, 61, 62, 65, 66, 68, 69, 123, 145
Kirk, William and Mary, 61
Kirk's Mill, 201
Kirk's Mill, William, 12, 61, 149, 154
Kittockton Creek Tract, Colo. Colvill's, 163, 189
Kleinhoff, John, 209

L

Larowe, Isaac, 72
Larrowe, Isaac, 100
Lee, 35
Leesburg, 61, 156, 224
Lewis, Thomas, 173
lime-kiln, 76
Little, Charles, 38, 123
Lord Fairfax, Thomas, 187
Lord of Tankerville, 29, 33, 44
Lovettsville Road (Rt. 672), 10
Lynch, Patrick, 149, 163, 189

M

Magruder, 35
Mandeville, Joseph, 219
Marberry, his survey, 62, 73
Martin Jr., John, 209
Martin, John, 98
Martin, Thomas Bryan, 36
Mason, Ann, 17
Mason, Mrs., 163, 188
Mason, Thomson, 17, 149, 150, 152, 161, 169
Massey, Lee, 17, 170
Mathews, Thomas, 6, 154, 175
Mathias, Jno. G., 76
Maxberry (Mayberry, Marberry), Samuel, 60, 63
Maxberry, his survey, 62
Maxberry, Saml., 61, 65, 68, 145
Maxberry's land, 71
Mayo, William, 5, 9
McCabe, George, 226
McFarlan, 132
McGeach, John, 187, 208
McGeach, Jos., 150, 151
McGeach, Joseph, 5, 167, 168, 169, 209
McGeach, Joseph, deceased, 174
McGeach, Mary, 52, 187, 192, 193, 196, 198, 199, 200, 208
McGeath, Jos., 48
McGinnis, Neal, 201
McHolland, Patrick, 162, 175
McIlhaney, John, 67
McIntyre, Alex, 6
McVey, Patrick, 204
Mead and Averill, 162, 164, 188, 190
Mead Jr., William, 46

Mead Sr., William, 46
Mead, Benjamin, 223
Mead, John, 31, 38, 45, 46, 47, 50, 51, 52, 90, 161, 218
Mead, John and Averill, Richard, 45, 162, 188
Mead, Mary, 47
Mead, Saml., 39, 47, 91, 128, 129
Mead, Samuel, 131
Meeting House (Fairfax), 62
Meetinghouse, 168
Meetinghouse, Fairfax Monthly Meeting, 45
Mercer, Anne, 207, 208
Mercer, Anne, deceased, 206
Mercer, George, 165, 191, 192, 193, 194, 195, 196, 197, 199, 203
Mercer, George, James and James as executor for Anne Mercer, 205, 208
Mercer, James, 191, 192, 193, 194, 195, 196, 197, 199, 203, 204
Mercer, John, 42, 92, 149, 152, 161, 162, 164, 165, 166, 187, 188, 190, 191, 192, 193, 194, 195, 196, 197, 199, 207
Mercer, John, & Co., 191
Mercer, John, & Sons, 161, 187
Mercer, John, and Cock, Catesby, 208
Mercer, John, and Cox, Catesby, 208
Mercer, John, and Sons, 52, 191, 200, 201
Mercer, John, deceased, 203, 205
Mercer, John, George and James, 200, 207
Mercer, John, James and George, 202
Mercer, John, James, and George, 201
Mercer, Joseph, 64
Mercer, Mrs. Ann, deceased, 203
Mercer, Mungo Roy, 204, 205, 207
Mifflin, Thomas, 155
Milford (Millford), 62, 72
mill, 75
mill dam, 98
mill-dam, 209
Minor, John, 26
Minor, Nich., 67, 150, 166, 167, 170
Minor, Nick, 32
Mitchell, Beth, 9, 25, 26
Moberly, 16, 40
Moberly, Saml., 17, 41
Moberly's dwelling house, 10
Mobley, Samuel, 18, 19
Moffett, Robt., 76
Monica, 37
Montgomery, Thomas, 37
Moody, Benjamin, 37
Moore & Phillips, 104
Moore Jr., Thomas, 218, 219, 226
Moore Jr., Thos., 52
Moore, Asa, 52, 101, 102, 220, 222, 223, 224, 226
Moore, James, 52, 100, 101, 102, 224, 226
Moore, Thomas, 219, 226
Morris, Elizabeth, 14, 17
Morris, Samuel, 14
Moss Jr., John, 150, 167
Moss, John, 32
Moxley, William, 96

Muir, George, 97
Mull, Geo., 209
Murrey, Samuel, 51, 218
Myars, Ann, 223
Myer, Jonathan, 175
Myers, Jonathan, 173

N

Nan, 37
Narrows, The, 101, 103
Neale, W.S., 104
Neilson, H., 155
Nelson, Arthur, 11
Nelson, John, overseer of the road, 11
Nelson's Ferry, 11
Nelson's Ferry, John, 11
Noland, Elizabeth Awbrey, 12
Noland, Paul, 15
Noland, Phil, 32, 170
Noland, Phillip, 11, 12
Noland, Phillip and Elizabeth Awbrey, 11
Noland's Ferry, 12
Noland's Ferry Road, 12
Noland's Island, 12
Northern Neck of Virginia, 26, 36
Northern Neck of Virginia, Proprietor's Office, 29
Norton, Edward, 48, 60, 61, 63, 64, 65, 68, 143, 144, 150
Norton, Edward and Elizabeth, 62, 67, 145
Norton, Edward, of County Armagh, Ireland, 60

O

O'Daniel, Henry, 34, 122, 129, 130
O'Daniel, Mary, 129

P

Packson, John, 100
Page, Wm. Byrd, 226
Pairpoint, Joseph, 221
Pairpoints, Joseph, 221
Pancoast, Asa, 193
Parker, Richd., 165, 191
path, 10, 165, 170, 171, 196, 198, 204
Patterson, Flemg., 124, 126
Patterson, Flemin, 223, 224, 225
Patterson, Fleming, 124, 125, 126, 127, 152, 225
Patterson, Flemon, 224, 227
Patterson, John, 31, 32, 33, 34, 35, 36, 42, 122, 123, 124, 125, 126, 127, 128, 129, 130, 131, 132
Patterson, John, his Reserve, 124, 133
Paxon, James, 175
Paxon, William, 102, 103
Paxson, William, 96, 98
Paxton, James, 19
Paxton, William, 99, 100, 221, 225
Peirpoint, Joseph, 225
Perry, William, 12

Peyton, Craven, 150, 152, 167, 169
Peyton, Francis, 205, 206, 208
Peyton, Henry, 205, 206, 208
Philips, Jenkin, 69
Phillips, Thomas, 102, 103, 226, 227
Phillips, Thos., 101
Philpot, 35
Pickerill, Henry, 69
Piercy, Richard, 25
Piercy, William, 10
Pierpoint, Joseph, 220
Plummer, Thomas and Ellen, 95
Poston, Leonard, 72
Potterfield, 75
Potts, David, 103
Potts, Jonas, 227
Poultney, 12
Poultney, Eleanor, 97
Poultney, Elenor, 17
Poultney, Ellen, 95
Poultney, John, 17, 66, 67
Purdom, Jeremiah, 99
Pyburn, Widow, 16, 40
Pyott Jr., John, 175

R

race (tailrace), 50
race (tailrace), the, 221
Ramsay, Capt. William, 37
Rasberry Plain, 149, 161
Ratekin, James, 96
Ratikin, James, 197, 198, 204
Ratliff, Joshua and Nancy, 75
Reed, John, the fence and house in the lot of land whereon he lived, 97
Reid, Walker, 103
Reynolds, Hannah, 60
Richards, Sampson, 76
Richardson, 27
Richardson, David, 13, 17, 18, 144
Richardson, Elizabeth, 220
Richardson, John, 162, 188
Richardson, Jonathan, 12
Richardson, Mary, 13, 17, 18, 144, 145
Richardson, Richard, 220
Richmire, Benjamin, 221
Roach, James, 69
Roach, Mahlon, 103
Roach, Richard, 19, 61, 62, 66, 67, 71, 151, 153, 155, 156
Roach, Richard, to build a mill, 67
Roache's Mill, 156
Roache's Mill, Richard, 61
Roach's house, 67
Roach's smith -shop, 67
Roach's, Richard, his smith's shop, 61
road, 49, 51, 71, 76, 94, 96, 98, 101, 103, 151, 168, 196, 198, 218, 220, 221
road from John Ball's to Joseph McGeach's corner to William Schooley in a line of John Ball's, 169
road from the mouth of Monocacy to the first mountain, 11
road leading from Farling Ball's Mill to John Hough's Mill, the main, 97
road leading from Leesburg to said Janney's Mill, 222
road leading from Mahlon Janney's Mill to Jonah Thompson's Mill, 100
road leading from Mahlon Janney's Mill to Leesburg, 223
road leading from Roache's Mill to Leesburg, 149
road leading from Roach's Mill to Leesburg, 156
road leading from Thomas Taylor's Mill to Fairfax Meetinghouse, 70
road leading from William Kirk's Mill to Mahlon Janney's Mill, 149, 154
road leading to Kirk's Mill, 201
road leading to the German Settlement, 102
road leading to the mill and across the Creek, 75
road or street, 224, 225
road or street, the main, 225
road that crosses said mountain (Catoctin Mountain), 149
road, and ford, 98
road, main, 71, 96
road, miller's house, limekiln, log house on the road, 76
road, mountain, 5, 201
road, proposed from William Kirk's Mill to the mouth of Catoctin Creek, 12
roads, parcel between the two, 201
Roberts, Richard, 11
Robinson, William, 205, 206, 208
Roch, Richd., 65
Rogers, Hamilton, 200
Rose, Alexander, 203, 205, 207
Russell, 19

S

Sands, 73
Sands, Benjamin, 69
Sands, Edmund, 60, 61, 62, 63, 64, 65, 67, 68, 69, 143, 145, 151, 153, 155
Sands, Edmund and Rachel, 66
Sands, Edmund, deceased, 70
Sands, Isaac, 69, 71
Sands, Jacob, 70, 71
Sands, Joseph, 62, 69, 70, 71
Sarah, 37
Savin, Sarah, 37
Saxton Jr., Charles, 154
Saxton, Nathanial, 155
Scheel, Eugene M., 35
Schooley, 169
Schooley, Dorothy, 127
Schooley, Garret, 127
Schooley, Nicholas, 126
Schooley, Samuel, 34, 122, 124, 126, 127
Schooley, William, 126, 165, 166, 167, 168, 171, 174, 193, 208
Schooley, Wm., 169, 170

Schoolhouse, 76
Scott, Daniel, 153
Scott, George, 153
Scott, John, 153
Scott, Mary, 153
Sears Branch (Steer's Branch?), 196
Sebastian, Benja., 43, 93
Seers Branch (Steer's Branch?), 193
Selden, Wilson Carey, 226
Semple, John, 37
Shaw, Middleton, 30
Shepherd, Thos., 67
Shibeley, Israel, 101
Shibeley, Jacob, 101
Shively, Jacob, 103
Shover, Adam, 133
Shover, Simon, 133
Shreve, Benj., 74
Shreve, Benjamin, 74
Shrieve, James, 71
Sinclair, 11, 12, 18, 145
Sinclair, Amos, 10, 13, 74
Sinclair, John, 13
Sinclair, Margaret, 18, 145
Sinclaire, 5, 9
Sinclair's corner, 12
Sinclear, Margaret, 17
Sinkler (Sinclair), 19
Sinkler, Margaret, 13, 14
Sinkler, Margaret Halling, 13
Sinkler, Margaret Halling now, 14
Smallwood, Bayd, 103
Smith, Catharine, 37
Smith, Catherine, 27
Smith, David, 17, 41
Smith, William, 225
Smith's Shop Field, 13
Spencer, 37
Steer, Benjamin, 96, 98
Steer, Isaac, 101, 102, 104
Steer, William, 74
Steere Jr., Isaac, 19
Steere, Isaac, 225
Steere, James, 153
Steere, John, 19, 68, 146
Steere, Rebekah, 19
Steere, Thos., 19
Stephens, James, 152
Stewart, Adam, 37
Stone, Daniel, 101, 104, 227
Stone, Edward, 104
Stone, Edward, his house, 104
Stott, 27
Stoutsenberger, 75
Sutherland, A., 72
Sutton, John, 219, 226

T

tailrace, mill, 51
tailrace, mouth of, 49

Talbot Jr., Joseph, 225
Talbott, Joseph, 225
Tankerville, 35, 104
Tankerville, his survey, 73
tanyard run near the road, 220
Tasker, Benjamin, 30
Tayloe, John, 9
Taylor Town, 62
Taylor Town Farm, 62, 75
Taylor, Ann, 74
Taylor, Harriet, 75
Taylor, Henry, 72, 74
Taylor, Henry, deceased, 75
Taylor, Jesse, 102, 104
Taylor, Joseph, 72
Taylor, Mahlon, 162, 172, 173
Taylor, Mary, 74
Taylor, Mary A., 74
Taylor, Mrs. Ann, deceased, 75
Taylor, Sarah, 75
Taylor, Thomas, 62, 69, 71, 72
Taylor, Thomas and Caleb, 72
Taylor, Thomas, deceased, 72
Taylor, William, 51, 218
Taylor's Mill, Thomas, 62, 70
Taylorstown, 62
Teel Jr., Joseph, 34, 122, 128
Teel, Henry, 128
Teel, Joseph, 34, 122, 128
Teel, Mary, 128
Teel, Peter, 129
Teil, Joseph, 131
Templeman, William, 44, 133
Thomas, Lord Fairfax, 25, 161, 187, 191, 192, 193, 197, 208
Thomas, Lord Fairfax and Baron Cameron, the Rt. Hon., 162, 188
Thomas, son of John West Jr., 37
Thompson, Amos, 187, 200
Thompson, Isr., 67
Thompson, Israel, 51, 52
Thompson, Jonah, 219
Thompson, Sarah, 224, 225
Thompson, the widow, 224
Thompson's Mill, Jonah, 100
Tramel, John, 17
Trammell Jr., John, 11
Trammell, John, 18, 19, 143, 144
Trammell, William, 34
Tuton, John, 14
Tutons, 10, 16, 41
Tutons, John, 10

U

Urquhart, John, 129

V

Vandevanter, Isaac, 209

Verts, Cunard, 101
Virtz, Cunard, 102

W

Walley, Henry, 25
Walton, John, 152, 153
Warner, John, 15, 40, 149
Washington, George, 37
Waterford, 45, 161, 226
Waterford, the little town called, 221
Waterford, the town of, 226, 227
Waterford, the village of, 224, 225
Watts, John, 16, 41
Wells, Levi, 31, 44, 94
West, 35, 68
West (Jr.), John and Catharine, 43
West Jr., Hugh, 39, 91
West Jr., John, 31, 36, 37, 43, 94
West Jr., John and Catharine, 31, 41, 90, 96
West, Catharine, 92
West, George, 31, 36, 44, 94, 122, 124, 126, 127, 132
West, H., 44, 94
West, John, 16, 41, 92, 97
West, John and Catharine, 42
West, John, and Catharine his wife, 93
West, Rev. William, 62, 70
Widow Pyburn's dwelling house, 10
Wilkinson, Joseph, 96
Willett, J., 226

William, John, 223
Williams, 73, 76
Williams, Benjamin, 187, 197, 203, 204, 206
Williams, Eneas, 73
Williams, Enos, 71, 72
Williams, Evan, 124, 125
Williams, George, 12
Williams, Jenkin, 69
Williams, John, 227
Williams, Joseph, 72
Williams, Richard, 62, 67, 68, 70, 71, 145, 156
Williams, Richard and Margaret, 69, 71
Wills, 27
Wilson, Cumberland, 37
Wilson, Robert, 152
Wilson, Stephen, 221, 223, 224, 225
Wilson, Stephen and Martha, 225
Wine, Jacob, 98, 99, 102
Wineburg, John, 99
Wise, Donald A., 25
Wood, Richard, 5, 10, 161, 163, 167, 189
Woollard, William, 156
Wright, Anthony, 99, 104, 224
Wright, Nancy, 99, 100
Wright, Patterson, 98, 99, 104

Y

Yates, Joseph, 48

About the Author

Roberto (Robert) Costantino is a graduate of Langley High School, McLean, Virginia. He attended Indiana University, Bloomington, and graduated from Loyola University, New Orleans, where he majored in political science (B.A.). Roberto also holds a graduate degree in Planning with a formal concentration in Preservation from the University of Virginia, School of Architecture (M.P.).

While a student at the University of Virginia, Roberto authored a book recording a historic landscape site under the direction of Professor K. Edward Lay, entitled, *Israel Thompson's Plantation*. It was entered into the permanent collection of the Fiske-Kimball Fine Arts Library, Charlottesville, Virginia. Furthermore, Roberto has authored the following books: *Miscellaneous Road Cases, Loudoun County, Virginia, 1758-1782* (Willow Bend Books, 2003), *The Quaker of Olden Time: The Life and Times of Israel Thompson* (Willow Bend Books, 2004), and *Colonial Catoctin: The Fairfax Family and Freeholders of Piedmont Manor and Shannondale Manor, Loudoun County, Virginia Land Book, 1743-1820, Volume 1* (Willow Bend Books, 2006).

www.ingramcontent.com/pod-product-compliance
Lightning Source LLC
Chambersburg PA
CBHW081418230426
43668CB00016B/2279